R.E.M. FICTION

R.E.M. FICTION

AN ALTERNATIVE BIOGRAPHY

David Buckley

First published in Great Britain in 2002 by
Virgin Books Ltd
Thames Wharf Studios
Rainville Road
London
W6 9HA

A catalogue record for this book is available from the British
Library.

ISBN 1 85227 927 3

Typeset by TW Typesetting
Printed and bound in Great Britain by
CPD, Wales

CONTENTS

For Louise and Elsa

ACKNOWLEDGEMENTS

First, I am indebted to my editor at Virgin, Humphrey Price, who oversaw the book's troubled pregnancy and complicated birth with creative, constructive and friendly comments and advice. Thanks too to his colleagues at Virgin: James Bennett, Julia Bullock, Rachel Bulbulian, Fiona McBain, Anna Martin, Jamie Moore, Becke Parker and Stuart Slater, and also to Martin Noble, who copy-edited the book. I'd also like to thank my former editor, Ian Gittins, who originally commissioned the book in 2001. Ros Edwards, my literary agent, was a model of good sense throughout, and her consistently upbeat approach raised my spirits on many occasions. She was ably assisted in this by Helenka Fuglewicz, Jo McGarvey and Julia Forrest at the office. Geoff Ward, who read some of the draft chapters, and Paul Du Noyer offered friendly advice and constructive comments and will be suitably rewarded with a pint or two of Cains next time we're all back in Liverpool.

Although this is not an authorised biography, R.E.M.'s manager, Bertis Downs, gave the all-clear for some crucial interviews with band members and associates, and was of immense help throughout the latter stages of the writing of the book. It was a pleasure to have contact with the unrock'n'rolly bunch of people that make up the Athens office, including a law school teacher (Bertis Downs), a philosophy graduate (management associate Kevin O'Neil), a post-graduate student in comparative literature (fan club manager David Bell), and an ex-art-school student (art director, Chris Bilheimer).

R.E.M.'s Mike Mills and Peter Buck were willing to spend hours on the phone discussing their careers. Mike was warm and generous, and Peter, outspoken yet kind, was one of the best rock'n'roll storytellers I have ever spoken to. Their insights form the backbone of this book. Bertis Downs also agreed to be interviewed, as did around three dozen writers, journalists, photographers, producers, engineers, music executives and friends. A full list can be found in the Documents section at the end of the book, but I'd like to single out two people for a special mention: ex-R.E.M. producer Mitch Easter, whose friendly, helpful manner and irreverent, though affectionate recollections made the early sections of the book possible, and Scott McCaughey, who has played with R.E.M. since 1995 and gave so generously of his time.

R.E.M.'s fans are among the best in the world. Two in particular have been unstintingly helpful in supplying me with material. Their names are Ole Skjefte and Werner Quadflieg. My gratitude to Paul Butchart too, who was always happy to be of service and helped me out so much in tracking down interviewees in Athens. Thanks must also go to George Dubose, who was involved in the first stage of picture research.

I should mention, and thank, a number of members of the Buckley family: Mum and Dad, John (for downloading all those R.E.M. lyrics!) and Beth, and Harry and Gill. My thanks also to Chris Andrews ('unofficial' photo advisor and Dexy's Midnight Runners fan), David Blackshaw (for great tech support and Weissbier camaraderie), Fred Sanders (personal time-management man), Graham Johnstone and Grant Coles (for their eagle-eyed detection of R.E.M. in print), and Matthew Hawkes, Liz Manning and Kate Monleon at the Open University for their encouragement and understanding. Many of the students I have tutored over the past three years took a kind and supportive interest in my 'second career' as a writer – my thanks to them too.

My daughters, Louise and Elsa, were converted to the R.E.M. cause early on in the project, with 'Stand' and 'All The Way To Reno' emerging as the family favourites. Finally, my wife, Ann Henrickson, took time to read various drafts of the manuscript. Her suggestions and corrections, and her patience and support, were absolutely invaluable.

David Buckley
Munich
April 2002

INTRODUCTION: THE ENIGMA CODE

David Buckley: How do you feel about the whole process of people writing biographies about you? There've been quite a few now, most of them written by Brits.

Mike Mills: You always were the literary ones, weren't you? [laughs] Well, I have a certain level of discomfort with it, but I would rather give you factual information than have you speculate. I certainly don't plan to reveal deep dark secrets – there are things that no one needs to know. But at the same time, on a factual level, I'd rather you know certain things than to try and guess them. It's just a question of how much. It's fascinating for me as a rock'n'roll fan to read biographies, but, as a person, it just feels very strange that anyone would give a damn.

Fiction has no claims to be 'complete'. In fact, it's one of the inspirations behind this book that no objective truth can ever really be decided upon, for when we try and reconstruct the past all we're often left with are competing, though equally valid, versions of personal 'truths'. Of course, we can try to verify that certain things did happen, such as the fact that Peter Buck's underpants were refrigerated in the early hours of 6 April, 1980 in Athens, Georgia (for more, do read on!). But ultimately the best a writer can do is to judiciously weigh up the competing oral testimonies of the key players. In the final analysis, there are silences and contradictions; the best one can hope for is to present *one* version of what happened, rather than *the* version. With R.E.M. some, but not all, of the leading figures refused to discuss crucial elements of the story on anything other than frustratingly superficial terms.

This book can therefore make no claim to be the sort of biography which trumpets the candid testimony that some rock biographies can mobilise (that would not, indeed, be R.E.M.'s style at all). Nor is *Fiction* interested in the multifarious side projects the band have been involved with for over twenty years (other books give in-depth coverage of these extra-curricular excursions). So, Peter Buck's astonishing capacity to play on what seems like everyone else's records, and Michael Stipe's excursions into art, photography and filmmaking, are largely absent from the text, at least for now. Instead, *Fiction* charts the band's history. It has had more co-operation from key figures than any previous work on R.E.M. But the gaps and silences remain, to be filled, perhaps, on another day, in another book, written after the group has ceased operations and is freer to discuss the past. In any case, I've always liked a sense of incompleteness. It seems so much more alluring to have things to wish for and wonder at, to provoke and to charm, rather than having life and culture spelt out and spoon-fed. And Michael Stipe knows all about that.

Michael Stipe is arguably the biggest rock icon of the last twenty years, an assertion perhaps only Bono could fairly challenge. The press-constructed version of him is a man whose eccentricities make him different from the rest of the population. To appropriate Winston Churchill's tart assessment of Communist Russia, Stipe's public know him as 'a riddle wrapped up in a mystery inside an enigma'. And while it is undeniable that Stipe has had an aura of personal mystique created for him, and has at times himself sought to pull the enigmatic wool over his public's eyes, he is ultimately only flesh and blood. *Fiction* portrays Stipe as a highly creative, sensitive, private man, but also, to some extent, a perfect pop mythologist.

I have no desire to preach to the R.E.M. converted. Enough of that goes on in the press already. Nor do I particularly care about the minutiae of what songs were played when, or what format which single was released in, or other nuggets of information which set some record collectors swooning. By this, I don't mean to be disrespectful to those who are interested in such things (although probably I just have been). It's simply that *Fiction* does not cater for this part of the (male?) psyche. Indeed, when I interviewed Mike

Mills at length for this book, I was amused to find that the co-writer of some of the best rock songs of the late twentieth century misplaces songs in his own *oeuvre* with refreshing regularity, placing 'It's The End Of The World As We Know It' on *Green*, and regularly seeking assurance as to which track was on what album. I found this charming, and it made me like Mills even more than I already did from reading his quotes and anecdotes in the press. The reality is that rock stars are not that different from the rest of us; they get muddled, they seek reassurance, they make mistakes. In fact, the disinterring of every shard of fact, every minute of their lives, every place accounted for, may to them feel more like surveillance than analysis. 'I was a fan of The Beatles more than anyone when I was younger, and I still have problems trying to remember which songs are on *Revolver* and which ones are on *Rubber Soul*,' admits Peter Buck. 'Especially with our stuff. I'll listen to a record and never listen to it again. Sometimes I can figure it out, sometimes not. I only ever go back and listen to stuff when I have to learn the song and remember what the chords are. The fans are more obsessive. I get fans asking me about things that I don't remember doing, and I have a very good memory.'

Fiction takes its title from an interview Michael Stipe gave in 1991, in which he mentioned that this had been one of the original titles for the band's global breakthrough album, *Out Of Time*. He wanted to make it plain, in artistic terms, that the songs of love (and love lost) on the album were in fact fictions, and not his own emotional map redrawn for public scrutiny. Stipe may, of course, have simply been lying for effect, which would have been more than fitting. When naughty Tom Junod admitted that the piece he wrote on Stipe for *Esquire* in 2001 was 50 per cent made up, and when Peter Buck waggishly commented to *Q* that they should hire a fiction writer to make up their story, this simply confirmed the choice of title. The pre-fame Peter Buck even spoke on how to misinform the public, through making up parts of the story. Peter Buck told me, 'I haven't constructed a great myth for myself, but I'm a good storyteller. I try to do my best to try and tell the truth, but I never let that get in the way of livening up a good story!' And as rock writer and former editor of *Record Collector* Peter Doggett wrote in 2001: 'The art of the biographer – and, for that matter, the autobiographer as well – is to deliver a fictional re-enactment of real life that has the taste and smell of truth. And the limit of biography is that fiction, no matter how intelligent or well researched, is perhaps all it can ever hope to deliver.'

R.E.M. don't feel as if their career should be treated as history, at least not yet. Biographies have a habit of hammering nails into coffins or proffering definitive stories of bands not yet ready to be definitive themselves. *Fiction*, I'd like to think, is work in progress, in the same way that R.E.M. is work in progress too. Unlike many fans and critics, I do not feel that this remarkable band's glowing career is behind them, although I do feel that there will be an end in sight at some stage. I can't see R.E.M. treading the boards at 55, playing their greatest hits – though I could possibly see them at 55 playing songs from a great *new* album. But it is more likely that the band will gradually, and gracefully, scale down its operations. To retain their level of popularity they need to commit to long and arduous world tours, and the years of feeling able to commit to such a schedule are already way behind them, as the three individuals settle down to parenthood, middle age and interests and loves outside of music.

I would, however, like to think that *Fiction* makes a first, tentative step towards assessing the band's music in a detailed, though non-specialised, manner and to critique the group's history in an affectionate but unfawning way. It's a remarkable story of four boys who, for the first ten years of their existence, sold next to no records in industry terms and spent the next ten as global superstars. It's also the story of some of the best rock music ever written. And it all starts in a second-hand record store many, many years ago.

NOTE ON METHODOLOGY

Fiction draws mainly on first-hand interviews and correspondence with the author, including interviews with Peter Buck and Mike Mills of R.E.M. When a secondary source has been used or referred to, in almost all cases a reference is given in the notes section on pages 331–45. Lyrical quotation is for the purpose of criticism only. For the lyrical transcriptions for all recorded material up to and including *New Adventures In Hi-Fi*, where, with the exception of one song, no official lyrics have been printed, I am indebted to a variety of internet sources, the most important of which is R.E.M. Guitar Archive: http://bubblegum.uark.edu/rem/ by Chris Bray (cbray@comp.uark. edu).

PART I
THE ICE AGE, 1979–85

1. 'SOMETHING BEYOND THE FLANNEL SHIRT', 1979–80

I

Sometimes it's hard to remember what an old-fashioned record store was actually like. In a twenty-first century of downloads and online purchasing, where formats are digitalised and shrinking in size yearly and popular music itself (according to the sociologists) increasingly means less and less to young people far keener to play on the Net than play some music, a depersonalised nature of acquiring and listening to music is the rule.[1] A generation ago though, all was different. Not necessarily better, but certainly different.

A small record shop in, say, early 1979, when new wave was just starting to sell, would be very different from the anonymous sprawl of rows and rows of product in a megastore: the walls plastered with flyers, picture bags competing for space with sick-green and snow-white vinyl, Debbie Harry and Devo and Kate Bush and Suicide and the Clash and Wreckless Eric and Gary Numan all peering down from the sleeves pinned up on the walls. A new release was an event, and would provoke 'listening sessions', late-night disputation, fallings out and makings up. People cared.

Back in 1979, you also had to dig around for your information. Two years before MTV, and light-years away from the bland Internet-led celebrity culture of now, back in new-wave USA, the arrival of a new record was a real event, the appearance of a rock band on the television occasion to get in a six-pack and get drunk with a mate in front of the set, and the arrival of a *bona fide* new rock band in a venue near you something of an epiphanic moment. If you lived away from the big cities, and were too young or too intimidated to drive the huge distances to the nearest urban sprawl with a rock venue sizeable enough to play host to, say, Devo, then your actual contact with any sort of new music could be extremely minimal. Unless, that is, you *worked* at being informed.

New wave music was written about in the hellfire club of Lester Bangs' *Creem*, under the custody of fevered fanzine partisans, stocked by specialist record shops and played by a few buccaneering DJs on college radio, but essentially, even as late as 1979, for most of the USA, challenging, emotional, motive, *new* music was firmly a minority interest, underground and buried beneath a pile of Rod Stewart, Journey, Elton John and Fleetwood Mac. For the new-wave-minded kid, this sense of excitement was felt even more keenly in seventies USA. UK glam rock filtered through, but a year or two after the event, so when a scene all their own emerged on the East Coast and spread and spread, for the Americans it was a culture-shaking event, a *big thing*. Buying these new artefacts was a difficult enterprise: walk into a shop to buy the latest Patti Smith, and the teenage, gum-chewing assistant would have most likely redirected you to the nearest Lynyrd Skynyrd. New wave had to be sought out and ordered, purchasing planned. It was like being in on a secret, a member of a Masonic lodge of music lovers.

By 1979, popular music had a history rich enough to fuel these teenage spats, those late-night disputations about the worth of each other's record collections. In fact, by this time, pop history was not so much progressing in linear time but folding in on itself. The signs that pop was meant to *replicate* had been there from the mid-1960s. UK writer Jon Savage's brilliant deconstruction of the Beatles' 1966 song 'Tomorrow Never Knows' in his book *Time Travel* pinpoints the moment when pop time changed from linear to serial, 'when directional was replaced by circular motion'.[2] Here, with 'Tomorrow Never Knows', was a record based on a rebounding rhythm – a pattern that recycled rather than moved forward – that made a mockery of the formal three-minute pop/rock structure. It did so by repeating time. It sounded nothing like the Beatles had ever recorded before. It sounded nothing like *any* pop artist had recorded before. A moment of high innovation, it presaged an era of pop time which moved in a complicated process of re-articulation.

Sometimes this took the form of pastiche or mimicry, sometimes brilliant collages of thoughts and ideas. What is certain is that by 1979 there was such a variety of genres and styles available to the pop performer that making new music was, for some, an act of musical archaeology as opposed to innovation. And those racks, stuffed full of Fleetwood Mac, of Joni Mitchell, of Kiss and of the Eagles, represented a library of recorded sound for the wannabe pop musician. And, if you scratched around, the racks also revealed Gang Of Four, Wire, the Sex Pistols, Suicide and the New York Dolls too. A great rock group now needed not just a sexy singer, a great virtuoso, or a sussed marketing scam to raise it above the thousands of others competing for needle time on a radio near you. It needed a pop *historian*, someone with a sense of what had happened and what could be done with it that might interest us. It may not have to be new or innovative in reality, but it had at least to *appear* to be different.

It's usually men who want to catalogue. You won't find many women with poorly-recorded hissy cassettes archived from 1 to 960, proudly presented in 24 rickety wooden cases. What's more, a tiny minority of male record buyers become *bona fide* rock aficionados. 'You mean you don't know who Henry Kaiser is?' they will ask in disbelief. 'Or Lee Clayton?' 'Or Fred Frith?' 'You mean you haven't got the bootleg of the Beach Boys' *Smile*? Have you really never heard Blondie's live version of "Heroes"? It really has got Robert Fripp on guitar, you know.'

One such person was undoubtedly a tall, good-looking boy called Peter Buck. With his high cheekbones and tall, sleek frame, Buck had the makings of a Keith Richard. He cut a raffish figure. A self-educated man, Buck had a short fuse and a withering line in put-downs for every occasion. 'Definitely a very intelligent guy,' was one opinion of him.[3] 'He could be rather sharp-tongued also, but he had a good sense of humour and leavened the sharp tongue with that and self-deprecation.' 'Peter is real funny and very well read,' was another assessment. 'He'd sooner read than watch TV. He's read a whole lot of books and is real good at being able to quote some literature.'

Like many self-taught people, Buck had a fierce, unconventional intelligence. Twenty-three and hyperactive, he presumably also had one of the largest record collections in Georgia. He was the kind of person who pored over sleeve notes, listening for hours to all sorts of music and sharply defending his likes and dislikes. For him, it was all in the detail. 'I'm a big fan of minutiae,' he later said. 'Fuck the whole concept of the record – what kind of guitar do you use on that song?' Those of an uncharitable disposition would brand such a man a sad, anally retentive muso, the sort of man who, in the 1990s, certain thirty-something British novelists would turn into someone weirdly admirable. Buck himself would disagree, perhaps rightly: 'I'm not one of those anal types of collector though that wants every different matrix number. I play records at parties when I'm drunk.'[4] What was certain was that Buck was on some sort of mission. He wanted to turn the library of sounds inside his brain into something with form, with feeling. But, how to do it?

Peter had been listening to music obsessively since the age of six. He grew up in California to the sounds of the Rolling Stones, Led Zeppelin, the Beatles, the Beach Boys, Jimi Hendrix and the Who, sounds which dominated non-commercial FM radio in the late 1960s and early 1970s. These staples of classic rock-radio formatting hot-wired the pre-teen Buck. In this, he was like millions of other kids of his generation. However, what *was* different was Buck's curmudgeonly eclecticism. Scrape away the veneer of hit radio and classic rock that was the given of the times, and musical tributaries are revealed, as well as sounds of different genres ripe for exploration for the music-hound too. On the recommendation of one of his high school teachers, Buck's musical ambit soon spread to contemporary jazz. As a 15-year-old, Buck bought John Coltrane's *A Love Supreme*. Years later, when he was just another middle-aged rock star reminiscing for the benefit of the nostalgia culture of American rock journalism rather than a Young Turk about to enter the music business, Buck told journalists Alan Reder and John Baxter that Coltrane 'was like a blast from another planet for me ... In retrospect, a lot of the sounds and ideas that come across in the music are almost philosophical in a sense. There are a lot of pictures of America in that thing, without him making any kind of conscious political statement.'[5] So, at an early age, Peter Buck was already fascinated by American imagery, the images that made his country distinctive and special. He would go on to develop the rare gift of being able to paint such images in sound.

Buck the connoisseur also had a taste for the Easybeats, the Troggs, the Monkees and the Yardbirds, who were perhaps not so much part of the musical terrain in late-seventies America. He also connected with the new, British, glam rock. Buck saw Bowie, T. Rex and Slade live, and had a particular liking for Ian Hunter's rockier glam outfit, Mott The Hoople. Glam was 'probably the last teen musical form I really liked', he would later concede.[6]

In 1992, he told British journalist Mat Snow: 'When Marc Bolan came out, I was about 14 and I thought, wow, this makes sense. I saw T. Rex live and everything. I thought, "That's what being a pop star is about – wearing feather boas and velvet pants and going on *Top of the Pops* swilling champagne." As an image, that was really cool, and living in Georgia, it was like Martians, a message from another planet. If people found his records in your collection, you were ostracised. In Georgia I had one other friend who liked Marc Bolan. We wore eye make-up and he had one thumbnail painted black. I had the New York Dolls and T. Rex and the Velvet Underground as well as Lynyrd Skynyrd. Marc Bolan summed up the whole English thing, like I guess people in England are fascinated by Southern blues, the whole voodoo thing.'[7]

Buck was a highly acquisitive and inquisitive man. He'd read the hip beat novels (Kerouac's *On the Road* was a prerequisite for an itinerant career in rock), seen the best films, was politically sussed and, more importantly, had soaked up the words of the rock journo gods as they came pouring out of the likes of *Creem* magazine, mixed with the sputa of Lester Bangs' twisted world. With so little decent rock music on the television, and so few gigs close enough to attend, the printed word was all. 'I got a huge amount of information from the print media,' Peter Buck confirms. 'I subscribed to the *Village Voice* for a couple of years, luckily enough for me, right when punk started happening in about '74, '75 and '76. I always had access to the *Voice*. So I was reading Robert Christgau, and Lester Bangs writing about Blondie – I think he reviewed the first Blondie record. I found out about Television. I was buying those records the day they came out, which for Georgia was pretty different. I read *Creem* magazine. I hadn't discovered the English papers yet, because I don't think they came to Georgia in those days. *Creem* was a big one, because they liked Iggy and The Stooges. So I got turned on to a lot of stuff.'[8]

Indeed, the acquisition of glam and new wave records carried with it a surprising risk factor. Today we are quite inured to the grotesque and the abject, and regard it as schlock irony, even if it isn't, as the mainstream success of Marilyn Manson shows. Back then, the purchase of an album whose cover depicted grown men in make-up (not Kiss, who were so obviously masculine in their war paint) was a terrifying prospect for punter and vendor alike. One music fan from the time remembers:

> When I was at high school my first interest in all this stuff was probably germinated by reading *Creem* magazine back when Lester Bangs was editor. Like a lot of people from that particular generation who got into music that was a big inspiration for me, just the way he wrote and the general tone of *Creem* magazine, which was very disparaging. I'd never heard of the Velvet Underground and the Stooges; it seemed really interesting but no one knew about them. Lynyrd Skynyrd were very big and when I graduated from high school in 1976, Kiss were really big too. There had been people into the country rock stuff, like the Marshall Tucker Band, and definitely the Allman brothers were quite big. Commercial hard rock like Deep Purple and Bad Company was everywhere too, not to mention the kind of artier stuff like ELP and Yes. And, yes, I can even remember people who thought David Bowie was pretty cool and also Lou Reed, who'd had a big hit with 'Walk On The Wild Side' around that time. They knew who David Bowie was for sure, but it was kind of like, 'Ahem, I don't know about *that* guy!' I can remember that, at our high school in '74, '75, we had a little bookstore there with a small record rack. What should end up at the front of the record rack but the New York Dolls' first album, where they're all dressed up in drag, and I remember that it sat there and no one bought it, including me! It would have been more than my life was worth to have bought something like that!

Peter Buck has similar fond memories. 'I'd be the only 13-year-old on the block going, "I think I need to buy this Iggy and the Stooges record." The guys at the counter would be like, "You better wear rubber gloves when you hold this album, kid."'[9]

The UK rather warmed to glam rock, but, in the USA, particularly the south, such outrage was not necessarily viewed with the sense of irony intended. Earlier in the 1970s, David Bowie had fallen foul of

American 'good ole boys' for arriving on a promotional tour wearing a dress. In the American south, denim and plaid shirts were for many a uniform, and southern boogie the only music that mattered. 'Everyone liked the Allman Brothers,' Buck would later say. 'I can't tell you why – that's all there was to it. It was a law.'[10] Deviations from the norm were deemed by some to be severe blows to the very moral fabric of society. It was in this climate of conservatism that the punk and post-punk generations of fans and musicians had to work to make alternative music heard.

II

Peter Buck himself was not from the South. He was born Peter Lawrence Buck on 6 December 1956 in Berkeley, California, and moved to the San Francisco suburb of Richmond when he was a toddler. In the mid-1960s, the Bucks relocated to Indiana for four years, then LA for about three, before moving to Roswell, Georgia in 1971. 'My best friend in high school was Charles Buckley,' recalls Buck. 'We looked exactly alike, exact same height, and exact same clothes. Unfortunately he dropped dead of an aneurysm at the age of 17. I think he had been in a car wreck a couple years earlier, but it might have been congenital. He just died and I was really sad.'

The teenage Buck may have been music mad, but it was his younger brother who showed the real talent as a musician. Quieter and more reflective than the quick-witted and quick-tempered Buck, Ken Buck, who went on to become a talented classical musician, outshone his big brother with his prodigious talent on classical guitar. Peter left school in the summer of 1975, and, just shy of his 19th birthday, enrolled at Emory University, with a vague plan to become an English teacher. He soon found a job in a local record store, Doo Dah's in Emory Village, to finance his studies, and began the search for the perfect education in sound, rather than the formal one in the lecture hall. By the spring of 1977 Buck had effectively dropped out of university, although his student days officially terminated in 1978, when he was hijacked by the lure of unlimited rock records at Wuxtry.

Via a short stint working at a record distribution company, Peter Buck found himself doing what he liked most: listening to records. In January 1979, he began work as a clerk at Wuxtry records in the Classic City, Athens, Georgia. 'I went to the Wuxtry in Decatur and they liked me because I had shopped there. I said, "I'm kind of between jobs, and I'm wondering what to do." So, I drove up and took it and, for me, it was a great education. I got to listen to records I would never hear, sitting in a place with piles of records from ten to six. It was a pretty loose job. I could dress any way I wanted to, and drink on the job if I so desired.' Buck didn't give up completely on his education (he also enrolled at night school at the university), but, for the whole of 1979, his main vocation was servicing the local population's musical needs.

Most small cities in America or the UK had their own version of the Wuxtry. Small shops selling new, rare and used records and promoting local music, they were pioneering businesses on the side of the home-produced talent, capturing and encapsulating any scene that was happening. However, this particular record shop was quite remarkable in one respect: it became the venue for a meeting of the minds that would help redraw the map of American rock.

Wuxtry Records (named after an old comic book) had shops in both Athens and Atlanta. Buck had originally applied to work at the store in Atlanta, run by Mark Methe, but Methe mentioned to Buck the existence of the Athens branch, which had two stores in the late 1970s, and Buck was keen to move down. His brother Ken was already a student at the University of Georgia in Athens (UGA), an institution which dominated Athenian life. Proprietor and co-owner of Wuxtry, Dan Wall, initially gave Buck a job as a clerk in his shop on Baxter Street in early 1978.

'We have always picked the "brightest" from amongst the kids who hang out,' remembers Wall. 'Knowledgeable and articulate – he seemed as if he could absorb our pioneering and unorthodox way of running a record store.' Soon he was asked to manage the smaller, second-hand record store in East Clayton Street, in the heart of town right next to the university. Buck listened to music all day long, bought anything new that filtered through to Athens from the various sites of new wave activity within the States, or came in on import from the UK, and, in his spare time, played guitar along to these thousands of records he encountered during his three and a half years at Wuxtry.

'At that point in time we carried mainly used records, comic books and sci-fi paperbacks,' recollects proprietor Dan Wall. 'Later, in our current location as well as our Atlanta store, we began carrying select domestic new releases and imports mainly in what was known at that time as the "new wave" genre. To Pete's delight, we were the only store in the Southeast to have a huge selection of 45s. We were also known for jazz and a huge domestic Beatles collection.' By 1979, Peter Buck turned himself into a one-man rock'n'roll almanac of sounds and songs.

At various times in the 1980s Buck would go back to working for Wuxtry, even after he became a successful musician. Buck would 'guest clerk' for the odd day until his celebrity status meant the demand for autographs blunted the sheer enjoyment he got from mooching around the record store listening to vinyl upon vinyl. 'I guest-clerked around 1986,' says Buck. 'I worked one day a week, Monday from ten till six and basically just got paid in used records.'

Buck had theories on musical history spilling out of him and could fight his corner on the merits and demerits of the most obscure of bands. If Buck had failed as a professional musician, he would surely have made a brilliant rock journalist. He simply adored music and was happy to turn any of his crash pads into junkshop record stores. Ten years later, when Buck was a millionaire, journalists and friends reported that his house was still essentially a record store writ large, containing tens of thousands of vinyl records. Buck could give you the history of each one of those records too.

Buck and Wall would spend hours in listening sessions, dissecting, analysing, categorising, and playing. Wall himself played in a variety of bands over two decades in Athens. In this small, close-knit community, musicians formed a floating population of entertainers who would play professionally or just for fun at cafés, bars and parties. Before long, Buck was a competent, albeit limited, guitarist. 'Peter could play,' affirms Wall. 'He taught me Freddie King's "The Stumble".' They would talk music too.

One of the themes that came up was the lie within the truth of popular music. To make it in the music world, a certain mythology was essential. 'I've seen things in print that I know are definitely not true,' says Wall. 'Peter and I discussed that before he was ever famous. We did have conversations about how it was important to lie to the press to build your own myth. It was just kind of a joke amongst us, how do you handle this, what do you say to critics and reporters? Just generally, to build a myth about yourself is the thing to do. I think when we were talking we would allude to the fact that

Bob Dylan always claimed that he was in minstrel shows with Woody Guthrie out West. In reality, they didn't meet until Woody was on his deathbed in New York City, so it was all made up, and that kind of thing Peter was well aware of.'

'I haven't constructed a great myth for myself, but I'm a good storyteller,' is how Buck now puts it. 'I try to do my best and tell the truth, but never let that get in the way of livening up a good story!'

The Side Effects' Paul Butchart is one of R.E.M.'s staunchest supporters. In fact, you can see him bobbing around on the first row of the audience on their live video, *Road Movie*. He's helped restore and decorate many of the local properties eventually bought up by the band and its entourage over the years. Back in 1979 he was just another young musician, the kind of guy who fooled around and skinny-dipped with the likes of Peter Buck and Mike Mills when they were all just ordinary folk. He cut a distinctive figure with his moustache and, despite his youthful years, his receding hairline. Later he'd be there when the band played their first gigs, pulling faces at them from the side of the stage. Today he's still a denizen of Athens and writes about the scene for various Athens-related Internet sites. He remembers the old Wuxtry fondly:

In 1979, the location of the Athens Wuxtry where the small Wuxtry now is was in the black wooden building next to the main Wuxtry. Its front door faces College Avenue, whereas the main Wuxtry's front door faces Clayton Street. The layout is very similar to this current store on College Avenue, as is the exterior appearance, which even retains the awning that was painted by local artist and musician George Davidson, though it is somewhat peeling. Twenty-plus years ago the entire side of the building would have been covered with posters of the various bands around town who had played in the last three months or so. There were so many staples in the wall that we used to joke how terrible it would be to be rubbed up against the building! The inside is so similar to the way it used to be that there are even posters hanging on the wall that I know have been there since 1980.

As you walked in the front door of the Wuxtry circa 1979, you'd find yourself in a room about 10 feet wide and 20 feet long. There was a shelf of records directly in front of the door and a shelf of albums along the wall just to the right. Just to your left was a glass display counter, behind which sat the ancient record player we used to listen to records on. The shelves had two layers, with the less popular recordings stored at the bottom. Another interesting architectural item is the step in the middle of the room that one must be careful not to trip over while perusing the selections. If I remember correctly, there were albums hanging on little wire hangers mounted in pegboard above the row of records on the right side of the room. A vast majority of the albums were used or promotional copies.

1980 was a great time to be collecting records, and many of us had huge collections of music from the sixties that we heard while growing up, as well as a very nice selection of the latest singles coming out of Europe and other enclaves of creativity from around the world which we had purchased at the Wuxtry and supplemented at Potters House. By that time I was listening to bands such as the Ramones, Television, Stranglers, Ultravox, X-ray Spex, Gang of Four, and Ventures, a combination of new wave sprinkled with sixties dance/popular music. I would have to say that this was the music most of us were listening to, rebelling from what was then the current mainstream. I remember going to the Wuxtry to trade my high-school Boston, Styx and Foreigner albums for Richard Hell and the Voidoids. It was easier for Wuxtry to sell those so they would give us a good price for them. It was there that many of us would hear the newest sounds and catch up on the latest gossip. It was here also where I first met Peter, though he later moved to the other store on Baxter Street, where he worked pretty much until he started making money while touring. That store carried more comics and most of the rejects and overstock from the other store. I remember visiting Peter here and showing him how I played 'Ghost Riders in the Sky' on guitar. I only knew a basic riff, but he quickly figured out the rest of the tune. There was a nickname for each of the two Wuxtrys. Downtown was known as 'Chuckstry' for Chuck Conley, who worked there and was in Athens' first 'punk' band, the $windle$. Baxter Street was known as the 'Buckstry' for Peter Buck who worked primarily there.

The Wuxtry clientele consisted of the 'townies', indigenous Athens folk into their music, and maybe a few of the conservatively clad prepies from the University of Georgia, whose taste in music stopped with the beach party music of the Drifters, Tams, Four Tops and Archie Bell & The Drells. The fraternity folk were sartorially irredeemable, as Paul Butchart remembers:

> They wore polo shirts with little alligators on and khaki pants. That was kind of their uniform. Whereas we would all shop at thrift stores and buy peg-legged cotton trousers with cuffs at the bottom, and shirts and skinny ties, so our style sort of emulated what was coming out of England, sort of like the group Madness. It would be go-go dresses for the girls and these sort of fifties-looking dresses too. The fraternity people all shopped at Sears while we all were buying at thrift stores.

'I'm sure every one of us had attended a party in a frock once in a while', says Peter Buck. 'I tended to wear it over jeans or something. I used to wear my girlfriend's clothes too – I was younger and thinner then. It was a party thing – it wasn't something I would wear to a premiere or out on the streets. I guess it's one of those transgressive boundaries which is always gonna set you outside of society a little bit. I can do this because I can. If you sell insurance you can't do that, but if you're in rock, you have a little more freedom and it's also saying, these boundaries don't mean anything to me.'

An important market for Wuxtry consisted of that small group of around 150 young people who would later be dubbed the 'scenesters', men and women in their early twenties, most of them enrolled in university classes and many of them attached to the University's vibrant and respected fine art faculty. The scenesters replaced 'Under the Boardwalk' with 'Mongoloid' and 'God Save The Queen', and hitched or drove up to Atlanta to take in gigs by Ohio's Devo or the Sex Pistols' show in Atlanta on 5 January 1978, a gig Peter Buck gatecrashed and was ejected from three songs in. It was this 'scene' that became a distinctive subculture within Athens. The scenesters dressed differently, they listened differently, and they even talked differently with little catch phrases, buzzwords and cool words. Paul Butchart:

The scenesters, people who were not in the new bands, consisted primarily of people who attended the University of Georgia Art Department, though there were also people who were not artists. A vast majority of them were students, as opposed to locals who were not in school. An art professor at the University used to host go-go dance parties out in the country at his home outside of town. People also heard the latest tunes from New York at a club known as Episode 247, and on WUOG, the university radio station which had begun to change its format from jazz to the newer sounds coming from the underground, beginning in the spring of 1978 with the show *New Wave News* hosted by Kurt Wood and another DJ called Bill. We would all attend the same shows and gradually got to know and recognise each other, though at the beginning we were all a bunch of individuals with no real group spirit. As the underground grew so did our camaraderie. We all felt that we were sharing in something special, something unique and different from the preppy, fraternity/sorority social lifestyle that ruled the University. Another unifying factor were the local record stores, where we would bump into people and catch up on the latest sounds. Both Wuxtry and Chapter 3 Records carried the latest imports from England and new music from across America, keeping us up with the growing worldwide underground.

Betsy Dorminey, now a successful lawyer and still active on the arts scene in Athens, remembers the Wuxtry clerk with affection:

I always thought Pete was cute. I found him attractive and I'm not the only one I'm sure. He was selling records in Wuxtry when I was at Law School and I have to tell you I hated every minute of Law School. If I had survived another week of Law School, on a Friday afternoon I would take myself to the second-hand record department where Pete presided and I would pick out a record for myself and bring it home. That was the reward for having endured another week of this deplorable experience that was Law School. Music was just in the air; everyone was in sixteen bands and we all wanted to play. I had bought this ratty old bass guitar. It weighed a ton and I fell over forwards when I held this thing. I wanted to play some music and I knew Pete was one of these people who would play guitar for hours, just doodle and doodle with it. He'd listen to uncounted hours of music and play and play and play. And I said, 'Pete, let's play sometime, I'll play my bass and you play your guitar,' and Pete said, 'No, I'm not going to play with anybody until it's serious' and you know, it worked out for him!

III

If Pete Buck wasn't ready to form a band, a previous incumbent of the clerking job at Wuxtry Athens had already done so. Her name was Kate Pierson and her wacky art-school band the B-52's had broken out of the mid-seventies Athens scene to achieve international success. 'Kate did not officially clerk but hung out every day after her work across the street at the Banner-Herald,' recalls Dan Wall. 'She always smelled of newsprint. Yes, she occasionally waited on customers. The main objective, however, was to climb the old elevator shaft up to the roof to smoke pot!'

The B-52's showed that, amazingly, the world could be brought to listen to a band from one of the unhippest regions of the USA.

On the face of it, Athens was a totally unremarkable town and few, back in the mid-1970s, would have predicted that it would become one of the USA's coolest rock venues. The Classic City, so named because of its abundance of architecture in neo-Grecian style, was a southern backwater, situated on the Oconee River and the Piedmont Plateau, 65 miles northeast of Hartsfield International Airport in Atlanta. Perennially hot and humid, Athens is a seemingly inconspicuous town surrounded by small farm holdings. Some find the lushness of the landscape agreeable. For others, the scenery amounts to a disorientatingly endless super-saturating green, as writer Geoff Ward remembers:

> Green. Trailing green. Miles and miles of it, between Atlanta (where our plane touched down) and Athens, Georgia. The airport at Atlanta is as big as a European town. It's a shock to hit the freeway and have everything dissipate into this endless monotonous greenness. The occasional Baptist chapel shining whitely, or some odd farm building with a corrugated iron roof. Guys who look like ZZ Top driving pick-up trucks, with fishing

rods and guns in the back. It's ALL THE SAME, for mile after mile until I began to wonder irrationally if the driver had somehow taken us in a circle. Paradoxically, this open road gives you claustrophobia . . . It isn't the rolling, alluring green of the UK or France, but a broken, slightly parched horizontality of trailing kudzu. A seeming infinity of scratchy broken netting. So when you get to Athens it's a relief. Taco Bell and the Bank of America and the mall and the parking lots and gantries and all the other signals of American sameness look like soaring minarets must look after a camel ride through desert, or like one of those Spanish cities that suddenly rises out of the plain. The heart lifts.

In fact, Athens was late to feel the full force of the consumerist boom: it only gained its first shopping centre in 1961. Its economic and social rationale was interlinked with the University of Georgia, founded in 1785 and established in Athens in 1806. Athens had grown in commercial and industrial prominence throughout the nineteenth century. The Athens Railway Company was founded in 1870 and by the 1890s the seat of Clarke County local government administrative region had moved there from nearby Wakinsville. Although a hearty textile industry powered the Athens economy, it would be the reputation of the University that secured the town's importance. A 1980 census confirmed that of the total Athens population of 42,449, over half were students.

The University was liberal and peacenik in the 1960s and early 1970s. 'Several students even occupied the university president's office,' recalls Paul Butchart, but by 1975, in the post-Vietnam, post-Nixon era, the campus had quietened down politically, if not sexually. Ray Stevens' 1974 'novelty' hit 'The Streak' had turned millions over the world on to the questionable delights of revealing all in public places. Athens, ever the good-time town, organised the world's largest ever streak as thousands of students ran bare-butted through the campus. Athens was also well known in the gay subculture as progressive and accommodating. There was still, however, pretty much nowhere for the night-owl partygoer to go: 'By 5.30 p.m. there was not a soul on the streets,' remembers one Athenian. 'Athens was only a happening town to those in the know. The Freddies and Susies [fraternity and sorority members] didn't know what was going on. They were too busy listening to their beach music.'[11]

The University is situated downtown, and most of the clubs, bars and venues that developed in the late 1970s and 1980s were within walking distance of the campus. Although firmly in the Bible Belt, Athens and the University had a tradition of free thinking. 'Athens is a pleasant, easygoing city,' opines writer and academic Geoff Ward. The city of today is 'college-dominated, but not in the edgy, town–gown sense you sometimes get in England, but in consumer terms – full of cafés, bars, unstuffy restaurants. My sense of Athens was of a predominantly white culture, a youth culture, car-owning.' Indeed, the black community, such as it exists, appears marginal to the life of the city. Few of the indigenous Athens rock bands that made their mark in the post-punk era attempted any racial barrier-breaking, or sought to reflect southern forms such as soul or gospel.

According to cultural theorists Richard King and Helen Taylor, this lack of racial cultural exchange is unusual in the 'new' American South, with its 'rich and variegated culture'. However, what Athenian pop culture does undoubtedly exemplify is the new eclecticism of the South. 'Contemporary Southern culture shows a healthy, latitudinarian attitude toward the attempt to mix high and popular culture . . . and [seeks] to deploy the present to interrogate the past.'[12] It is in this spirit of the desire to combine disparate elements to form something radical and new that Athenian popular culture became distinctive and vital. Not just music, but film-making, poetry, literature and the fine arts – all attempted radical, fun and powerful recombinations of past and present styles.

The result was that Athens took punk not literally, but with ample doses of irony and play. Rather than dress clonishly with safety pins, spiky hair and leathers, people dressed *clownishly* in thrift store clothes, glad rags to party in. They took what was good about punk (its spirit, its fun, the sense that there were no rules any more) and jettisoned the bad (the musical and sartorial Stalinism, the rhetoric that three chords and three safety pins were all you needed). With few venues in which to perform, and liquor laws that restricted the late-night sale of alcohol, Athens developed a vibrant party scene. From around 1975 onwards, the cultural life of Athenian teenagers and 20-somethings was situated in private homes, warehouses, lofts and disused buildings, anywhere big enough for a keg of beer and a space to dance.

The B-52's, formed in late 1976 by Kate Pierson, Fred Schneider, Keith Strickland, Ricky Wilson and his sister Cindy Wilson, were the first new-wave band to break from the Athens scene. Up in New York, post-punk groups such as Talking Heads had married jerky new-wave guitars with funky dance grooves and had begun to create a space for newcomers interested in something a little more eclectic than the Ramones. The B-52's appealed to the arty teenager and 20-something with their undeniably kooky and fun image. They had been playing in various guises since the mid-1970s, desperately trying to inject some much-needed energy into a knackered local music scene. Theirs was a self-conscious trash aesthetic – and *aesthetic* it was, for behind the party fun was an intriguing blend of the kitsch and the serious.

'We'd go to the university and on Sunday they'd show foreign films and they'd be there – real, genuine, happy people, they're really fun,' says the Side Effects' Paul Butchart. The world of the B-52's was one of show-tunes, banality raised into art, surf guitar and kitsch retro organ, camp theatricality and heady glam rock (Cindy's hero was David Bowie). They also had their finger on the pulse of avant-garde pop, as their signature song 'Rock Lobster' showed. The screaming, high-pitched mutant vocal squeals from Cindy were reminiscent of Yoko Ono's vocal pyrotechnics, which had seriously pissed off a whole generation of Beatles fans for over a decade. The album version of 'Rock Lobster' lasted an ear-piercing 6 minutes and 45 seconds and, in its twists, turns and lofty ambition, it became the scene's equivalent of 'Bohemian Rhapsody'. Only a million times more cool. Most importantly though, the B-52's made music you could lose yourself in on the dance floor and at the gig. After the B-52's, all Athens bands had to create a music that made you want to stamp your feet and go crazy.

The B-52's were an inspiration. Their success showed that a bunch of people who were not virtuosos could form a band, have fun, and make money, as Betsy Dorminey remembers:

Their success sort of opened everyone's eyes to say, you know what, we can do this here. Why not play in a band, why not just do what you wanna do? It's a low-cost living place so people can

waitress during the day, play in a band, go on the road, quit
their job, find another one, and manage to get by. And you need
that kind of flexibility in a place for people to get involved in
your creative activities whether it be music or art or
photography or whatever.

An important Athens venue was Episode 247, in the mid-1970s
the only place in town that played the underground disco hits. A
predominantly gay club, it was also the only venue liberal enough to
popularise new musical sounds. Just as, in the UK, John Lydon
remembers that the gay bars were the only ones in the mid-seventies
playing any decent music, pre-punk, so it was in mid-decade USA:
'It would be the place to go for many of the artists in town,' affirms
Paul Butchart. 'It was here that many people were introduced to the
"new wave" music that was trickling out of the Big Apple'.[13] Like the
Teddy Boy look in the late 1940s and 1950s, the mod look in the
1960s and the glam and punk rock styles of the 1970s, the gay
subculture played a crucial role in taste-making, since these subcu-
ltures were formed out of the fashion consciousness of queer culture.
The 'heterosexualisation' of the gay look was a factor in creating new,
hip, 'straight' communities. 'Beforehand, you listened to the Allman
Brothers and you wore flannel shirts and jeans – it was the tail-end
of the hippy era,' says Dorminey.

> You would not believe the people in this town who went
> *absolutely* nuts when David Bowie came out, and Roxy Music,
> and all that stuff. It was like 'Where has this been all my life?'
> The gay crowd always pulled us in that direction. They were
> more expressive, and had the attitude of, 'Let's party! Let's go
> shop at the thrift store!' So, after a while, everybody used to
> shop there and have fun dressing up. You *had* to go and get a
> two-dollar skirt and some crazy earrings and go to a party. And
> *everybody* had parties because the bars were not open
> downtown. So the gay subculture was influencing the somewhat
> larger subculture of the art-rock people, who were desperate for
> *something beyond the flannel shirt.*

The B-52's played their first show on Valentine's Day 1977 in the
foyer of an old house in front of no more than forty witnesses,

unveiling 'Planet Claire' and 'Rock Lobster' in the process. They played just three parties and made their official Athens debut at a club called The Last Resort. The show was broadcast on local radio. They cut their first single for Danny Beard's small Atlanta-based record label, DB records. Crucially, they saw the importance of extending beyond Athens, and beyond Atlanta, early on in their career. It was artistically and financially expedient, as the audience in Atlanta and Athens was simply too small to sustain a career in pop.

'We went to New York because there was no place for us to play in Athens,' affirms Keith Strickland.[14] By 1978, they had begun playing prestigious gigs in New York. CBGBs passed on them, but after a week's residency at Max's Kansas City, the band were snapped up by Chris Blackwell's Island label to record their first album. The B-52's continued to patronise and support Athens talent and, once established in New York, the group would put up bands when they were in town and help get Athens acts booked and listened to by record companies.

With the B-52's removed, the next new wave band to break were the Tone Tones, who were gigging in late 1978 and early 1979 and secured gigs opening for big names such as the Police, Joe Jackson and the all-conquering B-52's. They would be quickly followed by the art-school pop of Pylon, who played their 'coming out' party two years to the day from the B-52's' first tentative public appearance. The gig itself was in a room in the loft apartment of the group's drummer, Curtis Crowe. Since the only illumination for the room was a 40-watt light bulb, one of the scenesters waggishly called the venue 'The Forty Watt Club' and the name, if not the original venue, would become part and parcel of the Athens scene for the next decade.

IV

For any music scene to develop, though, the music has to be heard, and here local radio played a big role, and particularly a courageous young DJ by the name of Kurt Wood. In the autumn of 1977, Wood, then a journalism student at the university, applied to work at 90.5 FM WOUG, the local campus radio station, which had been set up five years earlier.

After I had been working there a little I made a proposition to the guys who ran the station. At the time, the station played progressive jazz and folk music, a lot of good stuff, and spacey rock stuff too, like Spirogyra. At this point it was late '77, and I was beginning to read magazines like *Trouser Press* and *New York Rocker*. In 1977 I started buying tons of records direct from UK record stores – Sex Pistols, the Clash, the Jam, all that sort of stuff. So I went to the guys who ran the station and said, 'Look, we gotta have some sort of show here for this new music because I like it a lot.' And they said, 'Well, actually, we *hate* it!', but they were fair-minded enough to say, 'Well, we're reading a lot about it and how punk rock is the future but, you know, I don't think these guys can play and I think it's a load of crap . . . but, some people are taking it seriously and it's definitely not getting played on commercial radio station at all. Maybe if you could do a show here, we could see how it goes.' And in February 1978, with another friend of mine who has similar taste, we did a two-hour show and we called it *New Wave News*. We got a lot of phone calls and a good bit of response so I think we did another one a month later, and then maybe one more after that and then the school year ended. By the fall of '79, I actually had a regular show at the station. At that point I was music director and could schedule myself at pretty much any time I wanted. So it was Fridays, 4 till 6. I had read somewhere that *Ready Steady Go* was always on early on a Friday evening just as the Mods were ready to go out on the town.

We had a B-52's practice tape that we played on one of those shows, as they never really played around Athens too much. They were a bit older than me and some of those guys like Keith and Ricky had been playing in bands since the early seventies. The Zambo Flirts, for example. They were like the only band in town. They *were* the scene. The first time I went to see them they played at this venue called The Last Resort, which was like a folk club. That was the first time they played in public in Athens, around early '78, and I went expecting to see something like the Sex Pistols. Of course, they were nothing like that at all. They were totally into sixties stuff, that Ventures guitar sound. They were actually more like a retro band than anything, although at the time people didn't think of it in that manner. They kind of grew out of that and moved along, but in the early days they were pretty primitive. I think they played their first gig in early 1977 and the house where they used to live was where Paul (Butchart) and I lived later on. In the year that followed they just played parties around town, because there really was no place to play. They were too weird to play in a hard-rock venue downtown which had heavy metal cover bands or hits of the day cover bands.

It's hard to overestimate the importance of open-minded DJs and music fans such as Kurt Wood, for, without their determination and enthusiasm, American rock radio would never have had an alternative scene. Back then, it was called 'college radio' and its existence helped break much of the best music of the 1980s. Athens journalist Ballard Lesemann agrees:

Kurt Wood still manages the Taco Stand today, great guy, great record collector, he used to play drums in the Woggles. He was there in 1979 and getting a copy of *London Calling*, *Setting Sons* or whatever, and putting it into rotation. They play all sorts of crazy stuff from across the spectrum that you can't hear anywhere else. Sometimes it'll drive you nuts and it's a bunch of noise or whatever, but they're playing it. It's all volunteer, all student. You hear people playing the records at the wrong speed, or fluffing up their announcements on the mic, and I don't mind that at all. It's the antithesis of the commercialised crap you hear on commercial stations.

By 1979 the B-52's were living in New York, having parted ways with their original local manager. But they left behind them a spirit of fun and creativity and a recognisable scene. Athens was a welcoming, bohemian oasis of liberality in a desert of southern hick republicanism, and the art-school crowd presented a viable alternative to the creepy conservatism of sorority/fraternity cultural politics. Rents were cheap and houses were cheerful. Curtis Crowe of the influential Athenian art-school band Pylon remembers: 'All the houses in Athens looked like the Munsters' house and they were all cheap. You can get one of these great big houses and put four to eight people in them and everyone would end up paying $75 a month.'[15]

By January 1979 [says Paul Butchart], there had only been four
bands that had played more than one show: the B-52's, the Tone
Tones, the Method Actors and Pylon. The 'coming out' party for
the post-B-52's scene was a Halloween show at one of the local
venues, called Tyrone's OC, in October 1979. It featured Pylon
and a new band, the Method Actors, a duo containing two of the
members of the Tone Tones, who had split up during the
summer. This brought the total number of people actually
playing music in the 'scene' to eleven!

The entire scene itself was still tiny, probably only 150 people in
crazy dresses, wigs or short hair, straight ties and snappy trousers.
After the success of the Halloween gig, Tyrone's made one night a
week free for the new music. The Athens scene finally had a regular
venue.

Meanwhile, back at the Wuxtry, Pete Buck was intrigued by a
young art-school student with blond curly hair cut short at the back
and left to tumble over his eyes at the front, a pock-marked but
striking face, simultaneously beautiful and ugly, and a diffident,
demure manner, who began frequenting the shop on a regular basis.
Very often he would come into the shop arm-in-arm with two
beautiful young girls, and quietly approach the record store clerk for
tips on new wave music. Perhaps he needed educating? Certainly, he
was curious and eager to hear new sounds. He was already well
known on the 'scene' and was actually earning his beer money
working in a local steak-and-ale joint with aspirant musician Paul
Butchart. His name was John Michael Stipe, and the two women were
his sisters Lynda and Cyndy.

'I was looking for someone to start a band with, and Peter was the
only person in Athens that would talk to me,' is how Stipe put it in
2002.[16] 'I mean, I was very, very shy. He worked in a record store.
He sat there all day with this kind of sneer on his face, kind of
strumming on a guitar. We struck up a conversation, and at one
point talked about starting a band. I called him Richard for the first
three months that we knew each other, and he never once corrected
me. He never said "My name is not Richard, it's Peter."'

'He was a striking-looking guy and he also bought weird records,
which not everyone in the store did,' is how Buck remembers the
pre-fame Stipe. 'He had interesting tastes and we got to be friends.'

Michael Stipe would be the first to admit that, back in 1978, he had a hole in his musical knowledge the size of Canada. Indeed, while Peter Buck was a pop polymath, Stipe's own handle on pop history was precarious at best, for the most part running the whole gamut from Patti to Smith. For example, according to some sources, Stipe professed not to have known that the title of R.E.M.'s Grammy top-heavy *Out Of Time* was also the title of a Stones song. Peter Buck later commented: 'I can honestly say that he's never played a Beatles record. I know he's heard some, but I do remember flying to England, probably in the nineties. We're off to the airport and "Tomorrow Never Knows" comes on. I turn it up and Michael says, "Oh, that's pretty good, who is it?" And I say, "The Beatles." He's not musically illiterate – he knows a pretty wide range of interesting music – but he's not like me, who explores everything.'

According to interviews given by the middle-aged Stipe, as a youngster he was more likely to have listened to the Banana Splits and the Monkees than to anything 'legit'. In 1978, at the tail-end of punk, a fellow internee at art school in Athens remembers Stipe holding a flame for Belgian Plastic Bertrand's novelty single 'ça Plane Pour Moi', which was about as unhip as you could get.

However, Stipe had already gone through an earthquake-like musical awakening a few years earlier. The arrival of Patti Smith in his life, particularly via the late Robert Mapplethorpe's cover shot for Smith's debut album *Horses*, severely rocked the 15-year-old Stipe. Mapplethorpe's androgynous cover bewitched him, and the music inside sent him spinning.

She looked like Morticia Addams [said Stipe to *Mojo* in 1996]. *Horses* . . . pretty much tore my limbs off and put them back together in a different way. I was fifteen when I heard it, and that's pretty strong stuff for a fifteen-year-old American middle-class white boy, sitting in his parents' living room with his headphones on so they wouldn't hear it. It was like the first time you went into the ocean and got knocked down by a wave. It killed. It was so completely liberating. I had my parents' crappy headphones and I sat up all night with a huge bowl of cherries listening to Patti Smith, eating those cherries and going, Oh, my God! . . . Holy shit! . . . Fuck! . . . Then I was sick.[17]

The above is a typical piece of 'Stipean' hyperbole: keen to make an impact or colour a point, Stipe explains and describes heightened emotional states or emotional turmoil or even acts of creation in vomitory, orgasmic, abject language. Situations break him up and reassemble him, like a shaman undergoing a cosmic reconstruction during a séance. We get his meaning though. Stipe, like thousands of other spotty middle-class kids, sheltered and protected and watered and fed, was suddenly confronted by a man-woman belting out raucous but literate and passionate music. This event of near-spiritual proportions did not, thank goodness, kill Stipe's love of plain, goofy, silly pop, which would remain with him into superstardom. Hence the Banana Splits tolerance. Much later, when he and Stipe were musician friends, Buck would comment: 'Now I know the things musically he doesn't like: anything that really smacks of rock'n'roll. I love the Rolling Stones and could make records like that every day, but he has no interest in that.'[18]

What the close encounter with Patti Smith reaffirmed in the teenage Stipe was his sense of isolation, and separation. He was 'alone in a crowd', and, like many of the best lyricists and pop icons, he would later connect with his public by acting as a conduit for this miserableness. Perhaps more so than any other rock star of the last twenty years, Stipe has expressed this sense of cultural displacement better than any other writer within popular music. He is almost never maudlin, self-pitying or trite, but can express genuine grief and sadness in his songs more convincingly than pop could possibly dare to believe. 'I realised I was an outsider and I felt separated from most people. This music made the separation worse, but it gave me an ace in the hole because I had something they didn't have. I had knowledge of this incredible thing. It was just me sitting in the Midwest wishing I was in New York.'

Stipe was born John Michael Stipe on 4 January 1960, the day that Albert Camus, the existentialist author of L'étranger (The Stranger), died in an automobile accident – those of serendipitous bent may see this event as fitting. Those who have time for astrology might also like to ponder how Stipe demonstrates the Capricornian traits of diffidence, separateness and shyness, papered over in public by a forced extrovertism. David Bowie and Elvis Presley were also born under the sign of the randy mountain goat. These are the sort of people who feel terrified at social events and parties, but when the mask is put on, and the audience awaits, they can command its attention.

Stipe was what is uncharitably called an 'army brat'. His father was a serviceman and, for a time, served as a helicopter pilot in Vietnam, reportedly helping to spray the defoliation toxin Agent Orange. We know from Stipe's gnomic reference that his dad is a 'math wizard' who attempted to explain the Vietnam war to his son using algebra, and that he has 'huge, beautiful ears. They're like satellite receivers!'[19] Stipe's own surreally dry humour (a trait missed by many) was, perhaps, inherited from his father. However, Michael Stipe has been very successful – more than most international rock stars – at keeping his private life private, so we know very little at all about either his parents, or his elder sister Cyndy, who works as a special needs teacher. We do know that Stipe is very close to and protective of his family, and vice versa.

Stipe was born in Decatur, Georgia, but his father's itinerant lifestyle meant that the pre-teenager got an early taste for touring, finding himself stationed in Germany in 1968, before moving back, very briefly, to Georgia. By high school, he was living in Collinsville, Illinois, a town near East St Louis, where he found the whole process of secondary education harrowing: 'It was a very outgoing, flamboyant, loud school, and I hated everything about it. I was very, kind of afraid of a lot of things.' The difficult, acne-attacked Stipe, with, if school photos are any indication, geeky glasses and the beginnings of an Afro hairstyle, looked as awkward a teenager as they come.

As a child, Stipe had shown little signs of musical competence, though a story related to journalist Paul Zollo, which may or may not be apocryphal, indicates that the youngster did play piano competently. 'I did play well as a child. I think it was when my parents bought a piano and put it in my room and I had this cow skull . . . I lived in Texas at the time and I had this cow skull that I carried with me . . . One night I woke up and the piano and the cow, whose name was Clyde, were staring at me. From that day on I never played piano again. Till I joined the band.'[20]

This anthropomorphic horror story may be true, but the simple fact is that we know very little of Stipe's early days. The tricksy, jokey comments he has vouchsafed to journalists over the years should perhaps be treated with caution. The fuzzy picture that does emerge is of a quiet, private and mildly eccentric adolescent whose lifestyle on the hoof made him reluctant to form long-standing friendships, except with those of his immediate nuclear family. The fact that his paternal grandfather was a Methodist preacher in Southern Georgia whom Stipe observed at first hand, should perhaps not be downplayed given the pseudo-bible-bashing stage persona Stipe would drop into in his late twenties, but the influence of Talking Heads' David Byrne, particularly in the video for 'Once In A Lifetime' in 1981, was possibly of equal weight. The overall conclusion is that we simply don't have enough detail to construct an accurate psychological map to orientate us through the eccentric twists and turns of the pre-fame Stipe.

What is certain, however, is that, by the late 1970s, and his enrolment at art school in Athens, those around him felt his quiet presence, his personal beauty and his arty eccentricities very sharply, despite Stipe's constant claims in the media that he is no more eccentric than the rest of us. Stipe, perhaps mildly hypochondriacal, and certainly self-absorbed, faddishly picked his way through life with an eye and ear for the exotic. Wuxtry Records had the aural exotica he was thirsting for.

'Michael always seemed like an original and non-conformist,' confirms Dan Wall, 'always into "charades". You always had to try to second-guess what he was thinking, he was always the odd man out, certainly then. He liked to hang in the store, conspicuously when Pete was working. They were on the same wavelength. Pete would hold the "right" records for him.'

Stipe's liberal, art-school background, encouraged by the likes of artist James Herbert who lectured at the university, further developed his distinctive approach to culture and to music. Like many tutored in an environment where the experimental and unorthodox are encouraged, and the ability to make cultural references from across a range of disparate styles and genres is rewarded, Stipe gave Buck something new in his life too.

V

Stipe and Buck struck up a friendship based on a mutual appreciation of popular music, and the latter would steer the former into new musical territories, advising and cajoling. Soon the discussion turned more frequently to the task of making their own music. Buck, as we have seen, was waiting for the right opportunity to take the plunge. Stipe had already cut his teeth, fronting some short-lived punk bands as lead singer, and was currently part-timing for an Athens group, Gangster. The name 'punk' should not mislead us into thinking that Athens-style punk was the granite-hard wall of lead guitar played by some exponents in the UK, or the bubblegum thrash of the Ramones. Athens, like its Celtic counterpart in the UK, Liverpool, had a decidedly melodic take on challenging musical styles, with melody, harmony and sing-a-long choruses *de rigueur*. In addition, Athens new wave put a premium on danceability and goofy fun. 'Athens new wave music does not attack', was WUOG's radio station manager's assessment at the time.[21]

The Stipe-Buck duo needed a rhythm section and they found one, circuitously, from contacts within the burgeoning, and rather mental, party circuit. At the time, Buck was living with a student called Kathleen O'Brien. Bizarrely, their home was in an old pink-washed church, which Dan Wall, the Wuxtry's proprietor, himself subletted. The church has been romanticised beyond belief by historians and fans of the scene. In fact, it was a monstrous, cold and rather unwelcoming dump. Peter Buck would later comment that the place was barely standing by the time he left in 1980, and indeed the site, minus the steeple, was demolished later in the 1980s. 'It was a real zoo,' Buck told *Rolling Stone* a little later in 1983. 'We lived with some girl who dealt drugs – all these sickos coming over at four in the morning with the urge.'[22] It was also, as Dan Wall remembers, an eerie place to be alone in:

St Mary's Episcopal Church on Oconee Street was the first actual denominational church in Athens (early to mid-nineteenth century). There was an actual condo-style square box built into the front with bedrooms, toilet and kitchen. Crawl through a hole in a closet and presto! you're in the back of the church with apse, bell tower, pulpit etc. Mark Methe and I cleaned it up and rehearsed jazz there, although we had to be careful with equipment because of the leaky roof. Sometimes at night there was the sound of a baby crying – later we learned from the old caretaker the legend of a baby buried beneath the church's floorboards. We used to tell ourselves it was the wind howling through the eaves but we always felt that we could hear the baby crying that was buried under the floorboards of the church. The legend was that the baby had been there a long time.

The living areas were spacious and there was space for three in a room – Kathleen, Peter Buck and his record collection. Surprisingly, Kathleen was an unreconstituted musical squarehead, as DJ Kurt Wood remembers: 'She was kind of a rock'n'roll chick. She was really into the Allman Brothers and stuff like that. After Pete had moved down there I think I was visiting and there were all these Allman Brothers albums and I was like "Wow, how do you guys get along?" "Simple," he said. "We don't discuss music."'

Kathleen also had a huge crush on a boy she had been in dorms with the year before, and would try to engineer any situation to be in the same room as him. His name was Bill Berry, a quietly spoken, rather charming guy, undeniably handsome, and the possessor of a set of eyebrows that joined in the middle. Rather than give the 20-year-old a sinister, Mr Hyde look, they suited his cute face perfectly. Bill was also a musician and, by 1979, a reasonably proficient drummer, having played in a group, the Wuoggers, which included Kathleen. That was, as Paul Butchart remembers, a strange affair to be sure: 'She used to work at the WUOG radio station and in a band called the Wuoggers, who were this campy art band who opened for the Brains, an Atlanta band. Bill was the drummer. There were like ten people in the band, a bunch of girls dressed up in catsuits.'

Berry's musical buddy was a slight, boffinish young man named Mike Mills. Yellow of tooth and pudding basin of haircut, Mills was also perma-friendly and, at the tender age of 20, already a talented musician. Bill and Mike had met years before at school, back in Macon, Georgia. William Thomas Berry was born on 31 July 1958 in Duluth, Minnesota, the home town of a certain Robert Zimmerman, born 17 years earlier. Berry was a musical child who spent his pre-teenage years fiddling around on the ukelele while his big brothers fed him a diet of Motown soul. In fact, although Bill would become world-famous as a drummer, he was just as accomplished on guitar and would later write some classic melodies on that instrument, and play impromptu acoustic sets at parties. Unlike the less than enthusiastic response from Peter Buck's parents, Bill Berry's household was musically proactive and, when he was about ten, his parents bought him his first drum kit. The Berry family relocated to Macon in 1972. In Bill Berry's high school class was Michael Edward Mills, born in California on 17 December 1958. Mills' dad was a

Georgian and the family had relocated to the South when Mills was a toddler. His parents were extremely musical, Adora being a talented pianist and Frank a commanding tenor who sang regularly in the church choir. The young Mills therefore had a classical musical training, although he kept an ear out for pop too. At high school he played sousaphone, before switching to guitar.

Berry, into drugs and teenage stuff, hated Mills, who was a model student polite to teachers and accustomed to straight 'A' grades. Mills, however, was quite capable of sending up his own sartorial nerdiness, and his self-deprecation and not inconsiderable personal charm masked an addictive and rumbustious nature. In years to come, Mills would be dubbed 'trouble' by the touring entourage, as his capacity for almost nonstop amiable partying was legendary. Back in high school, though, Mills and Buck appeared polar opposites.

'Well, Bill and I, when we knew each other in high school, were not friends because we were very different,' says Mike Mills. 'He was sort of the "JD" and I was more of the brainy kid, and he was on the wrong side of the law.' Matters came to a potentially ugly head when both lads answered an ad for an audition for a local rock band. The band was to be called Shadowfax, after Gandalf's horse in the *Lord of the Rings*. Guitarist David Clarke from the band still performs to this day. Berry claims that if he hadn't already set up his drum kit he would have left there and then. However, as so often in the course of human affairs, arch enemies found that they had far more in common that they had originally thought, and the two became inseparable buddies, spending their teenage years playing in various bands. At the time, Berry was competent musically, but Mills excelled. Bass guitar, piano, even a little bit of singing, it was all within the power of the classically trained Mills. He could read music. He was a true musician. He was a big musical catch.

So, in a rather different way, was affable Bill Berry, for Berry had hands-on, if rather limited, experience of the music business. Most students took part-time jobs to help keep them in beer and drugs, and Berry, who harboured serious intentions of entering the music business as a music lawyer, helped out at Paragon booking agency in Macon, Georgia. Paragon was headed by Ian Copeland, whose brother, Miles, was a budding rock mogul, and whose kid brother, Stuart, was about to hit the big time as drummer with the Police. Ian

Copeland flew out from the UK to take control of Paragon, while Miles was in the process of setting up his own label, I.R.S., as a conduit for new wave acts. Ian Copeland remembers Bill Berry, the quintessentially polite Southerner, as the gofer who picked him up at the airport and drove him back to base camp.

'There he was with one eyebrow, calling me sir . . . yessir, yessir,' Copeland told *Mojo*.[23] Berry also impressed Copeland as the only one at Paragon who understood, and liked, the new wave and punk records Copeland had brought back from the UK and had been so fascinated by. 'I used to drive people up the wall going on about punk. Bill and Mike were the only people I could get to come over and listen to the music! They used to jam on equipment that I had brought with me and we'd be playing the Ramones and stuff . . . In fact, Bill, Mike Mills and I formed a band called the Frustrations.' The period at Paragon was vital for Bill Berry. If Buck had the knowledge, Stipe the arty attitude and Mills the technique, Berry had the experience of what it was actually like in the music business.

VI

In January 1979, the inseparable Mills and Berry moved to Athens to enrol at the university, and in the autumn of 1979, Kathleen O'Brien introduced Bill and Mike to Michael and Peter. Unfortunately, Mike Mills was completely pissed, and could barely stand, let alone hold a conversation about the demerits of Suicide's first album with Peter Buck.

'I remember him sitting on the floor and yelling at somebody to get him his beer because he couldn't reach it,' recalls Peter Buck in 2002. 'Michael said he really liked my eyebrows and that's the reason we should get together,' Bill Berry told *Vox* in 1998.[24] Eventually the foursome got together, but it could have been oh so different. Stipe and Buck had already been in contact with two other local musicians about the possibility of forming a band.

'I could have been the drummer for a group with Peter Buck and Michael Stipe in it,' affirms Paul Butchart. 'The original next band in town, after the Method Actors, was going to be me on drums, Kit Swartz on guitar and bass, Peter playing guitar and Michael Stipe singing.'

However, when a rehearsal was called, Butchart and Swartz were nowhere to be found. What happened?

'I don't know!' laughs Butchart. 'It was probably some sort of anxiety, or there was a party that night and we decided to get drunk. There's no telling why we didn't show up. I still tell them I'd love to play drums!'

These were innocent and wild times in which to be young in Athens: unbridled hedonism, a pre-AIDS-era free-for-all of music, sex and drugs. There was a sense of share and share alike, keep it in the 'family', with the only real danger a dose of herpes. 'Back then everybody was sleeping with everybody anyway,' says one local musician. 'It was a very intimate family, so to speak. There were only 50 or 60 of us, so we had to get it where we could!'

Athens was also a drug-taker's Mecca, with hallucinogenics the favourite drug. This was a pre-ecstasy scene, but one which, in its use of mind-expanding drugs, formed a link between hippydom and rave. In the UK, fast drugs went hand in glove with the nihilistic aggression and sense of denial of the music. In late-seventies Athens, where a trippy party atmosphere prevailed, LSD and its derivatives powered the people on. A scenester gives the low-down:

In the early days, it wasn't ecstasy, it was MDA. Ecstasy was a derivative and created because the drug MDA was made illegal. They added another methyl molecule, changed it from methyl-di-amphetamine to di-methyl di-amphetamine so it circumvented the illegality of MDA and created a legal drug which was eventually made illegal. There's something written on a sidewalk here in Athens and it says, 'Love and Spiritual Development', which is what you could say those three letters did for this town. It was written by some local artist in wet cement – you can barely see it now but it's there, and it's right around the corner from Barber Street, when the scene was much smaller.

These were relatively uncomplicated, hedonistic days, with part-ner-swapping no big deal. 'Kathleen and I were kind of going out and Bill met her at a bar and kind of hit on her and he moved in with us, kind of,' says Buck. 'We weren't actually living together, we were sort of seeing each other occasionally, and then she started seeing him, and she wasn't seeing me. You gotta remember that we were all like 20 and 21, and it was 1979, 1980 and AIDS wasn't around as far as we knew. There was a whole lot of MDA circulating, which was basically ecstasy, so that kind of thing wasn't particularly unusual.'

For some, the hedonism reached its apogee on New Year's Eve in 1979, at a party held at the church, as Kurt Wood remembers, just about:

> The party on New Year's Eve – oh yeah, that was the *real* party. For me that was a really great party. I think Kathleen was working for a catering company at the time and she had finagled all the champagne that hadn't been used, and all this left-over food. I remember there was all this ham and roast beef. I can remember hanging out that day before the party with Pete Buck and probably Paul Butchart, making tapes for the party, probably Abba, the Monkees and the Archies, all sorts of cool pop stuff, as well as new wave and punk stuff, Sex Pistols, the Jam, the Ramones. We had these tapes to play so that we didn't have to change records when we chatted up a girl or were getting drunk or whatever. A lot of the food got thrown round the room and the champagne bottles got smashed. I think the tables maybe actually collapsed and all the food fell on the shag carpet. It was quite a mess, some people were dancing round, and stuff was going on in the back room, of a sexual nature. It was a great party!

In February 1980, O'Brien decided to hold another party at the church, this time to celebrate her birthday. It was scheduled for 5 April, and Kathleen was determined to have some live music. After the scene had descended on the Georgia Theater on 29 February to see John Cale in concert there was an after-show party to celebrate Kurt Wood's birthday. It was here that Kathleen plucked up courage to ask Paul Butchart, Kit Swartz, and Jimmy Ellison aka the Side Effects to play. Kathleen also asked Berry, Buck, Mills and Stipe if they would bite the bullet and play a set too.

At first demurring, the terrified twenty-somethings needed some severe pressurising before they agreed to step up to the mic stand and play. Ultimately they relented and spent the second half of February and the whole of March drinking beer and rehearsing. They had, even by this stage, already written a handful of original numbers. 'Within eight months of Michael and I meeting we were rehearsing and playing with Mike and Bill' says Peter Buck. It was the first part of 1979, maybe April or May, when I had met Michael. We were actually writing songs together before we met Mike and Bill. For example, "All the Right Friends", Michael and I wrote ourselves towards the end of 1979. That's kind of where we were then, it's definitely new wave, punk influenced, without fuzzy guitar. I thought fuzzy guitar was a kind of Deep Purple cliché, so I was looking to have a clean-sounding guitar.'

Wood: 'They were practising at the church maybe a couple of times a week, maybe from late fall 1979. We'd put some money together to get a case of beer, we would hang out and watch TV, take drugs or whatever, and by the time they played live they had it relatively together. R.E.M. practised at the back. You went through a hole in Kathleen's closet into the back area and that's where the altar was. That bit was kind of rotten and full of holes, you had to be kind of careful. When that party was taking place people were occasionally falling through the floor!'

The band began to define roles. Mills could play lead and bass guitar. Buck was hopeless on the bass and not exactly that proficient on lead either, certainly in comparison with Mills, but he would muddle through and eventually develop an arpeggiated and highly distinctive style. Just don't ask him to solo, that's all. Not only was this technically beyond him but it was against his punk religion – proper music was not of the virtuoso kind.

On the morning of 5 April, Wood invited the Side Effects into the WUOG studio, and the as yet unnamed headlining act of Buck, Mills, Berry and Stipe strolled in with them to be interviewed. Stipe and co asked the audience to vote on such names as 'Third Wave', 'Negro Wives' and 'Twisted Kites'. There was next to no publicity for the party up until that point. Paul Butchart:

One thing about Kathleen O'Brien's birthday party was that it was supposed to be a big secret. The reason for this being that at the time Athens was a party town and if you didn't want your party to go out of bounds, you only spread the news by word of mouth. One weekend before the party a lot of what I guess you would call townies went to see the Woody Allen movie *Sleeper*, about this guy that wakes up in the future. There is this one scene where someone shows the main female lead (I can't remember her name) one of those paintings from the sixties with the sloe-eyed figures, the ones with the big sad eyes. She looks at the painting and says, and I think this is close 'Wow! That is keen, no wait, that is more than keen, it's Kugat!', and so from that point on when something was deemed exceptional, we referred to it as Kugat.

Due to the secrecy of the party, there were very few posters made and those only by the Side Effects. They just had the name of the band at the top and a picture by Diane Arbus of a boy holding a hand grenade as the illustration. Each poster was hand-coloured by the band and put up. I'd say there were perhaps only 15–20 at the most. None of the posters gave the location of the event, but some people had handwritten on them, 'Only the Kugat will know'. Since R.E.M. didn't have a name at the time they put up no posters, but the poster that was hanging in the small Wuxtry downtown had handwritten on it 'with Twisted Kites', making this perhaps the only reference to the other band playing at the party.

According to Mike Mills, the band that played that night still had no fixed identity. 'We had no name. Peter wanted to call the band Twisted Kites. Nobody else liked that name, so Peter may have said in interviews that, just for that one show, we were called Twisted Kites, but we weren't called that in my mind. As far as I was concerned, we had no name.'

It soon became apparent that the party itself, rather than the small-scale secret gig first mooted, had been publicised across town. So, with a rudimentary stage area cleared for the bands, and kegs of free beer in place, some 300 people turned up to be entertained. In the audience was the Wuxtry's Dan Wall: 'I remember a rainy night. Where you might imagine huge stained-glass windows, this church had shutters. This was an old fan-yourself type of church – this was before air-conditioning. So, many people just hung on the windows outside and looked in, which is what I did.'

The first band on the bill was the Side Effects. Paul Butchart remembers the first-ever public performance of a band that would eventually morph into R.E.M.:

Time for our debut set, and the whole place is packed. There are even people hanging in the windows next to the stage, being careful not to fall through the holes in the floor. We are scared to death! We open with 'I Always Used To Watch You' and run quickly through our set, ending with a song the other guitarist would eventually name for us, 'Neat In The Street'. For some reason I think the idea of playing before the audience has given us some weird boost of energy. Finally our set is finished and everyone is screaming for an encore, so we play our first two songs over again.

The headlining band finally takes the stage for the first time ever. They play 'I Can't Control Myself'. Or maybe it was 'Nervous Breakdown'. It is hard to remember. Our set is over and the need to remain sober has long vanished. However, their set is just beginning, and for them it will be the first of many for years to come.

Although one cannot be certain of the exact set list, or the order the songs were played in, R.E.M. fans and collectors posit that the following songs were definitely played that rainy night almost a quarter of a century ago: 'I Can't Control Myself', 'God Save The Queen', 'Nervous Breakdown', '(I'm Not Your) Stepping Stone', 'Shakin' All Over', 'Secret Agent Man', 'With A Girl Like You', 'Dangerous Times', 'All The Right Friends', 'Different Girl', 'Narrator', 'Just A Touch' (later to crop up on *Lifes Rich Pageant*), 'Baby I', 'Mystery To Me', 'Permanent Vacation', 'Action', 'Honky Tonk Women' and 'Roadrunner'. By all accounts, they went down a storm, and played with good technique. They were certainly the best-rehearsed band on the bill, if not the most original in terms of material.

After the gig, the usual finale of booze and sex predictably closed the evening. In fact, as Paul Butchart remembers, Peter Buck himself had soon divested himself of his underpants. 'In the early days, it was just a core of 50 or 60 people; after the church party I was cleaning out my brother's van. I opened the refrigerator and there was some underwear in there and Peter Buck said, "Oh, that was mine, yeah I ended up going in there after the church party and we got it on and I didn't know what to do with my underwear so I put it in the refrigerator!"'

That unnamed band were just one of half a dozen or so neophyte Athens-based bands, and there was no sense that they were anything more than a competent covers band with a nice pop attitude and a cute lead singer. How wrong could people be?

2. 'WE JUST LIKE THE DOTS', 1980–82

I

The band that played the church gig in spring 1980 would almost certainly have been sucked into the relative obscurity of the Athens party scene and broken up within a year, had it not been for two unrelated factors that would project them out of the mire of mediocrity they were surely destined to inhabit. The first was an inspired name change. The second was the interest and support of a man from North Carolina whose entrepreneurial instincts and friendship went way beyond the call of duty and would continue to do so for the next 15 years.

The adoption of the name 'R.E.M.', originally often written in lower case (as the band's singer often couldn't be bothered to depress the shift key on his typewriter), was a defining moment. It's hard to overestimate the importance of selecting a groovy name for a rock band or act. Those that work sound natural, despite a surface silliness (the Beatles, for example). Those that don't (Crikey it's the Cromptons!) appear restraining and self-sabotaging, laughable and contrived rather than evocative and strange.

The choice of 'R.E.M.' as opposed to some of the other titles floating around at the time, among which were 'Slug Bank' and 'Cans Of Piss' in addition to the aforementioned 'Negro Wives' and 'Third Wave', was *not* meant to be a knowingly intellectual reference to a phase of sleep known as 'rapid eye movement'. It was simply a name plucked at random from a dictionary by Michael Stipe. The band liked the name because it was short, easily remembered and nonspecific.

'We wanted something short and small. The vogue at that point for punk or for that kind of band was to name yourself after something revolting – the Revolting Cocks,' is how Mills puts it. 'Basically, we didn't want a name that would peg us as one kind of band. That's what we were trying to avoid. We didn't want anyone to read the name and be able to tell what we sounded like. We didn't want anything that was stupid or limiting, and the open-endedness was very important as well.'

'*We just like the dots*'[1] was Stipe's typically gnomic explanation. You could read into it whatever you wished. For a band that would soon develop a cache of richly allusive songs, songs that provoked listeners into completing their muddied meanings, rather than foisting an interpretation on them, this was an inspired choice. It looked cool on posters, it looked good on album sleeves, it tripped off the tongue. The fact that, for those willing to do the research, it also alluded to a dream state, added a layer of allusion that fitted in with the trance-like structures of some of their songs, albeit on a symbolic level.[2] When Stipe commented to photographer and journalist George Dubose that ' "R.E.M." means nothing', he wasn't just being elusive for the sake of it. In a sense, just as their music left ample room for personal interpretation, so their name could mean anything and nothing simultaneously. The choice of name was also unwittingly apt since, technically, rapid eye movement is the physical manifestation of 'paradoxical sleep'. This is a phase that *appears* deep but is characterised by increased brain activity and eye movement so isn't strictly so. Stipe and co. would produce music just like this – music which appeared deep but was, in fact, just pop, or music which appeared superficial and light but which was also enduring and weighty.

Names can only get you so far, though, as One The Juggler would later find out. Indeed, talent can only get you so far too. What the fledgling rock act needs is a person willing to press the flesh, brown-nose the right people, be the telephone bullshit artist – in other words, someone with connections, drive, enthusiasm and an almost unquestioning loyalty. Such a man was Jefferson Holt.

Holt worked as a record store owner in Chapel Hill, North Carolina, and, at 28, cut an eccentric figure. His thin, tall frame, sallow complexion, spectacles and penchant for wearing rather straight blazers were coupled with all the foibles of the eccentric

Englishman (one of his favourites was Vivian Stanshall), mixed with a touch of James Stewart. Jefferson was a clever man, self-confident and self-deprecating. He was not averse to shaving off his eyebrows for a laugh. 'I worked in a record store called School Kids with Jefferson,' remembers Ann-Louise Lipman, one-time girlfriend of Jefferson, and a huge fan of the band in the 1980s. 'We knew each other for ten years. He's odd, but he's nice. He was very intelligent, from North Carolina, and he was working in this record store called Big Shot. We got to know each other and became friends. I remember him saying, "I think I'm going to go off with them," and I said, "Great, go, what are you doing here? Nothing, *per se*, just living in a college town and running after girls."'

Jefferson and his business associate, a long-haired, beer-drinking rock enthusiast by the name of David Healy, had seen the band live at a venue called The Station in North Carolina, on 19 July 1980. 'By the end of the night the windows were dripping with perspiration and the audience was dancing on the bar,'[3] says Paul Butchart. Bitten by the R.E.M. bug, Holt soon moved to Athens to be close to the next big thing.

There was, of course, a downside to Holt too. 'Jefferson could be self-centred,' says Lipman. His eccentricities also extended to an unorthodox and, some might hint, voyeuristic view of women. 'When I first met him, he would have this Polaroid camera and when girls came into the store he would take pictures of them. At the time I thought it was harmless, jokey and sort of endearing!' she laughs.

Musician Linda Hopper remembers Jefferson as the doorman at a club in Chapel Hill, North Carolina. 'I think it was called the Freight Train. It was the first time R.E.M. played there . . . and then the next thing I know he's down there working with the guys. He was about 27 or 28 and had been working at a record store, Chapter 3 in Chapel Hill, dying for a reason to get out of North Carolina. They all hit it off straight away, and I think it was through him they met Mitch Easter and stuff.'[4]

'Jefferson I thought was a straight-up guy,' remembers photographer George Dubose. 'He always maintained an authoritarian (but I don't mean a heavy authoritarian) air. The B-52's' first manager, Maureen McLaughlin, would go to the shows and spend more time dancing and chatting with her pals than sussing out the crowd to see who might be there from a record label. Jefferson I never saw doing anything but taking care of business at the gigs. I was surprised, when R.E.M. became big, that they took him with them. Whereas the B-52's allowed Maureen to be cut out by Gary Kurfurst [then the Talking Heads' manager]'.[5]

'He was the one who was really intent on making it happen for R.E.M. and he worked awful hard,' affirms Betsy Dorminey. 'He had a bigger equity position in that band than most managers do, but the other side of that story is that he really put his heart and soul into making it a success. Sometimes you have to give people a bigger share of the pie if you really want them to make that pie as big as it can possibly be.'

Prior to Jefferson Holt, the general dogsbody around R.E.M. was Kathleen O'Brien, one-time girlfriend to both Buck and Berry, who financed the phone calls and drove the band round their first few gigs that summer of 1980. While Bill Berry acted as unofficial booking agent, she pressed and cajoled and told the band they were great. For her pains, she was involved in a serious car accident in July 1980 when a car jack-knifed in front of her and crashed into the side of her vehicle. Her life was probably saved by the presence of Bill Berry's drum kit, which absorbed the impact.

O'Brien's role was taken on by Holt some time in the second half of 1980, who handled it all with equanimity, as Mitch Easter, the future co-producer of R.E.M.'s first three releases, commented:

I have nothing bad to say about Jefferson. He did drive a hard bargain, but that's fine, that was his job. He seemed to totally look after those guys, and the thing that was really great about him was that he had this bemusement about it all that was really becoming. There are so many things that can go on with a new band; people can be way too emotional or short-sighted. He always seemed to take the long view, and had a lot of faith in them even when *they* didn't seem to have much faith in *him*. Instead of being insulted by that he would sort of soldier on, and I'm telling you, if he hadn't have been there you would *never had heard of them*, I'm positive. They were just a bunch of young guys. I'm sure they would have gotten pissed off with one another early on, failed to show up for the gig or whatever, and broken up. Jefferson was this very calm, parent-like figure who made sure things got done. He just helped them in ways that I'm not sure they fully appreciated.

After the band had gotten signed and was doing some consistent business, I remember Pete Buck introducing Jefferson to someone with the words 'This is Jefferson. He's our manager for now.' Right in front of him, 'manager for *now*'. Somebody else would have said, 'Fuck you man!', but he didn't. Jefferson just laughed, because he just knew how they were. He was very classy; he never seemed to descend into that manager stereotype of just screaming at people or anything like that. He was just a good guy.

Holt became one of the R.E.M. gang. 'Jefferson was a funny guy, always laughing about something in a pretty nice way, not in a cutting way like Pete Buck can do sometimes,' recollects Kurt Wood. 'I remember hanging out with him the night John Lennon was shot, just me and him wandering around all night getting drunk and being out of sorts and upset.'

An indication of the potentially temporary status of R.E.M. can be found in the fact that Bill Berry was, in fact, hedging his bets throughout 1980 and into 1981. A March 1981 issue of *The New York Rocker* features three Athens bands – R.E.M., Love Tractor and the Side Effects – and Bill Berry is pictured in the first two of the three groups. Berry was apparently thinking of full-timing for Love Tractor as he wasn't sure which of the two bands was more serious.[6]

In the first half of 1980, all four members of R.E.M. dropped out of university. At one stage, Buck had three jobs: 'I was actually going into night school at the University of Georgia while the band was forming, and during the first six months of the band performing I was going to school two nights a week, working five days a week at the record store, and then playing live all weekend. It got to the point where I was having 120-hour weeks and sleep just wasn't on the cards, so school was the first thing to go.'

'I was on the honours programme, and I did very well on the honours course,' says Mike Mills. 'They were all small classes with pretty good teachers and you'd sit around and talk and it was great. The things I had problems with were the 300-people biology lectures which I couldn't get interested in and eventually that dropped my grade point average to the point where I was no longer allowed to participate in the honours programme. So, there was nearly no reason for me to continue in school, and the band was happening, so I quit. I was about eleven hours short of becoming a junior; I was almost through two years of school. I never majored. On becoming a junior, I would have had to declare a major and I guess that it probably would have been journalism. To earn some money I also worked as an inserter. The inserting machine is the thing that puts the little advertising supplements in newspapers – it actually lifts up the paper and slides in the adverts. I worked on that machine and stacked papers.'

'Michael was the last one to leave because he actually had a career in mind,' recalls Buck. 'He was an art historian and a photography student and was doing really well. I mean, he would have got his degree and probably some kind of masters and be doing something of that nature if he hadn't been in a band. He was the last to leave university. Bill and Mike dropped out the second they could and I hung in there because I wanted to finish the quarter and get "A" so that if I had to come back I could. At night school you can get "A"s if you're breathing, basically.'

R.E.M. were a competent band with an increasingly powerful stage presence, but it is safe to say that, without the intervention of Holt, they would almost certainly have found it difficult to attain anything other·than local cult status. The band Holt found in 1980 was nothing like a fighting unit. It's hard to underplay just how stinky and ragamuffin they were back in 1980. There are tales of Michael Stipe shaving in coffee because there was no hot water, and of him losing his one pair of trousers on a freeway. 'I had a pair of cotton black pants, and I wore them every day for months,' Stipe told *Q*. 'And Bill hung them outside the van 'cos they smelled so bad. And they flapped off on the highway. They were the only ones I had.'[7]

Paul Butchart remembers one gig particularly vividly:

When the Side Effects played a fraternity party once, our friends showed up because we had to make our own fun. I think we played our set twice. Some guy, one of the fraternity brothers, came up to me and said, 'Can I ask you a favour? Do you see your friends over there? Can you please ask them to leave? They smell really bad and they are really offending our audience.' And I said, 'Who?' and he pointed over to Michael Stipe and this other girl, she was French, I think. So I went over and said, 'Hey, sorry, but they want you to leave.'

One of the smelly escapades, which would stand them in good stead, had occurred back in the spring break of 1980, immediately before the church gig. Paul Butchart, Kurt Wood, Peter Buck and Michael Stipe had decided to head north; while the rest of student humanity headed south to hit the beaches, the Big Apple was their destination. This was a big deal for them. These four young bucks were not overly familiar with travelling outside the state boundaries and journeyed to New York in excited trepidation. Michael Stipe, ever the eccentric, spent virtually all his money in the first few hours buying trousers at a clothes shop. After several days slumming in the van, taking in, at Stipe's behest, a Klaus Nomi gig, grooving at a Pylon gig, travelling round the technological wonder that was the underground, checking out Harlem in wide-eyed amazement and generally culture-overdosing, these four hicks from the sticks wound up at an after-show party for Joe 'King' Carasco. And, who would be there but the great Lester Bangs.

Bangs, totally the worse for wear from alcohol, and matted in sweat, held court, firing off volleys of abuse at anyone daft enough to try to talk to a man so befuddled by drugs and booze that he was virtually ranting. Michael Stipe, starving hungry, arrived to find only the dessert trolley left to eat. It was this party that, seven years later, would be immortalised in the scatter-gun white rap of 'It's the End of The World As We Know It', as a dream recollection of a party surreally incorporating men whose initials were, like Lester Bangs, 'LB'.

'I had read all of Lester Bangs stuff in *Creem* and thought he was the greatest thing in the world,' remembers Peter Buck. 'Now here we were at this party, filling up on birthday cake and jelly beans. Lester was standing there, and every time someone walked by – it was like a mantra – he'd have some word to say to them. He called me a rotten cocksucker. I didn't take it personally because everybody else got it, too. I was like: "That's Lester Bangs! That's so cool! I was cursed at by my idol!"'[8]

The lads also left an impression on the olfactory faculties of the party's hostess, Kate Moline. A couple of years afterwards, Paul Butchart was chatting away to her when he was roadying for Pylon and Kate was also working for the band. 'It was her party and I remember going up to her to reintroduce myself. I said, "Hey, we were at your party, and Lester Bangs was there!" and she countered, "I know; you were the guys who smelt bad, weren't you?!"'

The New York trip would provide a dummy run for the future R.E.M.-ers. It would mark the start of a gruelling seven years of constant touring, sleeping in crappy hotels, on people's floors, in strange beds (allegedly, Buck would occasionally find himself in a bed with Mike Mills such was their poverty), of eating takeaway meals and of having to grab a wash and brush-up on the hoof. 'We only could afford one hotel room,' remembers Mills. 'We never lost money, ever, on a tour and we did that in the early days by staying in hotel rooms with two double beds. Peter and I stayed in one, and Michael and Bill slept in the other. Sometimes if we had a manager with us, somebody else would rotate out to the van.'

No one can say success came easily to R.E.M. They worked at it and took their art completely seriously. They also made it the hard way, through constant, gruelling touring, building solid support state by state, year by year, with little encouragement or empathy from the media, radio, television or even, at times, from the head of their record label.

II

The surprising thing about R.E.M.'s success, however, was that it appeared to be more or less instant in Athens and the surrounding territories, and this was, to an extent, resented. While other Athens bands played to small, if enthusiastic, audiences, R.E.M. drew bigger and bigger crowds. Their first gig as R.E.M. was on 19 April 1980 at a small venue called The Coffee Club 11-11 in Athens, which would eventually become one of the venues of the 40 Watt Club and was basically a warehouse rented by Rick 'the Printer' Hawkins.

'The venue had an espresso machine. We'd go in there and make coffee and hang out, and at the back there was this big empty room,' recalls Paul Butchart. 'There would be art shows and performance art people getting up on a chair and reading poetry. There was a jukebox and we'd be playing music and having dance parties.' Ostensibly, the show was put on to raise funds for Kathleen O'Brien, as one of the taps from the kegs of beer from the church party had been stolen and she had lost her deposit. It was brought to a halt just after 2 a.m., when the police raided it, apparently because the music was too loud.

On 6 May, the band supported the Brains at Tyrone's. 'I got them the gig,' says Dan Wall. 'Kate Pierson of B-52's fame shot part of the video and accidentally turned off the microphone. The tape exists in

Wuxtry archives, as do several others.' On 6 July 1980, the band took the next step up the ladder to play The Warehouse in Atlanta, after demoing some tracks at Wuxtry Records that day. The Wuxtry session was videoed with a view to using it as a promotional clip to get bookings, but this was never used. The film remains the earliest known video tape of the band. R.E.M.'s first trip beyond state boundaries was on 18 and 19 July, when they played The Station in Carrboro, North Carolina. By the summer of 1980, they were a happening band on the local scene.

'I don't look back on it much, but when I do I always think, yeah, those were kind of halcyon days,' says Peter Buck in 2002. 'The first time that we ever charged money for a show, it was sold out and that's unbelievable, that was unheard of. I think it was at Tyrone's. We played in front of 400 people on our first professional performance. We were famous in Athens. We had people asking for autographs after our first show. People were following us around, and we had groupies. It was weird. We weren't that great yet. But we were pretty cool.'

R.E.M. were also an unusually industrious band. 'We were working seven days a week, touring, playing,' says Buck. 'We threw away three albums' worth of stuff before we made our first single.' They had a policy of playing just about anywhere – clubs, bars, restaurants, chicken diners, pizza parlours, gay and lesbian bars – on any night of the week, for any clientele, simply to get heard. 'I remember one gig in 1982 in San Antonio somewhere where there was an air base,' recalls a wry Peter Buck. 'They just hated us, but they couldn't attack us because there were all these MPs [Military Police] there. Basically they had these MPs in front of us to prevent them from getting on stage and killing us. The major who took care of us was so nice and said, "Look we'll go over to the officers' club and get drunk, those people were idiots." Bill walked off stage so we got Sarah from Let's Active to fill in. They were yelling "faggot!" at us and we were playing up to it. It was pretty amazing. And we were getting paid quite a fair amount of money.'

By playing to indifferent or even hostile audiences, the band had to take each gig as if it were their last. They had to impress the sceptical, and they did so by getting the audience up and dancing. They broke pockets of resistance by the sheer force of their personalities.

'I remember seeing them at a venue called Toad's Place in New Haven, Connecticut. They were really just getting started, it was maybe 1982,' recalls Betsy Dorminey. 'New Haven's a funny town because it's got this really superb university and this ratty town around it! They weren't too well known, particularly in the northeast, so there was almost nobody there. But Michael gave it 200 per cent. They worked really hard and they were just delightful and wonderful and they worked so hard even if there was hardly anybody in the room. A tremendous amount of energy goes into what they do. About a year later they came back and they played a big hall on the campus. The place was packed and the audience went wild.'

'We'd done all the things that are ridiculous and numbing and embarrassing, all the weird little TV shows,' Buck told Q's Andy Gill. 'We did kiddie shows in 1982, with an audience of children. Three of the kids, incidentally, were the Beastie Boys – they were all, like, 15, these cute little child actors.'[9]

In Berry and Mills, R.E.M. had musicians with a mainstream sensibility and their versatility meant that they could accurately, if not always engagingly, cover songs from other groups, songs that would get the applause going and some feedback from an audience, however tiny.

'They did fantastic cover versions,' says R.E.M. producer Mitch Easter. 'Just the other night I was playing my girlfriend "I Can't Control Myself" by the Troggs, and I was telling her how R.E.M. used to do that. No one was covering that around that time. I'm sure that sensibility came from Peter, the record-store guy. He had this huge fondness for garage rock back then and I think that was OK, to do sort of garagey kinds of things.'

With other groups it was very different. Michael Lachowski of Pylon is of the opinion that one of the reasons R.E.M. were able to attain national cult status so quickly was this very versatility. On his own admission, Lachowski is a limited bassist compared with Mike Mills. The other musicians in Pylon were competent at playing their self-penned songs, but either unable or uninterested in playing covers just to curry favour with a conservative clientèle.

This special, out-of-category-thing was going on in Athens and people were open to hearing it, whatever it was. But when our band, Pylon, would go and play in New York, for example, we'd play our 40–45-minute-long set and we were done, that was our performance. Over the months as we found ourselves touring more in small markets, the set-up for rock'n'roll was that you played way more than 45 minutes. And, in some cases, bands were expected to play two sets. We learned early on that we were not like one of them, we were not that kind of band; we were not Lynyrd Skynyrd. We can play the *same* set twice, but we don't have any more songs.

The difference is that R.E.M. had members with huge record collections. They were incredibly elastic and were comfortable with different styles of music. As a result, they had the ability to present their original material and then pad the whole event with covers. This meant firstly that they could play in a college town in the southeast where audiences expected to be entertained for three hours and secondly, they could play songs that they were familiar enough with so that they didn't get beer bottles thrown at them. Thirdly, they were then able to fulfil their primary objective, which was to play their own material.

Pylon was picky: we only wanted to go where we were wanted. We had no missionary zeal; we had no desire to convert people who didn't care about what we were doing. We only wanted to go where really bright artistic people were going to think that we were the shit. In the meantime, when R.E.M. started, a little after us, they were out playing throughout North Carolina, Florida, Alabama, Tennessee, Georgia and they converted a lot of people who would otherwise have been completely unreceptive into thinking that they were cool themselves because they liked this R.E.M. band. Those people edged towards us so that eventually and consequently we were able to play some of those places. Not all of them, and not with as much success, but we would then be able to play some and they knew who we were and this was partly because R.E.M. came from the same town as us. R.E.M. converted people and they built up a huge amount of fans who have every right to claim that they were right there at ground zero with R.E.M. and they were crucial to that band's eventual commercial achievement.

Despite the fact that some fans of the new wave scene to this day still maintain that Pylon were the more talented of the two groups, the band themselves did not harbour ambitions of the lofty sort. They had no sense of really building a career, or a fan-base beyond those curmudgeonly arty eclectics who would understand the uncompromising nature of their music. They were called upon to support U2 on tour, but they didn't much care for the razzmatazz and the impersonality of playing to someone else's audience. As a result, Pylon became the art school favourites, while, for some at least, R.E.M., with their covers and poppy material, had sold out or, at the very least, were compromised. This is rather ironic since later in their career, R.E.M. would be identified as the only group who had remained 'true to their roots' and were 'both big and cool'.

Dan Wall recalls: 'Their sound was very easy to like due to the fact that not only were they playing several covers, but they were playing a sound that was similar to the popular music of the sixties. When they did become popular many people in the new wave scene were kind of resentful due to the fact that folks felt R.E.M. did not have the originality of Pylon or the Side Effects and therefore didn't deserve the popularity.'

However, some of the main players on the scene did not feel this alleged rivalry perhaps as strongly as the fans did themselves. 'There were a lot of bands in Athens,' recalls Lachowski, 'and everyone took lots of pleasure in supporting all of the music. I mean there were parties where *everyone* at the party would have been in a band practically. To us back then, the sorting out process had not happened. At the time, there was no appreciable difference between R.E.M. and Oh Okay and the Side Effects or whatever.'

R.E.M. were, however, developing as songwriters. Stipe and Buck had begun writing songs immediately they had decided to form a band. In fact, even before they acquired a rhythm section they had written half a dozen songs together. Mills and Berry had also presented pre-R.E.M. compositions. But the most exciting stuff was the new material worked on in the democracy of R.E.M. Berry, Mills and Buck had, by now, left the domicile at the church on Oconee Street to live on Barber Street, which became infamous locally as housing would-be Boho rock stars.[10] Peter and his girlfriend Ann Boyles lived next to Michael Stipe, who shared a house with a whole bunch of people, including Linda Hopper, who would form a band, Oh Okay, with Michael Stipe's teenage sister, Lynda, who was then working at the local Burger King. Mills was operating a machine at a local newspaper to supplement his income. It was all one big family, a creative environment perfect for the dropout students of R.E.M. to fool around with some new compositions.

The music seemed to come out easier if it was written by committee, rather than individual members coming in with completed songs, or songs written in pairs. They produced a body of work which, for the most part, did not get recorded, at least officially. 'Just A Touch' did find its way on to *Lifes Rich Pageant*, while another song, 'All The Right Friends', would be tracked as late as 2001.[11] The latter is an engaging piece of pop with a riff that would form the basis of 'I Took Your Name' much later in the *Monster*-era. Some of the other songs are juvenilia. Musically they are bright, breezy, new-wave*lite*, with Buck's arpeggiated style an instant musical marker and Stipe singing uncertainly at the top of his range. Interestingly though, Mike Mills' bass provides an unusual sonic reference which sometimes takes over the role of the soloing instrument, or decorates the songs in very unusual ways.

'They were written to play live, so they were great fun,' says Mike Mills of these earliest R.E.M. songs. 'There was a certain amount of naivety going on there, but it was fine because we were doing it at a time when anything was possible. When you're writing songs now, you're careful not to write something that you have already written. But back then it was just much easier to forge ahead. Sure, there are some that I might be a little bit embarrassed about now, but there are some that I would certainly like listening to too.'

What is also distinctive, as some critics have pointed out, is the gender-specificity of these very early songs. In interviews, Stipe has rightly pointed out that most of his could be taken as originating from either a male or female viewpoint. Until *Monster*, they were very often written in the third person, adding a sense of distance and history. Stipe was a chronicler rather than a protagonist. However, these first songs are laden with teenage angst and problems with girls, as well as other classic clichés of pop imagery.

The first song which unmistakably belongs in the tradition of music we now associate with R.E.M. is 'Gardening At Night'. Written in the summer of 1980, it was soon inserted into their live set, and was later recorded for the *Chronic Town* sessions. The inspiration for the song was apparently a story relayed to Michael Stipe by Pete Buck. Around town in the early hours in search of a beer to take home, Buck would often see a man dressed in a suit and tie attending to his lawn. This tale of eccentricity fired the singer's imagination. The lyric itself can be interpreted as being about the futility of certain human endeavours. With its wistful melody it was to form something of a blueprint for the future.

Another song which dates from that long, hot summer of 1980 was '(Don't Go Back To) Rockville', originally played live in a rock format. This time the addressee was a certain Ingrid Schorr, the song itself a plea from Mike Mills imploring Ingrid not to leave Athens to spend the summer in Maryland.[12] Once again, the lyrics deal with the pap of pop angst, but the song, later to be recast as country-pop on *Reckoning*, is noteworthy in that it is virtually a solo composition by Mike Mills, and therefore unique within their body of work.

'I thought that "Going Back To Rockville" sounded like a song title and, as I wrote it, I put myself in the place of what if I were really deeply in love with her and she was leaving me forever,' says Mills. Although the song wasn't autobiographical, Mills concedes that the two 'were very good friends', and 'dated also. There was definitely a lot of affection there.'

'Hey Hey Nadine' (also known as 'Small Town Girl' and 'She's Such A Pretty Girl') was also a naïve song based on the band's circle of friends. 'Yes, there was a friend of ours back then named Nadine Aldrich,' says Mills. 'She was this really neat girl from Waycross, Georgia, and it's as much about the name Nadine as it is about her. Nadine is just a great name!'

The band began gigging ever more frequently. Tyrone's, the popular new wave venue, played host to them on 4 October 1980, and the recording made of this gig is the earliest R.E.M. show in circulation. Although the bulk of the set is made up of tried and trusted covers such as 'Gloria', 'There She Goes Again' and 'Hippy Hippy Shake', the opener, 'Just A Touch', 'Gardening At Night' and the closing number, a new rousing instrumental named 'White Tornado', showed promise. By the time the band revisited Tyrone's the following May, such early classics as 'Laughing' and 'Pretty Persuasion' had also been added, along with the new show-stopping closing number 'Carnival of Sorts (Boxcars)' and a frantic slab of new wave called 'Radio Free Europe'.

By mid-1981, R.E.M. had morphed into something recognisable as a 'proper' band. By the end of 1981 they had played Tyrone's a staggering 19 times.

They got popular so fast, and they drew big crowds so quickly [affirms Kurt Wood]. The crowd they were drawing were kind of your average university students. There was a little bit of resentment there at first. Some of the people had been there at the very beginning. People get very protective of their scene, and when it spreads out, it's not their scene any more. It was more like that than anyone shouting 'you've sold out'. Their shows at Tyrone's were so crowded that you had to turn up early to get in. When Pylon played there were 50 to 100 people there. When R.E.M. played there'd be 200–300. There might have been a little bit of resentment that it happened so fast for them. It wasn't that they were internationally famous or anything but that, locally, they had made a very big leap.

There was, in fact, something of a new wave backlash against any band playing melodic pop. This backlash was also detrimental to the dB's from North Carolina, fronted by Peter Holsapple and Chris Stamey and, for some fans, serious contenders for R.E.M.'s constituency. Will Rigby, then the band's drummer, puts it like this:

When I moved to New York in '78 and started playing in a band, punk was the thing and a lot of people who were into that turned their noses up at anything that was melodic or Beatles-influenced. The Knack had a lot to do with that. The Knack had a huge hit with 'My Sharona' in 1979, and then all the record companies signed a lot of crappy bands that wore skinny ties. It was a flash in the pan, but it was *big* flash in the pan, and a lot of bands were signed that put out crappy melodic rock records, which at the time was called 'power pop' – a term I hate. There was bit of a stigma attached to making melodic rock, though, and although we were a little weirder than that, it was still basically what we did. R.E.M. never fell prey to that kind of prejudice because of their charisma.

Before an infrastructure was established in the late 1980s and early 1990s for 'alternative rock' acts, the life of an indie rock act was a life of hardship. Peter Buck might comment that it was still better than a 'proper' job, but, for the modest-grossing band, luxury was something only to be dreamt of. The gap between groups such as

R.E.M. and the biggest grossing acts of the early 1980s was vast. This was a time when the rock aristocracy could sell out stadiums with ease, but the gigging journeyman had little or no support. College radio and alternative music had yet to go mainstream. Jefferson Holt would chauffeur R.E.M. around in an old blue van. For the first two years of their existence, they did nothing else but play music and write material. On the road they would take it in turns to sleep in the van, while the others stayed in two crummy hotel rooms. They would wash where they could, often in the dirty bathrooms of the new wave clubs. Their food allowance was $2 a day.[13]

R.E.M. would endure, but their favourite venue, Tyrone's, didn't. It burnt to the ground.

> Everyone was upset [remembers Mike Mills]. The suspended heater broke off its moorings, fell on to the stage, and *bang* – there everything went. It happened at about four in the morning. It would have been better if people had been there because they would have been able to stop it . . . [the place] was great because the people that ran it would let anybody play there, and get the door [receipts]. You charge two dollars and you get all the money. I made $30 and I thought I was rich. They made their money off the bar – and they made a ton. The only thing that didn't burn down in the fire was my tab. They went sifting through the rubble and found it – $40.[14]

Will Rigby remembers how R.E.M.'s charismatic front man drew attention away from their less-than-polished musicianship:

> The very first time I saw them, Peter was not that good. You could tell what he was trying to do, but a lot of the notes he would miss. He was kind of ham-fisted on the guitar. They more than made up for it visually, and what they were going for was really good. There was nothing else like that going on, it was pretty original. The whole thing just kind of worked. Bill Berry was not a great drummer, at least when they started. He just did that thing where you play the bass drum on every beat, on most of the songs, which to me was really boring. He was probably the weakest part of the group early on. He wasn't bad, but he was kind of basic. Mike Mills was, at first, obviously the furthest

along in his musical abilities. I thought Stipe had a great voice, and the performance aspect was just astounding. By '84 he wasn't really doing it any more, but back in 1980 and 1981, he was in nonstop motion, he was whirling constantly. The very early R.E.M. was extremely visual, with Buck doing his leaps as well. It completely made up for their lack of musical prowess.

Stipe himself was emerging from his introversion to become an exceptional, and exceptionally eccentric, performer. He would arch, twist and tumble, his long blond curls whirling around. By the end of the gig, he would sometimes not be in good physical shape, having ricked his back. It was as if, on stage, Stipe became possessed by a spirit, something basic that animated him on a somatic, bodily level, which cut away his intellectualism and replaced it with something primal. He was bewitching.

R.E.M. were cultivating a recognisable look too. Although no designer boys in a world soon to be dominated by a material girl, with Buck's new-Romantic-influenced frilly shirt with French cuffs and Stipe's denims, the band were highly distinctive, as photographer George Dubose remembers: 'One thing sticks in my mind that made me realise one of the big differences between R.E.M. and preceding acts, and that was that the band cultivated a grungy look. Whether it was out of their poverty as students or contrived, I have no idea, but in all rock'n'roll's history, this image of knees bursting out of denim blue jeans and dishevelled hair was a new look that had never been seen before.'

Although far from being hell-raising, R.E.M. were no angels either, as one fan remembers: 'Stipe had this persona that would keep him removed a bit. But I think underneath it he was probably very nice. He had that hair back then, he looked angelic. Mike Mills – you would always see him talking. He was like the most personable out of all of them. As a college girl meeting this band he was the one who liked to chat up the girls! Bill was kind of adorable, and he had a lot energy that he had to expel, and Pete enjoyed his beer. But they were all kids. I don't think it was like the Psychedelic Furs, where the guy couldn't stand up. I don't think it was excessive.'

III

R.E.M. may by now have had a manager and a fan-base, but what they also needed was a booking agency, a single release and a record label. The former would be provided by Bill Berry's old friend Ian Copeland, whose FBI agency had replaced the folded Paragon. Under his guidance, the band soon began picking up prestigious support slots. On 6 December 1980, just eight months after the church gig, R.E.M. supported the Police at the Fox Theatre in Atlanta, an indication of their popularity and increasing maturity.

'They went down so well that the crowd demanded an encore and it got me in a great deal of trouble because they weren't supposed to play one. I was aghast,' says Ian Copeland. 'Had I not seen the crowd reaction I may not have taken them seriously because they were my buddies, so I loved them anyway, but seeing the crowd go wild convinced me.'[15]

R.E.M. were now ready to cut some tracks with a view to making a demo tape which would be their calling card in the industry. One track, 'Radio Free Europe', with its stunning bass run from Mills and ghostly echo of a chorus, showed that the band had progressed dramatically from the sop-pop of their earlier songs. In fact, when Stipe came up with the melody and lyrics, the other band members were reportedly awestruck. It was the first indication of Stipe's genius for plucking unusual melodies out of thin air and layering them over the basic track in idiosyncratic fashion. It's a song that the band occasionally play to this day, and rightly goes down as one of R.E.M.'s finest songs.

To record the song, the band journeyed to a small studio in Winston Salem. Drive-In Studios was run by 27-year-old musician Mitch Easter and was situated in the garage of his parents' house. Mitch himself had been playing music since the age of 13 and by 1981 was already a competent musician and had his own band, Let's Active. Although Let's Active would be signed by I.R.S. and would achieve moderate commercial success as a live act until their break-up in 1990, it is with his production work on R.E.M.'s early material that he is perhaps most closely identified in the public imagination.

'Somebody called me up about recording them,' recollects Easter. 'I guess it must have been Jefferson. They came into the studio, and when they showed up I found out that the way they knew to call me was through Peter Holsapple of the dB's. I never really talked to him about it, but I guess that was the link.' Easter immediately hit it off with R.E.M., particularly with Michael Stipe:

'He was the funny one in the band for me. I don't think anyone thinks of him as the funny one, but when he made a joke it always really slayed me. It was always the most intellectual somehow and it just hit me right.' When Stipe appeared for the first time at Drive-In, Easter thought immediately of a certain English rocker whose band, Mott The Hoople was beloved by so many in the USA: Ian Hunter.

'There was a photo of Ian Hunter in *Creem* magazine once which was captioned "a rare shot of Ian Hunter without his sunglasses". Of course, the shades are, in fact, on, and I always loved that. Anyway, that photo reminded me completely of Michael, or vice versa, when I first met him with his fluffy blond curly hair and shades. Michael had an eye infection and he thought his eye looked alarming, so when he arrived at my house in the evening, the specs were on and generally stayed on during the session. So, if you were me, you'd be thinking "Ian Hunter", you know?'

The instrumental, 'White Tornado', displayed a retro-naivety that automatically endeared itself to Mitch Easter. 'That was cute. They were these sincere, arty guys, but the fact that they were dabbling with some of this stuff, which was from another time that overlapped with my beginnings as a guitar player, was just charming to me. When I first started playing, I loved stuff like the Ventures. I didn't know quite what to make of them messing around with it, but I liked it.'

The band dubbed 400 of this three-song cassette, stickered with the labels 'Do Not Open' and one of these promotional copies found their way into the hands of an Athens law student named Johnny Hibbert. Hibbert thought the result of the first session was flat, so oversaw a remix.

'Neither of the "Radio Free Europe" mixes is particularly great, but the one I did I liked better,' Easter says. 'Just the presence of Johnny Hibbert was distracting, he wasn't my cup of tea. He came into my little studio and it was like, now the big city guy is going to do it right. We mixed the song for about 12 hours and really, there wasn't enough equipment to warrant more than 45 minutes. The thing we came out with was just a symbol of being tired. I don't think he fucked it up or anything, it just wasn't better.'

The single, released in July 1981, was greeted with dismay by the band. To them, it sounded awful, and whether it was the mastering or the pressing which was at fault, it disappointed them hugely.

Buck, ever the demonstrative type, broke one of the singles and nailed it to the wall.

It wasn't the mix, it was the mastering actually [says Buck]. Mike and Johnny drove up to this place in Nashville with this 80-year-old man who had a cigarette and who actually dropped ash into the first master, so he had to throw it away and start over! When he'd finished, he played it on this tin stereo thing and they're going, 'Yeah, it's fine.' But it was kind of muddy and hi-end. On one of those compilation albums I.R.S. put out it had been remastered and it sounded a lot better. But there's something to be said for the original sort of murky feeling for the first one. I'd been listening to records all my life and I could tell that the clarity wasn't all that great. Pylon was coming out with records that sounded just huge and spacious and beautiful and we had this kind of muzzy little thing. There were like thousands of guitars on there and it kind of just washes out, but that's as much our fault as anything.

Despite all this, the single surprised many by selling strongly in the independent sector. Although sales were confined to three main cities – New York, Atlanta and Athens – it went on to sell 5,000.[16] By the end of 1981, it had been voted single of the year by 200 critics in *Village Voice*. It had obviously got into the hands of the tastemakers if not the general public.

Holt felt the band was now ready to record some of the impressive cache of songs which had invigorated their live set. The feeling was, though, that although they were not ready to make an album, an EP was not beyond them. This was the tail-end of the new-wave era in which the EP had been an important format for showcasing talent and easily financed by small-scale record labels unable or unwilling to take a big financial risk. However, it was not certain who would produce the record. Mitch Easter:

I saw them play a few times after the first session for 'Radio Free Europe', and went to speak to them and felt pretty cosy about the thing. But when it was time for them to go in and record some more, they were sort of thinking about not using me. This was partly because there were other places to go which were more convenient for them, specifically this place in Atlanta – I think it went by the name of Channel 1. An engineer had started using this very old studio at night in order to record some of these new-wave groups like Pylon. When I got wind of this, I remember lobbying Jefferson out on the street in front of some club to come back up here. I'm not really that good at the hard sell, but that's the closest I ever came to hard-selling anything because I really didn't want to miss out doing more stuff with them. It just felt so comfortable and I suspected that not every session would be that good.

A relieved Mitch Easter got the job in the end, and in early October 1981, the band spent a long weekend with him at Drive-In to record the songs which would eventually form the *Chronic Town* EP. This venture was to be financed by David Healy, a business partner of Jefferson Holt's from North Carolina and an art student from Princeton, New Jersey, who had moved to Athens in the hope of setting up a fledgling record label, Dasht Hopes.

'I drove R.E.M. up to Drive-In Studios,' says Kurt Wood. 'I remember I had started working at his restaurant where I still work now, in fact I now manage it. They had this recording time set up on the Saturday and Sunday. They were going to drive up there but their van broke down. They came by at work and asked me if I could get off work and I drove them up in my dad's Volvo. Michael and Pete rode with me and they secured another car too. I actually hung out with Mitch's girlfriend, Faye, who was also playing in his band, Let's Active. When they were recording, we went out to the thrift stores.'

The stand-out song was 'Wolves, Lower'. With its beautiful counter-melody ('House in order, ah-ah-ah-ah!') it is an early R.E.M. classic and proof of a maturing talent. Nobody was quite sure what the song was about though:

I was really excited by that song [says Easter]. It's one of my favourite R.E.M. songs, it's so great. The first time I heard it was when they played it on stage. I thought, what an awesome song. It was sort of more advanced than the songs they had before. We recorded it twice, actually. We had to do it again because the first version was *incredibly* fast. Everything was so fast and poppy back then, you almost didn't realise it until you heard the songs later! I was probably too cool to ask what the song was about, though. There was an assumption that, of course, we all knew what it was about. It didn't take long before you realised that this *official mystery* thing was what everybody was going for, so I couldn't act as if I was mystified. I think Stipe wanted to try and make a play on the three little pigs, and it was some sort of metaphor for protecting your psyche.

Chronic Town was also characterised by homespun experimental-ism. Easter was enamoured of bands such as Kraftwerk and was always ready to try something more mechanoid in the studio. Part and parcel of this was to use rudimentary musical concrete techniques – any means to distort the fabric of time, or to layer slabs of 'found' elements: 'The session was just terrific because I felt that we knew each other a little bit better and I could start expressing myself too. I started layering on tape loops, and the session was certainly more of a stretched out kind of thing than the single was. We were all sort of beginners, but we were all sort of pleased with ourselves too!'

Easter also began the strange but true technique of recording Michael Stipe in the most extraordinary positions. In the early 1990s, Stipe would sing into a mic on a couch. For *Murmur*, he'd sing in a stairwell, and for *Chronic Town* he sang outside:

I remember that we were amusing ourselves by recording Michael's vocals in the yard at the back of the studio. There were all these cricket noises on the tape which sounded good. You can't really hear them, but I guess subliminally you do. I always loved those stories, which were probably untrue, about Syd Barrett hanging upside down in a shower stall when he sang. Stuff like that totally turned me on. All that homebrew stuff was really attractive to me, and the incredible thing was that, even as recently as then, you didn't have the studio stuff which allowed you to make these noises. If you wanted to sound like you were singing in a box, you had to stick your head in a box! We had that BBC's Radiophonic Workshop stuff and that was incredibly attractive to me. 'Wolves' has a psychedelic part in the middle. Part of that was backwards, and part was a tape loop. Those guys had never seen that and thought it was incredibly cool. Michael was still in art college then, so the mechanics of it –

chopping up the tape – was totally his cup of tea. That made him feel better actually. He was such a young guy, an art dude at the time. He was possibly feeling compromised just by being in a rock band, which was really a kind of conventional thing. By bringing in these art school techniques, he was much more at home and felt the record was much more his baby. All the process stuff he loved.

The song that yielded the EP's title was, of course, the live favourite, 'Carnival Of Sorts (Boxcars)'. With its lyrical themes of passage and travel it began a long dynasty of R.E.M. songs. Easter, however, thought the instrumental lead-in to the track was corny. 'Whenever they played live it was a great favourite and the audience would yell, *"Boxcars!"* It was a real crowd-pleaser. I always hated the fairground intro thing that they wanted to do though. There's this circus music-impulse in certain rock musicians, and it reasserts itself with great regularity. I always hate it, and people always want to do it! So, I could have done without that, but I liked the song a lot and it was really good live, really ferocious and fast.'

One of the tracks that didn't make the EP was a fun ditty, subsequently circulated by R.E.M. fans, called 'Jazz Lips'. 'That was a fun mess-around in the studio,' affirms Easter. 'My studio was always this repository for interesting gifts. I remember that someone had left one of those really great 1959 men's magazines and it had this obligatory story about the black American jazz dude and his Swedish girlfriend called "Jazz Lips". It was this hilarious post-beatnik hack writing. The text was what Michael sort of read as poetry over this track!'

This wouldn't be the last time Stipe would free-form on mic, reading a passage of 'found' text over an instrumental backing, and shows an early predilection for the ready-made.

The EP was all set to be released on David Healy's little indie label, but events were about to overtake him as a serious independent label were wooing the band.

IV

The promotional copy which contained 'Radio Free Europe', 'Sitting Still' and 'White Tornado' had been on the scene for several months in an effort to drum up industry support. In fact, these early demos have their fans. Will Rigby, the drummer with the dB's, rates the pre-*Chronic Town* material as the band's finest – ever. 'I get the biggest charge from the early crappy demos before they made any records. To me, it's the most exciting material. There are some exceptions such as "Fall On Me". Maybe it's nostalgia on my part. I didn't even think *Chronic Town* came out that good.'

'Ann Louise Lipman brought me a demo tape knowing that I knew people at I.R.S. Records and that, as a photographer, I had contacts,' remembers George Dubose.

R.E.M. played at a place called the New Pilgrim Theatre on Third Street at Avenue D, which is on a really bad neighbourhood on the lower East Side, a really heavy heroin-purchasing area. I introduced myself to them and told them that I had a photo studio on 34th Street, next to the Empire State Building, and that they were welcome to stay there. So, three of them moved in for a week or so. Michael Stipe had friends in Greenwich Village, which is where he stayed. I photographed the band in my studio, ostensibly for *Interview* magazine. It was the night after Bill Berry had passed out without removing his contact lenses, so he had suffered a laceration of the eye. On some of the photos he looks quite droopy-eyed, as if in pain, but he put up with it. I took their demo tape to I.R.S. Records, where I knew Ian Copeland, and was about to give him the demo tape when he said, 'Don't bother, I already have one.'

I was friendly with the owner of the Mudd Club, which was a famous New York punk venue. When R.E.M. appeared at the New Pilgrim Theatre in September 1981, I asked them if they wanted to play the Mudd Club, and they said sure.

So I phoned Steve Mass, the owner and said, 'I've got this band from Athens, Georgia, and they're like a mix between the Byrds and Yardbirds and they're really great. Can you give them a night at your club?'

And he said, 'OK, Monday.'

We all go to the club and it's Monday night, 10.30, and there's hardly anybody in the club. One of the bouncers comes to me and says, 'George, Steve wants to talk to you on the phone.'

Steve Mass says, 'George, you said these guys are really good.'

And I said, 'Yeah, they're really great.'
'How come nobody's in the club?'
And I said, 'Well, shit, Steve. Nobody's promoted this show.
It's Monday night in the winter, what can I say?'
So he said, 'Do I have to pay 'em?'
And I said, 'I don't know, I'll go ask.'
So I go over to the band and say, 'The owner's pissed off,
there's nobody here, I'm sorry about all this but do you guys
wanna play, he's not gonna pay you.'
And they said, 'We're all set up, we'll play.'
So they played for nothing! It's amazing how a band gets taken
advantage of, and this sort of thing is still going on today.

In the audience at the Mudd Club gig was the dB's' Will Rigby: 'A
lot of people who were dB's fans said that they borrowed from our
sound. I personally never heard it. The very first time I saw them I
knew there was something special about this band. There was
definitely a "greater than the sum of the parts" aspect of the band
from the word go. I always thought they were going to be something,
especially from the moment I saw them at the Mudd Club. Stipe was
like a whirling dervish on stage!'

According to Ian Copeland, R.E.M. were first mentioned to his
brother Miles at I.R.S. Records by Ian himself. Miles had been offered
the chance to work with an all-female group, the Bangs, soon to
become the million-dollar hit-making machine the Bangles, but
didn't fancy it, so the two reached a deal whereby Ian would handle
the Bangles in return for Miles signing R.E.M. This version of events
is disputed by Jay Boberg, Miles Copeland's young partner at I.R.S.
Although Ian and Miles Copeland obviously discussed signing the
band, it was, in fact, Jay Boberg who made it happen. As Boberg
points out, Ian Copeland was not even in a position to sign R.E.M.
'He couldn't sign bands, he was a booking agent. He had nothing to
do with signing bands to I.R.S. – not just R.E.M., but any other one
either, despite how history has been rewritten.' He continues:

A young man called Mark Williams had been working part-time
for I.R.S. out of Atlanta and he had met Jefferson Holt. He had
sent me this cassette and I contacted Jefferson to see the band. I
flew to New Orleans and I saw them in a little club called the

63

Beat Exchange – there were about four or five people and half the people who were there, including the club owner, were on smack. Jefferson was trying to work out the sound and it didn't sound great, but the band's star quality was so clear and the music was amazing. Afterwards I went backstage with my girlfriend, who was living in New Orleans at the time. I said, 'Hi, I'm Jay from I.R.S.,' and Michael Stipe said, 'Yes, we were afraid of that,' because they thought they sucked so bad, and the sound was so bad and there was no one there. I said, 'No, actually, I feel quite the opposite. I was blown away, and I thought you guys were amazing, can I talk to you about making a record?' The next day we met at this little café place in New Orleans. We sat there and talked about I.R.S. and what they were doing and what they were trying to do, and I said, 'I'd like to sign you guys.'

According to Buck, both Ian Copeland and Jay Boberg can lay claim to having 'discovered' R.E.M.

We were the first band that FBI [Ian Copeland's booking agency] signed that didn't have a record deal. Ian definitely signed us to a booking agency before Jay signed us. Jay had heard about us, and Jay came and saw us, and signed us, on his own initiative. He liked us so much that I don't think he even told anybody at I.R.S. what he was doing, which, I think, caused a little bit of a shit storm when he went back to LA. People who later became friends, like Michael Plen who worked in promotions at the label, used to say, 'God dammit, you can't keep on signing these bands nobody's ever heard of without telling us.' Then, of course, Michael Plen became our biggest supporter. So, it's one of those things that both Ian and Jay can both legitimately lay claim to having discovered us.

I.R.S. had to move quickly because other labels were also in the hunt for their signature. 'RCA records had been snooping around,' so Jay Boberg remembers. 'I.R.S. were the perfect place for us,' says Peter Buck. 'We had offers from major labels for hundreds of thousands of dollars and we turned them down for I.R.S. and a $7,000 advance. I think we got a new transmission in the van, drum cases, Mike and I each got a new amp and we paid off some bills. I don't think we saw a penny of it. We didn't want to go for a huge label. We were thinking I.R.S., Rough Trade, maybe another indie, there were only two or three we were seriously thinking about. RCA were really interested and we did some demos with Kurt Munkacsi. But it was a big machine, and basically we had a record, *Chronic Town*, that we wanted out that month and we didn't want to go through a process of having to have everything okayed. Friends of ours signed to a major label, the Bongos. They waited a year for their EP to get out and it pretty much killed any momentum they had.'

Of course, signing with I.R.S. meant that they had to find a way to extricate themselves from the legally binding contracts with both Hibtone and David Healy. In the neo-Darwinism of the rock music industry, it's simply a given that, if a better offer comes in, a more professional option presents itself, then loyalty and friendship count for less than hard-nosed commercial gain. Despite the band rhetoric of later years that they never compromised their purity, and never entered into the name-calling and charades of music business industry intrigue, their very early career presents an alternative case. To reach the next stage, they had to thank cordially those who had helped them and then move on, even if it meant that several who had helped got dropped along the way. They weren't grasping or unkind or even particularly materialistic. In fact, quite the opposite. But they were not wide-eyed innocents either. When the time came to negotiate with I.R.S. they drove a hard bargain. 'It is probably fair to say that the band bummed out Healy and Hibbert,' accords Mitch Easter. 'I don't know anything about how it all worked with Healy. Johnny Hibbert made out pretty well in selling rights back to the band, I think, although by now the money probably seems small.'

There's a sad footnote to the story, as Mike Mills concludes: 'David Healy was a very gifted painter and, for a while, a very good friend, but his behaviour became extremely erratic and I think he was drinking way too much. Some years on after we had lost contact with him he got sober and got married and resumed painting and contacted the office. I went up to New Jersey to visit with him to see how he was doing and to see his paintings. I loved his work and actually we ended up buying four or five of his paintings. Just when he got his life back on track again he was killed by a hit-and-run van while he was riding his bicycle.'

V

R.E.M. journeyed up to New York to negotiate the I.R.S. contract which they would eventually sign on 31 May 1982. A key player in these negotiations was a certain Bertis Downs IV. Downs had begun offering his services to the band on a voluntary basis some time after seeing them live at the Coffee Club in April 1980. 'I met Peter and Bill before they were ever in the band,' recollects Downs in 2002. 'I met Peter at the record store and Bill at the university. He was a freshman and I was a first-year law student. With Peter, we'd talk about new records and which ones to buy. Peter would kind of educate me.' A few years down the line and Downs was full-time, although he still teaches at the law school in Athens to this day.

'Bertis brought in an actual New York-based law firm who had had experience in the music end of things and who did the negotiation with them,' recalls Jay Boberg. 'It was indicative of how instinctive and smart Jefferson and Bertis were.' According to Boberg, the deal itself was for an EP and five albums, plus a greatest hits. The advance was small – less than $100,000. 'I.R.S. was not signing acts for large amounts of money,' concedes Boberg. 'Bands were signing with I.R.S. because they wanted to be on I.R.S., they weren't signing because they were getting an advance they couldn't refuse.'

The I.R.S. roster in the early 1980s showed a liking for left-field pop bands with a commercial edge – the (English) Beat, the Buzzcocks, the Go Gos, John Cale, and a Los Angeles-based group called Oingo Boingo headed by Danny Elfman, who would score several of Tim Burton's films. It was hoped that R.E.M. would fit in perfectly. *Chronic Town*, originally recorded for Dasht Hopes, was to be I.R.S.'s first release in the USA on 24 August 1982.

Jefferson Holt was unmistakably the captain of the ship and the sole manager of R.E.M., but the role of Bertis Downs, although secondary, was important too. Earnest and conscientious, Downs was the perfect foil to the more extroverted Holt. 'I studied at Davidson College in North Carolina where I read history and before that, I did the last bit of primary and secondary education in the suburbs of Atlanta,' remembers Bertis Downs in 2002. 'We spent four years in Taiwan before that, and that's where my father died in a plane crash. I was born in West Virginia and my father worked as a Presbyterian minister in the mountain region there. I was always interested in music. When I was at Davidson I did concerts and radio, and both

I did with my buddy from Decatur, John Huie. He went off and started working with Ian Copeland at Paragon in Macon, and I went to law school. I was studying at law school and whilst I didn't get involved in college radio there, I did keep up my interest in music, and I was involved in the concert division. John would say to me, "Why don't you work with that band Bill's got started?" So, John Huie was certainly somebody who gave me advice as a peer.' Betsy Dorminey remembers Bertis from his law school days as a likeable man who sacrificed a promising career in the legal business for the band he loved:

We were at elementary school for a year and he and I were at law school together. I liked him a lot; he is very dedicated. His father was a missionary and was killed very untimely when he was young. They were living in Asia, and then they had to move back to the US. He happened to be at my school because there was a centre for people who were missionaries who were returning to the US that was in the jurisdiction of my elementary school. Anyway they moved away somewhere else after that. This was in Decatur, Georgia, just outside of Atlanta.

I remember eating lunch with Bert downtown at one of these meat and three vegetables kind of places were you can eat for $2.95 or something, and debating with him the merits of the different bands. This was back in 1980. I was a big partisan of Pylon at the time; they were more an art rock kind of band. And he was saying, 'No no, R.E.M. are the greatest.'

I said, 'Yeah, I know, but I really love to dance to Pylon.'

Look how it came out: he's a multimillionaire and I'm a struggling lawyer! He was a good student and he was taken under the wing of one of the professors there. He had some very good career opportunities upon graduation, but he elected to accept a teaching fellowship position which paid peanuts, in order to stay in Athens and help the band to negotiate themselves through their first record deal and get themselves all lined up. So, at the time, he really made a substantial sacrifice in order to help his friends.

One of things that got him going too was yet another elementary school friend of ours named John Huie, who was the biggest kid in first grade. He was a classmate of mine from first grade on. John Huie and Bertis went to college together in North Carolina and got to be friends up there. John had gone to work for the I.R.S. record label, which was handling the Police. I think John was able to work with Bert to be a little smarter in dealings with the record companies and so on, and that added a lot of value to what Bert could bring to R.E.M. at that point. I remember Bert telling me that, in that business, if you were not prepared to sell your mother down the river then you shouldn't even try it, because the music business is a pretty predatory place.

This is a Southern thing and I don't know whether it's an Irish thing too, but, when two Southerners meet, particularly two Georgians, then the first thing out of their mouth is, 'Well, do you know so-and-so?' They try to get this feel for people. They need to get to know your people and your people need to get to know their people and that kind of relationship is very important. The fact that Bert had this relationship which predated everything with this guy in the record business was a big advantage.

As a person, Bertis is fairly intense and pretty serious. For a Southerner, he speaks quite fast. But he's a lovely person, very caring and very involved in the community. He's always been gracious to people, but he's pretty intent on doing a good job and doing his work. He's taken awfully good care of that band and everyone who works for it. One of the very first things they did was to make sure that the people who worked for them or with them had health insurance. Now this is something that not all small employers do, as you're not compelled to do that by law. But they took care that they had pension funds, and they invested carefully. R.E.M. have always done a stellar job looking after their staff and making them feel appreciated.

One of the first things Downs and Holt did was to ask the band to incorporate, even though at the time their entire assets only consisted of a $1,250 van. They also urged them to register their name as a trademark. This was important because of the existence of at least one other band with the name REM who had beaten the Athens quartet to the punch. John Ellis had left the Vibrators to work with Peter Gabriel and had begun a new project called Rapid Eye

Movement (or 'REM' – without the dots!). His electronic rock experiment was gaining attention in the UK indies, if not in the marketplace. REM had supported The Stranglers' Jean Jacques Burnel's solo tour in 1979 and had released a single, 'Babies In Jars'. Downs and Holt therefore moved quickly. If their name was not an original then it would need to be enshrined in law as a pre-emptive strike.[17]

Downs was also keen to see the band set up their own publishing company, Night Gardening. One of the first acts, as we have seen, was to acquire the publishing rights for 'Radio Free Europe' from Johnny Hibbert, something Downs had thought the band were ill advised to let go in the first place. But perhaps the most important move by the band was to make R.E.M. a true democracy. Jefferson Holt and Bertis Downs were to become unofficial fifth and sixth members of the band, and, although the details have never been released, it is rumoured that both had, if not equal, then near-equal royalty splits with other members of the band. For their part, R.E.M. decided to assign an equal writing credit to all members of the group, no matter how different songs originated. This sensible move stopped bickering and resentment before it could seep into the public domain. At various stages in R.E.M.'s career, some members would contribute more, some less, but the public didn't need to know about this. Rock historian Peter Buck had assessed the situation wisely, realising that bands tended to break up either because of drug abuse or from greed, so splitting the money equally was one way to ensure the latter didn't happen. The band were also lucky in the fact that, although Stipe was the sole lyricist and often came up with the melody vocal lines, Buck, Berry and Mills contributed about equally in terms of musical ideas.

Why did they sign to I.R.S.? Ultimately, it was because the label gave the band assurances that it would not interfere in the creative process. R.E.M. would be left alone to create, while I.R.S. would back them in their decisions. The deal was not generous. The small advance was a handicap, but the band would be rewarded by a bigger than usual percentage on royalties. They were up and running.

In an era in which photogenic pop stars were as much pop stylists and businessmen as writers and performers, the route R.E.M. proposed to take was an old-fashioned one, and not without risk. Two years earlier, when Michael Stipe and Peter Buck had first talked about forming a band, Buck had initially been reticent. It seemed to him that all rock stars were, in his charmingly direct way, 'assholes'. And he didn't want his rock band to turn into a 'bunch of assholes' either. So the blueprint for R.E.M. was that the group would not curry favour artificially with either its audience or the media in general. There would be no marketing scams, no crass commerciality, no tabloid revelations. It would be an understatement to say that the band were also not that enamoured with the whole concept of videos and their lip-synched phoniness. The result was that they decided to carve themselves a niche as an exciting rock act, but with the intention of playing good music and enjoying themselves and not, at least initially, with becoming a major act. They would live and die on the strength of their live performances. No one can accuse them of failing to deliver on this. The band built up a live fan-base throughout the remainder of the decade which far outstripped their actual commercial worth in the marketplace. Their success was almost completely based on this work ethic.

The decision to foreground performance and live authenticity was a double-edged sword. On the one hand, it enamoured fans and critics, who hankered after the sort of 'organic' folk consciousness of the hippy era which had been shattered by the new MTV-era pop. On the other hand, it severely limited their musical range, since so many 'commercial' options were self-denied. It also gave the band the appearance of purity and authenticity, attributes that many British music fans in particular, fed on a diet of irony and play, simply didn't get or found mildly distasteful. The agenda, which was crudely caricatured as rock + guitars + live performance = good, and pop + synthesisers + videos = bad, made R.E.M. initially seem like dinosaurs before they had even started. Mitch Easter found the band's purist attitude simultaneously endearing and constraining.

There was that really funny *nouveau* dogma that instantly swept in with new wave. Every time there's a new music scene everybody thinks they are forging entirely new territory. Part of that of course was the need to destroy the past. I would say that the R.E.M. guys were not total victims of that, but more victims of that than I was, because I was a bit older and I had also been playing in bands for longer than them, so I was more loosened up. In those days, you had to really watch who you mentioned or you got people really upset. Having said that, I used to have great sport with that, so, in the middle of every session I would do, I would mention a ZZ Top guitar tone or something like that, just knowing that it would piss 'em off. At the same time I thought it was important to sort of piss 'em off like that, not specifically R.E.M., I mean, but anybody, because I think that if you're going to make good music you can't be all prissy. So, the new wave was horrible like that. If you bent a string on your guitar you were trying to be a metal guy, and it was like, you know, 'fuck you man!' People used to get so wound up about it. I do remember that Michael later acted like he had never heard a Beatles song, so he was clearly playing that nouveau purist game a little bit.

VI

Finally, after two and a half years of playing together, the band were ready to record their first album. They had been wise to wait. An ever-increasing maturity and a singular approach to songwriting meant that, by the time R.E.M. entered the recording studios in December 1982 to record their first album, they had a consistent set of songs, many of which had been honed in live performance. Had they been pushed into recording an album's worth of music earlier, they might have failed badly, and again, we might never have even heard of R.E.M. as an international rock act. Back in the 1980s, you were allowed to take your time, to reach a certain maturity. The days of the super-quick sell and the super-quick record company drop were not quite yet part of the rock landscape. R.E.M. arrived just at the end of an era in which new talent was given time to mature.

The only matter to be resolved was the question of who was to take the band to this next stage. It was apparent that Mitch Easter was not a record company choice. His Drive-In Studio was comparatively basic and he was not a big name in record-producing circles. A man called Stephen Hague had a much higher profile. Hague later went on to produce classic pop records with the likes of New Order, but when he got his hands on R.E.M., it was a marriage made in hell.

With an ear for commercial hit radio and influenced by the electronica and pop sound of the day, Hague attempted to get the band to play technically correctly. This was a tortuous experience for them. With the exception of Mills, they simply weren't able to match the standards of even a run-of-the-mill session musician. Their music was about atmosphere, power, energy and feel, and if the odd drum beat was slightly out of sync, if the odd vocal was slightly off the money, then that was secondary to the overall concept of the song itself. But Hague made the band track the test song, 'Catapult', dozens of times, reportedly completely demoralising the hapless Berry.

R.E.M. implored I.R.S. to allow them to go back to the tried and trusted Mitch Easter. However, they demanded that the record be cut in a studio with higher technical specification and Reflection Studios in Charlotte was suggested. Mitch Easter himself had only had limited experience in a large studio and so decided to bring in his friend and mentor Don Dixon, already a talented and successful musician and producer, and five years Easter's senior. Easter, for his part, mischievously asked to hear the results of the Hague collaboration as soon as the new session began:

Of course, I was dying to hear it, and of course, I was hoping that the track would suck! I.R.S. had been totally horrified by the thought of some hillbilly from the South like me who they'd never heard of recording their new signing. It's just a classic thing to do, isn't it? They sign some band and then immediately not recognise what they are, simultaneously trying to sell them very hard from being from the South, then immediately hooking them up with a producer who had no idea what they were about.

He did the classic thing to alienate the band by having them repeat the basic track over and over again. All it did was to make Bill just miserable and when we started the new session he was convinced he couldn't play drums any more, which was just horrible.

The thing is, is that this was not funny to them. Even though it was over and they told I.R.S. that they were not using this for the record, it was still like they had spent a week with the devil himself, and they were trying to get their head around it. They were really upset. When they came into the studio I said, 'Please, please, please, I wanna hear it, please,' and it took a lot of work to get them to play it for us. It really was misguided, but you can see why it happened. It was like, the Thompson Twins are really happening – I'm going to make them sound like this. But I bet you that if there was a master tape of that that could have been gotten to, they would have destroyed it. It was like a blackmail letter or something, they were devastated by it.

It was in this demoralised frame of mind that the band began work on their first album proper in December 1982. All the willingness to experiment Mitch Easter had discovered during the *Chronic Town* sessions a year before had been bled out of them by the bitter experience with Hague. The atmosphere had been polluted, and Easter and Dixon encountered a band blinkered, but intent on making an album, as far as possible, in their *own* likeness, not that of another. The result would become *Rolling Stone's* record of the year for 1983: the underground classic, *Murmur*, which for some fans and critics, was the band's finest hour.

3. 'UH', 1982–83

I

The secret of great rock, like that of great comedy, is . . . *timing*. Had R.E.M. recorded an album in 1981, when they undoubtedly had enough material, their career might have ended before it really began. Their early songs showed promise, but they were nowhere near as strong as those of other post-punk bands, for example U2. In 'Gloria' one could hear greatness. In 'Carnival of Sorts', perhaps not. Fast forward to 1983, though, and the four individuals had grown up and matured as songwriters. They were ready and, more importantly, so was their public.

1983 was the year in which British pop dominated the American airwaves, but dismayed American journalists. Look at any chart week in 1983 and early 1984, and you'll see evidence of the remarkable Anglophilia of the American public. Culture Club, Thomas Dolby, the Thompson Twins, Duran Duran, A Flock Of Seagulls, the Human League, Dexy's Midnight Runners, the Eurythmics, the ex-bisexual David Bowie and the exhumed Kinks were shifting units in their millions. It appeared that the world was being swamped by a deluge of mascaraed, white, British electro-pop fops. Some 20- and 30-something critics didn't like what they heard or, more particularly, what they saw. This was the era of the pop *poseur*, driven by the explosion of formatting that was MTV. Those naughty synth-pop cats had truly queered the rockers' pitch.

There was a hunger for a reconnection with the past and, as if by magic, this was precisely what happened – the same sector at the same time in both the UK and the USA. Indie, or alternative, or college rock spawned the two monsters that made this serendipitous reconnection. The similarities between them were striking. In the UK the Smiths were seen as a band who made guitar pop and riff rock cool and, in the United States, R.E.M. emerged as a group in this same tradition. Both groups were fronted by keening, wailing lead singers totally devoid of the machismo of most punk and virtually all leather-trousered rock.

'Rock had become bloated and excessive, so thank God for punk,' Mike Mills would later opine. 'But the insistence on uniformity in punk and the DIY style of music bred something that had little to offer, including a lot of passionless synthesiser bands who had little to offer but video charm. So we came along at the right time.'[1] More than any other record from that time, *Murmur* would be the album that encapsulated the fightback. For good or ill, it was this album that was aimed full square at ironic UK 'New Pop', and struck a mortal wound. The legacy would be mixed but the effect seismic. By 1985 R.E.M. would be one of the biggest alternative rock acts in the world. But, similarly, Bruce Springsteen would be one of the biggest selling acts in the world too. A chequered-shirted man in jeans playing a guitar was the future of pop. Why on earth did it all happen?

Mat Snow, later editor of *Mojo* magazine, but then a journalist for the *New Musical Express*, remembers:

At this stage, R.E.M. and the Smiths were considered two sides of the same coin: four-piece rock bands with the traditional quartet line-up and the Rickenbacker-playing guitarist. This was very important because it straightaway made an atavistic connection to the classic beat era of the Beatles, the Who, and especially the Byrds. Both Johnny Marr and Peter Buck were very Byrds-influenced with their arpeggiated style, and, in R.E.M.'s case, especially in the early days, the use of the English/Scots/Irish folk scale. It was a significant throwback to sixties folk rock, but also it was radically different to what anyone else was doing in the contemporary rock sense. Obviously, there were folk rockers such as Richard Thompson, but it was seen as rather fogeyish stuff which had absolutely nothing to do with the cutting edge or the contemporary rock audience.

The mysterious quality to *Murmur* was also very important – the production and the mix had that kind of shadowy, half-heard quality which reminds me a lot, oddly enough, of the Rolling Stones' *Exile On Main Street* and, looking far forward, to Bob Dylan's *Time Out Of Mind*, which has a very stylised, spectral, ghostly quality, as if alluding to a past music, as well as the ghosts of people telling their stories. There was this quality of something weird going on beneath the surface which you can't quite pinpoint, but which is tremendously suggestive.

There was a bunch of us on *NME* and a bunch of people on *Melody Maker* such as Allan Jones, who fell in love with the thing. We really did think, not exactly that this was the future of rock'n'roll, because that had become a very clichéd concept, but that it felt like a reconnection to certain stylistic values of rock music, including a quality of Americana and mystery. It reinvented it and refreshed it at time when the broader context was British art school bands with a lot of gender role-playing. Like many, I felt a little bit disenfranchised by this because it was about a kind of clubby, posy feel which I suppose didn't connect to people like me, who were not just of the punk era but of the pre-punk era. I was a Bowie fan, but thought that Bowie had the last word on it. I liked The Eurythmics and thought there were other good bands, but what they were doing was very transparent; what you saw was what you got, oddly enough. The visual image and everything about it was so sort of packed and glossy that I felt that there was no depth really to be explored. The surface was very intricate, but it was really about exploration of that surface, whereas R.E.M. was deliberately foggy and shadowy and buried and allusive. That was interesting because your imagination had somewhere to go, and also your rock crit reference-mongering had somewhere to go.

So the arrival of *Murmur*, like the music of other acts of the time such as Cocteau Twins, Gang Of Four and Wire, was in the long tradition of records that were loved by critics and musicians, but almost completely ignored by the public. The world might have been listening to Genesis, Fleetwood Mac or Foreigner but you would never know that now if you read any history of popular music, because the actual rock literati that write the chronicles of today have impeccably minority tastes. R.E.M. fitted perfectly into this long tradition of underdog music, a lineage which dated at least as far back as the Velvet Underground, music unbought and unloved at the time.

However, Mat Snow's overall assessment of why R.E.M., 1983 style, were such a revelation does make a lot of sense. Not only the critics but ultimately the record-buying public were sick to death of irony within popular music. Back in 1972 with Bryan Ferry and David Bowie, it was witty and cool to be a dissembler. But a decade later, for many, it was a record stuck in a very familiar groove. R.E.M. would carry on the tradition of art rock in that they drew esoteric and exotic ideas from outside of popular culture and made them mainstream, but they did this, at least in the first 15 years of their career, with no sense of irony at all.

The most distinctive aspect of R.E.M.'s music was, for many, Peter Buck's playing – economical, arpeggiated, poetic. It reminded the 20-something UK journos of pre-teen days of the Byrds. The Byrds had straddled the pop/rock/country divide a decade and half before, bringing some sweet beauty and mainstream confidence to American pop, besieged and beaten by the new wave of Brit-pop excellence. R.E.M. would be cast in the same role. 'I liked the sound that R.E.M. made and I liked everything that was in that tradition of the Byrds-meet-Merseybeat,' is writer Paul Du Noyer's thesis. 'That's the line they come from, where the Byrds meet the Searchers, that's the line of American guitar music they embody and they produced some tremendous music in that line.'

For his part, Peter Buck vividly remembers being on tour during the summer of 1983 and reading Allan Jones's astonishingly positive review of the band in *Melody Maker* and feeling, well, a mixture of mild embarrassment and, one suspects, simmering resentment. Here was a band who were garnering the most unbelievably positive reviews, particularly from the UK press, at a time when in the USA they were no more than an opening act for the Police, and hating absolutely every minute of it. In fact, while *Murmur* had broken into the US Top 40 and had, if not made them a household name, at least given them a media presence, they were finding their brand-new fame hard to cope with.

'The people at our record company were just mind-boggled by the good reviews,' Buck said in 2002. ' "What's going on? You've never been over to the UK, right?" Well it was embarrassing but you have to remember I was making $140 a month. That was my full salary for 11 months a year, and none of us had any money. We'd get good reviews, but then we'd go into town and play to 50 people.'

II

The recording of the album was not without its trials for both band and production team. A test track, 'Catapult', had already been recorded and the band used the studio time to record a second song, 'Pilgrimage'. I.R.S., pleased with the results, confirmed Easter and Dixon as co-producers. R.E.M. turned up at Reflection Studios in Charlotte, North Carolina in January 1983 with plenty of material already composed and road-tested in concert. Since *Chronic Town* the band had made a determined effort to be less 'poppy', and were keen to make an album which had a certain unity. 'We felt really confident going in,' remembers Peter Buck. 'We had the songs and we knew what we wanted the record to sound like.'[2]

After the experience with Stephen Hague in Boston, R.E.M. were also in dogmatic mood. They knew what they didn't want, so what was left was where they could take their music. Michael Stipe told the *NME* in 1999: 'Well, I've got a tape in my head ever since I was 23, which goes: "We work by process of negation. We know everything we don't wanna do and what's left are our options." And those paths, which are often the hardest paths, are the paths that we took. But that's what put us where we are . . . And a lot of luck.'[3] 'We wanted to have this kind of timeless record,' added Stipe. 'We didn't want the mix to be totally radio-friendly.'[4]

> In America the new order of bands defined themselves as what they were not [confirms Mitch Easter]. And the hip bands were *not* all these rock clichés – guitar solos, putting your feet up on the monitor, smoke machines, and stuff like that. Of course, it took no time for all these bands to have smoke machines. You could make somebody furious by referring to any of this as 'show business'. It was a weird time. 'We're in the brave new world, and it's going to get polluted,' was their battle-cry. I thought, well, it's going to get polluted in any case in a year. How can you really believe that this is anything new? But they all did, and I didn't want to rain on anyone's parade too much.

Mainly I amused myself by talking about Led Zeppelin in their presence, just to make them uneasy, because it didn't take much!

What's more, I think a lot of these clichés are fun. People are going to want to jump about in their leather trousers and smoke machines. It's just not a problem. They were less sympathetic to any kind of new idea, that's what was frustrating. They had this sort of dogma that, if it came out of an electronic keyboard it was bad, but if you got the same sound by breaking a real-life light bulb, then it was OK. Although I'm only a few years older than Peter Buck, I keep on representing myself as if I'm from a different generation from them, and I felt like I *was*, because I felt so much less *pure*. I felt so much like I'd seen things come and go. At the same time, I had a little soft spot in my heart for the purity of these guys' opinions. On the one hand I thought, 'Oh, come on man, face it: everything's fake man.' But at the same time, I thought, when music can mean so much that you can be heartbroken over an issue like that, well, that's kind of wonderful, and I didn't really want to destroy that. I did not want to be too disrespectful. In a way that was part of the power of it all, of course, the boundaries that people put up.

These musicians were steadfast in their policy however. Bill Berry demanded to be recorded in a drummer's booth, a practice which, by 1983, was antiquated. He was also the most resistant to any sort of 'odd' musical suggestion.

'Berry seemed very stubborn and determined and feet on the ground and non-flighty,' was Easter's summation.

He was super-nice, but he was very earnest. If he said something to you, he meant it. We were recording 'Perfect Circle', and Don Dixon and I went in and did a whole bunch of overdubbing on this when they weren't around, knowing that this would probably piss them off. We were really pleased with what we did, but he was the one who opened his mouth when we first played it to them and said, 'You're kidding, right?' And of course I wanted to strangle him, because I thought what we had done was great. That led to Dixon really yelling at those guys and to us having our way.

Peter Buck would not solo, nor would he agree to his guitar being turned up to add colour to the songs, or to the use of fuzz. 'My feeling is that if I want to hear a solo, I want to hear a sax player, who has ten minutes to do it,' says Buck in 2002, still of the opinion that solos should not be part of his vocabulary. 'I see probably three bands a week and they each probably play about ten songs. Probably if they play ten songs they play eight solos. That's 24 solos a week, times 52. I can go a whole year and hear one solo that I think is interesting, which tells you how little use guitar solos are. I know that when guitarists rip into this hot solo, people go nuts, but I don't write songs that suit that, and I am not interested in that. I can do it if I have to, but I don't like it.'

As Peter Buck's friend, Seattle musician Scott McCaughey, in the nineties part of the R.E.M. touring and recording set-up, points out: 'Peter has never been a fan of the wanky guitar solo. I think he made that a point with R.E.M. right from the start: it was about songs and sound, and not whether you can impress somebody by your fingers sliding across the fretboard. That's something that made them unique, and certainly influenced a lot of the other bands around at that time.' The initial musical Puritanism was, one suspects, in part a result of Buck's own inadequacies as a guitarist. In the early days, it was not so much that Buck *wouldn't* solo, but that he *couldn't*.

Despite that, it was Peter Buck, more than anyone else, who was central to the group's sound, as Mitch Easter points out:

Peter Buck was always really easy for me to talk to because I love those chatterbox kind of guys. He had this loud, imperious opinion on everything. I don't think he took himself all that seriously, but he would say these things without a smile. He was always kind of edgy, and would pop up, describe everybody as 'idiots' or something as 'crap', which to me was kind of fun! He was very cut and dried about things: 'Let's get this done,' he would say, and he would get it done. As a guitarist, he was not versatile. But he did what he did with complete assurance, and he didn't sound like anybody else. The things he learned to do for R.E.M. were incredibly important to how they sounded.

Obvious to all was his deep admiration for the music of the Byrds, although Mitch Easter himself never thought R.E.M. sounded much like them. There were other influences too. 'I think Michael hasn't heard anything other than "Eight Miles High", but Roger McGuinn was a big influence on me as a guitar player,' says Buck. 'I just tried to soak up all the people who I thought were good, whether it be George Harrison, Steve Cropper or Roger McGuinn. The guy from the Lovin' Spoonful, Zal Yanovsky, I loved what he did.'

Mike Mills was essentially the closest thing the band had to a 'real' musician. 'He played his instruments with a sort of mainstream kind of confidence,' says Easter. 'He could be in R.E.M., but he could also be in a boogie band if you needed him to be. Mike Mills' persona is always jolly, and I think he must be a jolly guy. I've never seen him any other way. He's really smart and I got the impression from what the others said that when he was at school he was a nerd. I note in these old tapes that he's the one who counts things off, so maybe he had the "McCartney" role of being the competent/annoying one at times. But he was always so jolly!'

'Oh no, I'm not a big theoretician, and I'm not anal about my musical knowledge,' says Mills in 2002. 'As far as I know, my knowledge was never anything but a help. I brought, I guess, a degree of musical sophistication that wouldn't have existed otherwise. Now, sophistication is a relative term. Any real musician would not call what I do a sophisticated knowledge, but, relative to what the other guys could do it was, because Peter was just learning and was teaching himself, Bill had learnt a lot of music but that was from the drum point of view, and Michael was untrained in music other than what he listened to. So, I brought a little bit of this musical understanding which, to my way of thinking, made it easier to turn abstract musical ideas into reality.

Easter himself successfully managed to get some contemporary references into the sound through a certain naughty subterfuge: 'Fair enough, if you don't want synthesisers on the record, we won't use them, I thought. But I did get to sneak in my own stuff. Around the time we did Murmur I really loved ABC, I loved the way those records were done. The audible use of a vibraphone on Murmur was a direct reference, for me, to ABC. But I didn't say that to them. I thought, I can still have my way here, and I don't have to alarm anyone!'

With the synthesiser and sequencer banned, however, Easter nevertheless worried about the record's commercial appeal and I.R.S.'s reaction: 'I was a little bit concerned at the time that the drum sound wasn't up to date enough because we ended up making this dry record in a time of massive digital reverb and exploding noises. I was worried that we didn't have enough of that on *Murmur*, and worried that we really had made this sort of 1970s-sounding record. If you didn't know anything about them you probably would not know that it came out in the eighties. You'd think it came out in '72 or something . . . or now, even. I thought we had made this tame-sounding record, but in actual fact it had this art atmosphere partly because of that.'

Easter is right: the record is so devoid of the then commercial studio tricks of the trade that it does not sound of the time. It sounded anachronistic in 1983 but, by the same token, twenty years on it hasn't dated, a remarkable achievement since the then happening synth-drum sounds on other records of the day now make them sound like sonic antiques. This was an album of guitar rock, an unquestionably unhip strategy for the time, as co-producer Don Dixon reminds us: 'The eighties were tough, and Bananarama ruled. People weren't really used to these difficult-to-listen-to sounds. Mitch and I both still liked guitars, and guitars were not very popular at the time. They didn't have a keyboard player and didn't use sequencers at a time when that was at its absolute prime.' To augment the band sound, though, the four R.E.M.-ers were happy to use Dixon and particularly Easter as supplementary musicians and the results were often bewitching.

III

Murmur is perhaps not a consistently great album. '9-9', 'Shaking Through', 'West Of the Fields', 'Sitting Still' and 'Moral Kiosk' are clearly not up to the standard of the power-pop-greets-new-wave anthem 'Radio Free Europe'. But some of R.E.M.'s finest ever songs are on display here. 'Perfect Circle' was the song that was changed the most in the studio. Mitch Easter:

'We used two pianos on that song. One was a tack piano that was purposely out of tune, a sort of whorehouse piano where they put thumb tacks on the hammers, and it makes the sort of hollow, bright sound that you might hear in a saloon. Reflection had a piano that they kept in that condition as a sound-effects kind of piano, and they had their normal, nice piano. So it's those two pianos played by Mike and Bill at the same time. When they did that song on stage back then, they did it on a little Casio keyboard, so this was a massive rearrangement.'

'Perfect Circle' is a particular Buck favourite: 'I remember talking to Michael and we were watching these kids playing football or something outside this hall. Michael was working on the lyrics. The song's not about that, but it just reminds me of that day because we were in New Jersey, on the road, and we didn't really know anyone. You see these kids out who are not much younger than us doing this leisure-time fun thing and we were getting ready to play three sets at the City Garden nightclub in New Jersey. So, "Perfect Circle" always reminds me a bit of when and where this was written, the sun setting over these people, the figures running through the dusk.'

'Laughing' was also a standout. Here Easter and Dixon worked with the band to create aggressive layers of strummed acoustic guitar. 'We had our "campfire" guitars where everyone available would play acoustic guitar at the same time and we'd build up these "My Sweet Lord" washes of guitar,' says Easter. With 'Catapult', the producers suffered. The song was already a live favourite and trying to capture the energy of the performed version on tape was an onerous task. Buck was reportedly unhappy with the mix. Ultimately though, 'Catapult' suffered, as Easter concludes, 'mainly from the bad associations with the previous Hague sessions.'

'Pilgrimage', which had already been tracked at the test session, was yet another standout. 'It had a lot of things that were firsts for them,' recalls Mitch Easter. 'First of all we sneaked in the vibes, which doubled that guitar melody riff thing which I thought sounded good. We also had Bill singing the descending part that does have the Gregorian parallel part. Bill's voice is real loud there, he has this baritone voice that I thought was really good. I don't think that we had really used him before.'

The Gregorian modal reference was quite deliberate, as Mike Mills reveals: 'Yes, certainly, if you listen to Gregorian chanting, the sound of the notes and the melody is what's important. It became obvious to us that that resonates just as much with the human heart and human mind as good lyrics do. If you can combine them both, which we eventually did, then you're ahead of the game. We weren't thinking quite in those complex terms for "Pilgrimage". We weren't thinking, that's a subtle way to reach the human psyche, that wasn't part of the thought process. But we did want something that sounded like Gregorian chants.'

With the actual album in the can, it was time for some fun. Don Dixon liked putting his acts in slightly pressurised situations and, at the end of the *Murmur* session, he and Mitch asked the band if they'd like to lay down some extra tracks and B-sides just for fun. The idea was to do these very quickly, have a few beers, mix to two-track, and try and create the sort of homey spontaneity of a radio session. The results, on *Murmur*, were almost uniformly excellent, including the rather great 'Tighten Up', a cover of the instrumental hit from Archie Bell & The Drells, which was a slice of good-natured sixties silliness.

A forgotten classic from these sessions, though, is a ghastly version of the standard 'Moon River'. It is without doubt one of the worst things ever committed to tape. It is so bad that it actually goes off the scale, comes round the other side, and becomes good, a sort of 'malpleasurable' experience attainable only by truly great bad records such as 'Paralysed' by the Legendary Stardust Cowboy and several theme tunes to seventies BBC sports programmes.[5]

Central to the malpleasurable experience is the artist's serious intent. Despite the fact that the band had the wrong chords and played the song in the wrong key, their earnestness was unquestionable. After all, it was the first song that Michael Stipe remembers hearing as a toddler. Don Dixon still winces:

'Mike Mills certainly never bothered to learn the chords, but that was one of the great things about them. They were not intimidated by the fact that they didn't know them. They could be incredibly reverent to the ideal of a song, without taking the trouble to learn the song at all, and that's something that's not common. It's one of the reasons why this band has never been a musician's band. U2 has never been a musician's band either. You can respect them for what's going on, but guys don't sit down and carefully transcribe the Edge's guitar parts the way that they might Joe Satriani's. But there's little Joe Satriani music I personally would want to listen to. Michael was terribly sincere about that version. The fact that it was so wrong might appear to some people to be an insult. But they were not making fun of the song, or trying to insult it. There were so many mistakes that I don't want to enter into it, and the musician in me had trouble with that, but the producer in me felt that was not what them wanting to record that song was all about.'

Despite the group's determination to resist the parlance of rock'n'roll cliché, there was one aspect that made them immediately appealing, both commercially and creatively. They arrived in the studio as four completely distinct personalities. Unlike some bands (for example U2, where Bono would tend to dominate recording sessions), in an R.E.M. session a democracy of wishes was paramount. Here was a group that functioned as a musical democracy. Ideas were discussed and agreed, and no one viewpoint dominated. There were divisions of labour. It was up to Stipe to versify and come up with the melodies. It was Buck's role to edge the band in new musical directions. It was the task of Mills and Berry, as the more experienced musicians, to work more on the nuts and bolts of the composition.

Berry's role has often been undervalued. He would frequently write and record on guitar and keyboard. In fact the most beautiful piece of music on *Murmur*, 'Perfect Circle', was basically his. But it was this cartoon-like quality of the four members that immediately struck *Murmur*'s producers as curiously well-honed. 'What struck both Mitch and me was how complete each guy was as a character, each almost a caricature of themselves,' recalls Don Dixon. 'They were almost out of the box, individual equal cartoons. . . . They were all really, really distinctive personalities.'

'Probably the most amazing thing about them is the way they remained a band, as they had such different tastes,' agrees Mitch Easter. 'The one thing they always exuded about one another then was this funny kind of respect. They talked about one another dismissively, but it never went beyond that. You never started to hear, "Well, I'm working on my solo stuff right now." '

R.E.M. had a brilliant balance, even at this early stage of their career: Mills and Berry with their more mainstream musical talents, Buck essentially the rock theorist, and Stipe the man with his antennae up for any odd extra-musical references. It was no disadvantage that all four individuals were in their own way very handsome and photogenic guys too. There was no ugly sod to hide behind the drum riser or to position at the back in photos. In fact, the balance of their quite distinct features looked wonderful in photographs – Berry's cute eyebrows, Mills' pudding bowl haircut and schoolboy grin, Buck's tall, Rhett Butler swagger and Stipe's ocean of hair. Buck demurs concerning the group's sex appeal: 'We were young, and I guess that's 90 per cent of it. I would never consider myself as really good-looking and I don't know whether the other guys would consider it that way either. We were young, and on the road, and that's all it really takes!'

All in all, there was something very striking about R.E.M. By 1983, a small but recognisable fan-base was emerging and was growing. 'They immediately had this small, fanatical fan-base,' confirms Don Dixon. 'By the time they made the first record there were already a handful of girls in black parked outside all the time.'

The album's cover set the tone for the critical reaction to the band. Like Roxy Music and New Order, R.E.M. were convinced that the sleeve the music wore must be separate from the personalities that created the music. So, no cheesy band photographs allowed, at least not on the cover. Perhaps it was the cover, though, which first placed R.E.M. in that tradition of nonconformist art-school rock stars and so endeared them to the British music press. *Chronic Town* had only arrived in the UK on import, but with its spitting gargoyle (actually a famous icon of Notre Dame cathedral in Paris), its cover was only the first in a series of excellent artwork. Michael Stipe and, to a lesser extent, Bill Berry took it upon themselves to work closely with I.R.S.'s art department, and had stringently high standards.

As early as 1981 they had berated Jefferson Holt for having the band's name as 'Rapid Eye Movement' on concert tour posters. This was a band that packaged itself meticulously. The thicket of vegetation, tinted bluish purple, which adorns the cover looks like a photo of an alien landscape taken by an unmanned probe. It could even be seen to symbolise a sort of water-world, a visual representation of the wobbly, bubbly words contained inside. The vegetation is, in fact, kudzu, a Japanese vine that grows in Georgia. However, although the album consciously announces itself as from the South, the overall strangeness of the package disorientates and undermines any straightforward identification of the band with Southern traditions.

The back cover, on the other hand, is rather more literal, depicting as it does the now famous trestles. These trestles have attained a totemic stature for hardcore R.E.M. fans, and their preservation is a calling. It's a visible symbol of the connection between the band, their fans, and their home town. It was this sort of imagery that rooted them in the public psyche as a 'Southern' band.

IV

But the aspect of *Murmur* that so beguiled reviewers and fans was the astonishing vocal delivery of Michael Stipe. It was the profound literariness of the lyrics, at least the ones you could hear, coupled with the act of trying to hear them in the first place, that made the album essential listening. The lack of clarity could be infuriating, yet you listened on, ever hopeful of the penny dropping. Stipe's lyrics were the audio equivalent of a doctor's handwriting on a prescription. You could make out it was handwriting, but the words remained obscure, the meaning unclear, the code unbreakable. It didn't stop you trying to overdose on the non-meaning of the sounds of the words, though. It was reported that, in an attempt to make out the words, Elvis Costello had the first two albums on cassette on endless repeat. Twenty years later, it's still a nigh-on impossible task.

'I can't believe people on the Internet try to interpret different words and syllables,' said Stipe in 1999 before playing 'Radio Free Europe'. 'Some things make sense and some things don't. This . . . does not.'[6]

Stipe was, and is, a poor enunciator at the best of times. His flat speaking voice was in direct contrast to that of his co-producer, Mitch Easter. Whereas Easter's Southern accent had light and shade, and was interspersed with animated sections of reported speech and softer, more reflective passages, Stipe's voice just came at you in a straight line. George Dubose, who interviewed him around this time, had to throw the interview cassette away as it was inaudible and unusable.

Although a careful and highly articulate interviewee, Stipe punctuates his speech with stops and hesitations, as he pauses to compose his next move. This is the characteristic of many in the glare of the media. Politicians play for time using such cliché phrases as 'at the end of the day'. In Stipe's case it is an animalistic grunt, an 'uh'.[7] A little later, for example, the beguiling pseudo-Celtic 'Swan Swan H' was originally to be entitled 'Swan Swan *Huh*', giving an indication of Stipe's elevation of the guttural to pop art.

This lack of contour to his speaking voice is, of course, in direct opposition to his vocal style. His wailing, keening, arching vocal figures, which sweep up and down in melismatic fashion, are reminiscent of Celtic folk artists or Muslim *mujaheddin*. The northern European tradition prioritises the regular pattern of rigid blocks of music, with little stretching or bending of the notes, whereas in Celtic enclaves such as Ireland, or the Basque region, folk song prioritised the ability to hit a note and undulate around it. We can hear it throughout Stipe's singing career, as we can in the singing of Morrissey (of Irish descent), Björk (Icelandic), Kirsten Hirsch, Kate Pierson or John Lydon (also of Irish descent).

The lack of enunciation, and the resulting lack of direct literal meaning, made fans think Stipe was singing in a secret code, and this sent the literature experts in the music press into raptures of cogitation. In fact, some of the very earliest songs had either no words at all, or just approximate words that Stipe would extemporise. 'Let's be reasonable here,' Stipe revealed in an AOL chat room in 1994. 'You all know there aren't words, *per se*, to a lot of the early stuff. I can't even remember them.'

When asked by R.E.M. expert Kipp Teague about the lyrics to the chorus of 'Sitting Still', Stipe replied, 'Come on now. That is an embarrassing collection of vowels that I strung together some 400 years ago. Basically nonsense.'[8] This was the 'oral tradition' of his songs, existing only in sound, and not in print. Stipe would simply choose a combination of vowel sounds, or stretched out consonants, or alliterative and evocative patterns of words, that fitted the mood and the melody of the song he was singing.

However, this was the exception, not the rule. For the most part, each song had quite definite lyrics, which Stipe typed with loving care on an old typewriter at the studio in Charlotte. He took great delight in crafting and playing around with words, and the pride he showed in typing them out, and turning them into a document was charming and naïve.

Those songs that had definite lyrics were often deliberately recorded in such a way that it was impossible to make them out. ' "9-9" has a very distinct idea,' Stipe told *Rolling Stone* later in the 1980s, 'but, you know, it was purposely recorded so you could never be able to decipher any of the words except the very last phrase, which was "conversation fear", which was what the song was about.'[9]

Stung by the criticism that *Murmur*'s enigmatic quality was a lucky by-product of substandard recording techniques, Mills argues: 'No, those recordings sounded pretty close to how we wanted them to sound, it wasn't poor recording at all. We had contended early on that the voice would be another instrument, and therefore should not be a whole lot louder than any other instrument. That flies in the face of traditional recording, but that was how we felt. Michael was very unsure of himself as a lyricist and as a vocalist and, at that point, was using his voice more as a sound, rather than as a way to convey words. The words were not as important as the melody and the sound of the voice. Fortunately, he has a very rich voice, and he could communicate a lot of emotion without words, so we decided to use that as the way we sounded at that point.'

'When we were doing *Murmur* we knew that it was not going to sound like anything released that year,' is Buck's stark and accurate description. 'We wanted an air of mystery. We didn't want our record to be like the first Clash record, where it's kind of spelt out for you. There's no mystery to it, except for the fact that it's so great. We wanted people to listen to that record and think, "Jesus, what planet are those guys from?" And we consciously recorded all kinds of subliminal stuff and backwards things. Just strange little sounds that tend to pop up on the CD version more than they used to on vinyl.'

'You know, for the first album that we made, I didn't know the difference between the bass and the electric guitar,' is what Stipe said in 2002, probably with a heavy dollop of self-mythologising. 'I was so ignorant of music. I didn't sing words for the first two albums. I just sang and stuff came out about furniture and about bugs . . . it was nonsense, you know, but it was beautiful nonsense.'[10] Yet, Mitch Easter remembers quite differently: 'When we were at Reflection Studios, Stipe loved to sit down and play with this typewriter they had, one of those classic 1960s IBM office typewriters. He just loved typing the lyrics on it and looking at it. And I could totally dig his sense of style.'

What both Easter and Dixon were keen to do was to capture the broad picture. If they had paid too much attention to the detail, they knew they would kill R.E.M.'s fragile art, and particularly Stipe's confidence. This meant a minimum of vocal retracking. They would only fix up a vocal, or ask for it to be resung, if it was really substandard. Both producers were also keen to allow Stipe to express his words in the manner in which he wanted. Both were of the opinion that popular music did not have to be force-fed, or to sound completed, and that a rock lyric that was open to interpretation was nothing out of the normal. Hundreds of classic songs had left the listener puzzled as to their meaning.

One of the things I had been cursed with the whole of my life as a performer was having producers saying I wasn't articulating well enough [opines Dixon]. And I would say, 'Have you never heard "Little Red Rooster" by the Rolling Stones? What is going on here? Why are you trying to make this rock lyric clearer, it's not important.' What is important is that they believe that I believe what I am saying. I am not being hypercritical – I don't apply a different standard to the people I am recording than I do to myself. What I want to do is to believe that the person who's singing *believes* what they are singing, whether they do or not. There's a lot of acting involved in making records and that was something I feel R.E.M. pretty much understood.

This lack of clarity has, of course, given pop fans a lot of fun. On the Internet there are a number of sites dealing with mondegreens, famously misheard lyrics that attain a certain renown and that are, in fact, often more meaningful than the actual reality. From Hendrix's 'Scuse me, while I kiss this guy', and Bowie's 'ground control to Mao Tse Tung', to the Beatles' 'the girl with colitis goes by', the range is almost endless, and R.E.M. have carried on this tradition with some belters of their own.[11]

But there is a more important aspect to the fogginess of Stipe's words. For Stipe what mattered was not the end product, the literal meaning of the sentences he sang, but the *act* of singing them. The art was in the *process*, not the product. In semiotic terms, the act of enunciation was more important than what was uttered, the *enoncé*. Some critics would argue that popular music at its best prioritises this very aspect. Certain singers enunciate beautifully, telling stories through words, and the pleasure is in the song and the singer's skill at conveying literal meaning. However, for many music fans the true masters are those singers who distort, twist and generally play around with sound. Such singers refer to the *act* of enunciating, either through vocal ticks and mannerisms, or other earthy noises such as shouts, screams, moans, grunts and sighs. They draw attention to the act of singing, not the song itself. The B-52's do that with their screaming style and Michael Stipe is also in this tradition.[12]

The Athens-based artist James Herbert has said that the reason why there is such a diversity of artistic endeavour within Athens, in music, film, painting, sculpture or whatever, is because of the joy taken in the *act* of making, which is more important than the end result.[13] These cultural products may indeed have their worth in the marketplace, but they are not executed with that worth in mind and this is why Athens art tends to be homespun, quirky, eclectic and anti-iconoclastic. R.E.M.'s music was in this broad tradition too, at least initially. There was a sense of anyone can have a go; the act of trying was what mattered. It's no small wonder that punk rock's ethos played so well with the Classic City's liberal faction.

V

The impenetrability of the lyrics, taken with the decision not to print them on the record sleeve, reinforced the group's mystique. In fact, as the popular music critic Theodore Gracyk argues so convincingly in his major work *Rhythm and Noise: An Aesthetic of Rock*, it is this *lack* of clarity that separates 'serious' rock from 'pop'.

> Like opera fans, rock fans often consult the libretto when they want to know the words. In rock, vocals are often mixed as one element among many, rather than foregrounded with an instrumental background. Indeed, older recordings can seem quaint with their overemphasis on the vocals. One of the indicators used to distinguish rock from pop is that the latter emphasizes vocals and de-emphasizes the rhythm section. Clear enunciation is essential for pop, whereas rock singers are notorious for injecting a degree of incoherence into their vocals. In pop, the voice is thrust to the front and the lower tones which can mask it are kept to the back of the mix. Rock takes a more democratic approach and balances the voice against the other elements of the mix. There may be no attempt at clear articulation, and expression is conveyed by the tone and 'gesture' of the voice rather than the words. Among major rock performers in recent years, R.E.M. is conspicuous for not supplying lyrics. Their early records are also notorious for Michael Stipe's lack of articulation.[14]

Other music critics have also correctly argued that in rock'n'roll, words often act as 'music' and not so much as words to listen to; that they make their impact rather as a foreign-language opera might.

In spite of the ubiquity of lyrics and the fact that they do seem to receive the lion's share of attention in most rock criticism, [writes theorist David Shumway] it has long been a widely shared aesthetic principle that lyrics are not the most significant aspect of the genre. Records such as R.E.M.'s *Murmur* were praised because most of the lyrics could not be understood. Sociological studies have claimed to show that rock lyrics are routinely ignored by many listeners. Rock & roll lyrics may function mainly as 'music' just as scat singing does in jazz, or as foreign-language lyrics do in the experience of opera either on stage or record . . . But neither in opera nor in rock & roll are the lyrics merely an expression of music. In each case they contribute to the meaning of the performance even if their meanings are not immediately understood. Even if the listener does not know what the words 'Celeste Aida' mean when the tenor sings them, the opera *Aida* is still understood as a narrative. Similarly, while most listeners to 'Radio Free Europe' haven't any idea what the song is about, they already come to understand the meaning of R.E.M. as distinct from all other bands and performers of rock & roll.[15]

R.E.M.'s music creates a sense of identity. We know immediately that this is an R.E.M. track as soon as we hear it. It's this musical personality, this idiolect, which engages us. R.E.M. fans' passion for deciphering lyrics as evidence is a fun game, but ultimately misses the point. As stand-alone artefacts, the words themselves mean very little. It's the combination of words, music and iconography that makes the songs and the band what they are.

Thus, on *Murmur*, certain phrases are picked out and articulated, while others remain muffled. At this stage, Stipe was not exactly an excellent songwriter, but he was exceptional in that he had the ability to make individual lines hit the listener and become addictive and deeply evocative. ('Pilgrimage has gained momentum'; 'Laocoon and her two sons'; 'not everyone can carry the weight of the world'; 'a perfect circle, of acquaintances and friends'; 'Conversation Fear'; 'Up the stairs to the landing'.) The songwriter Billy Bragg once told *Mojo* magazine that 'Americans as a songwriting nation write in a very cinematic way, their culture is very visual.'[16] Stipe's work is a good example of this. A visual artist with a talent for art and photography, he uses the skills from these disciplines and applies them to music. Consequently, his words drift in and out of focus. Sometimes they are sharp and have distinct meaning, as if caught by a zoom lens. On other occasions they are blurry and indistinct and carry ambiguity. This makes us question how music communicates to us, and opens up the real joy of making personal, private meanings out of indiscreet public worlds of sound. The 'inbetweenness' embodied in the lyrics also makes us think of our own sense of awkwardness and indistinctness. Stipe's art is a world in which broad, rigid categorisation breaks down. It reflects his feelings of existing between and betwixt history, sexuality, society. It is a feeling felt by many of his generation, between baby-boomer and Generation X. It was this tension Stipe explored in R.E.M., the tension between a baby-boom optimism that the world could be changed for the better through direct political action, and the feelings of despair and cynicism characterised by the generation that followed it.

Usually bands build up a body of interpretation as songwriters reveal the motivation behind their lyrics. Although this body of work certainly exists for R.E.M., the commentary is often as misleading or opaque as the songs themselves. It's certainly been the case that no two members of the band have ever been able to agree on the meaning of 'Perfect Circle' for example. The meaning of the song is not contained in the lyrics so much at all, as in the 'grain' of Stipe's voice with its gentle, feminised, soft contours, coupled with the circular keyboard phrase that ripples and repeats through the song and which musically echoes the song's title. Indeed, it's this sense of completion and of repetition that is at the core of their music: 'Everything about R.E.M. is circuitous,' argues Stipe. 'It weaves in and out of itself and you always come back to where you started and start all over again. That's a great way to follow. It's hypnotising; it's music that draws you in if you're there to be drawn in.'[17]

On 'Laughing', Stipe said that 'the first line is about Laocoon, a freak mythological figure who had two sons. All three were devoured by serpents. It was a popular theme in Renaissance paintings. There's also John Barth's novel, End Of The Road, where a statue of Laocoon features. Oh, I did change the gender from a man to a woman.' Now, as a testimony of intent, this statement from Stipe is almost useless. He generally seeks to explain neither his lyric nor his motivation. What we do get is a sense of his cultural references, and this is where

Stipe's talent reveals itself in these early songs. The listener is not so much interested in the singer's own motivations or emotions or, in fact, in any direct end meaning, but in the strange pattern of cultural references and signifiers. These random, isolated allusions, phrases and statements don't head anywhere. They simply stand alone as vignettes to power our imagination.

It should perhaps be pointed out that, although posterity has been very kind to *Murmur*, as it has been to the band in general, and although the album was well received, it failed to break the Top 100 in the UK and was only a moderate commercial success in the USA. The band, and the album, had their detractors. For some the word 'enigmatic' was simply a synonym for 'badly recorded crap', and for others the act of constipated cogitation expected was simply a bridge too far. Paul Du Noyer, then a jobbing journalist and later editor of *Q* and founder of *Mojo*, gives it straight: 'I think Stipe's genius was to come up with random lines which drift across the melodies in a dreamlike fashion. This is quite affecting, but I never considered they were worth sitting down and analysing.'

Interestingly, with the exception of 'Talk About The Passion', *Murmur* is devoid of songs of a political nature or songs conveying a polemic charge. In fact, the band that transformed so rapidly in the mid-1980s into something akin to a protest band had no sympathy whatsoever with those punk and post-punk groups who were into reportage and activism. 'We never wanted to spell things out,' said Peter Buck in 1983. 'If you want that, go and listen to the Clash. They're a newspaper; we're not.'[18] They also said they hated playing large venues, hated pop videos and would never lip-synch. One by one, these sacred cows of rock authenticity would be violated.

VI

Michael Stipe was a very shy person. On stage, in front of just a few hundred people, and among friends, he could be fairly extrovert and loquacious. However, in a high-pressure media situation where he felt that he had to conform to the industry norm of what a rock star should be or do he floundered. Take the David Letterman show appearance in 1983. This was the band's first public airing of a new song, the totally beguiling 'South Central Rain', which had been inspired, so legend has it, by the spring floods in Georgia that year.

Hidden away from the camera's gaze behind a bonnet of curls that tumbled in front of his face, Stipe sings the song carefully but timidly. Then, when the band are interviewed on stage by their host, Stipe takes ten paces back and sits near the drum riser, utterly incapable of entering into small talk. Mainstream celebrity was a language Stipe couldn't speak until his own band had changed that mainstream to such an extent that he could talk his own language without fear.

R.E.M.'s support slots in 1983 for the Police had obviously made things even worse. As we have seen, Peter Buck hated playing to audiences that were not their own. The Police might have made great pop records, but, by 1983, they were a mainstream stadium rock act with little new wave kudos left. This alienated Buck. The sheer hollowness of playing to a sea of faces who greeted even your best songs with polite applause was dispiriting. It drove Buck to declare that he would never play a stadium again. It made Stipe so profoundly uncomfortable that he would play with his back to the audience, as Don Dixon reports:

'Their first big gaffe was to open for the Police. They weren't really ready for that kind of stage, and at the time Michael was not feeling real healthy. He was starting to realise that he was being compared to people, and he did not like it. I think he felt that he had invented some of the diving into the audience kind of stuff. When he got compared to people, he realised that he hadn't really invented it, even though in his own mind he may have. He didn't want to be seen as just another rock guy. He had a bit of an identity crisis during that tour which certainly carried on into the making of the next album, *Reckoning*. When I saw them support the Police, it was a shitty show. I don't think Michael faced the audience for more than 40 seconds in total.'

The result was that, by the end of 1983, the band, and particularly Stipe, were not in the best of shapes when it came to recording the follow-up to *Murmur*. The stakes were higher now: despite the accolades, the front covers and the five-star reviews, the debut album had only sold around 200,000 copies. For Mitch Easter, this represented a surprising success. Nevertheless, I.R.S. wanted more. For Jay Boberg, the record had actually under-performed and the company had found it very difficult to get the media into line:

'I think *Murmur* is maybe one of the top 10 records I have been involved with, but I thought it could have done better. It was very much a square peg round hole situation; the marketplace was very different back then. Stipe's singing was an issue. I can't tell you how many times I ran into various gatekeepers – the people in radio or in the marketplace that you're trying to convince to become R.E.M. followers, to play their music, promote their music or write about their music – who said, "This guy can't sing. You can't understand a fucking word he's saying, why are you bothering me with this?"

'I'd say, "Jesus, how can you say this guy can't sing? The melodies, the way he evokes emotion, you're just missing it, man."'

The band had been playing live now for months on end. For their next album, they wanted to project some of this energy onto tape. They also knew that it was their day of reckoning. A disappointing second album now, and their career, already somewhat stuck on a plateau of college radio respectability, would go into reverse. In December 1983, R.E.M. reassembled at Reflection Studios in Charlotte with the tried and trusted team of Don Dixon and Mitch Easter to prove that *Murmur* had not been a fluke.

4. SOPHOMORE, 1983–85

I

The appellation 'classic' can kill a record stone dead. Once a record has been given that highest commendation, there are often more pitfalls than pleasures for the hapless mortals entrusted with the task of the follow-up. Once you have attained greatness, the compulsion to overreach, and to overcompete, can be killing.

Some acts never recover from recording a 'classic' record, particularly if fate deals them the cruellest of blows and makes it their very first. Take the Stone Roses: their debut album was lauded, so it seemed, by millions of critics, though actually bought by significantly fewer people. It took them five years of in-fighting to produce another record, so self-consciously a 'son of' that they called it *The Second Coming*. They never recovered. A decade earlier, R.E.M. too became members of the same club of rock acts whose debut threatened to become a millstone. The music press had received *Murmur* as if it were a divine artefact forged from the elemental fires of the rock firmament. Journalists were as mad for a bit of authentic rock mystery and romance as they would be a decade later with Oasis. Everything about *Murmur* had fanned the flames of rock mystery: indecipherable lyrics, an unintelligible record sleeve, an organic rock sound, and tales of weird goings-on in the studio, with the lead singer reported, as it turns out incorrectly, to have recorded his vocal in the nude. It was an almost impossible act to follow.

Actually, Stipe's vocals, or at least a goodly portion of them, were not recorded in the main studio at all. Producers Mitch Easter and Don Dixon had to find an out-of-the-way area for him to work in.

This hidey-hole was, in fact, the stairwell at Reflection Studios. Stipe would be mic'd up to sing in a miniature private world under the stairs: a hiding place in which to create.

In order to have singers feel comfortable, it was not uncommon for producers to have to create a suitable physical environment, as Mitch Easter recalls: 'I always feel like there's a good place to be in the room for a singer and it is not the same for everyone. You can move a singer ten feet over, and, suddenly, they start singing better! At Reflection Studios the control room was higher up than the studio floor and there was a little stairwell that went down to it. He wanted to sing in there. I have no idea who thought of that, but he just loved it in there, because no one could see him. And I think he did turn off the lights, but there's nothing too radical in that. A lot of singers like to set up an environment wherever they are. One of the rumours I used to hear all the time was that he would do his vocals at Reflection naked. Well, I don't know what he did in there, we didn't see him!'

Stipe's timidity was just one aspect of his feelings of discomfort. It was clear that he was not the most cheerful of lads at the best of times. His feelings of separation were exacerbated by the fact that he was, in Easter's words, the 'art fart tolerating the barbarians', in a bemused, low-key kind of way. From this very early stage in the band's career, Stipe would cast himself as an *artiste* interested in pop as an important means of expression. It might be the medium with which he is most identified in the public imagination, but that isn't to say that Stipe himself felt he was *just* a rocker.

Stipe's frailties manifested themselves in a mild hypochondria. Easter and Dixon remember that the microphone had to be 'de-garlicked' between sessions, such was the pungent aroma that infused the equipment after Stipe had breathed fire on it. 'I don't know whether it had to do with health and the karma of killing animals, or if it had to do with fashion,' says Easter. 'I don't want to belittle a firm commitment to a cause, but there are a lot of guys, kind of arty guys, who are smelly and eat smelly food – it's part of their fashion, their attire almost! He spent time in the studio with Ann Kenney, who was a really intelligent, very likeable woman. I don't know what their relationship was, but he used to stay at her house. They would concoct all these horrific tastes out of soy beans and garlic and God knows what, and bring them to the studio in these Tupperware containers. He would sit around eating this nasty stuff all day long. He liked having his stuff around him!'

In fact, Stipe was not in a good shape during the recording of R.E.M.'s sophomore classic, *Reckoning*. The stakes were high. This art-school, college-rock band felt the weight of expectation, and so did the producers. Don Dixon remembers in particular being given I.R.S.'s directives for a more commercial sound. 'Jay Boberg arrived at the studio. Now Jay is a very nice guy, but he was record company clueless. They needed a hit and they couldn't aggressively attack R.E.M., because they were so protected from reality by Jefferson. But he could take me to the water cooler and tell me that the label needed a hit record.'

Easter too felt the 'Californification' of the popular music business was detrimental to creativity. 'I got along with Jay Boberg OK, and he was a friendly guy, but now and again he would express an opinion that would make me think, "holy shit", because it would strike me as really teenage. And that's the way the whole record business struck me. I thought these people in Hollywood were meant to be brilliant experts, but I can now see that they don't know shit!' The pressure was on for a more radio-friendly sound; but the facts were inescapable. R.E.M. could not be the Thompson Twins. They would not dress up in designer suits or get half-a-dozen voluptuous women to adorn their video shoot.

Peter Buck for one was grateful to Dixon and Easter for screening the band from the I.R.S. agenda: 'That's the reason why I have such great respect for Mitch and Don because basically they rolled their eyes and said, "We've got this bullshit message from your record company and we're going to ignore it." And it got to the point where, as much as I respected the guys at I.R.S., we basically tried to record the records so they wouldn't know we were recording them! One of the reasons we rushed through *Reckoning* was that we wanted to, but that we also wanted to have it finished before they showed up to listen to it. And we did. I think we had a month booked for the record and by the time Jay showed up it was the last day and we just played him the record. He really didn't have anything to say about it.'

Dixon and Easter may have felt under pressure from a record company eager for commercial music produced to a tight recording schedule, but concern was also mounting about Stipe. The band in general were physically and mentally tired after spending what felt like all of 1983 on the road, but Stipe was particularly frail. Just getting a useable vocal was proving a major operation. Don Dixon:

> One of the approaches we took would be that me and him would go into the studio early in the day, say 11.30 a.m. or noon. I would let him do his thing when there was nobody else around. The rest of the band would show up at about 3.00 or 4.00 and listen to what we had done. He was not feeling that good. When we got into the record he was kind of shut down, and it was difficult to get him to open up. A good example of this is the track 'Seven Chinese Brothers'. He was kind of singing 'seven Chinese brothers' so quietly that it wasn't useable. He didn't have to scream it, but he did have to have noise coming out of his mouth so I could get something on tape! So I remember walking through his little booth to climb up a ladder, ostensibly to change a reverb sound, but really just to do something to stop myself going crazy. I had to try something to juice him up because he just had no juice! I was turning up this crank on the reverb and I noticed this stack of old records that had been thrown up there. I just grabbed the one off the top – this old gospel thing by the Revelaries called *The Joy Of Knowing Jesus* – and tossed it down to the bottom of the stairwell to him. 'Maybe this will inspire you,' I said. The next minute he was singing good and loud, but he was singing the liner notes to the back of that gospel record over the track for 'Seven Chinese Brothers'! This became, 'Voice Of Harold' and was released a little later. After this, we were able to track the vocal for 'Seven Chinese Brothers'. Both were done within half an hour.

For their part, Dixon and Easter wanted to try to create something which captured the energy of a live performance, and *Reckoning* is a much more dynamic record sonically. 'We did less colour stuff on *Reckoning* because, for one thing, we didn't have that much time, and the band were starting to "feel its oats", as they say,' recalls Dixon.[1] Berry was moved out of the drumming booth and into the studio and the band even agreed to a bit of reverb on the guitars too. Dixon was enamoured of the technique of recording binaurally, as Mitch Easter remembers:

Don Dixon was interested in binaural recording, which was a means of recording stereo that was more like the way your ears hear it. The research on it was done in the 1930s. It became a recording technique found in jazz, and it's actually like a subtle stereo, so it's not really all that great for pop music. Now and then it comes into fashion – Lou Reed did a binaural record, for example. You can really hear the effect on headphones, it's a real natural sound field. Don decided that he wanted to do this with *Reckoning*, and he made this sort of fake binaural head out of a cardboard box and stuck two microphones in it. It was a pleasant sound. The drums ended up fresher sounding. Then there's the usual kind of crap on it that we mixed – delays and reverb – but overall, I think the drums do sound a bit more lively. I think it did fit, because the band did have that sort of coming-in-off-tour vibe about them at that point. A lot of the songs had the energy of the band on the move – they certainly didn't sound like they had been written at home.

Don Dixon also agrees that the intention was to take a snapshot of the band as a performing entity. Before *Murmur*, Dixon had not seen the band play live, so, with *Reckoning*, he had a different take on the band's strengths and weaknesses. For a start, he wanted the guitars to approximate their live sound, but he again met with some opposition:

Finally, on one or two songs on *Reckoning*, we were allowed to turn the guitars up – but then the label freaked out. R.E.M. were wrapped up in the idea of being leaders in *not* being a stadium rock band; it was so important that these guys were not seen to be part of this corporate onslaught. However, by the time we got to the studio, the band wanted to rock out a bit more. Mike wanted to approach his stage bass sound, so we created a sort of tunnel for the bass and mic'd it up in an ambient way so that it was livelier. I did some stereo binaural techniques which allowed Mike Mills to be loud but not be in the same sonic place as Michael. Mike Mills was often singing 12 to 15 feet away from the microphones that were recording his parts, but because it was in a stereo binaural field, we would tend to hear him as behind Michael. He could be loud without covering Michael's vocals up.

We were not trying to make a theme record; I was more intent on getting a bunch of songs that I liked. Nevertheless, what is good about doing records at this stage of a band's career is that they do tend to be snapshots of what they are doing live. R.E.M. had been playing a lot, so they did not have this pile of songs in the same way that they had for *Murmur*. But they weren't making stuff up in the studio; we still cut more than we needed.

II

While the music moved away from *Murmur*'s slightly airless feel, the subject-matter was a little darker. *File Under Water* is the legend on the spine of the album and, according to Stipe, its real title. For the band, water symbolised passage, movement, a state of flux. On the threshold of fame, the band knew they had entered a liminal state, and this disquiet translated itself into some of the songs. The scene that spawned them was also undergoing change. R.E.M. could never be thought of as anything but 'special' or celebrities back in Athens. People now started coming to Athens in search of the R.E.M. sound. Whereas, three years earlier, there was a sense of democracy, now the party scene had been replaced by something more professional. The innocence had gone. Paul Butchart: 'It is really difficult to pinpoint when Athens switched over from just a party music scene to a serious music scene. I would definitely say the rise in popularity of R.E.M. was *the* major contributing factor, though even in 1982 *People* magazine came to Athens to do an article about the music scene, which at that time consisted of about ten bands of about 45 musicians in total. Up to this point, most of the music groups had their origins in Athens, friends playing with friends and so forth. It wasn't until the summer of 1983 that people began moving to Athens because of the scene, to be part of it.'

The people were changing. Some, like photographer Carol Levy, would be gone for good. Levy had taken the band photo that adorned the back cover of their first single, 'Radio Free Europe'. A good friend of the band's, and particularly of Michael Stipe, she had been killed in a car crash when, with a carload of excited Athenians, she had driven up to Atlanta to see the film *Smithereens*, starring proto-punk Richard Hell. 'She was a friend to many,' recollects Butchart. 'She was an excellent photographer who took many pictures of early events during the growth of the scene as we know it. She always had a great smile and an easy-going demeanour. Her death along with Little Tigers keyboardist Larry Marcus came as a shock to all of our close family. They were riding back from a concert in Atlanta when the car in front of them swerved into their lane, causing their vehicle to lose control. There were three other people in the car, including Rodger Brown, who wrote the history of the whole scene, *Party out of Bounds*. The shock took years to disappear. Even today when friends get together to reminisce about our crazy youth we all remember fondly our love for Carol and Larry and our sudden loss of innocence at their passing.'

Levy and Marcus were killed the day *Murmur* was released, 12 April 1983. Rodger Brown tells how 'when she was buried in Atlanta, her graveside circled with weeping mourners, something crucial to the community was buried with her, an honest aggressive, hopeful voice . . . The spell of innocence that had fired the first furious scene was fading, ending. And the end came swiftly.'[2] In December, the group Pylon, for many the only serious rivals to R.E.M. in the Athens scene, split up, unable to get a major recording contract and, so Brown details, Jimmy Ellison, the former bassist with the Side Effects, was diagnosed with an inoperable brain tumour. R.E.M., at a crossroads musically and personally too, had, by the end of 1983, outgrown the scene which gave them birth. It is this sense of closure that pervades the song they would write for and about Carol Levy.

'Camera' reflects the band's sense of grief, not through the words (which don't refer to Levy by name, or the manner of her death), but sonically, in Stipe's haunted singing and the band's restless though jaded music – a rock'n'roll threnody. Stipe's bare and exposed vocal is set against the solemn, slow bass pulse at the start of the song (which in turn is reminiscent of Roxy Music's equally barren 'In Every Dream Home A Heartache', filtered through Siouxsie & The Banshees' 'Happy House'). Stipe's lyric is a snapshot in music of the dead photographer – roles reversed, media switched; 'If I'm to be your camera, then who will be your face?' Although not a sonnet, the song's words are elegiac: 'Will you be remembered? / Will she be remembered?'[3]

The chorus includes the words 'alone in a crowd', and could, actually, sum up a particular strand of what Michael Stipe represented to his public, a feeling of being disconnected and sad although connected with others through a shared culture. Sociologists talk about the 'atomised' individual, the person who is at once connected, via popular culture, to a network of like-thinking people, but also disconnected, because of the impersonality of that culture, the lack of real contact, face to face, which is popular culture's way. Today, the Internet is the logical extension of this feeling of being simultaneously part of and apart from a community. We can 'chat' to people, but we never see their living, breathing selves. People are reduced to a set of words and numbers on a computer screen. Songs such as 'Camera' and later, of course, 'Everybody Hurts', speak of the solitude and pain of a post-modern society where community life is being eroded. It's a trend that contemporary writers such as Robert D. Putman in *Bowling Alone* also say marks out American society, a society of the alienated, the alone, where activities that bond us, even if it's a fraternity of bowling chums, are almost a thing of antiquity.

In technical terms, however, 'Camera' was not one of Stipe's most convincing vocal takes. It needed fixing, but, for Stipe, it wasn't broken. Mitch Easter attests: 'When he sang that one, he sang it purposely before the band came in, early in the day. His vocal was so exposed on that track, and because of that, it could really show any technical flaws with regard to pitch. Michael's a good singer, but with that one we had to make him work a bit to make it a little more technically accurate. He wasn't happy about that. He was thinking more about getting the song across, at one point he refused to do it any more. I remember thinking, well, that's pretty good, I'm not going to argue with you at this stage. He thought he was getting it across.'

The song 'Harborcoat' was a musical development, in that it prefigured the intricacy of the vocal harmonising style which would be so important to the band's sound. It's the first of R.E.M.'s duologues, a conversation between the harmonies of Stipe and those of Mills and Berry. The vocal weave would be the defining sound of early R.E.M. (along, that is, with the neo-Byrdsian guitar). It can also be heard at the finish of 'It's The End Of The World As We Know It'. Mike Mills later told *Rolling Stone Online*:

I like 'Harborcoat' a lot. That was one of the best uses of
12-string I ever heard. With harmonies, you can go two ways.
You can harmonise with the lead vocal, which is fun, but what's
actually more fun is to create separate parts, an actual melody
that goes along with and is a counterpoint to the lead melody.
It's a weird thing because it's the sort of thing for me, the more
you try and work on it the further away you get from actually
having it right. It works best when it's something that you hear
in your head instantly and you go and lay it down, which is the
same thing I do with the bass. It's just much more fun to take
the structure of the song and to find the melodies that to me
already exist within the song; you just have to find them.

It was this sort of musical detective work, an intuitive response to
melody, that marked the band out as supremely talented pop
craftsmen. The musical structure to 'Harborcoat' might be less radical
than the weird chord changes and choppy rhythms of their signature
work, but the band were taking a certain pleasure in stumbling
across predictable chord changes which, for them, were something
new. Mitch Easter fondly remembers how the band would play their
'classic' R.E.M, quick-tempoed tracks then would become animated
when happening upon a quite clichéd chord development. However,
it was this beautiful counterpoint, with its echoes of Simon and
Garfunkel, which sounded so refreshing at the time within new wave
music.

A crucial element of the maturing R.E.M. sound was Mike Mills'
instantly recognisable, and oddly melodic, bass runs: 'I always played
a melodic bass, like a piano bass in some ways,' says Mills in 2002.
'I never wanted to play the traditional locked into the kick drum, root
note bass work. I always admired Paul McCartney and even though
I didn't like Yes, I really liked Chris Squires, so melodic bass playing
has always fascinated me. I just love melody.'

Another standout track, and one performed live for several months
before being tracked, 'Seven Chinese Brothers' has Berry's muffled,
simplistic thud set against Mills' unconventional bass licks, which
appear to be more like lead guitar than the traditional bass. Then
there's the astonishingly loud piano motif which surprised and
amused Mitch Easter when he relistened to the album in 2001: 'I was
totally surprised to hear that really loud piano thing, "bling, bling,

bling", before the vocal starts, which sounds great. I know there was much discussion about the drums being too loud on that one. As we mixed it, Stipe kept on coming back up into the control room to say, "the drums are too loud", and walking back out again! We fought with him the whole time we were mixing it, but we did get them down a little bit. Those were the drum-obsession years back then, and throughout the entire session the drums were starting to get on his nerves.'

The curious lyric is a reference to an ancient Chinese folk tale but, since the words are unintelligible, this is another song which communicates nothing on a literal level.[4] '"Seven Chinese Brothers" is your classic, model R.E.M. song, with the stiffer kind of rhythms,' says Mitch Easter. At that point they could crank out songs like this at any time they wanted to, and they were really good at it. But you could compare it to other songs of theirs. The rhythm is kind of stiff, and the little guitar melodies, the sort of winsome, cute melodies are there, and somehow it works because of the specifics of how they play.'

Yet another strong track was 'Time After Time', not the Cyndi Lauper song that lodged in the Top Three on both sides of the pond, but another classic, and underrated, R.E.M. smouldering, mantric beat with an exotic middle-eastern or eastern quality quite unlike anything else in their repertoire. Yet again, though, there was a disagreement about the sonics of the track. The middle-eight section contains a very short, and rather cool, section of semi-grunts from Stipe. Such non-literal moments, the yelps, screams, hollers and moans of pop, are what can make it special. But, on playback of course, Stipe wanted them turned down, and fixing them, back in those days, was a thankless task.

Mitch Easter: 'That song was probably my favourite thing on the record at the time. I thought it was beautiful. It seems like we spent time getting nice guitar sounds so that the guitars could build up and have different textures. We were doing a lot of guitars direct back then, without amps, so you got the super-clean sounds to contrast against the dirty sounds. Then, after we had finished and were happy with the mix, Michael declared that those "Hut hut" sounds he shouted out at the end of the instrumental break were stupid and too loud. The mix was already gone so we spent six hours matching the sound of the mix to the one second that it lasts so we could splice it in. We spent a whole afternoon trying to get those one or two seconds of vocals to match so we could turn them back down and insert them. The fear of those types of sound can be directly blamed on the band Big Country for their "shah" at the beginning of their big hit "Fields Of Fire", which the guys thought was incredibly hilarious. They were always making fun of that at any opportunity! But at the same time they were also very afraid of having anything which could be considered as the same type of exclamation!'

III

'South Central Rain' is the strongest track on the album, and contains the evocative line 'These rivers of suggestion are driving me away.' It's the epicentre of the album, the lyrics picking out the central themes of passage, redemption and purification almost in stream-of-consciousness fashion, before the four times repeated 'I'm sorry', a three-note figure which would be reused a decade later in another classic song (the melody for the first three syllables of 'And everybody hurts'). The music builds to a rousing and satisfying dénouement. Stipe is at the bottom of his register almost throughout the song, and, in fact, the vocal tracked for Reckoning is not as good as the live vocal he would sing when the band made the video for the song.

'South Central Rain' was correctly chosen as a single, but all discussion about miming to the studio vocal was off limits for Stipe. In fact, the whole idea of producing a video was painful to the band, as Jay Boberg sums up: 'They really had reservations concerning the whole concept of just making a video and adding a visual to their music.' Stipe stuck to his guns in refusing to lip-synch, so a solution was found whereby the band would mime to the backing track in the studio but he would sing a new vocal on top of it. This film would form the promo for the record. It's a simple idea well executed. Remarkably, Stipe's vocal is actually no clearer, and the lyrics to the song appear camouflaged in a wash of flattened vowels yet again.

Buck and Berry were however – God forbid! – sporting beards. A bearded new wave group! This really was a shock at a time when clean-shaven rockers were the industry standard. The only people sporting beards back in 1984 were either full-time folk rockers such as Ian Anderson or utterly irredeemable stadium rockers like Mick Fleetwood and ZZ Top. This was five years before the fashionable goatee and 15 years before the arch-slovenly beards of Oasis. 'That was the first song of theirs that actually got some American radio play,' remembers Mitch Easter. 'It was seen as one of the big songs on the record, and was one of their forays into normal songwriting. They were starting to get famous enough that kids would come to the studio and want an audience with the masters. I remember some kids saw these bearded men and they were clearly horrified, because that violated all the rules of the new wave scene.'

Buck was the most resistant to the new medium. In fact, he was the least happy of any of R.E.M. about having even promotional photos taken, despite being good-looking and having more than half a brain to counter even the most inane of questions floated his way by the press. For *Reckoning*'s inside cover shots we see the bearded Buck at the piano, an instrument which, at that point, he never played. Anything to be curmudgeonly or to take the piss out of his star image, was Buck's motto.

This was not, of course, the band's first foray into rock video, and nor would it be their video breakthrough either. They would have to wait another eight long years for that. Their first promo was for 'Radio Free Europe', shot at Reverend Howard Finster's Paradise Gardens, and featuring the Finster himself at the end of the film. Overall, it's totally unlike any of the videos then airing on MTV. There's no lip-synching, no fast panning, no supersaturating colour, no nothing. As such, like the song, it's dated remarkably well, and is a fine art film.

Finster, who died in October 2001, was a most curious figure. To some, he was an inspiration, 'a man of vision and feeling – a fine example to all', says Stipe. From an early age, Finster experienced visions (or hallucinations, depending on your medical stance on such matters), and the art he produced, trance-like, in an almost unbroken stream of consciousness, was simultaneously childlike and totemic. Finster befriended Stipe and produced the painting that the *Reckoning* sleeve would reproduce, badly, by all accounts. Later poached by Talking Heads, he produced the award-winning design for the front cover of *Little Creatures* in 1984. Athens lawyer Besty Dorminey reports: 'A friend of mine went to work with Finster as an assistant. There was some discussion about how much he was going to be paid, and then Finster told him that he would only have to contribute 20 per cent of his earnings to the church! I don't think as an employment lawyer that that would exactly pass muster!'

But for someone like Mike Mills, Finster was simply an inspiration. This is what he wrote back in 1985:

We go up and see him all the time. He very seldom leaves Summerville, but lots of art students from here and the University of North Carolina, South Carolina and North Carolina State all come down and help him with whatever projects he's doing.

He's a tremendous guy. His idea is that he is a traveller in space and was put here to bring the word of God to people through folk art. That's all he does. He sleeps about three hours a night and every waking hour he churns out his great folk art. For years he was a travelling evangelist and finally he had a vision. He is 'Howard Finster, Man of Visions', that is his title. His vision said: 'Don't travel any more. Sit here in Summerville and make your church and have people come to you.' He built a church by himself, three stories high with a big steeple, on his property. He buried all his tools in a cement walkway and said, 'I give up my tools. I don't need them any more because I'm dedicating my life to God.' He's selling in New York for unbelievable amounts of money. He was on *The Tonight Show* and blew Johnny Carson away. It's part of his religion – reaching people through art. He is making art to spread the word of God.

He helped Michael [Stipe] with the album cover for *Reckoning*. Michael drew the outline for this two-headed snake, and gave it to Howard to fill in. And Howard did – in incredible detail. It was screwed up in the way it was printed. What Howard did was so much more detailed than what finally came out.[5]

Texas-born photographer, Stephanie Chernikowski, who went on to work with R.E.M. in 1986, visited Paradise Gardens that same year:

In December of 1986, an acquaintance invited me to ride shotgun on a southbound journey to the earthly paradise in Summerville, Georgia, that Howard Finster calls home.

Around three in the afternoon on Saturday we walk into Howard Finster's home and studio. On the way in, we pass a free-form structure resembling a miniature Gaudi cathedral, the gates to Paradise Garden, and a real-life version of the 'mansion' that recurs in the paintings. Angels point our way and whimsical renderings of George Washington and Abraham Lincoln greet us at the door.

Inside the room is stifling. The space heater burns full tilt. Howard has arthritis in his shoulder and needs to keep warm. We find him hunched at his easel, an unfinished board on which a cut plywood 'Howlin' Wolf' hangs on nails. His painting hand is supported by the other to steady it; his failing eyes squint to slits. He looks up to greet us. A woman from Kentucky is introduced with '. . . but I cain't sell her nuthin'. Mah gallery in Palm Beach and mah gallery in See-attle and mah gallery in Los Angelees . . .' It is a rap he repeats regularly – demands exceed his ability to supply. Especially now, immediately before Christmas.

He seems to paint around the clock, pausing only to greet his endless guests and to rest briefly on the sofa when his body becomes too weary to hold him upright any longer. He eats when his wife brings a plate of food to the studio. From the time we arrive until we leave, to my knowledge he never sleeps at all. I am invited to sleep in the room off the studio. When I awake each morning, the paintings he has done in the night are the first thing I see. There are always new ones.

Howard announces that 'R.E.M.' came by last week to bring him herbs for his shoulder. That had to be Michael Stipe.

Monday, the morning of our departure, I am awakened by a fragile voice in the next room singing of another world. Like a snake who hears a charmer, I slither through the curtain into the room where Howard works to see a free-form wood scrap alive with joyful creatures and words of wisdom, 'Keep your Brain under Control' and 'Have a good cover on your head when the stars fall.' It has been an inspired night for him.

'Sometimes I hear voices,' he smiles when he realises I have entered.

Yes.[6]

The Rev. Howard Finster is nothing more than a long footnote in R.E.M.'s career, an eccentric Southern artist discovered by the esoteric Stipe. But it's the fact that Finster and other inspirational or just plain odd characters were discovered, and their experiences internalised by the singer, that is important. We are about to enter a new phase in Stipe's songwriting, a phase populated by myth, legend, fables, fictions, apocryphal stories of Southern eccentrics and wartime fables made real again over a century later. Michael Stipe was so important to R.E.M. because he had his eyes open to ideas outside of rock'n'roll and, in his own way, wanted to make that medium a wider receiver.

IV

Bootlegs of R.E.M.'s 1980 and 1981 gigs reveal that many of the songs recorded for both *Murmur* and *Reckoning* had in fact been in circulation for years before being recorded. 'Pretty Persuasion', for example, was played at Tyrone's in October 1980, and so too was '(Don't Go back To) Rockville'.

'Pretty Persuasion' was one of R.E.M.'s standout tracks in concert but, by early 1984, there was opposition from the band to recording it, as Mitch Easter recalls: ' "Pretty Persuasion" was an old song, and we had to talk them into putting it on the record. Michael hated it by then. I think Michael at the time was really worried about songs that had regular subject matter. I think the fact that it has this "she's got" chorus struck him as stupid, but it's great. They were really all or nothing about their songs – they were either "crap" or "really great", and that one was in the "crap" bin. They had done it as a live version at the end of the *Murmur* session, and the version for *Reckoning* is almost identical. It's kind of a rip-off of Todd Rundgren's "Couldn't I Just Tell You", though. The little guitar intro is almost note for note the same thing! The Todd Rundgren song is like him driving a stake into the heart of power pop to claim it for himself. I'm sure Peter Buck had heard it. I'm sure they weren't going to lift it or anything but anybody who hears the two songs would hear that.'

For Mitch Easter, 'Rockville', although undeniably catchy, needed a tighter arrangement. It was a pretty, country-flavoured song which, for many fans of their early work, is among their best tracks. In earlier live versions, the tempo is quicker, and although there's a phoney country twang in Stipe's delivery, the song isn't the rather mournful country and western work-out featured on *Reckoning*. It's a quicker, more urgent arpeggiated song with more spirit to it. The version tracked on *Reckoning* was intended as an affectionate doff of the cap to Bertis Downs, who was a country and western fan. It's an odd song in that it sounds like a cover version, which, in a sense, it is, since it's a restyling of an old live favourite. Mitch Easter, though, didn't feel that they realised the song's full potential in the studio:

It's a pretty good song, and if I'm not much mistaken, it's all Mike Mills' song. The little chord progression that leads into the chorus peaks my interest because it's got some interesting minor chords, and the chorus is simply undeniable – it's a good chorus and you're not going to forget it. You can instantly see the utility of that song for the fans, because it's so easy to get hold of. The only problem for me was that I don't think they really had the goods in order to play it. They kept talking of the Lovin' Spoonful a lot. They had this guitar player named Zal Yanovsky who did these countryish licks kind of well, and he was all by himself doing these in those years. I think Peter Buck was a fan of that guy, but he didn't really know what that guy did, and the only trace of it is at the end of the chorus, when Stipe sings 'waste another year'. Peter was really pleased he was playing like Zal at that point, but the problem was that there wasn't enough of it. The verses sort of lay there like these big gaps between the singing lines, and there's this half-baked piano and sort of nothing from the guitar. To this day, it still sounds unfinished there, but when you get to the chorus and the singing comes in it's really good. To me it's a song which they didn't quite have the tools to realise, but it is a good song.

But for Easter, the album's closing number, a band song about life on the road, 'Little America', was successful and touching. The band referenced manager Jefferson Holt ('Jefferson, I think we're lost'), cast in the role of the cavalry coming to rescue the four R.E.M.-ers from their touring tribulations: 'I really liked that one. It rocks out, and I love the way that, every time the "Jefferson" thing comes up, he sings it in a different way. Sometimes he doesn't say "Jefferson", and sometimes he doesn't say, "I think we're lost", but his little variations are really cool. I hate songs that are about being in a band, or songs about songs, but every now and again, it works, and this one does. It is a little travelogue about themselves. "Little America" is a chain of gas stations, by the way. They're out in the country in Minnesota and South Dakota: huge gas stations with crappy food, that kind of place.'

At this stage, R.E.M. were popularisers rather than innovators. They took well-worn styles and provided a new look, poppy enough to attract a mainstream college audience. R.E.M. were the acceptable face of the new movement of college rock.

Whisper it quietly: *Reckoning* might actually on balance be a slightly better record than *Murmur*, despite the attention given to the latter. True, it is not as original, but originality is, particularly within pop, an overrated virtue. True, it doesn't suck you into its world like the watery *Murmur* does and, true, the record was not as significant in terms of the overall course of rock history either. It didn't become a touchstone for would-be college rock acts in the same way *Murmur* did. But musically, comparing song with song, *Reckoning*, despite containing a few fillers like its predecessor, is perhaps very slightly the stronger set. Pete Buck has fond memories of the record: '*Reckoning* was one of those records that we wrote on the road and recorded in about two weeks. It's got a real haphazard feel to it, but I really like that record.'[7]

Despite the commercial success of 1991's *Out Of Time*, and the undoubted brilliance of later works such as *Automatic For The People*, *New Adventures In Hi-Fi, Up* and *Reveal*, these first two albums have many fans. For some, the band never managed to match their initial statement. Athens music critic Ballard Lesemann said in 2001: 'I don't think you can replicate *Murmur* or *Reckoning*. They came up with a lot from very little with those records and I still think they stand as their best.'

V

For the 1984 tour, the band would be supported by the North Carolinian band, the dB's. Peter Holsapple from the band had already opened for R.E.M. as a solo artist a couple of years previously and, at least on the 1984 tour, the dB's, if not an equal match for R.E.M. in terms of sales, were almost as big a band in college rock circles. As an opening act, they certainly gave R.E.M. a run for their money.

This was the band's fourth year on the road, and, like virtually all rock bands from the era, drink and drugs were taking their inevitable toll. Despite many a coy statement to the contrary, and although the band have distanced themselves from rock-star excess, the drug culture was part and parcel of their early years. The band are loath to talk about those years now in interviews. Buck, with typical humour, says that talking about the early days feels like talking about the American Civil War, so long ago does it seem. Typically, Stipe once said: 'I'm uncomfortable about dredging up moments and emotions from that far back. Suffice to say I was getting laid and doing a lot of drugs, travelling around sleeping on floors – it was great fun.'[8]

Mitch Easter: 'I don't know what people do and I never question it unless it's getting in the way, which it rarely does. Certainly no disco scenes and lines of coke on the console, they were too busy trying to make a good record.'

For Will Rigby, Stipe was emerging as a very forceful persona. 'He was aloof from the very beginning. He was the kind of guy who everyone wanted to be around, and it quickly got to the point where he had to ration himself out to people because he was in so much demand. He was kind of arty, and the other guys were more like regular guys. He was different. I really didn't know how to talk to him. I didn't feel like I could relate to him on his level.' Rock journalists began writing about Stipe's singular approach to the rock interview. Such eccentricity must have certainly stuck in the minds of writers more used to the sculptured suits of the Wham! era. Q journalist Adrian Deevoy remembers the young Michael Stipe: 'When I first met him in 1984, Stipe was 24 years old and working very hard at being misunderstood. He didn't say much, preferring instead to let Peter Buck do the talking, but when he did, it came filtered through a curious combination of chronic self-consciousness and childlike openness. He ended our meeting by saying "I really like your eyes." '[9]

Furthermore, although the band would attempt to portray themselves in interviews as being somehow outside of, or above, big business, as if their records were somehow made available by a process of barter, they were developing a very sharp business acumen. If the band would not accede to some of the more gross aspects of corporate rock, they were, conversely, not the ideological dreamers one might think. This first revealed itself to Mitch Easter in Stipe's eccentric designs for fashion goods: 'I thought the most eccentric thing about him was that he was the only one who really spoke about commerce. Not whether the latest record would go platinum or anything like that, but one of the things he used to talk to himself about to amuse himself was a line of fashion products. They were all weird, things like clothing that only used Velcro or fasteners. I think that and the fact that he was funny were things that I liked about him at that time. That still seems a bit under-appreciated to this day.'

Will Rigby also recalls how sussed the group was: 'I admired them for their business sense. Instead of taking 15 per cent of the gross, which is typical for a manager, Jefferson was an equal partner with them, and so was Bertis. I really admired that aspect of the way they set up their business. But they were always businessmen, they were very involved in all aspects of marketing and following everything from airplay to sales to advertising. They were always really super on top of it. I'm talking about members of the band. Maybe not in 1981 but in 1984 they could quote you sales figures and they would complain about things as relatively minor as a poster – "Tell I.R.S. you can't use that poster, that poster sucks!" – I.R.S. would just have to eat it and print up one they liked. They were very much on top of everything, in particular Stipe and Buck.'

In the autumn of 1983, the band made their first-ever trip to Europe. On 18 November 1983, they played on *The Tube*, perform-ing 'Radio Free Europe', 'South Central Rain' and 'Talk about the Passion'. It was the beginning of a promotional drive in the UK and mainland Europe, but poor distribution and patchy airplay meant that there was little real support. *Reckoning* would go on to reach Number 27 on the album chart in the USA in the spring of 1984, really a very good result for a college rock band, but only Number 91 in the UK, which was, by any standards, a poor result.

During the band's dates for the *Reckoning* tour, new material, already demoed and honed at sound checks, would be inserted into the set. 'Driver 8', replete with more surf-style guitars, was a fast and furious song in the old R.E.M. musical tradition. But Stipe's focus was changing. His new material would reflect an introverted, almost Messianic connection with the myths and legends of America's past, a sort of American gothic in sound. It was time to develop the sonic landscape of the group and to refresh the range of lyrical matter they dealt with.

Don Dixon and Mitch Easter were not invited to be part of this development. Easter remembers being told of the band's decision to record with the American producer Joe Boyd backstage at a gig.[10] He was disappointed, but not heartbroken. R.E.M. had given Easter his first audience: 'I would have continued working with them, of course, had I been asked to, and I would have come back at any stage. But I really don't think I had any grudge against them. I don't remember hearing their follow-up album, *Fables Of The Reconstruction*, and thinking, "Ha ha, it sounds like shit, they'll be calling me tomorrow!" Apparently I.R.S. was very much against them making this record with Joe Boyd and I hear they just went ahead and made it with their own money. I thought that was a great story if it were true because by then I was already feeling pretty grumpy about I.R.S. Moreover, I liked the fact that the band was in a position to control their destiny back then. The fact that they had picked an interesting, classic guy like Joe Boyd I thought was a good move.'[11]

For Don Dixon, there was even a sense of relief. The sessions with R.E.M. had been draining and it was time to move on too. 'Mitch and I were ready not to dive into the studio with them again. I was exhausted after both those records. They were very difficult to make, we were under a lot of pressure and we were not making a lot of money. There was a lot expected in a short space of time. I would have liked, one day, to have made a record where we experimented more, or looked at things harder, but one of my strengths is being able to see things quickly. Most of the time people will use me when they don't want to think about things too long, and they'll know I'll blast right through it.'

VI

For the next album it was decided, at Boyd's suggestion, that the band travel to London.[12] 'I think Peter Buck was a fan of the Fairport records,' recalls Boyd. 'I think they had been happy with the first two discs but I.R.S. put pressure on them to expand their audience by enhancing the production. I seemed like a good compromise – a kind of name (albeit fairly obscure in the commercial world of I.R.S.), but someone who wouldn't force them to alter their sound. I pretty much insisted on London. The time was short and I felt that in order to work quickly I needed to be in a studio I knew with an engineer I liked. I was booked already to do the 10,000 Maniacs album a month later, around the beginning of March, so I felt there was no room for error. They seemed to like the idea – at least before they got there!'

This would be the first time they had ever recorded outside the USA. The choice of Boyd was, at first, rumoured to be resisted by some at I.R.S., but the band were insistent that a man who had produced such classics as 'Arnold Layne' for Pink Floyd, and had worked with the roots and folk outfits the Incredible String Band, Richard Thompson, Nick Drake and Fairport Convention, would be perfect for the sorts of sounds they wanted.

The decision to record the album in London soon turned out to be a bad one, at least as far as the band was concerned. Road-weary and disorientated, they were thousands of miles from home. The early months of 1985 were bitterly cold too, and the band soon moaned about the cold, the rain, the snow, the awful English food, the unprepossessing studio (actually a converted church in Wood Green, London), the fact that the hotel was a long Tube ride away. In fact everything.

Now, for those of us used to the delights of a UK winter, it's hard to find much sympathy. What did they expect to do in early March in the UK, sip caipirinhas beside the pool? Nevertheless, this was a serious problem for the band. It was as if the inclement weather matched an emotional Ice Age of their own. For the music they began making was introverted, twisted, darker and sonically very different from most of the material that had gone down before. It was a turning point for the band. Mike Mills now sees the recording of *Fables* as marking 'Stage 2' in their evolution: 'To me the R.E.M. career almost felt like the first two records were of a piece. They were made with a great deal of innocence and naïvety in Charlotte with some old friends. Then, after *Reckoning*, that's where the big adventure really began. Everything started to take off a bit more after that.'

Jay Boberg of I.R.S., who flew over to see the work in progress, was of the opinion that another problem for the band, psychologically, was that they did not feel 'amongst friends'. In America they were at least known, and felt at home, but, in the UK in early 1985, they felt cut off from this support at a time when they were feeling in a gloomy frame of mind: 'I think when they made that record – and I was over there twice – on one visit to the studio the band was very down. It was cold and wet, and the English-damp-penetrating-into-their-very-bones vibe was how it felt *in* the studio. In Europe, we had tried feverishly to get excitement going on *Murmur* and on *Reckoning*, and although we had had some pockets of excitement and some pockets of success, the overall experience had been very difficult. I.R.S. was distributed by CBS records on the Continent and A&M in the UK, and, although we did have some underground and 'tastemaker' success, it was hard going. So, the band's overall impression of Europe and the UK was not easy. Whereas in the USA, by the time of the second record, *Reckoning* had sold 300,000 or 400,000 copies in its initial lifespan.'

With *Murmur* and *Reckoning*, the band had become a cult hit, but could anyone be happy to remain an act for minority tastes? Could R.E.M. successfully make the transition from critics' rave to a commercially successful act? Or were R.E.M. simply imploding, world-weary, road-weary, depressed and despondent. For, during those weeks in the late winter of 1985, R.E.M. came the closest they would do for over a decade to splitting up and losing the plot.

PART II
GLOBAL WARMING, 1985–94

5. 'GRAVITY', 1985–86

I

Michael Stipe does not feel comfortable writing about the upside of life. For him, the words that express love are often clichés, the ability to capture thrill and joy, without sounding maudlin, trite or overly sentimental, is a skill even some of the best songwriters don't possess. The language of the lover and the lovelorn in pop is worn out, stale. Stipe despised the continuous stream of what he regarded as schlock, put out by the likes of Rod Stewart, whose FM smashes 'Do You Think I'm Sexy', 'Hot Legs', 'Tonight's The Night' and 'Passion' were examples of how not to do it.

It would be another 15 years before R.E.M. would record an unabashed love song. The affectionate Brian Wilson homage, 'At My Most Beautiful', would be that song. R.E.M.'s first big international hit, 'The One I Love', although taken by many to be a missive sent from the heart to a lover, is, in fact, a cruel put-down. PIL might have sung 'This Is Not A Love Song', but R.E.M.'s anti-love song was more spiteful – 'a simple prop, to occupy my time' was what Stipe reduced his lover to.

What's more, when R.E.M.'s songs did talk about relationships, they were gender-unspecific, and this gives them their spice. Back in the mid-1980s, when Stipe's sexuality was never an issue with journalists, we simply assumed that the addressee of his lyrics was female. However, there's an open-endedness to these songs which undercuts such lazy assumptions. Sentiment can be misleading. 'Shall I compare thee to a summer's day?/Thou art more lovely and more temperate', wrote Shakespeare in 1609, yet this sonnet is supposed by many to be for a man, not a woman. Throughout R.E.M.'s career, with their first few unrecorded songs the only exceptions, Stipe's words were ambisexual, and, very often, shot through with a profound melancholia.

Very often pop's greatest moments come at times when the real-life trauma of the artist is laid bare on record. This is why John Lennon's *Plastic Ono Band* album, recorded after his primal therapy, is so much more emotionally believable than the love-crazed *Double Fantasy* recorded when he was a happier man. 'Remember' drips solitude and depression; 'Woman' is a pleasant tune, but a hackneyed lyric.

And so we come to R.E.M. in early March 1985, a band in crisis with a lead singer who claims to have suffered a 'mental, nervous, physical and mechanical breakdown' at the time.[1] Thousands of miles from home, distant from friends and familiar settings, R.E.M. may have been personally unhappy, but the odd and twisted album they made in the late winter of 1985, *Fables Of The Reconstruction/ Reconstruction Of The Fables*, although flawed in many ways, is one of their most underrated.

It's an album that engages the head *and* the heart. It's not an album of pristinely recorded and superbly realised songs, as *Automatic For The People* would be, nor is it an anxious, assertive and aggressive album like *Document*. It's a low key and, at times, poorly articulated record, but its themes of myth and legend are important ones, ones that engage with history and tradition: big themes for popular music. The dialectical title itself is a clever word-play: here is an album that announces itself as documenting the fables from the Reconstruction era, but also seeks to reconstruct these fables for a modern audience. Past and present, fact and fiction, are intertwined. As Stipe says, everything about R.E.M. is circuitous. It's this jumble of time-streams and traditions that makes *Fables* such a totem of postmodernity. In a sense, there is no history, only a 'depthless present'. The title's trickiness and allusive quality plays around with the fabric of time as if it were a toy.

The making of the album was a rite of passage for the band. It would be their last album of deliberate sonic murkiness, the last set of songs of tone poetry from Stipe. For, as the eighties unwound, the band would become ever clearer on the radio, and ever more vocal in the press. By the end of the decade, Stipe would be the spokesperson of his generation, his lyrics, although still baffling and opaque, now almost clearly enunciated and audible. But this was for the future.

According to Joe Boyd, there was no overriding concept to the album during recording stage. Like many other great conceptual records, the concept appears to have been grafted on afterwards by critics and fans, who have imbued the record with extra, hitherto hidden significance. In fact, the album's title was settled on after the album had been completed and arose after a phone conversation between Stipe and his father. It was the word 'reconstruction' that Stipe senior mentioned, in connection with carpentry, and Stipe has claimed that the album has less to do with Southern politics and more to do with the act of reassembly. Producer Joe Boyd says, 'If there was a concept, I was not aware of it. And I would doubt there was – there were about six other songs we recorded, some of which have since been released on collections/outtake things since, but which don't necessarily fit into any shape with the others.'

It is true, however, that Stipe took a genuine interest in the American South, approaching the subject not as a Southerner *per se*, but more as a tourist, historian or archaeologist. What comes across is the feeling that this wasn't the culture he *lived* in, but a *foreign* culture he wished to explore. His approach was thoughtful. Through his lack of specificity, he neatly sidestepped the risk of giving a crude characterisation of the South, or aestheticising it without remembering that region's brutal and complex racial politics. Having read about folk traditions and slavery, he was beginning to take an active political line as a liberal Democrat and had also befriended genuine folk artists such as the Reverend Howard Finster. But the songs on this album lacked any committed stance, and the result once again was a set of songs on which the words were muffled and concealed, buried beneath a busy mix, with beautiful couplets standing proud from the music to fire the imagination. This was essentially a set of fables with the lyrics as music rather than words. Ultimately, it was an intriguing meld of found elements thrown together. The result was an album of American gothic, recorded in London, with a European neo-surrealist cover depicting a tin ear!

II
The band had long outgrown the Athens scene, but had not yet shaken off the 'from the South' label. 'People used to say we were

such a Southern band, and it was like official . . . I don't know what they expected,' is Michael Stipe's curt assessment of the selling of a Southern band, made to *Rolling Stone* in 2001. 'There has never been a conscious attempt to sell the band as from the South,' was Downs' view in 2002. 'In the early 1980s, Southern bands meant the Allman Brothers and Lynyrd Skynyrd. We certainly weren't lumped in with that. Southernness certainly imbued their identity, but it wasn't part of this great master plan.' Writers and fans have so often simply bracketed the band as a 'Southern band', yet what does this mean? Was it simply nothing more than a neat marketing tag?

There's a hot-headedness to the Southern temperament which is mixed with a compulsion to confront and to rearticulate the region's singular past. As Athens lawyer Betsy Dorminey points out, 'If you come to the South you'll find that we're a Celtic group down here, much more than English. We're pretty much Scotch/Irish, that's the predominant ethnic character. The Irish character, the inclination to fisticuffs, hard drinking and irresponsibility – well, that's Southern.' However, this analysis does not explain the itinerant Michael Stipe. Although he doesn't match the maudlin Celtic stereotype, and neither really do the three other band members, the R.E.M. circle has always been a drinking one, if usually on a highly convivial level. And there is an expression of deep sorrow in much of their music. There is a Celtic influence to Southern culture for sure, and this has always been a theme musically in R.E.M. songs such as 'Swan Swan H', 'Try Not To Breathe' and 'Chorus And The Ring'. But you can hear the melancholia of the Celts clearest on *Fables*, in the lonely descending guitar riff in 'Green Grow The Rushes', or the hokey rootsiness of 'Wendell Gee'.

Yet, if we are to accept that the music references at least some of the traditions of the South, then their Southernness was very different from the redneck 'good ole boy' of popular myth. In fact, the band itself did not easily identify with any locale. It seemed to producer Mitch Easter that, if anything, they would be inclined to disavow their Southernness.

The 'Southern' business was funny. On the one hand, I always felt it meant nothing. I grew up listening to, and being inspired by, 'I Can See for Miles', which I guess is Southern – England! That meant more to me than, say, 'Dixie'. But on the other hand, there's no doubt about it that even the snappiest hipster from here is just obviously different from his/her equivalent in LA. I always felt like there was an 'off the beaten track' aspect to rock bands here, probably because there was no music business and therefore no force to consolidate a 'sound' in a commercial way, but at the same time, there were absolutely loads of string-instrument players, past and present. Maybe people were more eccentric (and naive sometimes), which fits with the spirit of that early 80s DIY requirement, and the manifestation in this area was that 'Southern pop' thing. Obviously, there is highly assembly-line music from the South – Nashville country, Memphis soul, stuff with a 'sound'. But there was no rock sound from here in those years beyond the last gasp of so-called 'Southern Rock' – and even that wasn't monolithic if you consider the jazziness of the Allman Brothers vs. the hillbilly Free-isms of some Lynyrd Skynyrd.

But as for R.E.M. – hell, only Mike Mills had a Southern accent! Peter Buck was totally un-Southern in demeanour, almost militantly. Bill maybe had a sort of 'soft' demeanour that's kinda Southern, and Michael I guess would need to be from the South, too, when I think of his style back then. But none of them were 'country', which is so often used as interchangeable with 'Southern'. I think those guys were 'Americans' who liked the spirit of Athens, GA.

It's important to remember that the South is still (forever?) the underdog, the weird, misunderstood, cliché-saddled part of the country. To this day screenwriters give the psycho killer a facile, overdone Southern accent for no good reason except it must play well with lowest-common-denominator thinking audiences![2] I swear, only after Carter was President could I travel around the country without my accent being cause for much hooha. I mean, puhleeez! But then the South got cool as a place to be from with your new wave band. Awright! I think the B-52's, Pylon, Love Tractor and R.E.M. all somehow benefited from being from the South. The time was right to take a look at, and enjoy, that part of the country. Who knows why? I think people got into this mindset of: leather jackets/tough = NYC or London; eccentric, cute, nouveau-beauty = the southern USA. I think people like this kind of categorisation. I guess I wouldn't expect R.E.M. to be from NYC – there's something pastoral in there that has to come from a quieter place. But hell, I dunno. It seems like we are all products of TV and radio as much as anything around us. And yet when you come here you will detect a distinct vibe . . .

So the pastoral quality of the South and the tortured beauty both played well with the audience. In creative terms, there was also a sense of, if not isolation, then separateness. The South was off the beaten track, an environment where a rock group could tour and make music, and could also make mistakes, without them damaging their career too badly. The centres of power in rock music were in New York and LA. Any locally successful rock musician or producer eventually felt compelled to work there. Although the South obviously had a rich tradition of blues, rock'n'roll and country music, and indeed has an almost undisputed claim to be the very cradle of rock'n'roll itself, it was still the case that, in the early 1980s, rock musicians tended to move away rather than stay put. Not so R.E.M., who set up camp permanently in Athens, Georgia, when the temptation, and indeed the logic, to move operations to New York must have been overwhelming. The fact that their Athens office would be listed in the phone book, would welcome well-intentioned fans and musicians, and would operate on a mostly small-scale level, helped ground the band and allowed them to retain a sense of identity when they did become a corporate rock act in the late 1980s.

III

Fables Of The Reconstruction is full of small-town scenarios and eccentric characters. The Otis Redding/Ray Charles pastiche/homage, 'Can't Get There From Here', affectionately references the lateral thinking of the Irish jokester in its humorous title. 'Old Man Kensey', about a real-life dog-kidnapper and acquaintance of Howard Finster's, and the banjo-led curio 'Wendell Gee', an epitaph for a car salesman who came from a local dynasty of Athenian Gees, and who in fact didn't die for another decade, also possess a winsome folksiness. 'Life And How To Live It' is about another old Athenian eccentric, Brivs Mekis, who divided his house into two halves. Copies of a self-penned book of manners, said to be racist and anti-Semitic and called *Life, How To Live*, were found in his house after he died.

Stipe later commented: 'Mr Mekis, of "Life And How To Live It", had actually divided his one house into two apartments, each outfitted differently than the other . . . I made it two houses for hyperbolic clarity.'[3] Another track, 'Maps and Legends', drifts musically with some beautiful harmonies, and is supposedly addressed to Howard Finster:

Called the fool and the company,
On his own where he'd rather be.

'Driver 8', on the other hand, follows in the tradition started by 'Carnival Of Sorts (Box Cars)' as another of the group's railroad epics:

Take a break, Driver 8,
Driver 8, take a break
We can reach our destination,
But we're still a ways away.

Roz Knight writes: '"Driver 8" mentions the Southern Crescent, the railway line through Georgia to New Orleans . . . The South has a long association with trains, dating back to the construction of railroads during emancipation and reconstruction. Railroads and trains are common themes in blues songs, signifying movement, power, and the broadening of horizons. Railroads also brought despair and sorrow as families saw loved ones leave to find work in the cities or to escape from Jim Crow to the North . . . The appeal of the railroads to travelling hoboes perhaps had a similar appeal to Michael Stipe. The sense of being between destinations and belonging nowhere is something he could identify with . . .'[4]

So, as hinted at by journalist Mat Snow, it's not a direct, but a diffusive set of images we get from the album. The music encapsulates the myth of a lost America that is immensely appealing to British journalists too: 'Stipe's projection was of a kind of eccentric historicism, if you like. You sensed what he was bringing to the party was a kind of cultured Americana which was too clever to be a sort of name-dropping. You sensed that he'd read some cool books and had some cool sepia pictures of West Virginia miners hanging on his wall! He seemed to be tapping into that particular Motherlode of the buried folk Americana, much like the Band did in the late 1960s, even though he wasn't nearly so specific nor, to be honest, as good a songwriter as Robbie Robertson.'

In *Fables Of The Reconstruction*, Stipe deals with fictions, with myths, 'maps and legends' and grand stories. The album also tapped into perhaps another major psychological state that defines Southern-ness: the paramount importance of memory, of reconstructing a truthful past in the light of so many cultural revolutions. According to cultural critics Richard King and Helen Taylor, 'Memory is of course a major concern, even obsession, in classic modern Southern writing.'

Writing in the 1950s and early 1960s, C. Vann Woodward in *The Burden of Southern History* identified memory as a central component of regional distinctiveness. 'This is not to say that Southerners have genetically programmed hyper-memories but rather to point to the fact that people, regions or nations to whom "history has happened" are forced to remember – or to misremember – "how it was" to the point that it often becomes "how we wish it might have been".' Though the neat divisions between myth and history, fiction and fact are never that easy to draw, much contemporary Southern culture still stands divided between a desire for a useable and for a truthful past.

Now, the South has manifestly been a place where history has happened and people have seen their lives yanked out from under them. The first obvious blow history meted out to the region was the Civil War and Reconstruction. The second, the period of the Civil Rights movement, roughly 1954–68, what Woodward and others named the 'second' Reconstruction, was also a period of heightened historical consciousness which made more explicit the political importance of collective memories.[5]

If R.E.M.'s music touched on this deep sense of the Southern 'bruised honour', of existing in relationship to a past that was, in a sense, negotiable, then, in its authenticity, its historical perspective and its use of folk, country and rock idioms, it also stood in direct opposition to much of the popular music of the day. In a climate which, unlike the UK, had never taken contrivance and artifice to its heart, America saw in R.E.M. all those universal pop truths – 'real' music, played on 'real' instruments, played as a 'band' – to counter what it saw as the endless procession of commercial pop then being churned out by MTV. In the post-*Thriller* 1980s, an era in which albums became nothing more than a collection of radio/television-friendly jingles, R.E.M. were thought of as a reminder of a more enlightened age, when an album was a collection of songs, an artistic statement, a book to read rather than a comic to flick through. In the words of rock writer Simon Reynolds: 'American culture critics generally seem to be oriented towards meaning, community, a lost 'organic' folk-consciousness. That is why R.E.M. are such totems, and why live performance is the guarantor of authenticity and value in rock. British writers are generally more tolerant of, even enamoured of, the elements of hype, contrivance, conceptualism, etc., in the pop process. Live performance is less important; TV, press and radio seem to be more central to the pop experience. In the UK, there tends to be more juice/*jouissance* in a piece of pop writing. UK critics gush, or lash out. US writing tends to be knotted with the effort of cogitation, of unravelling the resonances.'

According to the music critic Greil Marcus, what fires rock, and what certainly inspires much rock criticism, is the construction and maintenance of certain myths. A myth is a 'big story, a grand story, a story with room in it'. It inhabits that twilight zone between truth and fact. It draws us into its trajectory, it tells a story which reflects on, but is ultimately bigger than, personal experience. It is the story of 'pop transformation'. Without doubt, R.E.M. has left us with two decades of highly articulate and, above all, human and touching music. What is also certain is that they have made such music, in part at least, by dealing subversively and ironically with big ideas. For R.E.M. have delved into the myth of a lost America, the myth of a rock community, the myth of pop as poetry, the myth of rock untainted by commerce and outside of the holy trinity of sex, drugs and rock'n'roll. R.E.M., and particularly Michael Stipe, are the mythogenic totems of alternative rock.

However, it is a level beyond the lyrical that reveals the band's Southernness. The allusive and allegorical music on *Fables Of The Reconstruction* reveals its Southernness less in its storytelling perhaps than in its sense of possibility, as poet Geoff Ward so neatly puts it:

Of course they're liberals, and so is the prevailing culture, but of course the history of the State is a different matter. How is that played out in R.E.M.'s music? I'm not sure it is. The celebrated vagueness/open-endedness of Stipe's lyrics gives them a varied application, makes them user-friendly, like personalised mondegreens you can rewrite by the light of your own experience. That vagueness also allows R.E.M. to sidestep their Southernness, retaining only a marketable melancholy which could be attributed in some unquantifiable measure to their region, or could just index Stipe's alienation, or point to musical sources in the psychedelic area. The South is defeated, wounded, haunted. This is still a live issue. Northerners who settle there will routinely be asked their view of the Civil War, puzzling Bostonians and New Yorkers who simply thought that the good guys won, end of story. Southerners who believe intellectually in democracy, abhor racism and view Jefferson Davis as deluded still carry a sense of elegy and bruised honour that they can and cannot square with the politics of Union. It's there in the sad chords and cracked emotionalism of Stipe's voice, but somehow it isn't there, or it's avoided, or mythicised into dream, by the open-endedness of their music. It's the American dream.

In a curious way, R.E.M. also represent the sameness of the South to other parts of America. As King and Taylor wrote, 'the skylines of Southern cities not only all look alike but look like those of American cities elsewhere; not to mention the class and status uniformity of the upwardly mobile inhabitants of the cities and commuter suburbs: *Sleepless in Seattle* could as well have been *Sleepless in Charlotte*. Modernisation has proceeded apace and where the traditional South once was, suburbs have sprung up.'[6]

Geoff Ward links this trend to the music of R.E.M.: 'The South as a region comes second to the culture of mobility. This is a country where 20 per cent of the population move in any given year, often coast to coast. They don't need regional specificity, they need a system of easily recognised social signifiers that will get you assimilated as quickly as possible into the car pool, the schools, the Church. As the barman walks towards you to ask what'll you have in Athens his accent differs from that barman in Buffalo, but in essence it's the same bar. This uncanny replication is what shows like *The Twilight Zone* are really about. Maybe it's what the sad music of

R.E.M. is really about. Not the difference of the South, at all, but the sameness of everywhere in America, where every place is like home. But nowhere really is home.'

This sameness and sadness find expression throughout the band's career, but it all begins on *Fables*, an album of sonic straight lines, repressed tension. The swampy, unsuccessful mix is in a way its defining quality. Had it been recorded better it would have sounded less real.

IV

Although their music touched on such grand themes and schemes, for the four individuals themselves, the experience of working with Joe Boyd was a difficult one. Boyd was hired at the insistence of Peter Buck because of his track record of making innovative and uncompromising music. One of the most innovative singles of all time, Pink Floyd's 'Arnold Layne', had been produced by Boyd way back in 1967, and his subsequent work with the folk-rock pioneers Fairport Convention confirmed him as a producer with integrity. On being hired, Boyd flew out to Athens to meet the band. Everything was fine. They spent a day demoing and getting to know one another. Again, R.E.M. operated in a slightly underhand manner, concerned about outside interference from their record company. 'With *Fables*, we were technically going to England to do demos, knowing that nobody would be able to get to us,' remembers Buck. 'Jay called up Bertis or somebody and said, "I know what they're doing, I know they're making a record without telling me!"'

The consensus though, for all concerned, was that the combination didn't work as well as expected. The choice of studio was definitely an issue. Joe Boyd: 'I am very fond of the studio still. It was Livingston in north London. They booked into a hotel in Mayfair in the centre, and came out by car every day. I tended to come by Underground as it is much easier and more pleasant – you can read – rather than the long dreary car ride. But they insisted. Stipe started taking the Underground and exploring London in the mornings, but the others slept as long as possible and then had this long ride. And English winters are wetter than in Georgia, and the standards of central heating there are not the same as American standards . . .!'

'Because the dollar was strong we were staying in a place in Mayfair,' recalls Buck. 'I'd never been in a house that nice up to that point, but I couldn't afford to eat in any of the restaurants! I had to take the Tube out to Wood Green every day – which was a 45-minute trip – and then walk a mile to the studio in the snow. It sleeted every day and it was 20°F. We were always hungry because we never ate – there was never any food. On top of that, the songs weren't finished, and we had about twenty of them. It should have been a two-record set basically. We had one car, and basically Mike was the only one who had the nerve to drive in English traffic. Mike always comes in later than I want to come in. I'd leave the house at 12.30 so I could be there at a quarter after one to tune up or whatever, and Mike would motor in a little later in the day. I like to get up there early and on time and set stuff up and make sure everything's OK and tune guitars. Mike is much more like, walk in, plug in and start playing.'

The sessions for the as-yet-untitled album ran in a relatively orderly fashion from early afternoon through to about midnight. Stipe worked on honing lyrics but, according to Boyd, most of the material had essentially already been written prior to the London sessions. It had been written quickly, though. Some of the tracks, such as 'Driver 8', which musically is perhaps more akin to the songs on *Reckoning,* had been worked on during the previous year's tour and played live. Others, such as 'Old Man Kensey' and 'Wendell Gee', had only emerged in live sets at the end of 1984.

In terms of the creative dynamic, it would be Stipe and Mills who were the most proactive in the studio. 'Berry was just the drummer, was close to the others and occasionally vocal about things but generally took a back seat,' is Boyd's take on things. 'Buck was the intellectual of the group, but didn't actually have that much to contribute to the process, although I felt he had a lot to do with abstract leadership – such as suggesting me for producer! The real leaders seemed to be Stipe and Mills. The former was a very strong personality, but understated; unwilling to boss people around, but everyone respected him and sought his opinions. Mills was the practical one, interested in everything to do with the making of the record, kept spirits up, and was very level-headed and cheerful all the time. So my best communication was with Mills, then Stipe, then Buck, least Berry. Mills was always cheerful, and I just assumed the gloomy Buck and Berry were just the way they always were. Stipe seemed happiest to be in London, going to museums and meeting friends, while the others played pool and watched TV at the studio when not working.'

If the sleety English weather, poor food and unsatisfactory standards of heating were bringing R.E.M. down, then Boyd also had other things on his mind. His fledgling label, Hannibal, was strapped for cash and he was continually worried. Virtually all the money he received for the production work with R.E.M. was pumped back into the label. Also the fact that, by that time, producers worked for the band, and not for the label, meant that for a producer like Boyd, there was extra pressure. 'When I produced for major labels in the seventies, it was a different era, the producer worked for the label, as did the artist. By the mid-eighties, that had all changed; the producer worked for the group. I was never entirely comfortable with that structure, and probably will never do it again, but that was the deal and I felt my loyalty to the group. I wanted them to be happy, and was upset that they weren't.'

Problem-time came with the mixing of the album. Perhaps the biggest frustration Boyd had was with Stipe's vocal. 'The subsequent record had Stipe's voice very clear and present, which is what I had been arguing for.' Once again, the producer ran up against the band's reluctance to be heard! Boyd again:

The mix was difficult. Livingston had renovated the room we mixed in and I never got comfortable with the sound there. I prefer the other room and still use it rather than the one where we mixed *Fables*. The added problem was that I usually build a mix around something, making sure you can hear vocals clearly, for example. But Michael was still in his period of not wanting the vocals to be clear, so he argued against making them louder or brighter and clearer. And Peter was wary of turning up the guitar too much, which I understood. He is a good player, but not a 'guitar hero' you would want in the centre of a mix. With most groups the opposite happens: you start turning things up and then they are surprised when other things get quieter, so you have to bring out the 'a glass of water can only be full, not more than full' metaphor. With R.E.M. it was the opposite: you kept the voice and guitar down and then the rhythm section became loud, but they didn't like that, so I was groping for a handle on how they wanted it to sound.

The tracks I enjoyed mixing the most were those with an extra element – horns, banjo, strings – so that the mix had more elements to be interesting. I think those are the most successful tracks. I booked a friend of mine to write the charts, and some young English string players (one of whom I fell in love with during the session!), so the whole thing was removed from the privateness of the rest of the tracks. Peter really had fun with the guitar overdubs and Jerry Boys [engineer] and I had a lot of fun with the sound of the guitar and mixing it. I think that enjoyment comes through, which isn't the case, for example, on 'Driver 8', where we were pretty much doing what we were told and never got a handle on how to make it more interesting.

Boyd was, however, very much impressed with the balance within the R.E.M. camp. They were artistes as opposed to rockers. Although the mood inside the studio turned gradually to one of depression, Boyd was unaware of the alleged crisis, and the subsequent claims that the band were on the verge of breaking up, until much later. 'I did feel they had an extraordinary combination of humility and confidence. They were absolutely comfortable, it seemed to me, with where they were going. It was a surprise to learn later of tensions that surfaced during the recording both within the band and about the production. They didn't complain at all, although they did seem depressed by the weather and the commute, and, eventually, we all got depressed by the tracks. We did the tracks in the larger studio and then couldn't get back in there after the first week. I was more used to working with ace drummers, and the more we overdubbed and worked with the tracks later, the weaker they seemed. I wished we could have gone back to re-record some of them, but the right room was booked and there was no time.'

When I.R.S.'s Jay Boberg made a trip out to see them, he could tell that things were badly wrong: 'They didn't say "this guy's terrible". My reading of the situation is that Joe Boyd had not turned out to be what they'd hoped for. The personal chemistry between Joe and the guys in the band did not turn out to be right, which you can never predict. And now they were in England, which they found did not embrace them like the States did.'

'Jay from I.R.S. came once and I don't think he liked what he heard, but the group and management kept me pretty well screened off from that,' recalls Boyd. 'R.E.M. were the most together in terms of how to deal with the music biz of anyone I have ever met. They made the first EP with no advance and never took an advance from I.R.S., and thus could fend off unwelcome opinions.'

However, it was the combination of foul English food and weather that nearly finished the band off: 'I'd like to lay it at the feet of the English cuisine, but that was just a cog in the machine at that point – there were so many things going on,' says Mike Mills in 2002. 'The album's fine, it's just that the making of it was difficult. It certainly wasn't Joe Boyd's fault. It's a very specific record. I think that when you listen you get a feeling of the cold draughty studio in which we were working, and a lot of homesickness. We'd been on the road for most of the previous year, and most of the year previous to that. Just the fact that we were alone in London was difficult. We had never really spent time there, this was only our second or third visit. So we didn't know the city, we had no money, no friends. We just had each other and work, and we were all sick of each other at that point from all the touring. So, it was a sort of tough time, and that bleeds into the record. But, as I say, it's definitely a very specific album, it feels like that time.'

'It's a really dark, depressing and strange record,' says Buck today. 'I mean, what's not to like about that? I love Joe's work, but he had the unfortunate task of being saddled with the band when it was pulling in about eight different directions and had been on the road pretty much for five years constantly. We were all kind of unsure where to go and Joe was stuck in the middle and I felt kind of sorry for him, but we pulled a record out of it. I know a lot of my friends think it's our best record because it's so weird and creepy.' Berry was less charitable: '*Fables* sucked', was his blunt assessment.[7]

Joe Boyd, realising that the mix was substandard, desperately tried to fix things, but to no avail: 'I was unhappy with the final mix and took the tapes to another studio to try another mix after they left. It wasn't successful, but I was panicked about the record, feeling it was not as good as it should be and that we would all be embarrassed when it came out. I wanted to try mixing it again, but they said no, enough is enough.'

V

Fables has gone in and out and back into fashion. On release, the lifeless mix, the cluttered overdubs, and lack of 'bottom end' disappointed some critics. Don Dixon, who had co-produced the band's first two albums, was also unimpressed: 'It began to fall into some of the worst aspects of how records were sounding around 1985. Sonically there was this kind of thin thing going on. A lot of that is because of the approach producers were taking, of isolating all the instruments, of not having much what I call "sonic glue" – just the sound of the room around the stuff, the sound that you get when people play at the same time, the leakage. But it was a popular sound, and I think Joe was trying to make something that was a little more commercial for them, but those records end up being less timeless.'

For Athens rock critic Ballard Lesemann, however, the record is still an achievement to be proud of: 'I think it stands up. I kind of wish they had that sound now. Once they put out *Fables*, they stepped off into better recording situations.'

'When *Rolling Stone* and *New York Times* raved, I was so relieved – a huge weight off me, but I still felt unsatisfied with the mix,' Boyd recollects. 'Then it sold double the previous LP, so I felt better and better, but was shocked when interviews and comments let me know how unhappy the group were with it, as they had never said anything to me. They got some big award when I was in New York, and they thanked everyone but the janitor, but didn't include me, which was a bit upsetting. But we have always remained friendly, particularly Mills and Bertis Downs. I wanted them to be happy and was upset that they weren't. Critics have reassessed it favourably periodically, and the group seem to have come round to it. Some of them, like Stipe, have made a point of telling me that they didn't like it at the time, but have come to love it etc. I think Buck said something similar to me, so that makes me feel more that it was a job well done.'

The sleeve design for the album carried on the band's tradition of successful artiness. The curious tin ear is a nod to surrealism of the Dali kind. The cover artwork also shows a leather-bound book which has burst into flames on an old oak escritoire. Stipe himself is dressed as a Rudi Valentino figure (a look later adopted by Luke Haines of the Auteurs for their debut album). He himself admits that, on this album, he was close to demagogy – 'me at my most messiah-complex worst', was how he would later put it.[8] The overall package was weighty, the music, for the most part, detached and icy. It does not welcome you in, it does its best to catch you off-guard.

The key track on the album is the first one, and one of Boyd's favourites. 'Feeling Gravitys Pull', starting the tradition of R.E.M. titles with no apostrophe, is a serious and dour mid-tempo song with a discordant guitar line and harmonic from Buck, possibly a nod to Britain's post-punk avatars, the Gang of Four, and a dreamy, almost spoken vocal line from Stipe.

> Read the scene where gravity is pulling me around
> Peel back the mountains, peel back the sky
> Stomp gravity into the floor
> It's a Man Ray kind of sky
> Let me show you what I can do with it
> Time and stance are out of place here

This remarkable beginning sets the tone. Life is reduced to a drama, nature to a surrealist collage, and the fabric of time is disordered. Everything is disorientated and queasy. There's something elemental and eternal about Stipe's language, as if he were some sort of deity. Later, 'Oceans fall and rivers drift'.[9]

The music doesn't so much build as remain constant in terms of loudness and intensity. The violins surprise us, but the overall feeling is muted and downbeat. 'Feeling Gravitys Pull' is also the first of a number of tracks to reference 'gravity'. The song is an abstract expression of Stipe's desire to feel rooted and grounded. He needs gravity; he needs the pull of the Earth. Photographer Stephanie Chernikowski, who met and worked with Stipe in 1986, puts it like this: 'I remember a time when we were doing some editing. He put his hand on my arm, and it was like at that particular point he was doing it to ground himself, holding on to ground himself, to be *here*. The need to touch, to feel a part of the Earth.'

So many of Stipe's lyrics deal with, if not a fear, then an appreciation, of the human condition, with gravity being perhaps used as a metaphor for connection. Even a pop song such as 'Stand' is about direction, about orientation, about rooting oneself. 'The Lifting' from *Reveal* is another song that swirls and twists musically, with 'gravity' mentioned in the lyric. Other examples are 'Low Desert' and 'Leave' from *New Adventures In Hi-Fi* and 'Daysleeper' from *Up*. The sublime attraction of simply taking off, to escape gravity, is both a fear and a compulsion.

Despite the downbeat music and weighty lyrical matter, the record went on to become the band's biggest selling album up to that point, despite the fact that none of the singles off the record charted. 'It did better than the first two, about five or six hundred thousand copies, and eventually it was a gold record in America,' recalls Jay Boberg. 'It did not do better overseas. As I recollect, it did about the same as *Reckoning*, was my recollection of it. It didn't really open many doors there.'

The band was, however, undergoing a major crisis. 'I wasn't sure if I wanted to be in a band any more,' says Michael Stipe. 'I guess we didn't realise at the time how close they were to breaking up,' admits Downs.[10] As Mike Mills told *Rolling Stone* in 1987, 'A lot of things were catching up with us. We didn't realise we were going to be asked to do certain commercial kind of things, and we thought, "Is this what we really want to do?" It was maybe a crisis period, just an overall feeling of unease.'[11]

VI

By 1985, it was apparent that the band could not continue, or at least not in the same way. They were still relatively impoverished, still more accustomed to eating out of deli trays than in restaurants, still gigging at every possible opportunity. As soon as *Fables* was recorded, they went on the road yet again, this time on the *Reconstruction* tour. In 1985 Stipe, who had put on a few pounds, would sport first a close-cropped look with monk's tonsure, and thereafter a gaudy, home-made yellow-dyed look courtesy of egg yolk, transforming him into a grungy Simon Le Bon. It was during this tour, so Mike Mills recalls, that the band had their first 'clear the air' crisis talk, an attempt to find a way of continuing as a group. A running sore on the body politic of R.E.M. was the antagonism between Mills and Stipe:

Oh, there were a couple of occasions where we came pretty close to splitting up. In 1985 in Albany, New York, when we had a nice sit down and clear the air kind of meeting, that was probably the worst. There have been a couple since, but basically it comes down to the fact that you have to communicate. If you don't talk you are doomed. Secondly, once you do start talking you have a few decisions to make such as:

How much am I going to put into this? Is it worth it? Do I want to keep doing it? Once you answer those type of questions it's easy to decide what to do.

Now, Michael and I didn't get along in a lot of ways for a few years. We were very different people; we didn't really understand certain ways that the other thought. There was love there but there was also a great deal of oil and water for a while, but we both finally grew up. Michael was trying to deal with being a really shy person thrust to the front of the band. And I was trying to deal with how somebody had an attitude when it was unnecessary. But that's all ancient history. We've been as close as we could be now for as long as I care to remember.

Also, by 1985, the band had begun what music business folk call 'diversifying'. Peter Buck, Mike Mills and Bill Berry had formed the Hindu Love Gods with Warren Zevon. This would be the start of 15 years of constant moonlighting by Buck, who would play, produce and generally involve himself with dozens of splinter groups and side-projects. Later in the 1980s, Stipe himself is reported to have recorded an as-yet-unreleased solo album. However, back in 1985 it was clear that the band had reached a plateau of respectable, though hardly earth-shattering sales and appreciation. To go to the next level, and hit the Top 40 charts on a regular basis, would mean a consistent commitment to more touring and recording and, quite obviously, a more assertively commercial sound.

The band appeared unsure. Buck went back to work part-time at Wuxtry, where he claimed he was paid in records, to contemplate the next move. I.R.S. were becoming frustrated with the band's reluctance to 'pull the trigger'. All three singles from *Fables* – 'Can't Get There From Here', 'Driver 8', which was a US release only, and 'Wendell Gee' – had failed to chart. The answer seemed to lie in bringing in a producer with a history of making uncompromising music, but music with a more hard-hitting commercial sheen. Such a man was Don Gehman, and the result of the collaboration would see the beginning of R.E.M.'s assault on mainstream America.

6. 'THROWING A BABY INTO ICE-COLD WATER', 1986–88

I

Did R.E.M. consciously turn themselves into a pop group in the middle of the 1980s? Did they focus on the charts, on dollars and pounds, on becoming America's Greatest Rock'n'Roll Band? Did producers Don Gehman and, later, Scott Litt finally convince the band that music with a commercial sheen was not such a bad thing? Or was it the mainstream that moved towards *them*, their music becoming the blueprint for the emerging alternative rock scene? Whatever the motivation, it is certain that something very profound happened to R.E.M. between 1986 and 1988, for any number of self-denying ordinances were broken and sacred cows profaned. If *Fables Of The Reconstruction* had marked the band's period of greatest distance from the mainstream, then their next two albums, *Lifes Rich Pageant* and *Document*, would see them calling out to the world in a manner that shocked and disappointed some, but delighted and enchanted others, particularly those at their record label, I.R.S.

I.R.S. had seen *Fables* become their biggest seller in the States, but perform poorly in Europe, reaching Number 35 in the UK. Some critics regarded it as a dreary, poorly recorded album, and although it does have its admirers among hard-line R.E.M. fans, it is generally considered, along with 1994's *Monster*, as being one of their weakest. At the time, I.R.S. had a reputation for creative, bright and breezy pop music, very different from the music on *Fables*. For example, in 1982, the Go-Go's, with Belinda Carlisle and Jane Wiedlin at the helm, had scored a series of big American hits, aided by kooky splash-yourself-in-the-fountain videos. These photogenic female pop stars (who once took Polaroids of their own genitalia for a laugh) were the link between Blondie and Madonna, and proof that mildly left-field all-girl pop could sell in the video age. I.R.S. also scored hits with the likes of the (English) Beat, Oingo Bongo, Timbuk 3 and General Public. By comparison, as far as single sales were concerned, R.E.M. were underachieving. In fact, their image was that of a live-rock, album-based combo, with a small, but ardent following. It was not an act likely to appeal too much beyond their brethren. Not for nothing did their ex-producer Don Dixon dub them the natural successors to the Grateful Dead.

If R.E.M. sat uneasily in the I.R.S. roster in terms of their hit-single potential, then this is not to say that the band did not have its supporters within the company. Far from it, in fact. For some, the task of promoting R.E.M. was a personal crusade. 'It wasn't work breaking R.E.M., it was more like a mission from God,' says Cary Baker, former I.R.S. national publicity director. 'You got up in the morning, and you were driven to do it. We were so focused. I really loved the band and the band was responsible for me leaving a lifetime of family and friends in Chicago to work at I.R.S. I wanted to be a part of their success.'

I.R.S. would often suggest new ways of packaging and promoting the band's music, but any such suggestions would usually meet with polite, though defiant, resistance. The head honcho at I.R.S., the sharp-suited, silver-haired and potentially combustible Miles Copeland III, was not, however, altogether in synch with the band, as Cary Baker recalls: 'I was never sure whether Miles Copeland altogether got the band. Miles liked strongly defined singers, singers who enunciated for one thing, and I don't think he ever understood the image of Michael Stipe. Miles liked alternative music, but his vision of it was very commercial, which I think you can tell by the brilliant work he did with the Police and Sting. But that didn't matter because Jay Boberg was all about them and he ran the company day to day.'

Some of those who worked with or for him were far less sanguine in their appraisal of the dynasty-builder Copeland. 'Copeland is a sort of right-wing fascist. I think he's proud of the fact that he's a right-wing fascist and I don't think he'll mind me saying that about him,' says Don Dixon. 'I had to spend one night at his house with him going on and on about NATO and how nuclear disarmament was bad. It was kind of a difficult time, with me being the grotesque peacenik that I am.' Even his ex-partner at I.R.S., Jay Boberg, tempers his admiration, seeing in Copeland the image of a blinkered genius. 'He is extremely bright, very much a visionary, and says what he feels so directly at times that it can come across as rude. He's a very opinionated individual and doesn't suffer fools gladly. He can also be extremely myopic, focusing only on things that fit his agenda.'

According to Boberg, Copeland constantly ran up against a brick wall with some of the suggestions made to R.E.M. 'Miles was frustrated by their unwillingness to take the steps that would have brought them greater commercial success sooner. He would say, "Look, here we are just slogging our guts out, doing everything we possibly can, and if you guys would just do *this* (whatever that was at the moment), then it would make it so much easier, and we could all have so much more success. I know you guys want to be successful, but this would really help us." And the response repeatedly would be: "We appreciate how hard you're working. We think I.R.S. is the best thing ever. However, we really have to do what we feel is right for our music, and we don't feel comfortable doing what you've suggested, so we're not going to do that, Miles. Nevertheless, please don't give up; we're going to get there in the end." I think Miles found that really frustrating, not once, but ten times.'

However, it also appeared to I.R.S.'s Jay Boberg, despite overwhelming opposition to many of the promotional schemes, that, finally, R.E.M. were becoming more intent on breaking as a big band:

Very clearly when they got to Don Gehman, producer of *Lifes Rich Pageant*, and Scott Litt, who produced *Document*, there were two factors at work that had not been there previously. One was that the band *wanted* more and more to be successful, despite their assertions to the contrary. Michael Stipe in particular was starting to sense that they could be a big band, and I think he was really striving for this. And the second thing was that both Don Gehman and Scott Litt had much more dominant personalities in relation to trying to force R.E.M. to do things, and pushing them creatively and commercially. Both of those guys had had big commercial successes in the past, and both thought that this band could be one of the most successful bands in the world in terms of sales. Michael seemed to be more interested in commercial success than he had been previously. It doesn't mean that he became Madonna; it just meant that it was a gradual development. Michael definitely wanted success, albeit on his own terms.

Although the jury is out, it does seem that the band, if not compromised in their original vision, simply found elements of it untenable. They were evolving into a different type of rock group. For a start, the mid-1980s saw them finally get to grasps with video. Secondly, the band started playing ever-bigger venues until, by 1987, they were an arena rock act, albeit medium-sized. Thirdly, Stipe gave up on his seemingly unshakeable conviction that lyrics were meant to be seen (by him alone) and not heard, and began letting the naughty progeny speak louder and louder, first on *Lifes Rich Pageant*, and then particularly on *Document*. Fourthly, and perhaps decisively, the band decided that, since Stipe was now less a 'mumbler' than a 'ranter',[1] that the lyrics had better say something on a literal level. Now came the most dramatic change-around. For, although *Murmur* had contained the anti-poverty song 'Talk About The Passion' and *Fables* had 'Green Grow The Rushes', described by Stipe as a song about 'Hispanic guestworkers in America',[2] their next two releases would deal head-on with politics and with American life and culture. R.E.M. had always said that pop and politics didn't mix, but they were going to try and do just that. The attempt would be an intriguing one, and would result in what is perhaps the signature work of American pop of the late 1980s.

II
In May 1986, BBC Television devoted an entire evening and much of the early hours of the following morning to a history of music television. *Video Jukebox*, hosted by John Peel and the late John Walters, contained interviews with such videogenic artists as David Byrne, David Bowie and Madness, and included contributions from video producers such as Tim Pope, Russell Mulcahy, Steve Barron and Julian Temple. It was a fascinating retrospective. In 1986, MTV

was already five years old. Videos were becoming ever glossier, ever-more big-budget, and supremely self-referential. They had been around for so long that they had started to pastiche and parody earlier versions of themselves, and had begun to make fun of the whole process of video technique. Yet, for R.E.M., the medium was, if not new, then one that they had not as yet embraced. For a band with a lead singer so enamoured of the visuality of music, it was a surprise that they had been so coy. Maybe the band saw that the industry standard, in aesthetic terms, was so weak that they wanted nothing to do with the pop promo. However, by 1986, recalcitrant indie rockers or no, the band took their first steps towards video fame.

It wasn't that R.E.M. were not photogenic. Far from it. Stephanie Chernikowski, the New York-based Texan photographer who shot some of the seminal images of the new wave scene, remembers how poised they were:

Peter has this gallant demeanour when dealing with women. I was not being courted, but he still had this courtly charm that a Southern man like Rhett Butler would have – rushing in to grab my camera bags and that kind of thing. Peter also has that swashbuckling quality, whereas Michael is subtler. He loves his Mama and he loves women and women love him. Part of it is because he clearly relates to women extremely well. I think all artists have to have a very pronounced feminine quality. If gentleness and subtlety are feminine characteristics, and perception and emotion are feminine, then, yes, Michael has these. But I didn't find him girlish in any way. Michael has a very seductive quality. A friend of mine, Chet Flippo, who worked with Bowie, said that when Bowie talks to you it's like you're the only person in the room. Michael has the same quality. You can be in an auditorium listening to David Bowie or Michael Stipe and it's like you're the only one in the room. It's like you're the only one there – just you and that voice.

I often said that working with them taught me what a band was. They had such an incredible ability to play off one another. There was a real sense of teamwork; they functioned as a unit. You can see in the photographs that they compose themselves naturally into something that looks graceful to the eye.

With the advent of video, some artists, such as Christopher Cross, saw their record sales slump. A bearded, balding and slightly chubby 30-something singer-songwriter, Cross did not translate at all to the video glamour standard set by Duran Duran and Wham! But the members of R.E.M. were four striking, handsome men.

Their first pop promos had been art films. For *Left Of Reckoning* Jim Herbert shot a seamless photomontage of the band in Athens to accompany five of their songs from the album. The result would have worked well in a Sunday morning art-house showing next to a subtitled French film, but was useless next to 'We Are Detective' by the Thompson Twins.

The most unholy aspect of rock video was, of course, the dreaded lip-synch. Throughout the 1980s, Michael Stipe simply refused to mime, a decision that would please band egos, but diminished sales. Rather than accepting video as a pop construct, R.E.M. clung on to the idea of the song as performance. If they were unable to perform the song live, then they would simply not perform it at all. 'Performerless' videos can work, for example Paul Hardcastle's UK Number 1, '19', which featured clips from the Vietnam War, or the lyric-led video for Prince's 'Sign "O" The Times'. But, as a rule, viewers expected to see their performers create the illusion of authenticity by lip-synching.

What happened was a slow process of R.E.M. succumbing to the demands of the MTV era. In the second half of the 1980s, their videos would gradually become less impersonal and more rooted in the strategies deployed by video-makers, until we reach a point in late 1990 when the lead singer finally lip-synchs to a song, with astonishing concomitant global cash rewards. But that was for the future. 'The one thing I.R.S. did was to give them their artistic freedom,' says Cary Baker. 'If the videos weren't quite Madonna in their viability for MTV, we still worked them very hard, and MTV met us halfway, more than halfway.'

Some of their videos, such as 'Fall On Me', 'Talk About The Passion' and 'It's The End Of The World As We Know It', would still be visual representations with the band absent. But although the performers were absent, the videos had a narrative that the viewer could identify with. For 'It's The End Of The World As We Know It', a bare-chested adolescent boy with a skateboard is seen rummaging through a derelict building full of various broken, discarded, wacky and antique artefacts. 'I worked on that video with Jim Herbert,' says Michael Lachowski. 'The star of the video was a friend of mine. He got too much attention as a result of that, not all of it good for a kid in local schools in Georgia. He and I are still very close friends; he's about 28 years old now! I was thrilled to work on it because that song really stood off the album for me, and I loved it. I never tire of hearing it, either.'

The video works by mimicking the white-rap stream of conscious-ness of the song, through the assembly of found images held up to the screen by the boy. The video is suitably mainstream too in its self-referential nature. Just as the song is, in part, a pastiche of Bob Dylan's 'Subterranean Homesick Blues', so the video recasts the boy in the role of the placard-holding Dylan of the earlier video. So, unlike the art-house film for *Reckoning*, or the early atmospheric promo for 'Radio Free Europe', these videos tell a story.

A major feature of these late-1980s videos – and 'Orange Crush' and 'Finest Work Song' are in this tradition too – is the presence of perfectly physiqued young men, stripped to the waist. Although it would be lazy to equate these images with queer culture representa-tions in the media, there's no getting away from the homoerotic charge of those videos. If speculation about Stipe's sexuality was mounting, if reviewers of R.E.M.'s stage show would comment about his make-up and androgyny, then the videos appeared to confirm their speculations.

The video for 'The One I Love', the band's first major hit single, is the clearest evidence of a change in attitude. For while Stipe still eschews the lip-synched schmaltz of a Michael Bolton, he appears close to the picture plane, unquestionably the star, while a mini narrative of the song lyric works itself out around him. The video includes a group of young things dancing in proto-moshing fashion to the guitar fill – rock'n'roll community for the video age.

What we also see in the mid-to-late 1980s is Michael Stipe's developing interest in both film and photography. This was not a case of dilettante self-imaging, but a natural and predictable devel-opment. Financed by ever-increasing record sales, Stipe busied himself with more and more extra-curricular activities, whether it be the purchasing of properties in his home town of Athens or incipient mixed-media operations such as the company he founded in the spring of 1987 with Jim McKay entitled C00 Films (pronounced 'See

Hundred'). The company was 'designed to channel its founder's creative talents towards the creation and promotion of alternative film works'.[3] By the end of the 1980s, Stipe and McKay's company was producing pop videos of its own for artists such as Pylon and the Rollins Band, as well as R.E.M.'s video documentary of their 1989 world tour, and a feature-length film, *Lighthearted Nation*.

III

The band's willingness to accede to at least some of the demands of promotion developed at a time when they were changing their sound quite dramatically. In March 1986 the band demoed tracks for their new album, to be entitled *Lifes Rich Pageant* (once again with no apostrophe) after a line from Peter Sellers' character, Inspector Clouseau, in the Pink Panther film, *A Shot In The Dark*. The preproduction work was done at a venue that would soon occupy a central role in R.E.M.'s recording processes – John Keane's studio in their hometown, Athens.

'My studio is located in an old house in an historic residential neighbourhood,' says Keane. 'It was built around 1930, and is typical of Athens homes of that era, with hard pine floors, large rooms with 10-foot ceilings, and a large front porch. I moved in about 1980 with a couple of musician friends to help share the monthly mortgage payment, which was only $146.71! It had three bedrooms and a room we soundproofed so that we could practise. It wasn't long before the need arose to record some demos for my band (Phil and The Blanks), so I purchased a Teac 3340 4-track reel-to-reel from local musician Randall Bramblett and started educating myself in the art of multitrack recording.'

Buck had started to produce bands at Keane's studio in the early 1980s. In 1984 R.E.M. had tracked the song 'Romance' at the studio for a film project. In 1985, the band, minus Stipe, worked there on a recording with Warren Zevon under the guise of the Hindu Love Gods. But it was in the early spring of 1986, exactly a year after work had begun on *Fables*, that the band first used Keane's studio for a recording session. 'As usual, the guys were tight and well rehearsed. They really seemed to be hitting their stride with the new material. I think Don Gehman, the band's producer, was a little taken aback by their insistence on doing things their own way. They definitely weren't accustomed to taking directions from anyone. However, he did manage to take them to a new level with that album.'

Gehman had been producing records since 1973 and was used to making hit singles. He hadn't heard much R.E.M. before meeting the band, and had little interest in college rock. 'I was much more interested in the Bruce Springsteen/John Cougar Mellencamp/Bryan Adams phenomenon. I was looking for the three to five million not the 100,000 sales,' says Gehman. To Gehman, much of R.E.M.'s power was being dissipated in the studio and his task was to bring clarity to the overall sound. He was particularly unhappy with the way Stipe's vocal had been recorded on previous albums.

'I said to him, listen, I don't care if nobody knows what you are talking about, but I want them to understand the words, and I want your voice, which has a beautiful texture, to be well heard, not covered up in the mix. There's just no reason for this. It's just bad recording and bad mixing. Everything can be heard clearly and still be aggressive. I really thought we took it to a whole new level of craft, and that's the point that I am proud of. I showed them how to make records, and they showed me a side of their Zen style that I use to this day. It's about not always working at something until you get it, but learning to react to what your guts are telling you, being willing to take a new direction.'

'Don had just come off a series of very successful John Mellencamp records. To this day I can't recall who suggested him to us and why we chose him,' says Mike Mills. 'It could have been Jay Boberg, that would have made sense. We thought John Cougar Mellencamp records sounded OK. I had enjoyed working with Joe Boyd and I consider him a friend to this day, but we didn't want to repeat that experience. Joe wanted to work in England, we weren't about to go back there and make a record, so Joe was out at that point. We wanted a clearer, more powerful sound, and so we were willing to work with someone who knew more than we did, which is just about everyone at that point! To his credit, Don was also very good at getting Michael to clarify, as well. The word "clarity" really applies to what Don did for us in several different ways . . .'

Gehman thought his main sonic responsibility lay in bringing the instrumentation to life. 'I deployed various techniques to try and get the instruments to have more character, to have a sense of how it's being played so that it's not foggy. I like things to be crisp, and I like them to be punchy. Much as in the style of a Stones record, I don't mind things being ugly or harsh as long as they're balanced by other elements that are really sweet. I utilised a lot of colours, which is something they hadn't done in the past, and I also utilised the fact that Mike Mills could to some degree play anything that was in his hands. I always enjoyed recording really simple parts for lots of different instruments: he played piano, organ, pump organ, acoustic guitar, electric guitar, percussion instruments and all kinds of stuff that they hadn't fooled around with before.'

Despite the fact that he was technically weaker than Mills, Gehman also enjoyed working with Peter Buck: 'Peter is very dry. They're all very precise about what they want and Peter is no different. He always downplayed his talent. I was more accustomed to working with players who were a little more accomplished, but the rough and ready part of him was what was interesting to the band. We spent most of our time working on parts trying to get them interesting. We did a lot of work trying to double parts. He was a good writer and he had a great sense of style.'

Recording for the album took place in April and May of 1986 at John Cougar Mellencamp's scenic Belmont Mall Studios in Bloomington, Indiana, built for Mellencamp by Gehman. This was the first outside project ever undertaken at the studio. Work began in mid-afternoon and went on until the civilised hour of eleven o'clock. It took just five days to cut the basic tracks, but the mixing and overdubs took another fortnight, during which time some of the band members lost a little of their focus. 'I was certainly the first guy to stand up to them,' is Gehman's opinion. 'They were four guys who would always agree and at the same time always disagree, and it was chaos. I also started to realise that that was part of what made them work. I thought it was also unfocused, and it was driving me nuts until I learnt to have a good time with it.'

Although most of the musical parts had already been worked out, Stipe actually worked on the lyrics in the studio, and it was at this stage that Gehman began challenging him about them.

They would come in with these songs like 'Hyena' and I'd say, 'What are you talking about?' He would reply, 'I'm not going to have banal lyrics.' I'd go off with Mike Mills and we'd make textures and sounds, and somehow it fed on itself. He was writing lyrics as we were laying down tracks. So this was a process that evolved, and I became part of the creative process.

My issue was clarity, it had nothing to do with intent, although I did argue that the first single should at least have something that makes sense for the chorus line. I mean, give me a hook, come on! To my credit, later on in their career, they did do that, even though Stipe was constantly fucking you over with what he intended. He at least reached that place that most songwriters get to where they don't have to be literal, and their soundbites are evocative of something that pushes buttons. I remember sitting on the couch with him arguing that I didn't understand what he was talking about. I just remember the word 'banal' kept on coming up. He didn't want to write banal lyrics, in other words something literal. Whereas all I was looking for was, if it was metaphorical, that it made sense.

Stipe would later comment in interviews that the entire process was a traumatising one. 'It's a great-sounding record, but I really hated Don Gehman at the time,' he told *Uncut* in 1999.[4] 'He's a great guy, a fine producer, a good man, but he was sparring with me in a way that no one had up 'til that point. What he did was good for me as a singer and a lyricist, but he pushed me way too far and it took me several records to come back from that and recapture who I am and what I was trying to do. It was like *throwing a baby into ice-cold water* and just leaving it there. It was fairly compromising of me.'

According to Mills, though, the time was right for Stipe to clarify the meaning of his lyrics. 'After you've made three records and you've written several songs and they've gotten better and better lyrically then the next step would be to have somebody question you and say, are you saying anything? And Michael had the confidence at that point to say yes, when he wouldn't have had that confidence during *Reckoning* or perhaps even during *Fables*. By the time we had reached our fourth record we had all recognised that he was an extremely gifted lyricist and there was no reason why he couldn't clarify what he was saying and, to some extent, how he was saying it.'

Gehman was obsessed with getting as commercial a sound as humanly possible. 'Everything I did was about trying to get something that could be played on the radio. I knew that "Fall On Me" was the closest thing we had to a hit, but even that was a long shot. And I knew that I needed to make it work like a hit record would.' The resultant album is the first of R.E.M.'s career not to have a filler. Musically, tracks such as the aforementioned 'Fall On Me', 'Cuyahoga', 'Begin The Begin' and 'These Days' were perhaps the strongest of their career to date. The semi-instrumental 'Underneath The Bunker', a pseudo-Spaghetti Western comic cut, showed humour, 'The Flowers Of Guatemala' tenderness, while 'Swan Swan H' was more *Fables*-era pseudo-Celtish storytelling. The outrageously catchy 'Superman', a cover of a relatively obscure track from a band called Clique suggested by Buck, who picked up the record at Wuxtry, had a lead vocal from Mills, the first of his career. Buck even plays a guitar solo on one of the tracks, a move hitherto unthinkable. It's a very short solo, though.

Although the album remains a Mike Mills favourite, for Buck it was still just short of the stride he wanted to hit: 'For me it's not quite there yet. It's a good record and I think Don Gehman did a lot to help us figure out what we were doing in the studio and where we wanted to go. I think Don would say that we weren't ready to go for the throat commercially, which is true. He was a great teacher and a good friend. I really liked him. He would make us think about things instead of just doing them. Don has really clear ears and was good at focusing on things. So he gave us some tools which we were able to use to one degree or another in the future, and so did Mitch and Don and Joe Boyd too.'

The album, released in July 1986, was a solid seller, reaching Number 21 in the USA and improving on the sales of *Fables* markedly. The cover was another R.E.M. oddity, this time a punning shot of Bill Berry in black and white, with a hazy image of buffalo masking his face. 'Fall On Me' picked up considerable radio support but failed to break in the national charts.

Gehman was downcast. 'The moment after it was released I was disappointed that it didn't make the big step out but, looking back on it, its success worked to get them to *Document*. I think I was instrumental to all that happening. Whether it was my ego, I don't know, but I certainly cracked the ice and got things rolling, and maybe that was my function all along. Then Scott Litt came in and took it the rest of the way.'

Gehman was offered the chance to record the next album but passed it up. It was a decision he would very much regret. 'I was supposed to do the next record but I was making a Cock Robin record at the time. I made the wrong choice. It was a twenty-million-dollar mistake. I made a choice about whether they would continue and I just wasn't sure. I wasn't sure this was where music was going. Life's full of these choices. I've had a good career so I really can't complain. At the time I had two or three things on my plate and it was a choice between the next John Mellencamp record and the next R.E.M. record. Looking back, it would have been better not to have made the *Lonesome Jubilee* record and to have made *Document* instead.'

Lifes Rich Pageant was Gehman's only R.E.M. production credit, but it was a significant one. For many, the album defined the sound of new American alternative music, despite the fact that Gehman himself was not immediately attracted to the college radio sound. Musician Ken Stringfellow: '*Lifes Rich Pageant* was definitely a landmark record for many of the people I was playing music with at the time. It was strangely triumphant and anthemic in a way that wasn't a turn-off and wasn't cheesy. It was inspiring and focused and had a passion behind it that you wouldn't be embarrassed about.'

The writer Roddy Doyle penned a powerful tribute which sums up the charm of one of the finest records of the 1980s:

> For a short time in late 1986 a darkness, heaviness occupied my head. I dragged myself around, exhausted. I didn't want company, food, anything. I got through the working day, smiling, handed back homework I'd marked but hadn't corrected. At home, I'd stare for hours at the bars of the electric fire. It hadn't happened before; it scared me. There was nothing to show, nothing to tell anyone. The sound of *Lifes Rich Pageant* pulled my eyes away from the fire. It was fervent, determined music, and perfectly timed. 'I believe in coyotes – and time as an abstract.' I listened, felt the power of the songs, heard words rising through the noise. 'We are young despite the years – we are concern – we are hope despite the times.' These words seemed to mean a lot. 'Begin the Begin', 'These Days', 'Fall On Me'. Song on top of song, the music carried so much conviction and belief; it was so solid, built on a past, driving into the future. And what were the words about? Meaning disappeared under the music, and reappeared, like a whale's back, and went under again; snippets and phrases, bits of nonsense, small chunks of wisdom. 'Let's put our heads together and start a new

country up.' The glimpses through the sound were enough; this was music that gloried in the world, every little thing about it, the 'bone-chains and toothpicks'. Powerful, enthusiastic, calm and just plain good, it won me.[5]

IV

By 1986, although R.E.M. were still waiting for their first big hit single, the days of playing just about anywhere for just about anybody were over. The days of doing soundchecks in front of a load of grannies munching chicken, as happened when the band played an eatery in Nebraska called *The Drum Stick*, or at army camps, gay clubs, pizza parlours or folk clubs, had gone. There was, however, still room for a certain silliness. Mike Mills recalled a gig on Halloween in 1985 in an abandoned customs house on the pier, in front of a former European dictator with a prosthetic penis: 'It was a costume show and at the very last countdown Adolf Hitler pulled open his jacket and he had a four-foot-long rubber penis bouncing up and down. He won my acclamation: Adolf Hitler as well-endowed flasher beat out a woman who wore nothing but Saran wrap, a naked outer-space alien with antennae. She was going to win, but you couldn't beat Hitler with a massive prong. It was 120 degrees and we had to follow that. What a career.' By the time of the *Pageantry* and *Document* tours of 1986 and 1987, however, R.E.M. were becoming a major-league act.

Nowhere was this better evidenced than in the changing status of Michael Stipe. Like many celebrities who seem only to be comfortable in the company of other celebrities, he was secretly, or perhaps more accurately, privately dating Natalie Merchant from the band 10,000 Maniacs. He was also having to come to terms with the attention of fervent, sometimes rabid, fans who started making the pilgrimage to Athens, Georgia to walk in his footsteps. It was the start of the 'cult of Stipe', of a hardcore of fans who identified fiercely with their idol and pored over his every uttering, trying to break the code of his evocative, though seemingly impenetrable, lyrics.

A naturally shy man, although with a quietly dominating presence, Stipe had to begin a slow and painful process of learning to deal with his own stardom. The process of disentangling the 'public' from the 'private' self has kept the writing nation occupied for decades. The truth is that the version of the star that is presented to the public is an amalgamation of their private, everyday selves and the media persona they learn to adopt as a safeguard against intrusion. Many rock stars are cosseted creatures who unwittingly become detached from normality. Even the nicest of rock stars can fall prey to thinking that they are above their public.

If rock messianism is a fact, then rock stars develop different strategies to cope with it. When he first became a rock 'personality', Stipe was generally terrified and embarrassed by the attentions of his fans. 'One of the most profoundly terrifying experiences of my life occurred in a room at Radio City,' recalls Stephanie Chernikowski.

This is before they were megastars; this was on the *Document* tour. They were still at I.R.S., though Warner Brothers were courting them that night. Michael had been hovering with a couple of his friends and no one was approaching him. I just walked over and said, 'May I come in?' They separated and Michael stood beside me. I looked up, and it felt like the entire room was converging on us. I understood, in that moment, the absolute terror you must feel as a star. The Michael I walked around with in Athens was absolutely horrified by anyone treating him like a star. He had real trouble dealing with people who stopped him on the street, who were too worshipful. That night it was interesting because, yes, I felt his fear, but he rose to it, he accepted that position, he bit the bullet and he dealt with it. I don't think he wanted it, and I don't think it was anything that he had chosen for himself, but he was able to rise to it and to handle it. The reason why he was huddling in the first place was that I think he knew it was going to happen, and that he was going to have to deal with it. I often see this evening as a little metaphor for fame. I admire his ability as someone who had never sought fame, but had only sought to be an artist, to handle it as well as he has.

Michael Stipe was born in 1960, at the end of the baby boom, and a year before writer Douglas Coupland, whose novel *Generation X*, published in 1991, defined the generational disappointment that swept through America in the Reagan years. In the 1980s, it was clear that the promises of the sixties and early seventies counter-culture had not been kept. A decade of corporate suits, grasping politics and conscience-free social policy rendered America, and Britain for that matter, cruel and heartless places. What's more, there was a sense that this status was hegemonic – it was suddenly cool to be rich and to flaunt it – and that this was an acceptable standard of moral behaviour. This was an era in which style culture replaced political activism. By the mid-1980s it seemed that those who opposed or opted out of the political consciousness of the age had no place to go. A cynicism and simultaneous sense of helplessness took root among a section of Western youth along with, ultimately, a sense of nihilism and apolitical desperation. These feelings were acknowledged by Stipe: 'I probably embody that whole idealism/cynicism conundrum that my generation and people younger than me carry.'[6]

Mike Mills shared the feeling that the old activism was over and that pop and politics simply didn't mix. 'If you want to think about youth culture as one spearhead that's gonna make a difference in the world, it's not gonna happen,' was his 1985 take. 'The sixties were a time of political activism. It went from innocence to cynicism really quickly. And now the situation is not so much apathy as realisation and there's not a lot you or anyone else personally can do. Any rock star who thinks he's gonna make a big difference is deluded. Look at the biggest: Prince, Michael Jackson, Bruce Springsteen. Are they gonna inspire anyone to do anything? No! They're gonna inspire them to go out and buy a record – that's it. Millions have, and millions will. Great. That's what music is about; it's entertainment.'[7]

Stipe was never anything other than liberal and progressive in his views. Indeed, all the members of R.E.M. were 'on the same page' when it came to their political persuasions. 'One of my favourite R.E.M. moments occurred in 1984, right before the election,' remembers band friend Paul Butchart. 'Michael was hanging out outside after a show, and a few fans surrounded him, talking, asking for autographs etc. One young man, looking dazed and amazed to be so close to Michael, comes up to ask for an autograph, and my friend and I notice he's wearing a "Reagan for President" pin. We both make gagging gestures. Michael saw the pin, pointed to it and said, "God, I hate that guy." The fan looked crushed (imagine your hero saying that to you!), but I'd like to think that perhaps Reagan got one less vote.' But the alternative to Reagan, the Democrats, like the Labour party in the UK, were going through a deeply unelectable phase. With so little worthy of investment in the Reagan–Bush, Thatcher–Major years, many young people dropped out of political thought and action.

To anyone of a liberal or progressive political bent there was something radically wrong with Reagan-era America. Mike Mills' fatalistic stance of the middle of the decade was soon replaced by outright condemnation of Republicanism: 'He was just horrifying. I was aware of Reagan's effect on the country and it was not good.' Michael Stipe, at 26, had matured enough as a person to wish to vocalise this sense of disappointment through his work with R.E.M. The first stage of this awakening political consciousness was to establish a truthful history for himself and his public. Writing a song such as 'Cuyahoga' was evidence of this newly won maturity. The song, from the *Lifes Rich Pageant* album, shows the sense of outreach of the 20-something, the belief that life can be changed even through such low cultural things as a mere pop song. The Cuyahoga River in Ohio ran through Cleveland into Lake Erie, across territory that historically belonged to the Native American Indians. Earlier in the century, it had been so polluted that it would catch fire if a flaming torch was thrown into the water.

> Underneath the river bed
> We burned the river down
> This is where they walked, swam, hunted, danced and sang,
> Take a picture here,
> Take a souvenir
> Cuyahoga
> Cuyahoga, gone

In this song, Stipe confronts American youth with their country's history of mass genocide. The Land Of The Free may have been an Enlightenment project, but it was a project with evil at its root, as millions of the indigenous population were killed or depersonalised as white slave-holding culture established itself. Stipe's home state, Georgia, was the scene of one of the cruellest examples of American domination over the Indian. Known as the Trail Of Tears, in 1838–39 13,000 Indians were forcibly repatriated to territory west of the Mississippi River, and a quarter died from cold and starvation along the 800-mile route. 'There's a lack of history here which would be the American version of Catholic guilt,' Stipe told UK writer Jon Savage in 1989. 'I think that's a big flaw in the American dream. You are not taught about the annihilation of the entire culture of the Indians whose land this was.'[8]

With a present dominated by faceless corruption and uncaring politics and a past of deeply questionable morality, Stipe sings in 'Cuyahoga' about the need for starting over:

Let's put our heads together
And start a new country up
Our father's father's father tried,
Erased the parts he didn't like
Let's try to fill it in

The words of 'Cuyahoga' are words of optimism, partnership and community, set against an age of individualism. Its beautiful melody, its anthemic chorus and its sublime bass line from Mills all emphasise the song's centrality in R.E.M.'s canon of music.

Ken Stringfellow, then in his teens, but 15 years later a musician and member of R.E.M.'s recording and touring setup, neatly summarises why the song struck such a chord. ' "Cuyahoga" is an anthem but it's not self-congratulatory. It's about what's gone wrong with our country. It was an anti-anthem in a way, I guess. It took on an issue, but it was still unifying and powerful. That's a hard thing to do well.'

'Fall On Me', although less overtly didactic, may well be the finest R.E.M. melody ever recorded. The meld of harmonies in the middle eight as Mills contributes one of his trademark counterpoints, is almost unbeatable. The subject matter is allusive, but the theme of acid rain and eco-damage is definitely important:

Buy the sky and sell the sky
And bleed the sky and tell the sky
Don't fall on me

The theme of cleansing and renewal is also keenly felt in 'Begin The Begin', a brilliant *tour de force* of an opener, both a statement of intent for the band itself, heads down on a new music project, and a rallying call to American youth to make the change politically:

Birdie in the hand
For life's rich demand
The insurgency began
And You missed it
I looked for it
And I found it
Myles Standish proud
Congratulate me

Again, Stipe's surrealism touches on real-life historical events. Head of the Plymouth colony, Myles Standish was one of the first settlers in the New World, and died with Indian blood on his hands.

Like Springsteen and John Cougar in the States and Elvis Costello and the Clash across the pond, what R.E.M. were offering to their listeners were 'pockets of resistance'. From a pedagogical point of view, as academic Thaddeus Corneo writes,

> the typical content of this kind of music does offer teachers the chance to instruct adolescents about domination. Resistance to domination usually takes the form of a protest against some sociopolitical injustices like the decimation of the Brazilian rain forest, apartheid, US-backed Central American death squad governments, poverty, imposed paralysis of the American working class, or British occupation of Northern Ireland. Music brings these issues to adolescents as symbolic and emotional messages.[9]

Making political statements within popular culture is, of course, fraught with danger, and leaves the pop star open to accusations of double standards. Examples are legion: whether it be the rain-forest-championing Sting of the mid-1980s, who plugged his new album for fifteen years in an ad for fossil-fuel-guzzling Jaguar cars; or Pink Floyd's anti-war tirade *The Final Cut*, released by EMI, an affiliate of one of the largest arms manufacturers in the world. The lending of support to good causes by pop stars is therefore a tricky operation, and getting one's message across without sloganeering, a major obstacle. John Lennon's 'Power To The People' sounded dumb, despite good intentions and a great tune, while 'We Are The World' was a gruesome celebrity chum-up. Lennon's own 'Imagine', a communistic song, which imagined a world of 'no religion' and 'no country', was appropriated by the Conservative Party in 1987 during one of their election rallies. Aberrant readings of pop songs are therefore part of their meaning as soon as they become cultural property. Popular music is a poor vehicle for political messages because it is fundamentally designed to discuss the self, such is the overriding narcissism of the star-structure that gives pop its meaning.

What R.E.M. did was adopt what writer Simon Reynolds has called the tactic of 'entryism'. Entryist songs use the sweet melodies of pop, but the lyric of the radical political barb, so that songs in the 1980s by artists such as Hue and Cry, the Christians, Wet Wet Wet, the Style Council, the The, Deacon Blue, or the Beautiful South might on first hearing appear to be cheery and uncomplicated pop but, when scrutinised, are revealed to be carrying a didactic purpose. It's one way of getting the message across – a contentious lyric presented in a sugar-coated shell. And while R.E.M.'s music is more disturbing, more arty and conveys greater sorrow and yearning than many of those listed above, 'Cuyahoga', despite its metaphorical bent, is also partly in this 'entryist' tradition. Whether a format as hackneyed as the pop song could really shake the system is, of course, a moot point. In the mid to late 1980s other alternative bands such as Sonic Youth and the Pixies destroyed the pop song through noise, and created a music as 'political', sonically, as the entryists were political, literally. In 1987 Simon Reynolds wrote:

> I find myself steadily drifting back to the unfashionable conviction that radical meanings are betrayed by conventional forms; that if melodies, key changes, and vocal cadences follow expected paths they can only reinforce commonsense perceptions. I am drawn more and more to a resurrected belief in the marginal and its value-in-itself, beyond any consideration of its power to infect pop's arterial thoroughfares. A belief in the 'alternative' – not so much in terms of an independent business infrastructure – but in the sense of otherness: music that explores the otherworldly, or the other within yourself.[10]

It wasn't until much later in R.E.M.'s career, in the mid-1990s in fact, that Stipe's lyrics attained a richness and maturity that was matched not just by sweet melodies but by powerful deconstructive sounds.

V

The band's next album, *Document*, was the pivotal album in their career. Years of gruelling touring, and proselytising by I.R.S., would finally pay off as, by the end of 1987, R.E.M. would have their first Top 10 US hit single and a genuine big-selling album.

It's often thought that R.E.M.'s success was due to the support of college radio, and it is true that in 1987 the band's core support was in that area. But what is frequently overlooked is the fact that R.E.M. were also having big radio hits on AOR (Album-Oriented Radio) stations, the precursor to FM rock radio. Support from the pop stations came later, with the huge success of 'The One I Love', but to think of R.E.M. as simply an alternative rock act with little mainstream radio support is wrong. The head of I.R.S.'s radio promotion campaign until the beginning of 1987 was Michael Plen. Up until *Document*, R.E.M. had AOR hits, not Top 40 hits, as Plen recalls:

> There was college radio, where they were always Number 1, and then there was album radio, which was the early FM progressive rock format called AOR (Album-Oriented Radio) and this was pre-'alternative'. The only alternative radio stations that existed were WFNX in Boston and K-Rock in LA. There was about three or four alternative rock stations in America, it wasn't a format. All there was was album rock format, the people who played the Grateful Dead, the Police, Tom Petty and the 'hair bands', just mainstream rock, things that were not viewed as new wave at the time. That was the one format that all the R.E.M. records became hits on. The thing we broke R.E.M. as, and developed them as, was almost as being a mainstream rock band. 'South Central Rain', 'Can't Get There From Here', 'Fall On Me' were Top 10 hits on this format of radio. Every time we tried to take their singles to pop radio, it was like, forget it, other than in the South, in Atlanta, where they had a massive following. I.R.S. didn't have the money to do the things to get the records

exposed. I.R.S.'s job was like launching the shuttle. We lifted the record off, took it to a certain point and then A&M, who distributed our records and had a stake in our label, if they got a sniff of something, would take it the rest of the way. But A&M never really caught on to R.E.M. They never really put the strength of their promotion staff behind it. The common perception is that R.E.M. didn't get much radio support, but they definitely had radio success, it was just geared to the rock world.

'He worked really, really hard at a time when there was no money to spend on us,' says Buck. 'We always used to laugh at the "Plen Plan". We couldn't hire independent promoters because we didn't have any money. There was no money for ads in the papers, and we didn't expect it, so basically our plan was to stay on the road for the whole year and to do as many radio things as we can, and as many interviews as we can. And it really worked. We sold 100,000 records of *Murmur* in the first year – a record that was on college radio and nowhere else. That was pretty much unheard of. He really worked his ass off at a time when we were not an easy job.'

Choosing the right single was obviously of paramount importance. With this, the band maintained an uncompromising position. 'They would record the album and they would never tell you which songs to pick, but you could never tell them to remix a song,' says Plen. In the case of 'Fall On Me', I.R.S., for example, asked the band to make a change to the song's structure to make it more commercial. 'There was a long discussion about what could be done to that song to make it more appropriate for radio,' remembers Jay Boberg. 'At the risk of sounding like the big, bad, evil record guy, I was trying to get R.E.M. records played on the radio. And, incidentally, so were they. Nobody ever came out and said that, nor would it be appropriate R.E.M. ethos to say, "Yeah, we wanted to be successful", but believe me, they wanted to be successful. But they came back to us and said, "We understand that if we change the song slightly it might make it more palatable for the radio, but we like the song how it is." And I never brought it up again. Later when we ran into the inevitable roadblock of "this record isn't commercial enough" or whatever these jerky gatekeepers would say, I never went back to the band and said, "See, see, if you'd changed it."'

The only instance of band interference in the choice of single had come two years earlier when I.R.S. went for 'Pretty Persuasion' as the lead-off single from *Reckoning*. One night Peter Buck called up and said, 'Look, I know we're not supposed to do this, but we have a really strong feeling that "Pretty Persuasion" sounds like something from *Murmur*, and we don't want to go there, and can you make another decision?' At the end of the day, I.R.S. gave in and went with 'South Central Rain'.

Plen worked hard to make sure that radio cottoned on to the band's success, but very often the radio promoters were several steps behind the public. 'My job was to bring radio people to see the growth of R.E.M., and, over the years, I would take the same programmers to these shows and I made these people friends with R.E.M. In the end these people had relationships and they would always play an R.E.M. record when it came out. Then there would be guys who would say, "Oh, R.E.M. suck!" and would go to Richmond and they'd be headlining a 6,000-seat hall and the radio guy would say, "Jesus, they sold out 6,000 seats in our town and I'm not even playing the record! Holy shit, how did this happen without me?" "How could it happen without you?" I would say. "That's what I've been trying to sell you on. Basically, you're an idiot, you should be playing this." So they'd go and see the show, get blown away and the next day they'd add the record to the playlist.'

Despite this mainstream rock radio success, R.E.M. were undoubtedly a college rock radio phenomenon too. Astonishingly, a detailed monograph on the rise of alternative rock, *Our Band Could Be Your Life: Scenes from the American Indie Underground, 1981–1991*, by Michael Azerrad, hardly mentions R.E.M. at all. Perhaps this is a mark of how the public now perceives the band, as a global rock act rather than as indie pioneers. But the book, which is a valuable and detailed history of the likes of Black Flag, Hüsker Dü, Sonic Youth and Dinosaur Jr, is haunted by the absence of R.E.M. 'This book is devoted solely to bands who were on independent labels,' writes Azerrad. 'So R.E.M., for instance, didn't make the cut, since the band's pre-Warner albums were recorded for I.R.S. Records, whose releases were manufactured and distributed by A&M (which in turn had a business relationship with RCA) and later, MCA.'[11]

This alarmingly purist view of how rock is made is wrong-headed. Many rock acts signed to major labels make confrontational and uncompromising music, Neil Young being a shining example, while many acts who record for and are distributed by indie labels can make the biggest load of sexist, misogynistic and politically naïve trash in the world. But R.E.M's reduction in Azerrad's book to the status of Banquo's ghost is revealing in that there still appears to be a prejudice against the band. Just as in the early 1980s, elements of the Athens scene regarded them as too pop, and college rockers in the late 1980s saw them outgrow the genre that spawned them, so some critics obviously regard R.E.M. as compromised just because they're on a big label. It's a strange logic that one suspects Peter Buck might have used had he been a rock critic himself, since Buck's rhetoric is still overwhelmingly concerned with distancing his band from any notion that they are in any way compromised by big business. It is precisely because of those contradictions that R.E.M. are a significant band.

'The Azerrad book was a bit like the Last Supper without Jesus Christ being there,' says Buck. 'I'm kind of kidding. But we are the subtext to the entire book. Every single one of those bands signed a major deal because of us after we'd signed for our teeny independent. I'm pretty sure that Hüsker Dü, Black Flag, the Replacements, the Butthole Surfers were all on major labels before we left I.R.S., but we were perceived as this huge hit-making machine since I.R.S. was distributed through A&M and MCA. All the places that those bands played, other than Black Flag who paved the way, are places where *we* had been the first people to play.'

R.E.M.'s impact on college rock and indie rock and alternative rock was profound. It wasn't that bands began to copy them stylistically. Few did. It was their influence in terms of attitude. R.E.M.'s success showed that a band could reach a level of popularity without moving to LA, without acting like assholes, without making wholesale changes to a musical sound they felt comfortable with. The result would be Nirvana, a band that would break huge in a sector that R.E.M.'s success made possible, with music that was sonically true to its originator's intent, but commercial too.

VI

On 3 December 1987, R.E.M. adorned the front cover of *Rolling Stone* magazine. The legend read, 'R.E.M. America's Best Rock & Roll Band'. Despite protestations to the contrary, it was a status the band had worked for and dreamt of. 'We made a contract with the world which says, "We're going to be the best band in the world; you're going to be proud of us. But we have to do it our way"', was how Buck put in it 1985.[12] Securing the front cover had been a three-month-long mission for Cary Baker at I.R.S. Records.

I wrote a major proposal for *Rolling Stone*, and at the last minute there was a subject which dropped out which hastened the arrival of our cover, which was probably an inevitability in any case, because everybody knew this band was great. I wasn't quite sure of the band's news-stand market value yet, but R.E.M. ended up being one of the magazine's top-selling covers of that year. I did an extensive proposal whereby I compiled all the bands' previous press citations, all of its radio appearances to date, all of their radio stats and chart positions, their TV appearances. I put together the package from hell, by the way, with the help of Sheryl Northrop, who was working in my department. It wasn't every day that people came to *Rolling Stone* with a proposal that was this extensive. I mean it was over the top, there was far more information than we knew they were ever going to read, but we wanted to blow them away with information and I think we succeeded. We were helped by the fact that Buck was a born interviewee. I say this with the utmost affection, but he was a motor mouth. He was very bright, very extemporaneous, full of insight and very funny, whereas Michael was very much in his shell at the time, which of course has since changed.

It was perhaps fitting that *Rolling Stone* should champion the band in such a way. In the MTV-driven 1980s, the newspaper and its founding editor, Jan Wenner, saw the sort of music they admired marginalised. It now reflected trends, rather than created them. As rap was beginning to take over, R.E.M. were a trend to be admired. Granting the front cover to R.E.M. was hardly a proactive move though: '*Rolling Stone*'s proclamation at the end of 1987 that R.E.M. was "America's best band" seemed to arrive at least a year after any argument on that subject had been settled,' writes Robert Draper in his history of the rock newspaper.[13]

From that moment on R.E.M. were secure in the knowledge that the critics loved them. In the next two years, they queued up to bestow votive thanks on the temple of R.E.M. *Q*'s Andy Gill was mildly equivocal with his assessment 'The best band in the world? ... I think so' in December 1988, while by 1989 even the British broadsheet the *Observer* came right out with it: 'The Best Band In The World.' This was a mantle hitherto bestowed on no less a rock phenomenon than the Rolling Stones. But R.E.M. had barely sold a few million albums worldwide. They had had one USA Top 10 hit single, and had yet to even have a Top 40 single in the UK.

Concerns grew that the new album, *Document*, recorded in Nashville in the spring of 1987 and released that September, would be the last produced by the old-style R.E.M. The sound was now brutal, the drums thunderous, the overall package far closer to mainstream rock on several tracks, with even a U2-style harmonic flourish on the first track, 'Finest Worksong'. People remembered how groups such as Simple Minds had started, very much like R.E.M. had done, as purveyors of intricate and intellectual rock, only to turn into bloated stadium rock bores by the mid-1980s. Meanwhile the UK's direct equivalent, the Smiths, had announced that they were splitting up. For them, a breakthrough hit single such as 'The One I Love' simply didn't happen and, reluctant to commit to years of gigging to build up American support, the band split just before they would have achieved the huge success their music deserved. Now R.E.M.'s 'rivals' were U2. Bono and Stipe had emerged as political singers in a concerned world of white liberal guilt. R.E.M. fan and fanzine editor Paul Holmes remembers that R.E.M. were a safe haven for those fans who had a political conscience but who were frightened by those who wore their passions a little too much on their sleeves. 'Because of the time I got into them, I didn't really relate to them as an "American Smiths",' says Holmes. 'If anything, it was a "less up-their-own-arse U2", who I felt just took themselves way too seriously.'

Document is a very fine album. Like Bowie's *Low* or, much later, Moby's *Play*, the record is schizophrenic. The first half is accessible, the second more experimental. Thematically, *Document* worked better than *Lifes Rich Pageant*, which was simply a collection of excellent songs. 'Mike was listening to it again for a remastering for a hi-fidelity version recently,' says Peter Buck in 2002. 'He came in and said, "You know, that's a lot weirder record than I think we thought we were making!" Side 2 especially is just really weird, and

I think that's good. I always thought that Side 1 was a kind of mini-rock opera about America in 1987. I hate the word rock opera, but conceptually the songs are linked – we put them together on purpose. Side 2 has the hit single and the weirder stuff. If I was going to make a present of five of our albums to someone to show where we were, it'd be in there.'

Sonically *Document* is more sharply defined than *Lifes Rich Pageant*. New Yorker Scott Litt, promoted to co-producer in the absence of Gehman, created the most clarity yet on an R.E.M. album. John Keane remembers the band rehearsing some of the tracks earlier that year in Athens:

After *Lifes Rich Pageant*, the guys began booking the studio regularly for a week at a time to record demos for the next record. Their usual method was for Peter, Mike and Bill to come in and record instrumental takes of musical ideas they had worked up in practice. It was not unusual for them to record 20 or 25 different pieces of music. Rough mixes would then be given to Michael to write words and melody over. A few weeks later, Michael would come in and start trying out the melody and lyric ideas. Often he would come in by himself and just hum melodies or sing nonsense lyrics to get the feel of the material. Sometimes he would complete a full set of lyrics, only to scrap them and start over with a completely different approach. The songs that he was inspired to complete would then become candidates for their next record. The ones that didn't make it would often find their way onto B-sides or film soundtracks. I remember one song entitled (I think) 'It's Been A Bad Day', which was reworked in this manner and became 'It's The End Of The World As We Know It'.[14] Sensitive to Michael's need for space to focus and concentrate, I tried to remain as invisible as possible during these vocal sessions.

It was around this time that Scott Litt began to attend some of the demo sessions, forming a working relationship that would last through the next six albums. When the guys started cutting demos that would become *Document*, I remember being impressed by the intensity of their performance. They sounded hungry and aggressive, and they pounded through the songs, playing as if they had something to prove. Pete's guitar was becoming crankier and more distorted, and Bill was really punishing the drum kit. Michael's vocal abilities had reached an amazing level. I remember being particularly enamoured with 'The One I Love'.

As soon as you put *Document* on the turntable, the impressive, gigantic sound is what hits you foursquare. The tone is immediately set by 'Finest Worksong', later remixed with a horn section for single release, and one of R.E.M.'s best songs. The thudding drum figure and insurgent one-note guitar riff from Buck makes the opening sound like a Mayday call, a distress signal for America. Like 'Begin the Begin', it's an utterly brilliant opener, with much the same intent: 'The time to rise has been engaged', but the lines 'What we want and we need/have been confused, been confused' struck to the core of the Reagan-era politics of greed as successfully as any moment on the album. This was a musical documentary of a modern-day America in decline.

While 'Finest Worksong' alludes to the Protestant work ethic and the dignity of labour in an age of mass deindustrialisation, 'Exhuming McCarthy' looks back to the witch hunts and demonisation of the Commie-bashing 1950s. Stipe's twisted historicism punctures modern-day style culture, while simultaneously reminding us of the perils of the Cold War mentality. 'Disturbance At The Heron House' contains peculiar anthropomorphic images of an Animal Farm of the oppressed and manipulated. 'Strange' is a successful cover of an old Wire song, which fits the overall mood of disquiet perfectly, while 'Welcome To The Occupation' is a classic entryist song, with a sweet melody but a dark commentary, this time a surrealistic statement of anti-imperialism directed against US foreign policy in Central America.

The quartet of songs which conclude the album are R.E.M.'s weirdest to date. 'Fireplace' is rooted by Berry's odd drum figure, an ominous melody and gorgeous sax runs. The lyric is partially based on an eighteenth-century speech given by Mother Ann Lee, leader of a religious sect, a communistic group who, according to Mills, 'didn't believe in using electricity'. According to R.E.M. biographer Marcus Gray the Shakers 'originally fled to the New World to escape persecution in England'. He goes on: 'they were pacifists, small "c" communists . . . but they also renounced alcohol, smoking and sex, practised faith-healing, and earned their vibratory sobriquet from their behaviours when in a state of spiritual exaltation.'[15] Steve Berlin of Los Lobos stars with his brilliant saxophone fills throughout this underrated R.E.M. song. 'Lightnin' Hopkins' is one of Berry's finest moments, while 'King Of Birds' is, in part, a reflection of Stipe's morbid fascination with earthquakes, a phenomenon he claims to be able to predict or sense as they happen around the globe. The September 1986 Mexico quake was the impulse here – 'a hundred million birds flew away'. The line 'standing on the shoulder of giants leaves me cold' was lifted from a quote by Sir Isaac Newton, and would later become an album title of one of pop's most referential/ reverential acts, Oasis, in 2000. 'Oddfellows Local 151', like 'The One I Love', had already been previewed on the previous year's *Pageantry* tour. It's a downbeat ending, a snapshot of the tramps and winos who were cluttering the streets of Athens. It was a picture of a heartless American society in crisis.

But it's the two hit singles from the album that tower over the set. 'It's The End Of The World As We Know It' was a moderate hit as second-choice single, but has now simply become an R.E.M. classic, the band's adrenaline rush at the end of each and every concert. A brilliant, scatter-gun white rap of a dream-state stream of consciousness and a light-hearted stab at the macabre, after the World Trade Center attack of 11 September 2001 the song became for some the anthem of 'Indieamerica', as an alternative to 'God Save America'.[16] Michael Stipe vomits list upon list of directives, people seen and places visited, in that strangely ironic, modulated shout-singing style, in a 1980s take on the Dylan blueprint of two decades earlier with 'Subterranean Homesick Blues'. In the right hands, this sort of white talking jive is effective in turning the rock lyric into stream of consciousness. Billy Joel would use it the same year on his 'We Didn't Start The Fire'. A little later, UK dance act the Beloved would dream through 'Hello' using a similar technique. Perhaps most successful of the lot was the minor classic 'Endless Art', a creepy litany of dead composers, artists and cultural icons compiled by Irish band A House. But with Stipe, this *Sprechgesang* is given a comic edge.

The song came to Stipe in a dream, a recollection of his first trip to New York six years earlier. The words come from everywhere. 'I'm extremely aware of everything around me, whether I am in a sleeping state, awake, dream-state or just in day-to-day life,' is Stipe's self-assessment. 'There's a part in "It's The End Of The World As We Know It" that came from a dream where I was at Lester Bangs' birthday party and I was the only person there whose initials weren't L.B.'[17]

'The One I Love' is the record's pivotal song and marked a sea change with R.E.M. It's a great song, with a fantastic riff from Buck, impassioned singing from Stipe and altogether in-yer-face production from Scott Litt. The music is strangely familiar too, like a mix of Steve Miller's 'Rockin' Me' with a bit of 'Scarborough Fair'. The folksy nature of the melody would later be teased out by the band in various live acoustic treatments. Its lyric is one of utter contempt, as Stipe uses his amour as a time killer before casting him or her off:

A simple prop
To occupy my time
This one goes out to the one I love
Fire!

'It's probably better that they think it's a love song at this point,' Stipe told Q magazine. That song just came up from somewhere and I recognised it as being really violent and awful. But it wasn't directed at any one person. I would never write a song like that. Even if there was one person in the world thinking, this song is about me, I could never sing it or put it out. . . . I didn't want to record that. I thought it was too much. Too brutal. I think there's enough of that ugliness around.'[18] It was certainly the first R.E.M. song that sounded like a massive hit single and I.R.S. knew they were on to a winner.

'*Document* was R.E.M.'s go-forward album,' says Cary Baker. 'It took a lot of money to go to CHR (Contemporary Hit Radio), but no expense was spared in breaking "The One I Love".'

Was there a conscious decision by the band to be more radio-friendly? 'Yes, but that came from the band, it did not come from our prodding, everything physically came from the band,' states Baker. 'As far I am aware, I.R.S. never hinted to the band that they should make a more commercial album. We like their albums just fine.'

However, to some, it was the sound of compromise. A song with such a simple, even simplistic, lyric, a guitar solo from the solo-hating Buck – it had pop-radio smash written all over it. Was it a betrayal? Mitch Easter:

To me, it was such a radical change. I know that's silly, because I'm not the kind of person who thinks, 'that band sucks', just because they've got a major deal. I wish success for people. But it was such a change. The vocals went from admittedly pretty unintelligible to beyond anything Tom Jones ever did. It seemed a little bit crass. It was almost like, 'Right, now we're going to rule the radio. Let's do something where we can't go wrong. Let's have a verse that has about eight words in it and we'll repeat it over and over.' I think it's a good song, but I thought it was a bold move that was somehow unnecessary. They were already an established band then, and they could have called the shots a little more. If they're doing this because an A & R person has told them to, why now? And if they have gotten into this frame of mind, then, what next? Are they going to start doing dance routines? I am enough of an old hippy to feel a little bit alarmed when I think something is commercially motivated. But then I do understand that it's a good idea to be huge, it gives you leverage for what you want to do in the future. I think it's also maybe because that song's big, climactic word is the word 'fire', which is this big classic rock word. Let's put the word 'fire' in there because everyone likes it. All sorts of thoughts and worries went through my head when I heard that song.

Was there a sense that the hook, the 'fye –yer!' was too cliché, too *Unforgettable Fire*, too stadium rock? 'Uumm no, but I would say that's probably about as far in that direction that we would go,' says Mike Mills honestly. 'It had a solo and it had "love" in the title,' concludes Buck in 2002. 'It certainly wasn't a cynical ploy. It's kind of an anti-love song, but believe me, when we play it, people hold hands and look at each other and sing it into each other's eyes.'

Both the album, *Document*, and the single, 'The One I Love', went Top 10 that autumn of 1987, and the promotional tour saw the band play to bigger and bigger venues. Support act for both the *Reckoning* and *Document* tours were the dB's. Drummer Will Rigby tracks the seismic change in American pop in the mid-1980s.

We toured with them in '84 and '87 for about a month or six weeks each time. In '84, they were on I.R.S., and we were on Bearsville, which at that point was in its last throes of being distributed by Warner Brothers, and Warners had one employee in the whole company working on college radio. The whole college radio thing was super-underground back then. By 1987 that had changed, but in 1984, it was below the radar of the major record labels. We were opening for them, but we were getting just as much airplay on the college record stations, although we weren't getting the record label support they were. I have a copy of the CMJ [*College Media Journal*]. It was like the *Billboard* magazine of college radio. They compiled the charts of college radio airplay. I have a chart where the dB's are Number 1 in airplay on college radio and *Reckoning* is Number 2. On that tour, we were really giving them a run for their money. We were getting as much airplay as them in some markets. We weren't selling anything like them, their rise towards stardom was pretty steady and they were well on the way. But, because we were opening for them a lot of people who were coming to see them, were coming to see us too, because they were hearing us on the same radio stations.

I do remember Michael Stipe saying one night, 'Oh, you guys really blew us off stage tonight.' There were times when it was pretty competitive, although not in a bad way, not cut-throat or anything. It was very fraternal. We were more musical equals in 1984. Whereas in 1987 they were big. In fact, 'The One I Love' went Top 10 while we were on tour and that was their first Top 10 single. By that point it was a whole different ball game. They were playing much bigger places and we were like this little opening act that nobody really knew because the fans were much more mainstream radio listeners as opposed to college radio listeners, who were really willing to dig our music. I don't begrudge R.E.M. their success at all, but there were nights on that 1984 tour where they were really given a run for their money by us, because we were right there with them in terms of college radio airplay. A few years later, not only were they so much bigger and, if anything, we were smaller, but the whole industry had changed. There was a focus on the college radio market and there were huge departments and major labels to push records there. The Nirvana thing opened the floodgates, but it was like going on so far before that. Even between '84 and '87 there was a huge difference between how major labels thought about college radio. In 1984, we played a couple of clubs, but mostly campus small halls, around 2,000 seaters, but in 1987 it was like 5–10,000 seaters, and some of them were even bigger than that.

It was on the *Document* tour that Stipe really emerged as a consummate rock performer, an assured singer and a formidable rock icon, as journalist Ballard Lesemann confirms: 'Once they started doing "The One I Love" and "Fall On Me" and that kind of thing, that's when Michael Stipe had come out of his shell from being this Jim Morrison fey kind of arty-farty guy on the mic with his hair down in his face to being a real front man. He actually projected, performed and sang lyrics. Maybe you didn't understand the lyrics and you formed your own meaning out of it, but the vocals were out front and that's when they became a *real* rock'n'roll band.'

R.E.M.'s critical success was indisputable, and their commercial power was growing. However, could I.R.S. Records, the label that had guided them through the first six years of their recording career, take them into the big league? The band's recording contract with I.R.S. had expired, and what followed was a desperate attempt to persuade R.E.M. that their future lay with the creators of their success.

In the spring of 1988, I.R.S.'s Jay Boberg flew to Athens on several occasions in a desperate attempt to try to persuade the band to sign on the dotted line. But R.E.M. did not want more of the same. They were about to enter a new phase in their career, as serious contenders for the crown of Genuine Global Rock Phenomenon. They had decided that I.R.S. would not be there to see the job through.

7. 'THE MAYOR SAYS HELLO NOW', 1988–91

I

There comes a time in the life span of many successful rock groups when painful decisions or switches in allegiance have to be made in order to 'move on to the next level', as record business people say. It might be the removal of a trusted musical colleague (such as the jettisoning of Mick Ronson by David Bowie), a change of manager, a change of location (look what Berlin did for U2), or even a change of drug (witness the change in the Fab Four from speed-freak Mersey Beat to the kaleidoscopic LSD-injected *Sgt Pepper*). But very often, it's simply a change of record label that does the trick. So it was with R.E.M. Their five albums for I.R.S. had made them a name in alternative rock. The next three, with a major label, turned them into a rock institution.

For R.E.M., the main consideration was not financial *per se*, but a feeling that their music wasn't being heard by enough people, particularly outside the US. Simply put, they were with a record label that was not big enough to ensure that their music hit the radio stations and, more importantly, the record racks, in Berlin and Paris as efficiently as in Dallas and New York. 'The red phone doesn't sit on your desk.' That was how one of the members of the band explained the real reason behind the band's decision to break with I.R.S. in the spring of 1988 to a distraught Jay Boberg. Boberg had spent weeks flying back and forth between LA and Athens in a desperate attempt to persuade his charges to remain within I.R.S., but to no avail. 'We had an incredibly good relationship – it was like family, like brothers,' says Boberg, still, one suspects, saddened by losing his favourite band to a rival label.

We had a vision and helped execute it for one another. I knew we couldn't have done better. If we were doing a figure-skating routine, we would have got a perfect six. But we still lost out, because of factors beyond our control. I.R.S. offered what we thought was as much money as Warner had offered, so I'm not sure that it came down to the money.

They told me before they told Warners that they were going to leave. I remember somebody saying to me, it was either Michael or Peter Buck at the final meeting in Athens, that, at the end of the day, the red phone doesn't sit on my desk. In *Batman*, the red phone went straight to the bat cave. That was a reference to the fact that I.R.S. is a distributed label and internationally at the time they were distributed by CBS, with whom we'd both been frustrated. We had had many problems with the international affiliates of CBS in terms of whether or not they were really chasing the R.E.M. records and really putting the money behind it that they needed to. One of the band members said to me that at this point in their career, while there were many companies who could have taken them to the next level, there was no company who could have done for them what I.R.S. did for them at the time. I was really sad. It taught me that it was impossible for I.R.S., as an indie, to compete with the big companies.

'When we finished our contract with *Document*, we were done. It wasn't a foregone conclusion that we were going to go, but we kind of felt that we probably would. We switched labels because our records were just unavailable in Europe,' is Peter Buck's take on the situation. 'It used to drive me nuts, when we toured Germany, say, and played to 200 American servicemen. They'd be saying, "My God, I can't believe that we get to see you in front of 200 people, when in America you play to 20,000." Then I'd go into a record store, and I'd be completely unable to find any of our records anywhere. We'd play in Finland to 500 people because our records essentially weren't out there.'

In interviews with the media since then, the testimony of the Copeland brothers, Miles and Ian, has cast doubt on Boberg's version of events. According to Ian Copeland, what actually happened was that I.R.S. knew they would be losing out to Warner Brothers and were told by them that they would double any offer I.R.S. could make.[1] Ian Copeland reports that, with this in mind, I.R.S. made the band one final, lucrative offer, which was rejected; they couldn't possibly have made good on this, it was done simply to get a better deal for R.E.M. from Warner Brothers, to ensure that the band kept on-message with regard to the future exploitation of their back catalogue, a process which would yield several compilations in the next few years.

'I wouldn't be surprised if Miles had upped an offer. But we were getting offers from all over the place, and we did not accept the biggest. I won't name the company, but I had this instantaneous personal dislike of the person at the company we were talking to, and they offered us more money. Bertis and Jefferson went around to every single company that expressed an interest in us. They said to us, we're not going to prejudge, we'll talk to these people, and we'll narrow it down to the five companies that have European distribution and who seem to know what you guys are about. People promise you all kinds of stuff, but to a certain degree you have to go on trust. Even though we've always had in our contact that we've always had complete artistic control over what we do, that still doesn't mean that they won't fuck with you if they feel like it. I felt really comfortable with Lenny and Mo. They let Randy Newman do what he wants to do for years. I think we could have squeezed more money out of a different label but we felt good at Warners,' says Buck.

The whole atmosphere at I.R.S. appears to have changed the moment they changed distributors. Former R.E.M. producer Mitch Easter was still signed to I.R.S., along with his band Let's Active. He is in no doubt that the entire character of the label underwent an overnight transmogrification:

Their distribution changed to MCA in the USA, and when that happened the whole tone of the place went down the drain. They just lost their coolness overnight. A&M has a really appealing location in Hollywood; it's the old Charlie Chaplin

studios and it's really cute. I.R.S. had a little building on the
A&M lot, and everything was just so cool. When they moved
out to MCA, it was on a much bigger film lot and the whole
thing had this 'business, business, business' feel about it. All
they were talking about was Belinda Carlisle going to Number 1
with this dreadful song, and 'Why can't your band be more like
this?', that kind of depressing, anti-art stuff that saps your spirit.
That period produced the deathless comment to me from Jay
Boberg that I should try and turn myself into the American Mark
Knopfler. Now that made me want to jump off a bridge right
there and then. Mark Knopfler is just fine, but that's *not* for me.
I thought holy shit!, if that's how they see us, it's hopeless.

For Peter Buck too, I.R.S. had morphed into a different kind of
label. The pressure on R.E.M. was to keep I.R.S. in the black: 'It was
the perfect label for us but their label mission changed halfway
through. When they signed us they said we're gonna sign young
bands, we don't expect you to have a lot of hit records, we just want
you to make good records, go on tour and work your ass off because
there isn't gonna be any money. And that's what we wanted, we
wanted creative freedom and that's the main goal for us. Then one
or two records in and the Go Go's had sold 6 million records. All of
a sudden people at the label who didn't know anything about music
were saying, well, where's your hit single? But that wasn't the point.
In the end there was a huge amount of pressure on us to support the
business that had grown to this big level. I personally liked all the
people a lot. I just think they grew too fast and didn't have anyone
to back it up sales wise.'

Like Mitch Easter, the band were also far from happy with the
switch in I.R.S.'s distribution, as Buck adds: 'A&M were very good
but MCA really didn't show any interest. I remember when *Lifes Rich
Pageant* came out, maybe it was even *Document*, and I was talking to
someone who was very high up at MCA and they said, "Do you
know, we're just not going to push your record because it doesn't
have any hit singles." I said, "Gosh we sold like 600,000 of the last
one without any hit singles." Then they told me that their record for
the year – the one they were going to put all our money behind –
was Charlie Sexton's first record. I was kind of insulted. He plays
with Dylan now and he's great, but it was insulting to hear that they

were going to put all this money into the first record from an 18-year-old kid.'

What was certain was that many at I.R.S. were utterly demoralised to lose R.E.M., as I.R.S.'s Cary Baker remembers: 'We were called into the office one day by Miles when Jay was still in Athens speaking to the band, and he announced that the band had left. I think everybody was crestfallen. I just went home that night, poured myself a drink and stared at the wall. I was supposed to meet some friends at a Don Dixon and Marti Jones appearance that night, but I just couldn't go. At that point my soul left my job at I.R.S. and it became a bit of a "J.O.B.". At that meeting Miles was trying to rescue our morale, but there was also a part of him that was a little nonchalant about it – like, hey, they were just one of the bands on this label and we've got others and we'll get through it. And I don't think anyone in that room really felt that way.'

Warner Brothers won the signature, beating off Virgin, Sony and several other labels, because they offered the band total artistic freedom. Other labels in fact offered the same thing, but the band didn't believe them. In Warner president Lenny Waronker, the label had a personable figure who had also been a record producer and who connected with the band. And in artists such as Neil Young and Randy Newman, it had a prestigious roster of rock acts with credibility, artists who were not dropped if a particular record failed in the marketplace. What was more important to Warner Brothers, R.E.M. were convinced, was the quality of music artists produced, not sales.

The size of the Warner deal is unknown. Reports have placed it anywhere between $6 and $12 million. Jay Boberg puts it much higher at $22 million. The Athens office refuse to discuss any financial details pertaining to the band, claiming that they are contractually barred from doing so. 'Twenty-two million is definitely wrong,' assures Peter Buck. 'That is much higher than we got. I don't know if they did match what we ended up getting.' Ask Michael Stipe why the band signed with Warners and the answer is simple: 'Bugs Bunny.'

There is no doubt that 1988 was a watershed year for the band. For the first time they had the financial security to match their creativity. Their next album, *Green*, and particularly its successor, *Out Of Time*, would be the products of a new maturity. Work on making the records was conducted at a less frenetic pace, and there was money to finance the whimsical and the experimental. For their part, as musicians, R.E.M. wanted change – to enrich and expand the band's rock sound with unusual and unexpected pieces of new orchestration and instrumentation. By 1991, the band was making music that was so intricate, and so disconnected from the grand rock gesture, that it was pretty much designed not to be played live. This new music automatically drew parallels, not altogether unfavourable, with the work of other rock *auteurs*, such as the late-period Beatles, who swapped the stage for the studio. All this did no harm at all to the band's public image as 'serious' rock musicians.

For the band, and, one suspects, for Peter Buck, this was a confusing time. Now signed to a major label, the band was accused by a small section of their original fans of selling out. In interviews R.E.M., and especially Peter Buck, would be both defensive *and* aggressive about this. True, the old, and always untenable, distinction between challenging, independent music and corporate, big-business garbage was collapsing in the minds of the consumer. But the big labels still had an air of capitalist complicity about them. In interviews a prickly Peter Buck felt compelled to justify his position as millionaire rock star, financed by a massive dollar-chomping record label, playing in a band that supported 'the common man' and was on the side of progressive politics.

Today, Peter Buck maintains that the band handled the situation with integrity, and put loyalty and artistic freedom above personal gain. 'I think we were a little defensive because we'd signed to a major label and everyone was like "Oh, they've sold out." We signed to a major label, Warner Brothers, after Hüsker Dü, after the Replacements – everyone else had done it too. We had people coming to us from a major label from our third record on saying, "We can get you out of your deal with I.R.S., they're in breach technically in several ways and we'll pay the legal fee if you sign with us right now." I think a lot of people would have done it. But we didn't, we honoured the contract, we liked those people and we did our five albums and greatest hits. I was only defensive in that people just assumed that it was over, and then we went on I think to make our best records, so I think we answered in that regard. I'm used to that huge crowd thing now, but back then it was kind of tough. It was ironic that I'd do these 20,000 seat shows then go to a club to see a band play with 150 people and probably have a better time.'

II

R.E.M's new album was recorded in Nashville. Their first for Warner Brothers, it was surprising in that, although their public political profile was at its highest, the songs on the album were, with only a couple of exceptions, apolitical. Sure, the album cover, with a typical perverseness a murky *orange* in colour, had images of foliage and eco-friendliness which echoed the title, but one would be hard put to see it as a political album in the tradition of *Lifes Rich Pageant* or *Document*. Instead, this was the first album that attempted to break the mould in musical terms. Reportedly, Stipe told Berry, Buck and Mills, 'not to write any more R.E.M.-type songs'.[2] The result was *Green*.

On *Green*, the music develops in three seemingly contradictory directions. Songs such as 'Stand' and 'Pop Song 1989' are ironic pop songs, and catchier and breezier than most in the R.E.M. repertoire. 'Turn You Inside Out' and 'Orange Crush', with their hard-hitting big guitar and big drum sounds, look back to *Document*, while the beautiful 'You Are The Everything', 'The Wrong Child' and 'Hairsuit' are pastoral acoustic numbers featuring Peter Buck on mandolin, and look forward to *Out Of Time*. 'The Eleventh Untitled Song', with its weirdly off-kilter drum beat (played by Buck, as Berry refused to play it), ended the album on an emotional high, but sounded very different from the rest of the material. So, sonically, *Green* is all over the place, the result being a fascinatingly eclectic album rather than a unified artistic move forward.

Mike Mills argues that the album was experimental: 'I think *Green* is haphazard, a bit scattershot, but that's because we were experimenting with things. A couple of songs feature the mandolin, and I like both of them a lot. There's some accordion on there and we have some pedal steel. We have always been interested in realising songs as fully as possible. Now that doesn't necessarily mean putting more things on them, but finding things that will make a simple barebones song into a beautiful creation. I'm sure there are times where we've put one or two more instruments more than we should have done on a song, but then again I haven't listened to *Green* for years. But I recall liking it very much.' Producer Scott Litt generally concurred with the overall assessment that although the record has 'some great things on it', it was 'not a fully realised album'.[3]

The original idea was reportedly to have had one side of electric and one side of acoustic songs, but this formally coherent plan had to be dropped when not enough of the acoustic ones were considered for release. There was just enough on the album to keep R.E.M. in that liminal state of being 'the acceptable edge of the unacceptable stuff', as Peter Buck told writer Steve Pond in that career-defining *Rolling Stone* interview in December 1987.[4]

Traditionally it's been Peter Buck who takes the lead in suggesting new musical territories for the band, and, as long as the other members don't have a problem with them, Buck is generally able to please himself in terms of the texture the records have. In the autumn of 1987, he had splashed out $500 on an 'oddly-shaped Italian mandolin-cum-lyre'.

'I was just wandering round New York and saw this very strange-shaped instrument like an Italian mandolin and I learnt how to play it,' recalls Buck. 'I was playing a lot of acoustic music with my friends in Athens and that was where I was heading a little bit at the time.' Buck's mastery of the instrument would bring rich rewards, adding a melancholia to three of the tracks on *Green*. In addition, Mills added some accordion into the mix. There was a sense of play in their music, as new instrumentation was brought in, including cello and pedal steel. Since Berry was equally at home on acoustic guitar and piano, and Mills could play virtually anything, the policy of the switcheroo became part of the band's working practices from this period onwards.

Released in November 1988, *Green* was R.E.M.'s poppiest and most accessible album to date. 'Stand', a huge American hit, was a splendid pop song. Being simultaneously stupid and profound, it had all the necessary ingredients for pop greatness. The ending is amusing, the final consonant so perfectly vocalised that it is hard not to think of it as a send-up by Stipe, bearing in mind his mumbling past. Lyrically, 'Stand' is geographically organised. Stipe writes about the need for orientation in one's life, as if based on a series of steps for an unknown, invented, dance. It's another classic duologue, a conversation in music between Stipe and Mills:

Stipe: 'Stand in the place where you live'
Mills: 'Now face North'
Stipe: 'Think about direction
Wonder why you haven't before
Now stand in the place where you were'

Above left R.E.M.'s original manager, Jefferson Holt, with beer in hand, partying in the early 1980s.
Above right A young, and hairy, Michael Stipe. Both © Terry Allen
Below The whirling dervishes on stage – Michael Stipe and Peter Buck in an all-action early R.E.M. show.
London Features/Anna Summa

Left The band backstage at The Park West in Chicago, 1983. Note the big hair.
© Linda Matlow/Pix International

Below left Michael Plen of I.R and Michael Stipe goofing in photo booth at Atlanta Airpo circa 1985.© Michael Plen

Below Learning to be a star – Michael Stipe backstage, aga at The Park West, Chicago.
© Linda Matlow/Pix International

Below Welcome to Howard Finster's Paradise Gardens, Sumerville, Georgia, 1998. © Heather Unbehaun

bove Stipe at a rock festival in Minneapolis, mid-1980s. © Michael Plen

elow A chunky Stipe, circa 1985. © Debbie Leavitt/Pix International

Above A sleeker look for R.E.M. in 1986. © Paul Natkin

Above Mike Mills and Michael Stipe on the *Pageantry* tour, 1986. © Paul Natkin

Left Stipe sings 'World Leader Pretend' on the *Green* tour of 1989. © Ebet Roberts

left The band in their global breakthrough year of
91. Note Bill Berry's bug-eyed stare and mullet!

right Michael Stipe having a bad hair day in 1993.

ve Stipe, Mills and Buck, together with Tarsem
andwar Singh collect an MTV Music Award in 1991
the brilliant 'Losing My Religion'.

Charlotte, NC (FP) Throughout

#	Song	Notes
1	I TOOK YOUR NAME	Carnival/loops
2	KENNETH	
3	CRUSH	Hula
4	DRIVE (FP)	Circle
5	I DON'T SLEEP	Furniture (or fish+boots)+flowers
6	WAKE UP BOMB	Flowers + flowers
7	UNDERTOW	Shim
8	RELIGION	(IJ)
9	BINKY	Scratch things
10	BLAME (FP)	FENCE
11	STRANGE CURRENCIES	SURVEIL. [35mm]
12	REVOLUTION	
13	TONGUE *MB*	X-RAY + fish
14	MAN ON THE MOON	MERCER
15	COUNTRY FEEDBACK	PARKING
16	ONE I LOVE	5 boys
17	ORANGE CRUSH	Fish + fish
18	GET UP	
19	STAR 69	Tooth pix (IJ) / LEONARDO
1	LET ME IN	SUN + LEONARDO
2	EVERYBODY HURTS	NYC / BEES
3	SOUTH CENTRAL RAIN	(IJ)
4	DEPARTURE	MAN RAY
5	END OF THE WORLD	"?" (IJ)

A B I C I D E

Left Apart from the almost traditional closer, 'It's The End Of The World', R.E.M.'s sets have tended to be mixed bags, as this set list reveals. © Paul Butchart.

Bottom left 'You, you will be my queen'. Stipe's 'hero' Patti Smith photographed in 1996.
© Kevin Mazur/ London Features.

Below right Just before the break-up of the R.E.M. nuclear family. From the left: Bill Berry, Bertis Downs, Michael Stipe, Peter Buck, Jefferson Holt, Mike Mills.
© Kevin Mazur/London Features.

Bottom, right Superstar friends: Stipe and Bono. Bono would later testify as a character witness during Peter Buck's trial in 2002. 'Perhaps one day U2 and R.E.M. will merge and just form one huge super group - R.E.U.2.M?' says writer Paul Du Noyer in an era of the Time-Warner/AOL global merger.
© Kevin Mazur/ London Features.

ve Scott McCaughey and Peter Buck rock out during an impromptu Minus Five gig staged during a
off' from the *Monster* tour in 1995. © Marty Perez.

w Bertis Downs, the linchpin of the R.E.M. team: music fan, law
lar – he is admired throughout the music industry. Downs claims
not in the music business, but in the 'R.E.M. business'. © Bertis Downs.

Above The first concert without
Bill Berry. A saronged Stipe and
a soaring Thom Yorke perform
together during R.E.M.'s
perplexing Tibetan Freedom
Concert, Washington DC, June
1998. © Kevin Mazur/ London Features.

Above left Mike Mills and Michael Stipe share a tender moment on stage. As was customary during the *Up* tour, Mike and Michael would do 'Why Not Smile' together between the main set and the encore, and would usually kiss dramatically afterwards. The photo was taken on 9 September, 1999 at the Meriweather Post Pavillion, outside Washington DC.
© Ethan Kaplan

Above right Stipe waves to the audience at Ea Court, London on the successful *Up* tour of 1
© Awais Butt/ London Features

Below The band as a trio at the Marge Simps ADR Studios in Los Angeles in July 2001, be interviewed by Fox Television for an electron press kit for the Simpsons. They were there t day to record the voice-overs that featured in 'Homer the Moe' episode. © Ethan Kaplan

Mills: 'Now face West'
Stipe: 'Think about the place where you live
Wonder why you haven't before'

The little interjected commands from Mills (and Berry?) are the sort of deft touch at which the band were becoming so adept. The result is a song which has the silliness of the twist married to the call-to-arms of a protest song. 'It's about making decisions and actually living your life rather than letting it happen,' Stipe would later tell *Q*'s Mat Snow.[5] The video, directed by Katherine Dieckmann, featured a number of happy people doing a silly dance to the song's directives. In another dollop of postmodernist play, the viewer is being asked, in the era of slick *Thriller*-style choreography, to enjoy the self-conscious spectacle and stupidity of badly performed dances. The video also testified to the band's continued unwillingness to lip-synch in their videos. In fact, when they appear, fleetingly, at the end of the video, jumping towards the camera mimicking the dance routine, they look so self-conscious as to be quite unsettling. Stipe's smiling face gives way to *faux* shyness as he covers up his face, like an embarrassed 13-year-old. A gesture which was superficially intended to show the 'real' Stipe behind the allegedly po-faced veneer merely revealed yet another level of the contrived. Stipe was 28, and this sort of feigned embarrassment was odd.

On one level, the band recognised the inherent silliness of the record. At a live gig in June 1989 in Copenhagen, Stipe introduced the song in his trademark flat Southern drawl and, it must be said, with no little comic timing:

This next record stands alongside such great classics as Gershwin's *Rhapsody In Blue*, Samuel Barber's *Adagio*, the *1812 Overture* with real cannons. This song stands as one of the most artistic, one of the most ingenious, one of the most inspired, and yes, one of the most audacious pieces of music ever written by man.

To highlight the fact that R.E.M. had an underappreciated line in the droll and bizarre in their back catalogue, they followed 'Stand' that night with the equally silly 'Underneath The Bunker' from *Lifes Rich Pageant*.

On another level though, R.E.M. expected us to laugh at the mock sincerity of the silliness. We were supposed to chuckle, not at the silliness of the song, but at the fact that this was a serious group self-consciously parodying the silliness of a pop song in a serious way. R.E.M.'s jokiness was no laughing matter.

'Pop Song '89', in fact played on the 1987 *Work* tour, was another self-conscious slab of pop pastiche, this time with the Doors as the inspiration. The astonishing video for the single featured three topless women and a topless Stipe dancing to the track. It was, as Mike Mills says, an anti-sexist video: 'We hated videos so much, and the majority of them had all of the same images: scantily-clad women, breaking mirrors, all this slo-mo stuff, and it was just really *stupid*. So, the video was an exercise in mocking the genre. Michael said, well, if the girls are going to go topless, then I am too!' One of the topless women was Michael's close friend Caroline, who had also starred in 'The One I Love' video. The original video was promptly banned by MTV, but was later aired with black censor's bars placed over all four sets of nipples, including those of Stipe! The single flopped.

'Get Up' was a better song though. Although yet another exercise in pastiche (the intro sounded, perhaps unintentionally, very like the Stranglers' 1977 hit '(Get A) Grip (On Yourself)'), it captures our imagination through clever lyrical interplay by Stipe:

Dreams they complicate my life
Dreams they complement my life

Dream states play a central role in Stipe's creativity. So many of his songs have either been inspired by dreams, or reference them.[6] In fact, this particular song was written for Mike Mills, but this fact wasn't revealed to the boffinish bassist until a decade later: 'I didn't realise until we were on the last tour, I guess it was '99, or maybe the one before that. We were doing that song, and Michael said it was about me. And I stopped the show and said, "What?" And he said, "You didn't know?" And I said, "You never told me!" So apparently, "Get Up" is about me, 'cos I love to sleep. It's not so much how much I sleep; I just don't like getting up in the mornings. I just prefer being awake at night. I love the night time, whether I'm out or whether I'm alone in my house by myself. Alone in my house at night is one of my favourite times. But I prefer to stay up late, and then I end up sleeping late. But I'm not so bad as I used to be. For some reason, I love staying up late in my house in Athens. I get to bed around two, or three, maybe later.'

Two tracks relayed an opaque political message. 'Orange Crush' was a superb rocker. With Berry's insistent, gunfire-mimicking drumming and Buck's almost U2-style guitar work, it was a minor UK hit single. Their performance in the late spring of 1989 on the high-rating show *Top of the Pops* was crucial in introducing the group to a new post-acid house generation of would-be rock fans. Placed next to the sludge of the Stock Aitken and Waterman boy and girl bands the sight of Stipe screaming into a loudhailer was a reminder of pop's original, dangerous power. The lyrics referenced Agent Orange, the defoliation agent used by the Americans in the Vietnam War to reduce enemy cover and destroy food crops. The chemical also had a long-lasting effect on the ecosystem, contaminating water supplies and fish stocks, as well as the airmen and soldiers who came into contact with it. Stipe has hinted in interviews that his helicopter-flying dad had administered the biological weapon.[7]

'World Leader Pretend', a languid commentary on Cold War mentality, sung confidently by Stipe, is arguably the lyrical highpoint of the record: 'I raise the wall, and I will be the one to knock it down'. For his part, Mills was initially disappointed by the transform-ation the song underwent at the hands of the lyricist: 'I loved the song, I didn't like what Michael did with it. I wanted it to be this sort of pop hit, and Michael did this sort of sombre vocal on it. I wasn't real happy about that, but the more I listened to it the more I liked it, and I love it now. It's much more of a downer song than I wanted it to be, but it's a very good one nevertheless.'

In a well-meaning, though perhaps mildly insensitive move, the vice-president of sales at Warner Brothers, Charlie Spinger, invited the staff of the I.R.S. label, still mourning the loss of their prize asset, for pizza and beer and an exclusive advance listening of the new album in the Warner Brothers conference room. Cary Baker appreciated the gesture and attended. 'It was hospitable, but I missed being the one who extended the hospitality on the band's behalf,' says Baker. 'It was bittersweet. Especially when I heard the album and it was predictably great.' Jay Boberg stayed away. 'I couldn't go. To this day, I've never had a bad thing to say about R.E.M., nor had

I then, but I couldn't bring myself to go. I felt so disappointed, let down, disillusioned.'

Green was finally released in November 1988, and although it improved on the sales peak of *Document* worldwide, it failed to reach the US Top 10 or the UK Top 20. Apart from 'Stand' in the USA, none of the singles made a big impact either, but the astonishingly positive press more than made up for this relative lack of commercial success. Andy Gill, writing for *Q* magazine, awarded the album five stars: 'It's their best album yet, no doubt; the kind of record which, once you live with it a day or two, will soon become part of your family. Are R.E.M. the best band in the world? I reckon so.'[8]

III

Peter Holsapple, who had opened as a solo artist on the *Chronic Town* tour way back in 1982, and had played on *Green*, was now asked to be the fifth member of the touring party, replacing Buren Fowler, who had played guitar on the *Work* tour in 1987. Holsapple told *Mojo* in 1994 that rehearsals were 'minimal'. 'For the *Green* tour we did three without Michael and one with Michael, and then a kind of dress rehearsal at the first place we were going to play to make sure the stage gear was up and running. But in a way the lyrics and the vocal float on top of the music – in a spiritual sense as well as a musical one – so as long as the underpinnings are there, it works.'[9]

The *Green* tour was R.E.M.'s biggest and most visually expressive to date. Production values were considerably higher than on previous R.E.M. tours, and the clever use of back-projections, art films and sloganeering was a dry run for U2's bigger and bolder *Zoo TV* tour of 1992. Stipe was at his most eccentric. His thinning hair worked up into a quiff, in what one future R.E.M. associate, artistic designer Chris Bilheimer, calls 'the worst hairdo in the history of mankind. I think that might be a direct quote from Michael, I know he's said it before in the press. He had the sides shaved, the hair on top and then the really long braid at the back.' His eyes heavily mascaraed, he took the stage in the full spirit of fun in his raffish pastel suit. But he commanded the stage like never before, and with an intensity that unsettled.

'I could turn you inside out / But I choose, not to do', he sang through a loudhailer, his voice eerie, his demeanour threatening, the lyric, about the inequality in the power nexus between the unfettered ambition of the performer and the blind devotion of an imagined audience, made chillingly real. Stipe's power was not just figurative. The loudhailer made the gap between the amplified performance and the audience even more imbalanced. For 'World Leader Pretend' he stood rigid, to attention, beginning and ending the song by smashing a cane on to a chair. For 'Stand' he danced that stupid dance, while for 'Swan Swan H' the gothic spirit of the backwards preacher overwhelmed him and he twisted and contorted as he glared at his audience and spoke in tongues.

The reconstructed opening of 'Feeling Gravitys Pull', all-wailing avant-rock guitars and with ominous drumming from Berry, was the show's most extreme moment musically, while old favourites such as 'Perfect Circle' were reminiscent of a pristine pop sensibility. This was R.E.M. at the crossroads. Just as their new album *Green* was a jumble of styles, so was their stage show. The overall atmosphere was, for the first time, imbued with a certain artifice. Stipe's wildly stylised, deliberately dumb dancing, his flailing singing style and his hip-swivelling postures made his a compelling performance. For the rest of the band it was, in the main, business as usual. The only real show of theatricality from the other three members came from the trademark Peter Buck leap into the air.

The shows were a triumph, with *Green* and *Document* providing the bulk of the repertoire. One of the striking features of R.E.M. at the time was that, although vigorously and, some would say, ruthlessly separatist in their attitude to the music business, they were paradoxically open-minded when it came to repertoire. The band, as we shall see later in the book, were touchy when it came to the possibility of bestowing song-writing credits on outsiders, but they connected readily with songs from outside their *oeuvre*.

In the main, they were competent interpreters of the music of others. The resounding comedic failure of 'Moon River' aside, the cover versions to be found on the odds-and-sods collection, *Dead Letter Office*, released in spring 1987, which included versions of '(All I Have To Do Is) Dream' (Everley Brothers), 'Crazy' (Pylon), 'King Of the Road' (Roger Miller) and 'There She Goes Again' (Velvets) are all embarrassment-free and mostly fine. Live, the band could be heard building on this ever-growing repertoire of covers; the Boss's 'Born To Run' morphing out of 'Ain't No Sunshine' with earnest Peter Gabriel's 'Red Rain', demented Iggy Pop's 'Funtime', and departed Syd Barrett's 'Dark Globe' thrown in for good measure. R.E.M. were music fans, so it came as no surprise to see their live set enriched or, on occasion, diluted by the addition of cover versions. They had started out as predominantly a covers band in any case, so the continuation of this tradition was a logical development.

It's true that a sizeable part of R.E.M.'s public were either unaware of the band's commitment to liberal causes, or enjoyed the music regardless of their convictions. But no one was left unaware of the band's political mission. Throughout the 1989 tour, Stipe informed his audiences of a whole range of pressing socio-political issues against a background of political indifference to the manifestly gloomy predictions of global eco-meltdown being carried in the media. The Brave New World of technological freedom, championed by the technocracy of post-war America, turned sour in the seventies. Rachel Carson's prediction, back in 1962 in *Silent Spring*, of the dangers to the ecosystem of unfettered technological expansion was manifesting itself in the destruction of the environment. Stipe's self-imposed brief was to educate his people, calling for boycotts of offending multinationals such as Esso/Exxon after the Alaskan oil spill and raising awareness of the progressive platform that existed. Indeed, the increasing politicisation of R.E.M. came at a time when the rock music industry itself was beginning to reflect a burgeoning global concern about environmental issues. An Amnesty International tour of 1988 was said to have added around 200,000 new members to the organisation in the USA alone.[10]

In November 1989 at a gig at the Fox Theatre in Atlanta towards the end of the tour, the band played the whole of *Murmur* in order, then the whole of *Green*. For the band, both albums were thematically linked. '*Green* had so many connections to *Murmur*,' says Stipe. 'It was very much at the back of my head the whole time we were working on it. From the album cover to the topics of the songs and the way the songs were carried out, to me, there's a great connection there. Signing to a new record label was a new start for us.'[11]

The 1989 tour would be exhausting for all, but particularly harrowing for Bill Berry. In Munich, Berry was taken seriously ill with a high fever. His condition worsened to such an extent that he began drifting in and out of consciousness, suffering hallucinations, and broke out in a rash of red spots. The medical team in Germany treated Berry as if he had a viral infection, but were unable to diagnose the illness. Eventually he was correctly diagnosed as suffering from Rocky Mountain Spotted Fever, a potentially fatal condition caused by a tick bite. He had contracted the illness, which has a week-long incubation period, while gardening back home in Georgia. Peter Buck remembers the trauma only too well:

He was pretty close that time. If they hadn't have given him the right antibiotic, then he might have died. He was pretty damn sick. One of us actually said, 'This might be Rocky Mountain Spotted Fever' and the German doctor actually said to us, 'I'm the doctor and you are *not!*' Fine! We called a doctor back in Athens and he said, 'Well, it actually sounds like it is Rocky Mountain Spotted Fever,' and he called someone he knew in England, who called up the German doctor and just reamed him, and said, you shouldn't even be practising medicine, you should get to a butcher's shop! It turns out that they were so bewildered and gave him such a wide array of antibiotics that they hit on the right one, tetracycline. But Bill just hated those guys. They didn't want him to leave because they wanted to test him some more. They'd never seen anything like this before so they'd wheel him out the door and there's doctors trying to take blood and Bill would be swatting at the guys, telling them to leave him alone, saying they'd almost killed him and stuff.

This rather frightening brush with death aside, 1989 had been a startlingly good year for the band. One could put forward a reasonably convincing case that the *Green*-era R.E.M. had the biggest impact on fellow and would-be rock musicians of any version before or after. In the UK, *Green* was the first album to tap the wellspring of support that would grow and grow over the next five years and that would ultimately outstrip the level of acceptance of the band in their home country. Neil Hannon, who would later become the singer-songwriter of the Divine Comedy, talks with reverence of the night the *Green* tour made it to Dublin. 'The sight and sound of this brilliant band at the height of their powers had a profound effect on me. The most obvious was the complete mess I made of my A levels that followed shortly afterwards. In the long term it proved to me that music can be both inclusive and cutting-edge; that popularity and art don't have to cancel each other out.'[12]

IV

In the late 1980s, Stipe struck a determined figure, walking round the streets of Athens, his hair dyed orange and tied into a ponytail at the back, wearing thick spectacles and big boots, his big suits crumpled and still carrying the air of thrift-store chic. He still drove an old Volvo round town.[13] This was Stipe on the edge of rock'n'roll mainstream celebrity, the glossy Sunday-supplement treatment, the tour launch from a Dublin castle, the lip-synched big-budget videos, the designer clothes and the glamorous photo-shoots. He was now almost thirty years old. In the bars and clubs of Athens he would greet old friends with enthusiasm, but would give dullards and drunks short shrift. He was slowly becoming a rock star, and beginning to develop the defence mechanisms needed to deal with the 'cult of Stipe', and those fans so bewitched by his persona that their fandom bordered on pathology. Dubbed 'distiples' by the press, this band of hardcore Stipe-worshippers would henceforth be an ever-present factor in the life of Stipe.

Bill Berry had been married to Mari for four years. Peter Buck had split up with his girlfriend Ann some time in 1986, and had married Barrie Greene, owner of the 40 Watt Club, in the spring of 1987. Mills' son, Julian, had been born in 1989. Michael Stipe was busy on the dating scene and had been, for a while, the secret love of Natalie Merchant from the band 10,000 Maniacs. R.E.M. were now four grown-ups, the years of hedonism now largely behind them. The R.E.M. culture was a boozing culture, as the band was out most nights when in Athens in the bars, convivially chatting away. They were as unaffected as any wealthy rock stars could be. And they were, to all intents and purposes, workaholics rather than alcoholics.

R.E.M. did not squander their newly won wealth. Rather than shift operations to New York or LA, a logical move for any big rock band, they stayed local. There was a precedent for this in the style of management developed by U2's Paul McGuinness, who based operations out of Dublin, but it was still rather a novelty to find a name rock act with a 'homey' style. In the 1980s R.E.M. were permanently on the road and it simply made good sense, on a personal level, for them to base their managerial seat of power in their home town too.

The band members began acquiring properties in and around the Classic City. Peter Buck's house was a thing of rare splendour, a cross between a steamboat and a Gothic pile, with a tower, a big porch all round and impressive tall windows. 'It looked like something out of a Charles Adams cartoon,' says Athens-dweller Betsy Dorminey. 'There is a tower with a little deck off it. The Jester family built that house.'

'It was really cool at "Buck Mansions",' remembers musician Nikki Sudden, who stayed and played with members of the band in 1990. Peter said, "Stay for two weeks, stay for two months," and I ended up staying for three! Peter was generous – he ended up paying for a first-class plane ticket to LA, paying for my hotel when we went over there. He had a beautiful old house and had a widow's tower, where the widows of the Confederacy used to go to look for their men returning, who never came back. Bertis Downs lives in the house next door.'

'Buck's house was called a Queen Ann Victoria, Imperial Style,' says Paul Butchart. 'Bill Berry's house was built in 1864 and it was called a Greek Revival. Buck owned another house too, where his brother lived. That's the house featured in the Athens *Inside Out* video.'

All the members of the R.E.M. extended family lived the good life. 'I can remember one great night at Mike's house – everyone ended crawling under the piano because they couldn't stand any more,' recollects Nikki Sudden. 'Jefferson had this really opulent house that he spent so much money on. The house had ornate glass everywhere so you could see from one floor to the next. It must have cost him millions.'

As we have seen, Stipe ran his film production business in Athens, and also became a local entrepreneur. 'I used to wait tables from 1994 to 1998 at a place called The Grit, and I used to see Jefferson Holt in there at the time,' says Ballard Lesemann. 'Stipe owns the property but he doesn't own the restaurant. The couple that owns the building are Ted Hafer and Jessica Greene. Jessica is Barrie Buck's sister. We used to get phone calls from people all the time asking if Michael Stipe was hanging around and one of us would get on the phone and imitate his voice, "Uh, I can't speak right now." I remember during the 1996 Olympics in Atlanta that somebody was trying to secure an interview, so I did the interview in his voice, and I don't think he even knew that. It was some writer from New Orleans!'

Stipe's house was a private space, hidden behind a fairly impenetrable wall of bamboo. 'He's the kind of person who needs his privacy,' affirms Dorminey, 'and I guess the only way to get it when people are that hungry for every little second with you is to throw out some false things to put people off the scent, so you can have some breathing room. Well, if it were me, I might do the same thing. It's like building up a big fence of brambles round your property to keep the people out. You want to maintain some sphere of privacy. The disadvantage of people who are famous is that other people come to them knowing a lot more about them than the other way round.'

For his part, Bill Berry had some odd ideas with regard to home removals. Wealthy rock stars have a tendency to have crackpot ideas and outrageous demands. Elton John once famously complained to his hotel room service that the wind was blowing in the wrong direction. However, very few have been quite so eccentric as to have their house removed and rebuilt, floor by floor, in a different location. But it's all true, as Betsy Dorminey confirms: 'There was a house of a certain historical value that was getting ready to be demolished by a church of all things, and the workmen uprooted it piece by piece and carried it off!'

Despite their vast wealth, all four band members could still be spotted on the town, in the bars and clubs. To some, they gave the impression of mid-30-somethings who had never grown up. UK journalist Mat Snow, who came out to interview them in the early 1990s, says:

> I had a really good time, mostly thanks to Peter Buck and Mike Mills, who remain my two favourites. They're both very, very smart cookies, both big rock fans, especially Buck. Back then, at their height – when they were selling most records and also when their records were of a high quality – they were very self-assured without being cocky. I think the collegiate background really helped, oddly enough, in that they had stayed true to their school and a certain type of studenty, not dressing-down exactly but . . . they weren't living in Hollywood. They were very into the student life. In many ways they were like those perennial students. You go to a college town and you see people still there, ten years later and they can't move on because they're having too much fun. You're hanging around bookshops and coffee shops and you're going out drinking and

taking drugs and there's women you can lay and there's the nice atmosphere of a liberal arts college establishment. They had that sense about them; that they were musicians, and millionaire musicians at that, almost felt incidental.

For Nikki Sudden, their, or rather Michael Stipe's, self-assuredness crossed the boundary into arrogance: 'They did two secret gigs at the 40 Watt while I was there. I went up to Michael Stipe afterwards, the next day, and said, "I thought you were really good last night," and his words were "Thanks, we always are." I thought, thanks a lot, I won't bother paying you any more compliments.' Stipe's coolness might be attributed, according to Sudden, to the way he viewed other musicians who wanted to record with band members as a potential threat. But it might also be evidence of an attitude problem, an ego, a competitiveness that showed itself at certain times and to certain people.

V

By 1990, not only were the members of R.E.M. local and global heroes, they were also respected citizens. Their opinions carried great weight politically, and their words and lyrics were greeted by the music press with grave and deep reverence and speculation. '*The mayor says hello now*,'[14] was how Bill Berry wittily described the band's newly won respectability, but it was a respectability built on solid hard work. Rich entrepreneurs they may have become, but R.E.M. were also vociferously politically active. For them, 'think global, act local' was no rhetoric. In fact, for a few years post-*Green*, the band not only punched its weight locally, but also gave its support to a variety of good causes at national and international level. This political activity should, however, be seen in the wider context of pop activism in the 1980s, and also, the inherent and, so it seemed to many, insidious hypocrisy of the music business. At the height of apartheid, Queen, the show-stealers at Live Aid, found it quite acceptable to play Sun City in front of an all-white audience.

Protest and pop had achieved some sort of reconnection in the 1980s, but there was an overall feeling that the chosen spokespeople had, in the main, neither the deftness of touch, nor the fire in the belly, of their counter-cultural forebears. Plus, they were marginal and marginalised. Anglo-American youth were supporting Reagan/

Bush and Thatcher/Major in their droves. Stipe's revolt was less bound up with style than, say, Morrissey; less to do with the imaginary and more to do with practical support. Together with their legal and managerial entourage centred around Jefferson Holt and Bertis Downs, Stipe and the rest of R.E.M. not only vocalised a sense of outrage at the Reagan/Bush era but also funded attempts to fight Republicanism on a grass-roots level. And, while Morrissey's brilliant vignettes came laden with emotional difficulties and camouflage, Stipe, although richly allusive himself, at various stages dropped the guard of self-protection, stripped away irony, and sang songs of unfiltered power and political passion.

So, from the late 1980s onwards, the band busied themselves with local politics, adding their voices and their money to the liberal democrat cause. When journalist Andy Gill visited the Athens office in the early nineties, the evidence of band philanthropy was all around:

the Earth Day Award for Environmentally Responsible Business; the Athens-Clarke Heritage Foundation Inc. Award for Support of Historic Preservation in Athens; similar plaudits from the Georgia Environmental Council and the Georgia Special Olympics; a signed photo of the Athens YMCA basketball team that the group sponsors; a letter from John Cage thanking them for donating a tape-loop to one of his projects; and – perhaps most desirable of all – a signed photo to the band's manager Jefferson Holt from none other than Burt Ward, better known as the Caped Crusader's sidekick Boy Wonder.[15]

In Bertis Downs they had a trained advocate who would attend local meetings and speak persuasively in public for various good causes. At the top of the list was the issue of historical preservation. Athens was a discrete entity, a historically rich and beautiful city, but its close proximity to Atlanta meant that there was an ongoing struggle in the minds of many Athenians between wanting the town to be prosperous and wanting to retain an identity separate from that of the state's capital. Central to this assertion of civic pride was the importance of retaining existing historical artefacts such as the impressive neo-Grecian architecture, which the 'good ole boys' of the Republican cause, funded by big business, would cheerfully demolish to set up a new fast-food chain outlet. 'Mike, Michael and I have all lived close together in the same neighbourhood, in the same houses that we bought in the mid-1980s,' says Bertis Downs in 2002. 'We care about our neighbourhoods.' He goes on:

Athens is a very interesting town. It's about one hour fifteen minutes away from a huge metropolitan area. We have the advantage of being able to go in to Atlanta for entertainment, sports and the airport, even dinner and a movie, but we're not a suburb. The cutting issue of local politics in the last few years has been us retaining our special identity, not to be reduced to one of the faceless millions of suburbs that surround all the major cities of America. Happily, we still have about 30 miles of countryside between the outer limits of Athens and the suburbs of Atlanta. Over the years we've gotten into all sorts of disputes, from radio towers going up in historical locations to a civic centre being built where they were going to tear down a bunch of warehouses and a firehouse, to various candidates getting elected to office. Almost always the issues to us seem to be growth, that is, inappropriate growth, versus preservation and quality of life, right down to issues such as bicycles and traffic control. We're not experts in these things, but we are keenly interested and we go to meetings and try to read up. We've sponsored speakers coming to town, held workshops, given money at different times to different organisations and it's all been done for one reason – altruism. Well, it's partly altruistic, because we want to help out the town, and it's partly selfish, in that we want the town to stay special and a place where we want to live. We've put our money where our mouth is and tried to keep Athens a special place.

R.E.M., a multimillionaire rock group signed to a multinational and multimillion-dollar record label, a label with corporate interests as diverse and as potentially destructive as any big business, saw no contradiction between being on the side of the little man in Athens, but on the side of capital when it came to their own business. The alternative, to set up their own record label, retaining almost complete autonomy, did not appeal to them. It would have forced the band to agree on policy as a four-piece, and the perils of having to agree would have proved divisive. That said, the band have retained the tightest of controls over their music, refusing to license songs for advertising (an approach by Microsoft in the mid-1990s was apparently rebuffed), and have also consistently refused any corporate sponsorship for their tours.

'Bless R.E.M. for sticking around – mostly,' says Betsy Dorminey. 'They've been model corporate citizens. They've spent all sorts of money on local charities and helped old buildings and have been very, very socially responsible. For example, in the late 1990s Bertis fought against a large public hospital which he lives close to and which has been trying to gobble up the neighbourhood there. He was one of those people who would stand up and speak very effectively at community meetings to say, "You don't need to demolish all these houses to make a parking lot, you can leave them as houses." There was a move to demolish a hotel and to turn it into a drug store. The neighbourhood was against it, and Bert was very effective in communicating with the drugstore executives that they would not be making a good move. As R.E.M.'s lawyer he had a lot more credibility.'

The individual band members have also put their wealth to active use in the 1990s to help local people, as Betsy Dorminey reveals:

There was an old girls' school that had an interesting, round, theatre-chapel type building. One of the locals, an older man who has since died, although his widow still lives here, had been a very strong and early proponent of preserving buildings in the community. He had undertaken to get funds together to restore this building. If you go into that you can always see that Michael Stipe has made a contribution, Bertis Downs has made a contribution, and their names are on the wall along with all the other little names who have contributed to the restoration projects. You'd expect most of their money to go up their noses. I expect Bert has a lot to do with the fact that the impulse has gone all the way to fruition.

They're really putting their money where their mouths are, which I think is much more admirable than the usual liberal line that 'the government should pay for x, y'. They're not saying there should be government healthcare to look after the people who work for me, they're saying, I'm going to establish a programme that's going to supply pensions and health care for the people who work for me, which Bertis did at the Athens office. They're using their funds to do privately what a lot of the liberal elite think should be done at the taxpayer's expense.

There was a story in connection with a little building that Michael owns. It houses, I think, his studio upstairs and a natural foods grocery store downstairs. It had been owned by a little old lady. Her husband had died and it was on the market and a lot of people were interested in the property, it was a neat little building. My understanding at the time was that he paid well over the asking price for the building because he thought the widow should get that money. Now that for me really is putting your money where your mouth is.

For the local Republicans, R.E.M.'s support for the Democratic faction was a colossal headache. Matters came to a head when the Democrats put a certain Gwen O'Looney forward as their mayoral candidate. O'Looney, who lives just a few doors down from Bertis Downs, was not only a woman, but also an ex-hippy, into the counterculture and all its freethinking. A graduate of the University of Georgia, she was with the Red Cross for over a year during the Vietnam War, and had worked in Atlanta and New York before coming to Athens in 1980 to work as a social worker running drug and child abuse prevention programs. When O'Looney ran for mayor in 1990, very few gave her a chance. However, she was elected twice during the nineties, each time by a tiny majority. R.E.M.'s advocacy and money were crucial, and probably tipped the balance in her favour both times. For the first time, the Athens Republican elite had to work with a true progressive, and Athens Inc. were right behind their new liberal mayor.[16]

'Gwen was never taken seriously,' recalls Bertis Downs. 'She was a woman, she was a social worker, and every single mayor up to this point had been a white man, typically from the conservative establishment. She won twice and won the first time with the prominent backing of the band. They gave her some credibility and early donations, which helped her get her message across to about 51 per cent of the population.'

In the late 1980s and 1990s, R.E.M., and particularly Michael Stipe, would espouse good causes increasingly visibly. Voter registration, safe sex, Greenpeace, environmental disasters – all were valid enough issues for Michael Stipe to talk about on national TV, often in the form of short messages to camera shown on the likes of MTV. At the MTV video awards in the autumn of 1991 he was dressed in half a dozen T-shirts which he removed one by one for the camera, revealing directives such as 'rainforest', 'love knows no colours' and 'handgun control now'. He was brilliant at slogans, though one of his best, from back in 1988, 'STIPE SAYS / DON'T GET BUSHWACKED / GET OUT AND VOTE / VOTE SMART / VOTE DUKAKIS', went unheeded.

R.E.M. were a liberal, democratising voice within the music business. The band felt a genuine affinity with the disenfranchised: 'Well, just because these things [social ills] don't touch us personally doesn't mean we aren't affected by them,' Peter Buck contended. 'You've got to believe that what's happening to the lower man is an indignity to all men.'[17] The Reagan/Bush years were politically reactionary, the Gulf War at the end of 1990 and beginning of 1991, a forceful show of American Imperialism under the leadership of George Bush, the last US president old enough to have served in World War II. R.E.M., along with the likes of U2, Tracy Chapman, Sting and Peter Gabriel, became the public face of music industry liberalism. 'If you asked people in the town and in the government whether Athens Limited is a political force, they'd say, absolutely,' says Athens-based journalist Ballard Lesemann. 'I think that's a real asset.

> For example, the building (a cool two-storey building from earlier in the century) which houses the Grit restaurant would probably have been torn down. Whole neighbourhoods have been refurbished because of their attention. It is weird to remember that Pete Buck especially used to say that he couldn't care less what some rock star says about political stuff, it's none of their business, how dare they? But when they got into a position where they were millionaires, they probably felt an obligation to do something assertive and to be active one way or another. I don't think they're doing it to pat themselves on the back. A lot of them give to charities, particularly AIDS foundations, because they've lost a lot of their friends through AIDS. Bill Berry donates a lot of his time and money to a

Tourette's charity in town. A close friend of his, Rick Fowler, a recording engineer and musician, has Tourette's and was misdiagnosed for a long time. So, I think they do practise what they preach. If they were in it for the money, purely, then they wouldn't be making the music they're doing. They'd be cranking out the same old music that got them signed to the major deal anyway.

Although the band presented the media with a united front on any political action they might take, there was, of course, dissension over certain issues, as Mike Mills reveals: 'Actually, what you normally get is that one person is against something that two, or, pre-1997, three, might be for. But out of respect for the people who disagree, those discussions tend to stay in-house, just because we'd rather not let people know where the divisions lie, so people can't exploit them for their own purposes.'

One such issue was scientific experimentation on animals. In 1990 Peter Buck told *Rolling Stone*: 'Michael is involved with People for the Ethical Treatment of Animals – we're not. I agree with a lot of their goals, but I wouldn't feel real comfortable supporting them, because I'm wearing suede shoes. I eat meat, you know? I am against most testing on animals, but I have some friends who have AIDS, and I'm not gonna say you should stop using animals for AIDS tests.'[18]

The downside of this reasonably high-profile activism was that it opened up a can of worms concerning personal motivation. To some R.E.M. were, on the one hand, issuing statements on the environment, on big business, and castigating conservative politics, and on the other hand profiting from the benefits of being signed to a major label, Warner Brothers, the very personification of the capitalist structure that caused such inequality in the first place. R.E.M's supporters could, however, rightly claim that the band were bringing much needed attention to a whole variety of important issues at a time when the debate within youth culture was sterile and when youth felt demotivated. R.E.M. may have been a major rock act, with all that that entails, but their support of causes was discreet and consistent. They did not lease out their music to be used in commercials, nor did they accept corporate sponsorship for tours, or guest as music-biz celebs to wail to some appalling song recorded for charity. And they were not afraid to speak their minds, even to their political allies. As the straight-talking Peter Buck recalls in connection with Tipper Gore's misguided Parents' Music Resource Center, an organisation set up to proscribe 'dangerous' music: 'It probably wasn't a very fair thing to do because we had this disagreement at a benefit and they were invited,' recalls Buck.

> But I thought to myself, she's a very smart woman. I respect her and her husband. So, what does she decide to do with her time? Basically she gets all these right-wing idiots together, makes them a political force, and then lets them go. I told her that it was insane, that she was wasting time with these people, and that there were hungry children just two blocks away from this fuckin' place. I told her that the educational system in this country sucked, there was no health care and all you're worried about is people listening to records? And she gave it to me right back! She wasn't overly polite about it either. I respected that in her. Then Al came over, and there's actually a picture of me pointing a finger at her and her pointing her finger back at me. At the end, we shook hands and walked away. When somebody who's really bright, and together, and on the right side, decides to waste her time like that, it's galling. I voted for Gore, but I didn't go out campaigning for him and I know a lot of people didn't because they thought, Tipper's gonna be in there and what's she gonna do? She'll go right back to blaming the record industry for children being shot to death. If you're worried about kids, why don't you get some handgun control going? But that's not a popular stand in America, so forget it.

VI

After the *Green* tour, the band had unofficially decided to take a year off, an extended sabbatical and the first in their decade-long career so far. Financially secure and successful, for the first time in their careers there was no need to hurry into another album or promotional campaign. The 'Groundhog Day' scenario of album/tour/album had been an enormous strain on them.

But, within six weeks, the band, minus Stipe, were back demoing songs at John Keane's studio in Athens, Georgia, at the start of possibly the most creative three years of their career. 'Oh, I just recall this as a wonderful time,' says Mike Mills. 'We were one of the biggest bands in the world. We were doing music that was creatively very satisfying. We were enjoying ourselves very much.'

'My job in the band is to get people excited about doing things,' says Peter Buck. 'I do a lot of pre-work. I write a lot of songs beforehand and arrange things, while the other guys tend to come in and feel the moment and then work, which is a perfectly valid way of doing things. I was thinking of doing something more acoustic that time. Having said that, on the first day of rehearsal – well, Bill and I are always earlier and the other guys are always late – he sat at the drum kit and I picked up the guitar and we played for about two minutes. Then he just looked at me and said, "fuck this". He threw down his sticks and picked up an acoustic guitar. I walked over and picked up my mandolin. Every year playing 150 shows as a rock band was too much – we just thought it was time to do something a little different.'

Peter Buck, the musical conceptualist, had decided to move the band further in the direction of the acoustic songs on *Green*. Mills was happy for Buck to take this lead: 'We've always been interested in how R.E.M. can do different types of music. I enjoy playing so many different types of music that I don't have a problem with whatever Peter wants to play. If I ever have any strong desires to suggest a direction we should go in, I would certainly do that but I enjoy Peter's creativity and I enjoy the directions in which Peter wants to go.'

One day during one of those demo sessions for the new record, Peter Buck played a doleful, yearning and utterly bewitching melody on the mandolin which was to become the sonic centre of a new song. With no chorus, it would have a lyrical theme of emotional possessiveness and an almost spiritual intensity. It was above and beyond what would pass as a radio hit in 1991. One of the serious songs in pop, it would be one that changed their lives unalterably, for both good and bad.

8. 'THAT'S ME IN THE CORNER', 1991–94

I

Between 1991 and 1994, the world went mad for R.E.M. and R.E.M. went a little mad in return. With an estimated 30 million album sales in this period, but, significantly, no major tour, R.E.M. asserted themselves as rivals to U2 for the title of biggest rock band in the world. This was not, however, achieved without a price.

In early 1992, Peter Buck attended the Grammys, just one of dozens of award ceremonies to which the band were invited during this period, in his pyjamas. He had put on a bit of weight, grown his hair longer, and his sideboards bushier. Later, there were tales of him spending six months in bed ordering pizza and drinking red wine. There were silly tales of him as a heroin addict living on the streets of San Francisco. There were also true stories, in 1993, of him packing his bags, leaving his wife, Barrie, and heading off to drink tequila with cowboys for six months in Texas and Mexico. Peter Buck mentioned one obsessive fan in New York who had pretended to be him, as he told Mat Snow in 1992: 'This sort of thing goes on and I find it amusing. We live in a weird world anyway, and what I do makes it that much weirder.'[1] In 2002, Buck revealed:

> I had an impersonator. I think it was in the mid-80s. People would come up to me and say, you owe me twenty dollars, and I'd say, what are you talking about? One of the people who worked for us went up to this guy and talked to him for a full minute before she realised that it wasn't me. He apparently had

it down really well. His girlfriend called the office one day and said, 'Is Peter still with the band?' They said 'yes', and she said, 'Well, where is he?' 'Well, he's in Europe, on tour with the band.' 'Well, I've been living with this guy called Peter Buck who plays with R.E.M. I thought we had this great thing. When he went out to get cigarettes, I looked in his wallet for an address and I found his driver's licence. It says his name is something else, what do I do?' And they said, 'Get out of the house right now, and call the cops.' I don't know if they ever charged him with anything.

The whole thing was weird, but it didn't really affect me. It's not as if the person had stolen my whole identity, he had just pretended to be me. It may not be fandom, it may just be a con guy. The poor bastard probably figured, he has to look like me, he might as well get something out of it. Apparently he was really good. In the mid-80s every time I'd go to New York because it's a small club scene up there I'd bump into people who would say, you owe me 20 dollars for a cab, or, you owe me 50 dollars for speed. I'm like, 'What? I've never met you before in my life.' On a couple of occasions I've bought people drinks and said, sorry, it's not me. I don't have to borrow money from people. You know why they picked me, though? Because I'm less famous than Michael and I wore thrift store clothes in those days. We didn't have our pictures on the records, so it was kind of easy to get away with it.

Funnily enough, we got a phone call two years ago from our English record company asking whether Peter was still married. 'Yeah.' 'Where is he now?' 'He lives in Seattle.' Apparently I'd been photographed on the cover of some magazine with an Italian starlet that I'd got engaged to. It wasn't me, and I felt sorry for whoever the starlet was. I had to write her a letter.

But, back in 1992, there were few thoughts of a jocular nature for Buck, whose marriage to Barrie was over. 'I think the bad time was before we split up to tell the truth,' says Buck today, now a father and happily remarried. 'I actually felt really liberated when I packed my bag and moved out. I'm not blaming her and I'm not saying it was all her fault or all my fault – these things happen. Sometimes people don't realise that they're not suitable for one another until it is too late. It was kind of tough, and kind of rough, but once I had actually packed my bags, got out of the house, threw myself in the car and took off, I felt great. I was still a pretty young guy. I had made millions of dollars and was driving this car, sleeping in 19-dollar-a-night hotels, and drinking tequila with old cowboys. It was kind of cool.'

Although, in interviews, Buck had professed his love for Athens, and Mike Mills had predicted gloom and doom in at least one interview should any band member leave town, the fact was that remaining in Athens with his ex in town was not an attractive proposition. Barrie Buck would take over the beautiful house the two had shared and would continue to run the 40 Watt Club, while Buck would fall in love with Stephanie Dorgan. Dorgan would run the Seattle venue, the Crocodile Café. They would have twins, named Zoë and Zelda, in 1994. For Buck, life in Athens had simply become too public:

> Ever since we got successful back in 1983, some people do get resentful. It's a really small town and a huge amount of attention is focused on R.E.M. It got to the point where I couldn't blow my nose without it making the newspapers. I remember the thing that really blew my mind was that I went in a shop and they had T-shirts on sale and I bought some T-shirts and the next day someone came up and said, 'I hear you spent about a thousand dollars on clothes yesterday.' I said, 'No, the T-shirts were on sale for $2.99 and I bought 30 of them.' So that's 90 dollars'-worth of T-shirts, which I wear to work every day.
>
> Every taxi driver in town knew our address. Kids would come into town and drivers would drive them by, and people would show up at our porch. At two in the morning there'd be a knock on the door and there'd be five kids from Gaston, Alabama. It all got really small. I mean, the dating scene in a small town is just ridiculous. And I had personal reasons. I love Seattle and I love the West Coast. I love the South too and I'm glad to be back, but I can't live in a small town again.

Michael Stipe was learning very quickly how to deal with fame. His approach was to put on something of an act for the media, to reinvent himself as a mystifying anti-hero, down with popular culture but up with the latest Hollywood show gossip. His circle of friends seemed to confirm the belief that famous people can only really be friends with other famous people. He hung out with Kurt Cobain and Courtney Love, with actor River Phoenix, and, on one occasion, with miserablist Mancunian singer Morrissey.

'The temperament is the same. The sense of rationale is the same. I was surprised that it was so easy and compatible,' is how he recalled the meeting.[2] He would cold-call famous people and befriend them. The need to be almost exclusively around creative people over-whelmed him. His features had become gaunt, his face a little lined, his goatee turning grey. He refused to give interviews. His thinning hair was almost permanently concealed by a variety of sloganeering baseball caps. He wore one at the Brits, and at the Grammies in early 1992, with the stark legend 'White House Stop Aids'. Freddie Mercury died in November 1991 and the media speculated all too intrusively on Stipe's physical wellbeing.

'When I met Stipe for the first time in 1985, I thought he was shy, diffident, awkward, but trying to communicate,' recalls UK journalist Mat Snow. 'Stipe the second time I met him was very different from the first time. He was playing a part, in 1992. He was perfectly pleasant but the deal was that he wasn't going to be interviewed. He was hanging around the R.E.M. office and we exchanged small talk and I was trying to lead him into saying more, but there was no way he was going for it.'[3] Stipe had always been an odd interviewee. One suspected he found the whole process painful at worst, tiresome at best. Interviewers commented on how Stipe would drift off in deep concentration, struggle to find the correct words to express his ideas. His language was a strange mix of the arcane and the trivial; not many rock idols of the 1980s used the word 'herewith'. Stipe avoided all talk of his sisters, his parents, his partners, and his down time. He spoke exclusively about his art, but in such a way as to avoid attributing any literal meaning to any song he had written. He was, in short, a paradoxical and intriguing interviewee, and one who gave little away. The fact that he refused to give interviews for *Automatic* merely added to this sense of the enigmatic.

Although Buck's personal life was going through an upheaval and Michael Stipe was undergoing something of a personality change, it did not dim their creativity in any way. In fact, if anything, it appeared to enhance it. For their friend Bill Berry, however, it was very different. The spark was going out of him. Slowly but surely, he was falling out of love with the band that had made him a household name. He became less interested in playing gigs, less interested in listening to new music, much happier back home in Athens. 'Even when we were doing *Automatic For The People*, which most people think is our best record, he was ready to get out of the studio really fast. I don't think he worked past five or six on any day. He'd say, "I'm done, I'm gonna get something to eat and go home." He just wasn't into it.'

Finally, the remaining member, Mike Mills, was about to undergo something of a character change, morphing from a bespectacled 20-something boffin into a heavily ironic showman. Still single, he was the hardest partygoer in the band, and perhaps the most personable, certainly the most accommodating to approaches by fans for autographs and five minutes of his time. Fast-talking Peter Buck could be hilariously funny, but he had an edge to him which Mills manifestly did not. Both grounded R.E.M., while Stipe and Berry became increasingly more eccentric, operating 'a little closer to the fringe', as Mills would say. By the end of 1993 Mills would have split up with a long-standing girlfriend, and grown his blond hair long, to look like a Las Vegas version of Colonel Custer. In the autumn of 1993 he road-tested his famous nudie suit (for more on Mills' Nudie suits, see p. 245). Brash and brazen, Mills was sartorially sending up his nerdiness.

And, although this may be idle speculation, it also appears that the Jefferson Holt/Bertis Downs management team was also undergoing something of a change too. Downs' public profile was much higher, and that of manager Jefferson Holt concomitantly lower. As ever, any dissent or disharmony within the ranks would be kept well away from the media. For the moment at least.

II

The blame, if that is what it is, can be levelled fairly and squarely at one song, one video. 'Losing My Religion' made the difference between a successful career at the margins of popular music, and massive, mainstream popularity and acceptance. 'There've been very few life-changing events in our career because our career has been so gradual,' opines Mike Mills. 'If you want to talk about life changing, I think "Losing My Religion" is the closest it gets.' Whereas Michael

Stipe might be bothered in Athens by a relatively small number of overzealous fans, now he would be looked at, spoken to, pleaded with and admired around the globe.

'Losing My Religion' is one of R.E.M.'s best songs, maybe even *the* best – a song with no chorus and a mandolin as the lead instrument. It modulates between major and minor chords and fits Stipe's keening voice perfectly. 'It was written on the mandolin,' affirms Buck. 'I know it reaches people, and I love playing it, but when we play it it's like just the big hit and you get this energy. I'm not sure I feel the same feelings I felt when I first wrote it, or when I first heard Michael's lyrics, but because it is an audience favourite it always gives you a huge boost of energy.'

The vocal itself was a single take, and is all the more powerful for it.[4] There were simply no other songs like it in the spring of 1991, and it stood out in all its strangeness, reaching the Top 20 in the UK and Top 5 in the USA. The success was all the sweeter since sage Warner Brothers had told the band that their choice of lead-off single would be commercial suicide. The single sold strongly throughout the world, but, more importantly, it provided the perfect advert for the accompanying album, *Out Of Time*. Some pundits might have predicted a global tour to cash in on the success of both album and single but, really, there was little need. MTV guaranteed the band exposure and, for the first time, mainstream rock radio came to the band's rescue with heavy rotation for the album's singles. '*Out Of Time* was, and still is, by far and away the biggest hit we've ever had,' says Mills. 'It was worldwide, it was massive. Without "Losing My Religion", *Out Of Time* would have sold two or three million, instead of the ten or so it did. But the phenomenon that is a worldwide hit is an odd thing to behold. Basically that record was a hit in almost every civilised country in the world.'

Stipe's brilliant lyric simultaneously commented on his own stardom and updated the love-song-as-surveillance strategy developed on the Police's 1983 lyrically creepy 'Every Breath You Take', a song Stipe has admitted was a prime influence on his own lyric.

That's me in the corner
That's me in the spotlight
Losing my religion

Trying to keep up with you
And I don't know if I can do it

Stipe the pop star and Stipe the lover are transfixed in the glare of the klieg light of his lover's gaze. The song is a metaphor for Stipe's fame: one is seduced by it, one welcomes it, but it comes at a price: the loss of privacy and the loss of identity. 'Losing your religion' actually means to be at the end of your tether and was a Southernism even his fellow band members thought obscure.

Ironically for a band so antagonistic to industry-norm videos, it was the video for 'Losing My Religion' which would make the single such a massive commercial success. It was the band's first-ever lip-synched video, thereby making the entire performance simultaneously more intense and also more human.

The inspiration for Stipe's astonishing performance is perhaps an equally astonishing performance by David Byrne of Talking Heads. In the 1981 video for the classic 'Once In A Lifetime', Byrne can be seen contorted, twitching, sweating, his body jumping as if subjected to electro-shock therapy. Byrne returned the camera's gaze with a glare so penetrating and so unsettling. His performance was based on that of a preacher. The sheer showmanship, commitment and rhetoric of the performance (if not the content) given by preachers had made a deep impact on Byrne, and for 'Once In A Lifetime', he stylised the preacher-performance as pop performance. Stipe's performance in 'Losing My Religion' comes from the same tradition of mimicry, and it is no less powerful in its effects. Hitherto Stipe had absented himself from videos, or had appeared sheepishly in the margins. Now he too fixes the camera's eye in this confessional. He twists his torso, flails his arms in arcs, and rotates across the floor-space like a top. His legs and feet seem nailed to the floor. A more idiosyncratic performance one could hardly imagine.

What R.E.M. did with the video was what pop stars at their best always do and that is to make the genre a wider receiver for cultural ideas. In this instance, they drew on high art and translated it for MTV. This wasn't dumbing down so much as enriching, taking the mannerism of the Italian artist Caravaggio and the experimentalism of Russian filmmaker Andrei Tarkovsky and turning them into something special, something pop. Central to this translation process was the video-maker himself, Tarsem Dttandwar Singh, a 30-year-old

Indian director with a penchant for the quasi-religious. The video itself unravelled through a series of pietas, or mini tableaux. Tarsem Singh won six Video Music Awards for his brilliant work.[5]

Out Of Time was a fine record and a huge international hit, but it alienated certain sections of the traditional R.E.M. fan-base. Representative of this viewpoint is writer and academic Geoff Ward. 'I abandoned them after *Green*,' he said in 2001. 'I felt in the eighties they were the only new band really worth listening to, and they became part of my life-soundtrack. However life wasn't that good for me in the eighties, and it suddenly got better in the nineties. So I probably stopped listening because I felt free of the 1986-9 period, when I was very fucked up and miserable. So it wasn't their fault. Having said that, I didn't like the one with "Losing My Religion" and "Shiny Happy People" half as much as *Green* or *Fables Of The Reconstruction*. I know that's a bit like saying you never liked David Bowie after he started wearing make-up, but there you go. I thought it was calculating and commercial, and that they'd lost their interesting swampiness.' In the first half of the 1990s R.E.M. would develop a huge fan-base, but the original cult following started, one suspects, to drift away.

Of course, the next single didn't help. 'Shiny Happy People' is probably the only real musical mistake the band ever made. Released in the summer of 1991, it became another major hit, and the first R.E.M. single to reach the UK Top 10. It was also, to many, proof positive of the band's new over-commerciality. The riff, the vocal duet with the self-consciously screwball Kate Pierson of the B-52's, the lyric and the oh-so-ironic video were turn-offs. 'By the time they did "Shiny Happy People" I had kind of signed off,' concludes Athens journalist Ballard Lesemann. 'Maybe it's in the spirit of fun. You had Kate from the B-52's singing on that record, but at the time I thought I'd rather listen to an old record by the Fall. They got a little goofy.'

Over ten years later, it is a song the band members now feel unfairly stereotypes them. It was, after all, a rather brave song. As one critic commented, probably apocryphally, writing songs to make teenagers depressed is about as difficult as shooting fish in a barrel. Writing songs about happiness, fun, joy or plain silliness without them sounding trite and misguided is a very much more difficult task. 'It's a good song; it's a quality piece of work,' says Mills. 'The trouble is, it's hard to write happy positive songs. It's easy to write angry, dark songs, but it's hard to write happy songs and, when you do, people assume that you're taking the piss, and that one really isn't. It's sort of a happy song and, as such, it seems a little out of place in our *oeuvre*. People seize on it for a number of reasons. I just think that it's a really great song that I don't really want to hear again!'

R.E.M. had recorded some tongue-in-cheek stuff, of course, including 'Stand', 'Pop Song '89', and 'Underneath The Bunker'. The difference was that 'Shiny Happy People' was the song that hit pay dirt. 'You know, it's a great song, I don't ever want to play it live, but it's certainly entered the lexicon,' says a resigned Mike Mills today. 'I certainly hope that that isn't the first thing they think of when they think of R.E.M., but sometimes that's just the way it is.' One imagines that Jay Boberg and the rest of I.R.S. were in a state of apoplexy when they heard the single. For five long years they had dreamt of just one unadulterated singalong pop single to plug, and then, three years after leaving the label, here it was. 'Fucking ironic', is all Boberg says.

It wasn't so much the song that caused the damage, but the video, possibly the gayest ever to be given such exposure on international television. Stipe sings with a smile so beaming and so manufactured, while 40-something Kate Pierson resurrects the good-time Athens party scene as pastiche. Mills plays an upright bass and long-haired Buck a mini-sized mandolin, while Berry stares to camera with *faux* gormlessness. Dancing around them is an assortment of brightly dressed, smiling everymen and women. The video's supersaturated cheesiness is actually quite depressing.

Within weeks, fast-talking, wisecracking, leather-jacketed Denis Leary began pummelling the song in a series of MTV monologues. The band couldn't complain; the channel was, after all, supporting them to the hilt at this point. But Leary's withering, high-profile attack on the band raised the twin spectres of 'sell-out' and 'backlash'. Were R.E.M. really bothered by Leary? 'Nah, not really,' says Mills. 'I mean, he was kind of annoying, but I didn't give it a whole lot of thought. I only saw it once. I just thought, here's another guy full of hot air.'

'Shiny Happy People' was the low point on an otherwise strong R.E.M. album. If *Green* was pleasingly eclectic, and still carried the brashness of Indie-America, *Out Of Time* was more of a piece musically, more matured, but perhaps with less vibrancy and less daring. 'With mandolin, you tend to use more breathy, wooden instruments,' concludes Peter Buck. 'So there are acoustics and strings and stuff.'[6] Ten years on from 'Radio Free Europe', this is the sound of technically excellent musicians with a desire to explore non-rock elements, and *not* the sound of alternative rock. 'I never use that word,' says Buck. 'I mean, I don't know what that word means. For me it's just a classic rock album. It's of an ilk, if not as good as, things by Nick Drake or Van Morrison, although not influenced by them, because I know that Michael has never heard Nick Drake, and I doubt if he's heard more than one Van Morrison song.'

Seattle grunge, Nirvana and *Nevermind* would explode later in the year and initially make R.E.M.'s new music sound quaint by comparison. John Michael Stipe would certainly disagree with this assertion. He told journalist David Stubbs that ' "Losing My Religion" came at a point when alternative music had finally, after however many years, been co-opted into the mainstream . . . but there were so many bands who fell by the wayside who could have and should have been heard by a lot more people – but never were.' So, R.E.M. were simply the fittest in the indie gene pool. They survived when countless other strains of the college rock bacillus died out. This may be true, but the new R.E.M. music, although hardly traditional middle-of-the-road fayre, had none of the new-wave youthful aggression of *Document*. That said, in the first half of the 1990s, R.E.M. were definitely hip. Mike Mills puts it like this: 'Sometimes, if you're in a band, it's your time. And from 1990 to 1995, that was pretty much our time. It was just the shape of the wave, and that's how it goes for most bands. We did some incredibly good work, we were touring, and we were fashionable. All those things just came together at that one time.'

Out Of Time had some unexpected musical excursions, such as the dalliance with rap on 'Radio Song', a collaboration with KRS-One which was a wearied, though ironic, attack on the current state of pop radio. The unity of sound was, in part, to do with the fact that, whereas on *Green* the non-rock elements such as the accordion and mandolin were often used at the overdub stage as strange sonic sweeteners, on *Out Of Time* the band wrote in the rehearsal studio on mandolin, organ and acoustic guitar. These instruments were now at the *start* of the process, rather than at the end. They made tracks such as 'Half A World Away', a song with the added oddity of a harpsichord line, one of the most beautiful ever recorded.

'I think *Out Of Time* was certainly more realised than *Green*,' concurs the album's producer, Scott Litt. 'You see the balance shifting from guitar records to more involved/produced/arranged records. So *Out Of Time* had real string arrangements with 12 or 14 or 16 pieces on a lot of the songs, and violins and violas and cellos.'[7]

Although the music showed a new earnestness, the lyrics were typically playful and kept us all guessing. The band toyed with the idea of calling the album *Fiction*. Stipe wanted his public to know that the love songs on the album were not drawn from personal experience but were imagined states for imaginary people. He told *Q*'s Andy Gill: 'I wanted to call the album *Fiction*. I thought that was descriptive – all the songs are basically fictions, they're all love songs. At one point we thought of calling it *Love Songs*, but that seemed a little too stupid. And *Out Of Time* seemed appropriate: thematically, the record deals with time and memory and love . . . One of the reasons for writing an album of love songs is that I didn't want to be known as just the political activist singer of a band. I think it's important to point out that just because I've moved to an I/me lyrics or I/You type of lyric doesn't necessarily mean that I've experienced everything in those songs . . .'[8]

The emotional highlight of the album is unquestionably 'Country Feedback', an astonishing song, recorded in one take, and totally improvised at John Keane's studio in Athens. Stipe calls it one of his 'vomit songs', an almost unconscious out-spilling of a jumble of emotionally surrealistic images, free-formed on mic. 'Sometimes I just open my mouth and *blaagh*, there it is on the page,' Stipe told *Q*'s Adrian Deevoy.[9] '"Wendell Gee" is like that. "Country Feedback", which is my favourite R.E.M. song on record, is like that. That's so beautiful. "Try Not To Breathe". "These Days". I just woke up and there was writing on the page and that was the song.'

'By 1991, I had purchased an Otari 24-track machine and a Trident mixing console. This enabled me to make more professional sounding recordings, and get more serious major label projects,' recalls John Keane. 'It also made it possible for R.E.M. to do part of their albums here, in addition to the demos. Sometimes the demo versions would end up on the album. This happened with several songs, including "Country Feedback". Peter, Bill and Mike had just laid down a nice acoustic track, onto which Peter suggested I overdub a steel guitar. Once Michael had added the vocal, Bill looked around and said, "You know what guys? I think this song is finished. We don't need to re-record this one"'

'"Country Feedback", for example, was not even a song. It was words on a page that hadn't even been put into an order,' is how Stipe described the composition to journalist Paul Zollo. 'And I went into the sound booth, strapped on the headphones, sang it, and that was it. That was the version we kept . . . The words were written down on a piece of paper but I had no idea how many times I was going to repeat a certain line, or that "it's crazy what you could have had" would be used over and over again.'[10]

Although 'Losing My Religion' is the song most of R.E.M.'s public would pick as a favourite from *Out Of Time*, hardcore fans, and perhaps some of the band members themselves, might disagree. Fan Stine M. Olsen says that its magic is not fully realised until played live: 'My favourite R.E.M. song is the live version of "Country Feedback". It's a song I listen to when I need to heal myself, when I go through really hard times. The song lets me get in touch with my emotions, so that I can work with them and then move on. The song has a cathartic effect on me, more than any other song. The structure is actually very simple, as it is the same chord pattern repeated over and over. But the melody builds up to a climax (when Michael hits that high note "it's *crazy* what you could have had") and then calms down slowly, ending with a guitar solo. The lyrics don't make any literal sense to me, but they still make sense in a way. The way Michael sings the song is also very important. He looks so emotional when he sings it, so you get the feeling that he feels something very strong for this and he really means it. Too bad Peter's wonderful guitar improvisation is not included on the album version.'

The song was indeed a test for Buck. His beautiful guitar lines use feedback to stunning effect as he follows Stipe's haunting vocal as it twists and circles and folds back in on itself. Live, he often sings it with his back to the audience, emotion so raw that the singer has to avert his gaze. 'It's a love song, but it's certainly from the uglier side,' Stipe told *Q* in 1992.[11] 'It's pretty much about having given up on a relationship.'

We've been through fake-a-breakdown, self hurt
Plastics, collections.
Self help, self pain

EST, psychics, fuck all.
I was central. I lost control. I lost my head
I need this. I need this.

'Country Feedback' showcased Stipe's ability to encode his unconscious onto tape. 'Me In Honey', on the other hand, is testament to his astonishing ability to hear melodies where none had existed. Stipe was given a piece of music based on the repetition of just two chords, and on top of it he grafted an astonishing melody which, when the time came to track the record, he would sing with Kate Pierson. The two voices float on top of the basic pulse, their keening, melismatic style reminiscent of Celtic folksong. 'It just rocked. It felt great, over and over; the riff, the repetition of it was beautiful. To me. I like really dumb, repetitive things[12] . . . With this record particularly I've chosen a certain point of view, or character, that I want to get across,' Stipe opined. 'For instance, in "Me In Honey", the idea of pregnancy from the father's point of view. Which, as far as I know has never been seriously addressed in music. With the dubious exception of Paul Anka's "Having My Baby".'[13]

Out Of Time is curious in that it has less of Michael Stipe than any other R.E.M. album before or since. 'Radio Song', 'Shiny Happy People' and 'Me In Honey' are duets. Mike Mills sings the breezy 'Near Wild Heaven' (at one point considered for the album's title track)[14] and 'Texarkana' (which he also provided some lyrics for),[15] while 'Endgame' is an excellent instrumental. 'Belong', again with some banshee-like wails from Stipe, includes a semi-mumbled recitation rather than a traditional vocal performance.

It's an album that has gone down as being a rock landmark but, on reflection, even one of the band members agrees that that assessment might be a little too generous: 'When we did the record I felt proud of it, but in retrospect it does feel a bit patchy,' says an honest Peter Buck. 'I wouldn't say it was one of our weaker efforts though. People always put it on the classic list, but, well, *Automatic* is a lot better. There is a lot of good stuff on *Out Of Time*, but now I think of it, I probably would have just stuck on all the B-sides like 'Photograph', 'Free World Baby', 'Fretless'. We were changing from one kind of band to another kind of band, so it's a kind of interim record.'

III

Out Of Time was a transatlantic Number 1, yet the band hardly celebrated the event at all. Other major rock acts might have turned the occasion into a massive media jamboree, but for R.E.M., it was simply a pleasant development, a time for personal satisfaction. 'I was there in Georgia when *Out Of Time* went to Number 1 in America,' recalls Billy Bragg. 'I think Peter had a beer and that was about it. Don't get me wrong, they were ever so pleased about it, but they were more concerned about getting into town for this meeting where the council were debating whether or not to knock down the old fire station. And they went to the meeting and invited all these wonderful Southern middle-aged ladies who'd come to town to defend this historic building back for a party.'[16]

There was no tour in the offing, but the band did play a series of one-off promotional shows. In London that March, they appeared twice as Bingo Hand Job, with Billy Bragg, Peter Holsapple, Robyn Hitchcock & The Egyptians and the Chicksaw Mudd Puppies sharing the fun. These intimate gigs at The Borderline have gone down in fan legend yet, at the time, they garnered mixed reviews. For some the 'relaxed' atmosphere was more akin to a 'shambles'. Jefferson Holt took the stage to introduce the band as they played acoustic versions of mostly newer material. 'It's great to be back here at Wembley,' joked Stipe. 'It's great you could come out. I hope nobody paid too much money for a ticket.'

The following month they recorded a set for MTV *Unplugged* in New York, solidifying their credentials as authentic rockers who could play 'proper' tunes live. This was music that could be busked on acoustic guitar. In an era of digitalisation, recycling, sampling and rap, it was a reminder of pop's original power to charm through song, rather than through sound collage. Whether this made it better is very much an open question. For every R.E.M., a band brimming with ideas and beautiful melodies who chose, for the moment, to perform in a more acoustically driven mode, there were hundreds of groups and seemingly thousands of journalists who championed the new authenticity; as if any artist who sang with 'real instruments' was automatically a superior version. In the first few years of the 1990s the battle lines would be drawn between the technologically mediated and the traditionally motivated.

Peter Holsapple, who appeared on the same stage as Bingo Hand Job, was now unofficially the band's fifth member. A talented singer-songwriter in his own right, he had played on the *Green* tour, and the *Out Of Time* album. However, the rather abrupt termination of his tenure as valued sidekick provides something of an insight into the inherent problems of accommodating extra members within the band set-up.

The band had a history of producing new material during sound checks. For example, 'Driver 8' from *Fables* had been composed to a large degree while sound-checking on the *Reckoning* tour the previous year. According to one version of events, on one occasion on the *Green* tour, Peter Holsapple began playing a bass line that would eventually find its way on to the final version of 'Low', the moody, slow-paced, deliberately dirge-like song on *Out Of Time*. Holsapple asked, perhaps with some justification, for a songwriting credit, but his request was turned down flat.

R.E.M. had long established a precedent that all monies should be divided equally, but only within the nuclear family of Mills, Buck, Berry, Stipe, Holt and Downs. True, Jerry Ayers, a member of Limbo District, had been the sole beneficiary of a writing credit for 'Windout' and 'Old Man Kensey'. But Holsapple's case was different. Here was a friend who had played with the band for a number of years. As a longstanding songwriter, surely he would know what constituted arranging and what constituted actual songwriting? As R.E.M.'s career progressed they felt the need to explore new musical possibilities with new musicians. But this desire to enrich their experiences was potentially at odds with their original and, so it seems, unshakeable conviction that everything had to be kept in-house. At the root of the dilemma in compositional terms is the grey area that exists between composing and arranging. Current R.E.M. collaborator Scott McCaughey puts it like this: 'In general, I have too much respect for R.E.M. as songwriters to stick my nose in where it isn't wanted. Michael may sing or read a lyric-in-progress to me, or Peter or Mike play an instrumental song idea, and invite comment. I usually end up voicing encouragement, because they know what they're doing, and I almost always dig it! I fancy myself a pretty good (if weird) lyricist, but what Michael comes up with usually blows my mind. I can't imagine thinking I could do better.'

According to Peter Buck, Holsapple was not in on the composition of 'Low' at all, and demands made by Holsapple's manager as to the involvement of his charge in future R.E.M. records were deemed unacceptable. Buck gives a fascinating insight not just into the Holsapple disagreement but also into the perils of working with session musicians and what constitutes songwriting within the R.E.M. camp:

I think we kind of patched it up. I wrote that song 'Low' and taught it to people in the band while on stage. Michael wrote the words. A year later, basically everybody who had worked on that record came to us and said, we need more money because that record did so well. Peter Holsapple said, well, I co-wrote it. And I said, no you didn't, because I wrote it myself and I taught it to you, Mike, Bill and Michael, and then Michael wrote the lyrics. I explained to him that the reason that Mike and Bill get credit for songwriting is that they slept on the floor with us and made $5 a week for years, whilst he was getting a fair amount of money to back us up and he didn't have to do all the hard work. And he understood, I think. I honestly don't think he had anything to do with writing the song. We were going to hire him again to play on *Automatic*, and his manager, Jimmy Ford, said, 'Look, you'll have to submit demos to me, and if the demos are even a little bit different from what's on the record, then he's going to get a songwriting credit on anything that's changed.' I'm friends with Peter, Mike has lent him money, but I'm not going to send demos to some guy's manager. So we said, no thanks, we can't work under those circumstances.

I do sessions all the time with people, and I have never asked for a songwriting credit. I've actually written bridges and rewritten songs for people. If you're getting paid a lot of money per week or per hour, it's kind of a given that, if you add something to it, it's still their song.

My feeling is this: there are different ways that people record. Some will go into the studio and will not really have an idea of what they want to do. They say, well, we've got a couple of chords, let's work on them. I'm not that kind of person, I've got it pretty well formed out in my head and I know exactly how it's going to go. I'll sit with people and teach it to them on their instrument, note for note, and what comes out is really close to what I have in my head. That doesn't mean that things don't change a little bit, and people have latitude in coming up with their parts. But that's what a session musician is.

What is tough is when you have someone who's making a whole lot of money per year who's hiring someone who's making a lot less money a year, and songs kind of appear out of jam situations. That's an iffy prospect, and that never happens to us. If we're jamming, I'll never use anything from that. That's quite a perilous situation when you're using people who are not in the core group, because you never know who will come up with a riff that will change the song or rhythmically change it. On 'The Lifting' [from *Reveal*], Joey [Waronker] started playing that weird beat and we speeded it up. My demo was slower, and we were trying to make it faster, but I wouldn't have come up with that beat. But, Joey knows that's not songwriting. Songwriting is coming up with the chords, melody and words.[17]

With Holsapple out of the equation, and Buck in the middle of the personal trauma of a failing marriage, the band reconvened to record their eighth album of new material. When the session began, Buck once again took the lead in suggesting a new direction. Although, after the intricate sound of *Out Of Time*, there was initially a strong case for making a rock'n'roll album, it soon became apparent that the new material was even more downbeat and introverted than before.[18] R.E.M. decided to hire John Paul Jones, bassist and keyboard player with Led Zeppelin turned producer and arranger, to orchestrate four new songs. Scott Litt was retained as producer, his fourth album at the controls. This new album, though, would be a song suite, a seamless collection which moved away from *Green* and *Out Of Time*'s jerky switches in style.

In terms of atmosphere, the new material echoed earlier work, perhaps matching the template of *Fables Of The Reconstruction* and parts of *Lifes Rich Pageant* in its sorrow and pain. Again there was a high casualty rate for would-be songs. Buck, Mills and Berry worked on several dozen songs, possibly all of equal merit, but only those that inspired Stipe would be fertilised by the addition of melody and lyric. With no tour planned, the band decided to record the album in several locations, and to enjoy the good life while doing so. Preproduction work took place at John Keane's in Athens, then sessions moved to Daniel Lanois' Kingsway Studio in New Orleans, Bearsville Studios in Woodstock, overdubs at Criteria in New York, Miami, strings at Bosstown Studios in Atlanta and mixing in Seattle, at Bad Animals. R.E.M. may not have been touring, but they were recording on the road.

IV

Automatic For The People is regarded by Peter Buck and Mike Mills, and by most critics, as being the finest R.E.M. album ever recorded. With one exception, the music on *Automatic* hangs together beautifully. What makes the album is its atmosphere – sombre, withdrawn and contemplative. Each song is like a poem or a sonnet. Each compresses emotion; the beauty is in the tension, then the release of emotion. Most of the songs on the album are tributes or memorials or testimonies to people, places and states of mind. On 'Try Not To Breathe', an elderly man holds his breath and tries to imagine what it will be like when he's dead. 'Monty Got A Raw Deal' portrays media intolerance of homosexuality. 'Man On the Moon' is a eulogy for a dead comedian and, by default, a dead pop star, both of whom, according to urban myth, are supposedly still alive. 'Sweetness Follows' is an epitaph to give solace to the bereaved. Like a photograph, 'Nightswimming' recaptures the spirit of lost youth. 'Find The River' is a testimony to the human spirit's endless quest for spiritual enlightenment, and was released as an epitaph for a dead friend. These are big themes, handled brilliantly by Stipe as lyricist, and mounted near perfectly by the band. Like the sonnet, these songs are a 'moment's monument'; they make everlasting fleeting feelings of sorrow, pain, regret and love.

'I love the seductive, melodic quality of their music,' says photographer Stephanie Chernikowski. 'I love the brooding, I love the darkness, I love the incredibly deep sorrow. I think that, when you're down, music like that keeps you alive.' This is why *Automatic* has taken root in the hearts and minds of so many people. It's R.E.M.'s most human, and humane, album.

The low-keyness of the album was not wholly reflected in the band imagery of the times. For the first and last time in their careers, the band was promoted with a stylish left-field cool. The Anton Corbijn shots which adorned the CD booklet of *Automatic For The People* were moody black-and-white studies of four successful and unconventionally glamorous rock stars. They captured the band unprepared and off-guard, but they were mounted with a new sense of the chic. The homespun nature of their 1980s iconography replaced by stylised poses from the man who had turned Depeche Mode from Essex Boy sartorial misfits into icons of nineties cool. The Corbijn images of R.E.M. were a testament to the band's colossal international status. This was a band at the very peak of its career.

R.E.M., together now for a dozen years, began to speak of an end to the whole band project. Stipe told *Rolling Stone*: 'We have a pact to keep going until the end of the millennium. Then we'll break up. That way, we'll hopefully avoid being one of those dumb bands who keep going, not realising how bad they are.'[19] *Automatic*'s themes of loss and mourning reflected the band's sense that the rock world that had given them life, was changing unalterably. It has that whole sense of loss, of turning thirty,' opines Buck. 'The world that we had been involved in had disappeared, the world of Hüsker Dü and the Replacements, all that had gone, all those bands were breaking up or in the process of breaking up. We were just in a different place and that worked its way out musically and lyrically.'

With speculation in the media at its height concerning Stipe's health, the context in which the album was received was of endings and closure. Even the Manic Street Preachers, arguably Britain's best new group at the time, got in on the act. On 11 December 1992, in a statement that matched Elvis Costello's 1979 comment to members of Steve Stills' band and Bonnie Bramlett that Ray Charles was a 'blind, ignorant nigger' for shock value, bassist Nicky Wire told 2,500 fans at the Kilburn National: 'In this season of goodwill, here's hoping Michael Stipe goes the same way as Freddie Mercury pretty soon!' A pissed-up Costello had made the remark in the course of a pub argument. Nicky Wire, actually a closet R.E.M. fan (the Preachers' 2001 song 'Year Of Purification' sounds like a *Reckoning* outtake), made it on microphone to thousands of fans. In deep shit, he was asked to quit the group, so widespread was the disapproval of his remarks. Wire's comments were stupid and sick, but the actual target wasn't so much Stipe as rock-star hypocrisy and, in true Manics style, the end was meant to justify the means. 'I'm sure Stipe hasn't got AIDS anyway, that's one of the sick things of it all, he's just using his sexuality to make a point again.'[20]

Peter Buck, for one, was extremely angry, at least initially:

My first inclination was, do you know what? I'm gonna get on an aeroplane, fly to Wales, go to his front door, and I'm gonna punch him out! Then I thought about it. I don't know the guy. He seems like a smart guy. I'm sure he was baiting the audience and people have done that before. I don't think you should judge someone by the stupidest thing they've done in their life. Elvis Costello had his little stupid things in the seventies. His point was, it's OK if you lambaste Glastonbury or Phil Collins or whatever, but one of the sacred cows . . . ? Well, they're one of those bands who said all rock'n'roll is homosexual. Well, I've always believed that to be true. It just seemed a stupid thing to say about Michael considering what he'd said in the past. I've seen those guys, I've done award shows with them and none of them can really look us in the eye. But I don't hold it against them.

It was generally surmised that Stipe was, if not gay, then at least bisexual. By not making any kind of public statement quashing the rumours of ill-health, was he merely milking public sympathy for commercial gain? Stipe answered the charge, but not until much later: 'Rumours went around that I was sick with HIV – I wasn't and I'm not but I really don't want to answer it. To go public and deny I had AIDS would denigrate those who are suffering from HIV and AIDS. I didn't want to be like that (makes pushing away motion). I didn't want to dignify the rumour. When I did speak I think a lot of people were relieved, I didn't realise there was actual concern for me.'[21]

Did any of the band members give credence to the idea that Stipe might be dying? It seems not, as Peter Buck assures, but it was a crazy time, a time when malicious rumours troubled the band and their family and friends:

Not to be rude about this, but he's closer to being a hypochondriac than he ever is to being sick. He's the healthiest person I know, and he sees the doctor all the time. I knew that he wasn't [HIV-positive]. The fact of the matter is that we hired a private detective to find out where this stuff was coming from. We kind of figured it out. I don't know the guy's name, they wouldn't tell us, I think they were afraid that we would go and beat him senseless. But it was a guy in LA who was calling up mutual friends of ours and saying, oh, Michael's got AIDS. He was also saying that I was a heroin addict and living on the streets barefoot. This was at a time when we had sold 20 million records in three years. People would call me about it and I used to say, well, you know, I've made so much money that I could check into the Four Seasons Hotel and have it sent over in a wheelbarrow. For years that was the thing: Michael's dying and Peter's a junky living on the streets. It was basically this one guy who was semi-associated with us, who we'd once met or something. I think Michael might know, but I certainly didn't know. He would call up and say, 'I'm a friend of Peter's, I'm really worried,' or 'I'm a friend of Michael's, I'm really worried.' Then these people, who were indeed friends of ours or who had met us, would flip out. They would come to us and talk to their friends, and it kept spreading and spreading. It was weird – just this one guy and all those rumours. Years later people still talk about them, and that was ten years ago. You've just got to accept those things; these things happen.

With media speculation and concern for Stipe growing, the new album simply seemed to reflect the funereal themes hinted at in the media. There's a trademark minor-keyness which casts a ghostly, melancholic and sorrowful shadow on the proceedings, and, as Mike Mills remembers, a musical unity too: 'There are some keys that Michael often likes to sing in, but that has changed over the years. You'll find that on *Automatic For The People*, a great many of the songs are in D or G. In fact, that's the first question the tennis star Jim Courier asked me when he met me in the early 1990s, why are all the songs on *Automatic* in D and G!'

The album's opener establishes the creepy tone. 'Drive', the first single and, like 'Losing My Religion' a song with no chorus, is, in its bleakness, one of R.E.M.'s strongest songs. Buck's acoustic guitar gives way to a blistering guitar part and a soaring orchestral arrangement by John Paul Jones. The song plays around with David Essex's 1973 hit 'Rock On', both musically and lyrically (with the 'hey kids!' refrain and the echoey vocal), but the overall mood is one of gothic introversion, underlined by images of torture and druggy decay and Stipe's intensely unsettling moan which closes certain lines of the verse. 'The David Essex reference was very deliberate, but it's also a whack at George Bush,' says Mills.

Smack, crack, bushwhacked
Tie another one to the racks, baby
Hey kids, rock'n'roll
Nobody tells you where to go, baby

The change of tense from present to past conveys a sense of decay, of the finite, a sense that maybe you've rocked your last roll. If this was a lyric written by a terminally ill person (as was suspected at the time), then it was chillingly apt.

Maybe you did, maybe you walked
Maybe you've rocked around the clock
Ticked, tocked, ticked, tocked.

The basic track was a first take, and set the blueprint for the album: chamber music meets rock. 'The idea of putting string arrangements on every song really started with Peter,' remembers Scott Litt. 'That was a live recording. The electric guitars are overdubs, and then we overdubbed strings as well. But the basic track, which was Peter playing acoustic guitar, Mike playing bass, Bill playing drums, and Michael singing, is a live take in the studio.'[22]

'I was just looking for this thick tone,' says Peter Buck, 'and I remembered that Brian May had used a coin, so I played it with a coin to get a kind of heavier sound. But I didn't base it on anything by Queen, although I do like Queen quite a lot, the earlier Queen.'

The video, filmed in LA by Sheffield-born Peter Care, consisted of a stage-dived Stipe held aloft by a sea of fans. Picked out by searchlight and drenched in cold water, it was a powerful image of the pop icon supported, both literally and figuratively, by an obsessive audience. The outstretched hands moving in waves towards him, the video takes on a bizarre quality, the crowd reduced to a living organism, a unity, a whole, rather than a collection of individuals.[23] The arty video was actually terrific fun to make. Work went on till six in the morning, and everyone got drenched in water, band included. In a typically friendly touch, specially printed T-shirts were distributed to commemorate the day.

But it would be 'Everybody Hurts' the album's fourth single, and biggest hit, which would provide the most affecting video. A heartbreaking song, it started out as the runt of the litter.

' "Everybody Hurts" was something that Bill brought in,' recalls Buck. 'He didn't really know how to approach it. It was kind of a country song, and I kind of suggested an Otis Redding, "Pain In My Heart" sort of atmosphere for the song.' 'When we wrote it, we all switched instruments,' Buck had told Mat Snow back in 1992. 'Mills played drums, I played bass and Bill played guitar, and the demo was just the worst thing you've heard in your life – we were dropping beats, making wrong notes. We had to stop at one point, we were laughing so hard. But for some reason it really hit with Michael.'[24]

And hit it did. 'Everybody Hurts', is an R.E.M. classic. Stipe takes all the themes in pop that had long been dismissed as cliché, that stockpile of images with trite written all over them, and turns them into something simple and beautiful and raw. Lines such as 'When you think you've had enough of this life to hold on – hang on' are denuded of all schmaltz. In the heavily ironic 1990s, people were not used to a piece of artwork that can bring tears to the eyes, even after repeated listening. A plea to a would-be suicide case to 'hold on', 'Everybody Hurts' is the musical version of Clarence, the guardian angel who visits the helpless Jimmy Stewart figure of George Bailey in *It's a Wonderful Life*. In an echo, perhaps unintentional, of Bowie's 'Rock'n'Roll Suicide' ('gimme your hands, 'cos you're not alone'), Stipe sings, 'No, no, no, you're not alone'. In its general spirit and sentiment, the song also echoed the plaintive Peter Gabriel duet with Kate Bush from 1986, 'Don't Give Up'.

The video is simple, and simply distressing. A traffic jam of cars occupied by the bereaved, the emotionally tortured, the forgotten and the lovelorn forms the *mise en scène*. In a stroke of surrealistic genius, the participants take control, abandon their grid-locked cars to take control of their lives, break free from their sorrow and walk unafraid into the future. The video brilliantly articulates the feelings of deep sorrow followed by consolation and, ultimately, release contained in the lyric. For anybody who sees in MTV an unending flow of mediocrity, then in R.E.M. one sees art. The video, directed by Jake Scott, son of Ridley, won four MTV music video awards in 1994.

R.E.M. are aware from the letters they have received and the comments made to them by their fans that the song has meant a great deal to many people, and has, on more than one occasion, perhaps even made the difference between life and death. 'I'm certainly aware of that,' affirms Mike Mills. 'I've gotten enough letters from people who have told me that. There's universality to that song that's kind of undeniable and it feels good to be able to touch that many people that deeply.'

'I'm not ashamed or afraid of my emotions. And I'm not afraid to express them,' Stipe told Paul Zollo shortly after the song was released.[25] 'However you are taking chances of coming off really vapid or maudlin from time to time. And I would accuse myself of having done that a few times. Mostly though I've been OK about it. I don't like being whiny in songs. And I don't like being misread. Like "Everybody Hurts" was a real coup in that it could very easily have been really sappy and whiny and maudlin and stupid and for whatever reason it doesn't come across that way to most people.'

V

Other tracks on the album have moments of emotional intensity to rival 'Everybody Hurts'. 'Try Not To Breathe's' remarkable lyric is framed by a quite beautiful melody. It's possibly the best R.E.M. song never to be released as a single:

> I will try not to breathe,
> This decision is mine I have lived a full life
> And these are the eyes that I want you to remember

Old age, dignity, and death with dignity were themes hardly ever discussed in the popular music of the day. The song's beginnings were far more mundane: 'When we were making the demo, the microphones were really close to the guitar, so I tried not to breathe into them,' said Peter Buck. 'And on the tape I say, "Try not to breathe." Michael said, "That's a good title," and like an exercise he tried to think about why someone would try not to breathe. It's about an old man who's imagining himself dead and holding his breath to try to imagine what it's like to be gone.'[26]

'The thing I remember about "Try Not To Breathe" was that when I was doing the background vocals, it was just Scott Litt and myself because everybody else had gone to dinner,' says Mills in flashback mode. 'And I just kept on working and working, trying to find something that would fit. I was trying to feel a little John Lennon creeping in there, so when I finally hit that little riff Scott and I looked at each other and knew that that was the one – "the something to find" bit.'

'New Orleans Instrumental Number 1' continues the spectral mood of the album. Mills remembers: 'We did pre-production at Daniel Lanois' studio in New Orleans, a town that we all used to really love. There's a lot of ghosts in New Orleans, of one form or another, and it was a beautiful old-style house we were working in.' 'Sweetness Follows', an emotional song about grief and loss, is poised and graceful, and moves the R.E.M. sound closer to chamber music than folk or rock. 'That's a beautiful song,' agrees Mike Mills. 'The cello – it's just a beautiful touch.'

Stipe had been talking to someone who had the still from the film *The Misfits*, and the experience formed the inspiration behind 'Monty Got A Raw Deal'. The experience of 'in' gay actor Montgomery Clift is the thematic starting point to yet another beautifully crafted song. 'You know, knowing it's about Monty Clift, you can go anywhere you want to with the lyric,' says Mills, reminding us that no R.E.M. song is ever *about* just one thing. 'But yeah, it's just an idea what the poor bastard had to go through.'

With its wash of vocal harmony, 'Star Me Kitten' was an attempt to re-create the aggressively lush sound of classic rock hits such as 10cc's 'I'm Not In Love', regularly voted the best record of all time in UK polls, until ousted by the likes of the gruesome twosome, 'Bohemian Rhapsody' and Robbie William's 'Angels'. In an era in which even Frank Zappa had a 'caution: parental advisory' sticker placed on one of his albums, the band decided on a tactful substitution for the title with the word 'star' replacing the actually sung word, 'fuck'. Shortly before his death, Bill Burroughs produced a version of the song for an *X Files* soundtrack. It's hardly a tender song. In fact, it sounds as if it's being sung by a deviant or miscreant persona and, as such, prefigured Stipe's writing for the next R.E.M. record.

Automatic contains two up-tempo numbers. 'Man On The Moon' is now an R.E.M. classic. They'd be lynched if they didn't play it live and it's one of Mike Mills' favourite R.E.M. songs. It originated with Bill Berry, who contributed a sizeable part of the music. 'He started playing the verse part that kind of went from C to D, and fitted in the other stuff – the chorus and the bridge around it and the B sections,' recalls Buck. 'Bill wasn't that big on finishing songs. He'd come up with stuff and quite often show it to me. I'd say, "Yeah, that's a chorus, this is a verse, let's change keys and have a bridge here".' The band worked on it towards the end of the recording session, with Peter Buck writing the bridge. It was almost left off the album though before Stipe turned the song into a tribute to the late comedian Andy Kaufman. 'It's the one where everything else on the record had been done except this track,' affirms Mills, 'but there was basically no vocal yet. We were leaning very heavily on Michael saying, we really want this track on the record, you need to write some lyrics to it [laughs]. On the very last day he came into the studio with these amazing, amazing lyrics. He threw them down, and we threw the backgrounds on, and basically it was mixed and ready to go.'

'Man On the Moon' is now part of the canon; 'The Sidewinder Sleeps Tonite', a Top 20 UK hit, is not. 'No, we don't play it live, it was one of the few songs of Michael's that really didn't connect with me lyrically. I couldn't really get a hold of that one. I just don't think it's a great song all the way round. It's catchy, it's memorable, but I was just not a huge fan of it musically or lyrically,' says Mills. Peter Buck is not overly fond of it either, opining that it doesn't fit thematically with the rest of the album. This was a shame since 'Sidewinder' is a much better pop song than, say, its counterpart on the previous album, 'Shiny Happy People'. Punchy and vibrant, it's a happy song that doesn't sound trite. The subject matter (a homeless man who spends his time in a phone box) is classic Stipean eccentricity, and the interpolation of 'Wimoweh' inspired. The chorus of 'Call me if you try to wake her up' was written by Stipe to be deliberately unintelligible. With its nine syllables rushed over seven beats, it sounds like the ravings of a madman.

No, 'Sidewinder' is fine, it's the plodding, heavy-handed political rocker 'Ignoreland' that is the album's only real mistake. We can excuse R.E.M.'s failings, however, as the Reagan–Bush years were indeed so ghastly, and America seemingly so outrageously lacking in any sense of propriety, particular with regard to its own foreign policy and sense of history, that the dying regime deserved such a battering ram of words. America is a country able to ignore reality, to ignore what is going on in foreign countries in the name of American interests, and to ignore the fact that taxes on the poor had been raised, because the rhetoric claimed that taxes had been lowered (which they had, for the super-rich). Stipe feels better for having shouted, and wants us to use the song to vent our anger. But this is not the call to arms we would have been given when Stipe was a younger man and dreamt big dreams for his country on 'Cuyahoga' and 'Begin the Begin', and was proof that, for now, in 1992, pop and politics didn't match for R.E.M. The not wholly disagreeable music sounds muffled, and weirdly pomp-rockerish. 'That one was a tough one,' concedes Mills. 'We had a lot of trouble mixing it, and we disagreed about how it should sound. For me, it is a bit out of place, but we were so damned angry at Reagan/Bush that we put it on anyway.'

Much better are the two beautiful ballads that conclude the set, particularly 'Nightswimming'. The musical, with its circuitous piano line, reminiscent of 'Perfect Circle', was actually almost discarded. 'I was playing the piano bit at John Keane's studios and I remember Michael hearing it and liking it,' says Mike Mills. 'But I never thought it would amount to much because it was just a circular thing that kept going round and round and round. But it inspired Michael.'

The lyric looks back fondly, though perhaps not without regret, to the hedonistic days of late-night swimming romps in a lake near Athens called the Ball Pump.[27] It's a song about youth, about the less complicated world of a decade earlier. It's a farewell to youth as the band enter their mid-thirties, that awkward limbo world of neither young nor middle-aged.

'It's based on true events,' affirms Mills. 'Well, there was a lake just a few miles out of town where all our small circle of friends would go skinny-dipping after the clubs closed. There'd be us, Paul Butchart, DeLoris, the Love Tractor boys, the girl that "Camera" was written about, Carol Levy. You see, the big thing was that, back in '79, '80, '81, there were only really about 50 to 75 people that were into this kind of music. We'd go to the parties, we'd go to the clubs and we'd go to the Ball Pump, and there would be any number of these same 50 people, so it was a very tight circle of friends.' Peter Buck is typically far less dewy-eyed about that period, though even he concedes it was a significant time in the life of the band, a time of hedonism before AIDS, adulthood and addiction took their toll:

We would play on a Friday night, then drive out to the Ball Pump, go swimming naked, and then pair off. It was a pretty idyllic, carefree world, but then again there were a lot of people who went through that who destroyed their lives too. It was an amazing time for us. We all came out of it unscathed, but were a little more hardworking and smarter and focused. It was kind of like the Summer Of Love 1967 in 1980 and 1981 Athens. Everybody was really having this wild time and there was a lot of ecstasy around. Meanwhile we were working 360 days a year and we were part of it and not part of it. We'd come back into town and see people who had tried to commit suicide while we had been gone, so it wasn't all sweetness and light. None of us were ever heavy drug users, it was more the early eighties psychedelic thing. That kind of just ended. We were on the road for so long that, basically, we were in a van going from place to place, where the drug of choice is generally Budweiser out of a bottle. Like San Francisco in 1967, people started doing tons of coke, and then they started taking heroin to come down. We'd come back every six months and see it. There were these sorority girls who were out of their mind on heroin. And you thought, 'This is stupid.'

The second ballad, 'Find The River', has become an anthem, and a staple of the R.E.M. live set. Mike Mills: 'I think it's incredibly evocative and emotive, and very well realised. It's actually a demo as well. It's pretty much the demo version of the song. The thing about us is that we try and make the verses as interesting as the choruses. One thing about the way that we wrote was that, since we were writing without lyrics and melody at first, we always wanted the song to be interesting without the lyrics and melody. We had to be happy with what we were writing before we gave it to Michael. We could have done these three-chord things and said, OK, make it interesting, but, for us, we always wanted to try and have something interesting already there. I think that's why there's such depth to the songs.' Musically, the songs on the album were already well constructed and vibrant even before Stipe overlaid his lyric and melody. With such care and attention spent on the musical weave, it's little wonder many of these songs are timeless.

The packaging was a winner too, the bolted steel star an eye-catching design. The album title referred to a soul food restaurant run by Dexter Weaver (or Weaver D as he is known outside his family and friends). Weaver D's Delicious Fine Foods can be found on Broad Street, Athens, and Weaver is often asked to provide the catering for local R.E.M.-linked events. The restaurant itself, along with the Church (or what's left of it), are now landmarks for the R.E.M. fan. His catch phrase was 'Automatic'. Weaver D explains: 'I worked at a fast-food chain many years ago, and the manager informed us that if any of our employees didn't report for duty then all his employees had to work a double shift *automatic*. I also used to sell leather goods years ago on the streets, you know, leather neckties and things like that, and a man once informed me that if I didn't have a product on one day then I would have it on the next. So, I just combined both these things into the slogan 'Automatic For The People', meaning 'ready, quick and efficient'.

Of course, R.E.M. had to ask for permission to use the slogan. For Weaver D it was a life-altering event. 'Michael Stipe and Bertis Downs came into the restaurant the day after I had been burgled,' remembers Weaver D. 'They said, "we'll give you a sizeable amount of money for the use of your slogan". I immediately went into a coma! They asked me to get in touch with them in a few days and ask them for an amount that I needed. And I did. We worked it out.'

Weaver D's Delicious Roasted Peanuts were given away to media and radio in the autumn of 1992 as part of the press package marking the album's release. They now sell for $20 a bag at music auctions. In fact, Weaver D's is part of the R.E.M. pilgrimage in Athens. Not only does it sell high-quality soul food, but the R.E.M. connection means that fans and documentary film crews regularly appear outside the restaurant. Weaver D himself is a Motown fan. He doesn't know much R.E.M. music at all.

VI

R.E.M's most visible period of political activism was coming to an end. In fact, as the years went by, R.E.M. became more, not less, committed to political causes. It's simply that their charitable donations and support from now on came to be conducted on a more low-key, low-profile basis. The days of the grand gesture were drawing to a close. The band had simply grown tired of, and a mite cynical about, the impact their more vocal championing of causes was having. One final flourish came after 12 years of Republicanism, with the election of a Democrat President, Bill Clinton. And the saxophone-tooting Clinton was down with popular culture in a way that Bush and Reagan, already old men, patently could not be. After 12 years of misrule, of 'read my lips, no more taxes', of 'let's bomb Russia', of economic depression and political desperation, you didn't have to be a rocket scientist to work out that Clinton had to be a good thing.

In 1992, Vice-President-elect Al Gore, perhaps the stiffest American politician of his generation, visited Athens in search of some heavyweight youth culture backing. The result, at least to journalist Ballard Lesemann who witnessed the rally where Gore and R.E.M. shared the rostrum, was an embarrassment. 'It was kind of dorky in '92, when Al Gore, who was running for Vice-President, comes to Athens and Michael Stipe's on the stage with him. There's literally thousands of college kids out there, and Al Gore's trying to be hip, saying, "Do you know what? Bush and Quayle are *Out Of Time*, ha ha!", and corny shit like that. I'm sure Michael Stipe was thinking along with the rest of us, "Oh my God!"'

Mills and Stipe travelled up to Washington DC for the various showpiece events scheduled around Clinton's inauguration in January 1993. Buck turned down the offer and, instead, began his six-month sabbatical from the band in border country. 'I don't have any interest in meeting presidents or whatever,' he says. 'I'll vote for the guy, but I'm always disappointed with them when they get in office, because no matter what they say they're going to do, they're kind of wishy-washy. I'm just not interested in politicians.' Stipe and Mills, however, played a version of 'One' with U2's Adam Clayton and Larry Mullen Jr under the name of Automatic Baby at MTV's Rock and Roll Inaugural Ball in Washington DC. In May 1993 Berry, Mills and Stipe were given a tour of the White House and were feted on the White House lawn.

Some time around the end of 1993, or the beginning of 1994, Stipe, now 34, decided that, rather than enduring years of being tonsorially challenged and having to adopt that most loathsome of hairstyles for men with receding hair, 'the sweep over', he would simply shave it all off. Stipe wasn't bald, but his hair was thinning, and had been for five years. Having a baseball cap welded to his head was one option, but he'd been trying that for the last two years and was fooling nobody. Of course, some pop people use their chrome dome for dramatic effect. Eno, for example, 'ingeniously transformed his into some sort of monument to his enormous intelligence – as if the sheer force of his powerful mind has expelled the very roots from his head',[29] as Q's Phil Urr waggishly put it. With Stipe, on the other hand, his shaven head made him look sly, sexy and punky, in other words perfect for the new image and the new music the band began working on in preproduction in the autumn of 1993. Stipe unveiled his new look (along with his mum) in February 1994 in New York at the *Rock the Vote* party MTV held to honour R.E.M. for their work for voter registration at the last election. Clinton sent a videotaped message to be shown at the reception.

Automatic For The People had been a huge success just about everywhere, most particularly in the UK. *Out Of Time* and *Automatic* would eventually stay in the UK album charts for almost 300 weeks in total – an astonishing achievement – and the latter topped the UK charts on four separate occasions. R.E.M.'s music was now bought by just about everyone. Long-standing fans enjoyed the music's sorrow and gloom, new fans simply enjoyed the carefully crafted melodies. That R.E.M. were becoming hegemonic is shown by the following anecdote reported by journalist Jon Wilde.

'After the release of *Automatic*, R.E.M. were voted Top Act by the Metropolitan Police Gazette. Commented its editor, Detective Sergeant Philpot: "R.E.M. pulled two-thirds of the vote, which was a surprise because I'd never heard of them. However, my wife tells me that they write toe-tapping tunes and meaningful lyrics. That probably explains the breadth of their appeal. They're welcome to pop into any police station in Britain for a nice cup of tea and a fig roll or two." So, there we have it. R.E.M., the Great British Bobby's favourite, and the friendly face of caring America, the smiling side of alternative pop and the doyens of carefully crafted pop. How soon it would all change.'[30]

PART III
BIODEGRADING? 1994–2002

9. 'LOOK OUT, THERE'S A MONSTER COMING', 1994–96

I

In *Pygmalion*, George Bernard Shaw wrote wittily of how, in an act of almost Frankensteinian proportions, flower-seller Eliza Doolittle was turned into a 'duchess' in a Wimpole Street laboratory. Shaw created Eliza Doolittle at the very start of Western society's preoccupation with the 'star-making machinery', just before Hollywood became the multimillion-dollar machine we now know and love/hate, and just before the advent of the first celluloid stars of the silent film era. Fifty years on, sixties pop culture was starting to reflect on this stardom, and on its manufactured quality. Dating from 1967, 'Look Out There's A Monster Coming', a song by those English fruitcakes the Bonzo Dog Doo-Dah Band, sung by the late, great (and seriously out to lunch) Vivian Stanshall, eerily presaged how pop would develop in the two decades that followed. He addressed a theme that had always been part of popular culture, but which would come to dominate it in the years ahead: the limits of the pop imaginary. Just how far could popular culture go in creating a pretend world (and a remodelled person and personality) in real life? Stanshall told the tale of a cyborg – half man, half accessory – whose fascination with the mod cons of self-improvement transmogrified him. At the start of the song, Stanshall sings

> My image was wrong, I didn't like me
> So I changed my personality

However, by the song's dénouement, the accessorised sad-case is reduced to a modified mutant. It's a line that a certain Michael Jackson may have taken greater heed of if his own alleged facial reconstructions are given credence.

Please be gentle with me
I come to pieces literally,
Look out, there's a monster coming.

The mid-sixties was the time when cheap fashion hit the high streets, putting enormous pressure on the young to be fashion-conscious. On one level, Stanshall is merely poking fun at the shallowness of this. But his lyric hit on more than the desire to be chic and trendy. It also spoke about how popular culture could transform the everyday, how the process of becoming a star could be manufactured for us all.

The idea that rock stars could remake themselves artistically and sartorially, if not biologically, became essential, first in the 1960s, with the Beatles' bewildering array of musical costume changes, then in the 1970s, when rock stars such as David Bowie and Bryan Ferry wrote songs that deliberately drew our attention to the processes of remake/remodel. As we have seen, R.E.M. had been born into a quite different era, one that rejected the posed nature of rock music. Their music was arty, without the artifice. It was sincere, poetic and, at times, transcendent, without being ironic or theatrical. All this was to change. For, in 1994 and 1995, Stipe became a dissembler, a role-player, and R.E.M.'s music turned with it.

U2, surprisingly, were the first to jump ship, with *Achtung Baby*, one of the best rock albums of the 1990s, if not *the* best. The rootsy sounds of their previous album, *Rattle And Hum*, had been replaced with generous dollops of Eno-inspired late-seventies art rock, matched successfully with the funky dance beats that were breaking out like a dose all over guitar-rock at the time. Recorded at the Hansa studios in Berlin, the site of production of one of the finest alternative rock albums ever, Bowie's *Heroes*, U2 chopped up their sound and remade it for the 1990s, with Eno's help of course. What's more, to our eternal gratitude and relief, Bono finally recognised that he was in fact a bit of an absurdity, and began sending up himself (or an archetype of the earnest rocker) quite deliberately. At the same time, he sent up the rest of eighties rock earnestness too, so successfully that many rock listeners who had previously given up on U2 as hopelessly up their own arses suddenly thought they were vital and cool. Bono was The Fly, Bono was Macphisto, and Bono brought character-playing and silliness back to rock – and did it rather well. R.E.M. followed suit. U2's *Zoo TV* tour had sourced bits from various segments of popular culture, but had definitely been inspired by R.E.M.'s *Green* tour of 1989. For R.E.M.'s part, Stipe, perhaps unwittingly, reflected Bono's new sense of play and parody in his own work, for the first time very obviously written in character. *Monster* was the result, a triumph of style and contrivance over musical content.

R.E.M. and U2 were never really in direct competition though. Somewhere around the late 1980s, U2 became so commercially successful, and so obviously the biggest band in the world, that R.E.M. could never hope to achieve the same level of global fame. For a few years in the early 1990s, however, R.E.M.'s sales matched, and even outstripped, those of U2. With U2, one sensed a determined effort to be the biggest rock group on the planet. With R.E.M., one sensed that the aims and goals were different, less grandiose, less rock'n'roll. Apart from a generally healthy artistic rivalry, U2 and R.E.M. were the best of buddies. Theirs would be no Beatles/Stones or Blur/Oasis face-off. Rather, the two represented something of an alternative-rock luvviedom, both on the same page politically, both making music which was for a mainstream audience from a mildly left-field tradition of art pop/rock. Their music was melodic enough to connect with FM rock radio, but also sufficiently layered with intricacy and complexity to appeal to the serious rock snob too.

The two bands operate in the recording studio in rather different ways. While R.E.M. is a democracy, with U2 there is an enlightened despotism at work. Mark Howard, who worked with R.E.M. on *Automatic* and *Monster*, and with U2 on tracks from their 2000 album, *All That You Can't Leave Behind*, says: 'With R.E.M., there was an equal balance between all of them when it came to their songs and ideas. It wasn't like that when I worked with U2. Bono was the leader. Bono pushes the song. With R.E.M. it was kind of like an open group and everyone discusses it. In an R.E.M. session it's easy-going. With U2 it is down to earth, but it's full of tension. You're flying by the seat of your pants. Bono has a million ideas and he's got to try them all. You'd finish a track and then suddenly Bono would want to take the drums from the end and put them at the beginning, or redo a part, or whatever. He's always moving on. With R.E.M. it's much more kind of, this is what it is. The tension is not as intense.'

II

Work began on the new record in the autumn of 1993. A few months earlier the band had convened in Acapulco during Peter Buck's six-month sabbatical, and had devised a plan for the next two years, of an album followed by a world tour in 1995. Berry in particular was keen to tour, and was insistent that the next record had to rock. According to Stipe, the sessions for *Out Of Time* and *Automatic For The People* had begun each time with the intention of making a rock record. Each time, they ended up not making that record. The general feeling in 1993 was that another slowly paced album would be one too many. Having hit upon a winning artistic and commercial formula for *Automatic*, there could easily have been a temptation to record a 'son of' as follow-up. With typical curmudgeonly stubbornness, the band did the very opposite, following up their artistic masterpiece with an album so contrary that it didn't really even sound like R.E.M. at all. These were songs stripped of almost all the intricacy which had come to be associated with the brand name. Overdubs were kept to an absolute minimum. Timbres were grungy and dirty, Buck's lead guitar distorted, Stipe's vocals like before, further back in the mix, while, all along, various other elements played against this neo-glam rock sound – odd pulses, electronic beats, one-chord solos, drifty, repeating patterns of an almost avant-garde rock bent. This was a new sound.

'That was a "rock" record, with the rock in quotation marks,' is how Peter Buck now puts it. 'That's not what we started out to make, but that's certainly how it turned out to be. There's a nudge, nudge, wink, wink feel to the whole record. Like, it's a rock record, but is it really? "I Don't Sleep I Dream" is sort of rock, but it's totally discordant, and there are eight guitars hammering away on one chord. I remember when Thurston More saw us play it, he said, "What was that Philip Glass kind of thing you ended the set with?" I thought that was kind of cool, because, yeah, there was some Philip Glass in there that I knew was there, without referencing it. That and

Glen Branca, because I actually saw him perform once in New York in the 1980s, the 18 guitarists all tuned to an open E. So there was a little bit of that on that track in particular. It is our least direct record.'

The problem of course is the relationship between Americans and irony. The Brits are so used to having their pop music in quotation marks that 'honest' outpourings of rock emotion tend to be automatically disregarded as phoney. In America, the reverse is true. Fans and critics alike seek authenticity, frowning upon pop which is all surface and no substance. This was a major problem for R.E.M., because their new album was deliberately written to tease and provoke, and to source contrived and uncomfortable celebrity situations.

'People in America especially, they're so stupid. They can't get anything that has two layers,' says American musician Ken String-fellow, later part of R.E.M.'s touring and recording set-up. 'They see everything as it is presented to them, and they can't even read subtext. They couldn't get anything other than just looking at Michael Stipe on stage on the *Monster* tour and saying "What *is* he doing?" They couldn't get whether it was a reference to anything. Although the songs on *Monster* were popular as rock songs, the imagery around them was lost on 99.99 per cent of America. In Britain there's a bit more of a novelistic approach. There's a lot of intricacy that's much more pronounced in British culture than American culture. It's just a little more literary. And word play and being clever with your speech is respectable, expected even.'

So, what was so different about *Monster*, what was it that they didn't get? Released in September 1994, work on the album had begun almost a full year beforehand, with preproduction taking place in Kingsway Studio New Orleans, under the supervision of Mark Howard, who had also worked on *Automatic For The People*. As Howard recalls, the sound on the new album was more experimental: 'The bass had this tremolo sound on it. It was a more inventive session for them. Scott Litt came in when we were done and I handed it over to him. I played him all the tracks we'd laid down and he was pretty much pleased with everything.' Jefferson Holt and Bertis Downs also called in to hear the new material. 'They always travelled together,' says Howard of the then indivisible management twosome. 'They attended the session with Peter's guitar technician, Microwave. I had a preconceived idea about Holt and Downs from seeing them on television, and I just thought they'd be stuck-up or bigheaded. But it was the total opposite. They were more down to earth than a lot of other people I had ever worked with.'

Howard witnessed the birth of an experimental album, observing how Stipe worked from scratch to build up lyrics, while his friends traded musical ideas: 'Mills is very strong creatively in terms of melody, he and Peter Buck, they're the musically strong writers. Michael would be lying on the couch, singing. The studio didn't have a control room. It was open, like a big ballroom, and I went over to him with a microphone. He said, "Can I sing lying on the couch?" I said, "Yeah man, go for it!" So, I recorded it. If the band's playing, working out their parts, and you have lots of lyrical ideas and you don't capture them, then they're lost for good. Being able to put those vocals down helped him write the lyrics to a lot of songs on *Monster*. None of the vocals were actually used on the finished versions, because he asked me to erase them. In the past they had had problems with bootlegs and people getting hold of tapes. These were more like a scat, a sketch around the song. I videotaped something too, but they asked for the tape back!'

In February 1994 the band moved from Kingsway to Crossover Soundstage in Atlanta to continue work on the album. But the recording of the album was blighted. On Halloween night, 1993, Stipe's close friend, the actor River Phoenix, died from a seizure after a drug overdose. Stipe was devastated. 'Find The River', the sixth single from *Automatic*, was released a month later as a tribute. Then, in the spring of 1995, Mills fell ill. 'I had diverticulitis, an inflammation of Meckel's diverticulum, so you can look that up in your Gray's Anatomy, if you've got one.[1] I was only at the hospital for maybe three or four days, but it held up preproduction a little bit.' Then Berry had to return home to Athens with a bad dose of the 'flu. Stipe interrupted the schedule to visit his sister Lynda, who had given birth, and, in April, Buck returned home for the birth of his twins, Zoë and Zelda.

Overshadowing all this, however, was the tragic news which broke on 8 April – the suicide of Kurt Cobain. In Stipe, Cobain had found a role model. Tired of the existing Nirvana sound, Cobain had wanted a more experimental approach. Just as R.E.M. were heading towards a rock sound, Cobain looked at *Automatic For The People* and saw rich possibilities. The two had talked about a musical collaboration, and Stipe had sent Cobain tickets to fly out from Seattle to join him in Atlanta that spring. 'We'd been talking about touring together, and Kurt and Michael had talked about working together,' affirms Mike Mills. 'I think that there would certainly have been some sort of collaboration between ourselves and Nirvana had that continued.'

R.E.M. had been an influence on Nirvana and bands of their ilk; not, perhaps, musically, because early nineties music was not colonised by Byrds-influenced jangly pop, but in terms of attitude. 'You could stretch a point and argue that Nirvana were as much influenced by R.E.M. as they were by the alleged LA hardcore,' says writer Mat Snow. 'I think what R.E.M. did was not so much influence but to inspire a great number of rock'n'roll acts who were in some ways no more than bar bands with a twist to say, hey, it can be done.'

So, Cobain followed in Stipe's footsteps. He played around with gender, was famously photographed in a frock, and his vocal delivery, jumbled, garbled and slurred, was filtered through the wearied defeatism of his generation, and was reminiscent of the impenetrability of the early Stipe. 'Smells Like Teen Spirit' was a masterpiece of unintelligibility. Cobain saw Stipe as a man who had dealt with his own success with humanity. For his part, Cobain was riven with uncertainty and self-loathing, his career an unsolvable riddle. By early 1994, Cobain had become one of the most visible, and richest, corporate rockers on the planet. He had become that which he had set out to replace, and he hated his new role. Seven years Stipe's junior, Cobain was emblematic of Generation-X cultural politics, the politics of inertia, inaction, and nihilism.

Stipe could identify with this disenfranchisement, but, crucially, he was born in time to be touched by just enough baby-boom optimism to be able to see the merits of speaking out and direct action on social issues. Cobain, born after the baby boom but close enough to it to retain an interest in oppositional politics, was nevertheless a far more defeatist, world-weary and negative individual who reflected back on to Stipe a generational disappointment and a confused set of priorities.

At the very end of the session for their last album, R.E.M. had recorded a joyous tribute to a dead icon, 'Man On The Moon'. This time, the last-minute addition would also be an elegy, but no joyous celebration. In 'Let Me In', as chill a moment as any in their work, R.E.M. perform the obsequies, and bury Cobain in sound.

In 1994, Peter Buck and the Cobains were neighbours in Seattle. The Cobains had moved into 171 Lake Washington Boulevard East in 'ritzy Denny-Blaine, one of Seattle's oldest and most exclusive neighbourhoods', writes Charles R. Cross. 'Though Peter Buck of R.E.M. owned a house a block away, he and the Cobains were the exceptions in the neighbourhood, which was occupied by old money scions, society matrons, and the sorts of people who have public buildings named after them.'[2] In the first three months of 1994, Cobain was closing for business. He cancelled the Nirvana tour after playing *Terminal Eins* in Munich that March, turned down *Lollapalooza* and refused to practise:

'The only musical project Kurt planned was with R.E.M.'s Michael Stipe. Stipe had gone so far as to send Kurt plane tickets to Atlanta for a session they had scheduled in mid-March. At the last minute, Kurt cancelled.'[3] The extent of Cobain's R.E.M. infatuation can be gauged by the fact that the record he was listening to immediately before his death was *Automatic For The People*. 'Courtney would later find that stereo still on and this CD in the changer,' records Charles R. Cross, Cobain's eloquent biographer, in 2001.[4]

R.E.M. actually used one of Cobain's guitars on the album. 'He had a Kurt Cobain line of guitars and there were two prototypes,' states Buck. 'Courtney wanted me to have one of them because Kurt was a fan, and we used to live next door to each other. And so, with the song ostensibly about Kurt, without telling anyone I just kind of figured, well, Mike, why don't you use this guitar that Kurt's wife gave me? So I set him up with this crazy sound, and he played guitar and I played organ on it.'

After Cobain's death, Stipe would frequently be seen in media situations with Courtney Love, Cobain's widow, whose own group, Hole, was a sizeable, and critically lauded rock act in its own right. It was speculated that their relationship had gone beyond the platonic stage. Whatever the details of their relationship, it seemed to some that the whole idea of a Nirvana/R.E.M. liaison, and indeed of a Love/Stipe mutual appreciation society, was desperately close to the sort of rock aristocratic chumminess that was so loathed.

'I guess for me, I felt the most skin crawling when I saw Michael with Courtney Love and they're referring to each other in terms of how much they love each other,' says original R.E.M. producer Mitch Easter, no lover of Courtney or her music, or, perhaps more accurately, what the new breed of nineties rockers represent. It was a world of designer angst, when Hole, along with Trent Reznor and Marilyn Manson, made good music without it appearing in any way connected with the lifestyles they lived.

III

With *Monster*, its press and its yearlong tour, Stipe's public persona, like his lyrics, became confused. On the one hand, *Monster* was meant to be a sexy but detached comment on the nature of celebrity, and on the creepiness of fandom as pathology. Written in character, it set the real Stipe at a distance from the mask adopted for each song. On the other hand, Stipe's real-life demeanour seemed to confirm the suspicion that there was more than a hint of the real Stipe in the soupy world of *Monster*. Stipe, now 35, shaven-headed, lean and goateed, appeared like a born-again punk rocker in printed T-shirt and with quizzical glare. Journalists commented that, in interviews, Stipe could be temperamental, could drift off or snap with undisguised annoyance, or nervously talk around his feelings for Cobain and Phoenix. There was now, more than ever, a perception that R.E.M. was *Stipe's band*. 'It's strange when *Rolling Stone* announce their songwriter of the year: Michael Stipe,' a resigned Peter Buck told *Q* in 1995. 'Even Michael goes, "Well, those songs are presented to me to write lyrics to."'[5]

The *Monster* tour, launched with surprising ostentation at Luttrellstown Castle in Ireland, would see the band play night after night of high-energy rock to huge audiences, a scale of public acceptance that far outstripped that of their previous world tour, six years earlier. Buck however was exhausted before the show even got on the road: 'I had new kids; I was so busy that I couldn't even think about the professional end of it. The Castle thing was fine, it was just that I didn't have a baby-sitter, my wife was exhausted, I had twins and it was like, fuck, I don't know what I'm going to do! I got through it though.'

On its release, the new album caused a general wave of disappointment among fans and critics. It was certainly *not Automatic For The People* 2: 'It's a kind of cynical record in a way,' says Mike Mills with a mischievous laugh. 'The trouble with *Monster* is that it came immediately after *Automatic For The People*, and everybody wanted another *Automatic*, and they didn't get it. The contrast is so shocking. It's not like it's a smooth transition from one to the other, it's like a left-hand turn. *Monster*'s a very sexy record, there's a lot of hip-swivelling songs and a lot of dirty, grungy guitars. Not grunge the movement, but grungy in the sense of dirty and noisy. It was an album that was made to be taken on the road. We hoped we had songs that were fun to play live and not be overly studio-complicated.'

'I don't think it's our best record but I think it's better than a lot of people give it credit for,' is Peter Buck's assessment now. 'Some day there'll be a box set and there'll be four or five songs left off from that record and people will think there's some pretty cool stuff. We had about twenty songs.' On re-examination, *Monster* might be an under-written, under-produced and flawed set, but it swings with a vibrancy and a magic all of its own and, both lyrically and musically, it uneases and unravels celebrity more than any other rock album ever has.

Perhaps the key song on the album is 'I Took Your Name'. Does this song describe just an infatuation with another person, or does it describe the mood of the obsessive fan, the stalker, the fan who identifies so completely with the star that the two personalities merge together?

> I wore the clothes you wanted
> I took your name
> If there is some confusion, who's to blame?
> I signed your living will
> I smile your face
> I'm ready to close the book on NASA in outer space

The song, its sly riff an echo of the much earlier song, 'All The Right Friends', was a surprise opener on most of the *Monster* dates in 1995. 'Strange Currencies',[6] another R.E.M. song written in 6/8 time, updates the melancholy of 'Everybody Hurts' and does it well. This is stadium-rock balladry, with opportunity at the end of the song to sing along, as the lyrics cut out and the band repeats the overwhelming riff of the chorus. Once again, Stipe sings in character, and once again the emotional attachment borders on pathology. Is the persona here in love, or possessed? Is he rational or pathological? Is this even a love song at all, or merely a story of unhinged possession, an expression of Stipe's own discomfort with his status as media player?

The fool might be my middle name
But I'd be foolish not to say
I'm going to make whatever it takes, ring you up, call you down,
sign your name, secret love,
Make it rhyme, take you in, and make you mine.[7]

Another tremolo-heavy song earlier in the set, 'Crush With Eyeliner', deals with one of *Monster*'s other central themes, the interplay between the natural and the created, between the real and the fake, the themes looked at earlier in connection with loopy Vivian Stanshall and his 1967 blueprint. One of the central songs on U2's *Achtung Baby* had been 'Even Better Than The Real Thing', a glorification of the fake as superior to the real. Now Stipe answers the song with more explicit words of his own:

What position shall I wear?
And cop and attitude (you faker)
How can I convince her? (faker)
That I'm invented too?
I am smitten
I'm the real thing (I'm the real thing)
We all invent ourselves, and
You know me.

R.E.M. had been well and truly weirdified on these haunting songs of possession, double-bluff, personality construction and pathology. Stipe had fought shy of writing in the first person earlier in his career; now his songs were littered with personal interjections, but the 'I' wasn't him at all. In the records before and after *Monster*, Stipe would write in character too, but these later characters, for example the aspirant starlet of 'All The Way To Reno', were abstractions of himself, close to, but not coincidental with, his own character. The characters on *Monster* gave the impression of being beasts, crazies, stalkers and egomaniacs. They couldn't be anything like the 'real' Stipe, could they?

'The whole record was a kind of reaction to having people following us around to a big degree, making the news in all these weird ways,' is how Buck puts it. 'When I read the lyrics I thought, all these guys are totally fucked up, I don't know who they are, because they're not Michael. I would say that this was the only time where he's done characters that are creepy, and I don't know if people got that. He was getting out his things by acting out these parts that are not him. He took the mantle of front person to a degree he hadn't done in the past. Someone has to do it, and it's not going to be Mike or me, and to a certain degree on that record, and probably that tour, it was less like him than ever before or since. It is a record that is our least direct and our tour was the least direct. If you've seen us since then, Michael has been far more himself on stage. I think it was all character-driven in a way – let's be someone else for a while.'

The song with the strangest origin is the album's only big hit single, 'What's The Frequency Kenneth?' A superb riff drives this slightly pedestrian rocker through its four minutes, padded out, it has to be said, by a leaden solo from Buck. Mills is more than happy with the album's opener, though: 'It's a great song. A lot of that song was mine actually, and I remember trying to teach these convoluted chords which didn't seem to make much sense. But when we got everything together it held together nicely. Great video, too.'

The title, if not the song itself, pertains to a weird incident concerning droll CBS anchorman Dan Rather. Late one night in 1986 while walking on Park Avenue, he was punched from behind and knocked to the ground. Rather fled into a building and his assailant gave chase, punching him several more times and asking 'Kenneth, what's the frequency?'[8] It is now thought that Rather's assailant was William Tager, imprisoned for killing an NBC stagehand in 1994. According to the website RatherBiased.com, 'Tager was convinced the media had him under surveillance and were beaming hostile messages to him, and he demanded that Rather tell him the frequency being used.'[9] A good sport, Rather appeared with the band in 1994 on CBS's *The Late Show with David Letterman*.

The video for 'What's The Frequency Kenneth?' was the first time many R.E.M. fans had seen Stipe in all his Dalai-Llama-like glory, or the hitherto sartorially muted Mills replace gawkiness with cartoon-like costuming. He now looked simultaneously cool and amusing. Mills hit his mid-thirties suddenly single after breaking up with his long-standing girlfriend and, on entering another phase in his life, decided to change image too. In came the tousled long hair, the General Custer beard and the Nudie suits, five of which were bought for the planned tour:

Well, they're known as Nudie suits. Nudie was known as the rodeo tailor and he did all these country stars' outfits, and Elvis and stuff like that. He had a tailor named Manuel, and Manuel is the person I got my suits from. Manuel has a store in Memphis, Tennessee, and that's where I went to buy all these suits, because Nudie was dead and gone by the time I started buying them. You've got to have a sense of humour. I think they're beautiful and really fun to wear, but they're also supposed to make you smile.

I guess I was coming out of a long relationship there. Basically, one of the great life lessons I have learnt is to let things go. I was never really an anal person, but I had these sorts of rules about myself. Then I realised that these were very confining and there was no reason to be the way I had been in terms of how I looked in general with the hair thing and the suit thing. I finally had the self-confidence to do something like that, part of my thinking was that I didn't want people to be bored because they were stuck on the bass player's part of the stage!

Elsewhere on the album, the lyric is more sensitive, and less concerned with the double bluff. 'Tongue', with much of the original music brought in by Bill Berry, is a song about how plain and dumpy girls have nothing left to offer other than sex in order to win affection. It's a sad song, and the music – piano-driven, soulful, mixed with Stipe's falsetto – isn't completely successful, but it stands out on *Monster* as a poetic moment amidst the role-playing.

Ugly girls know their fate
Anybody can get laid

And later Stipe sings:

Call my name; here I come
Your last ditch lay, will I never learn?

'It's a very powerful song,' accords Mike Mills. 'It was written on the piano at the house of the girl that I ended up breaking up with. It had nothing to do with any of those aforementioned things, that's just a side note.'

IV

There's a general sense in the R.E.M. camp that *Monster* is not one of their strongest records. There is, however, also a sense that the album contains material that has been undervalued. 'I don't think it's our best work; songwriting wise, I think it's a little underappreciated. I don't think it sucks,' says Mike Mills. 'It may not be our best record but there are some good songs. I think "You" is a very good song, but it never gets mentioned by anyone, ever.'

With its big, bold riffs (the best of which graces 'Circus Envy') and pared-down arrangements, this was, as Peter Buck sarcastically commented at the time, music to sell hamburger and beer to on hot summer nights. They needed a repertoire of aggressive songs which would replace the baroque'n'roll of their previous two albums. Despite its loud, skewed rock sound, *Monster* was both too subtle and too contrary for its audience. It was too subtle because, for it to be enjoyed, it demanded an acceptance of a certain irony within the music and the lyrics. It replaced the earnestness of *Automatic* with distance: the songs, written in character, were songs of fame, lust, sex, personality crisis – all filtered through the ironic prism of Stipe's imagination. They were, perhaps, themes which a mainstream audience found it a lot more difficult to empathise with. After *Monster*, people didn't trust R.E.M., as fan and musician Ken Stringfellow eloquently describes:

Artists are here to provoke and confuse us. But R.E.M. have never really been seen the same since. I will say, though, that, as a fan, the record and the images around that time confused me a little bit. I can see that they were trying to do something larger than life. Just talking to fans around me, I think that, ever since that period, people have been a little mistrustful of them to some degree. Hence, the next record, *New Adventures In Hi-Fi*, was a very honest, quite open, regular guy sort of record, and a great one. I don't think *Monster* was an attack on their audience, but maybe you could see it as an attempt to really go out on a limb and do something that they had never done before, which again is a sort of 'contrived' image. I don't mean that in the pejorative sense. It's simply that something that's created and artificial is a weird turn for them to take. You can understand why it was so attractive for them, because it's the last thing you'd expect them to do.

Monster was to some degree an attempt by Stipe to put clear blue water between himself and the sort of 'undesirable' people his mainstream audience now contained. In rock history artists have been known to pander to the mainstream once their cult status has developed into global success. R.E.M., so it seemed, deliberately moved into territory which was designed to alienate the unwanted. In 1999 he told the *NME*: 'In a way we were like the jukebox band, the soundtrack to Reagan and all those people who were nothing like us, nothing that I agree with, nothing that I look like, nothing that I want to see. And I became a little bit of a contrarian purposefully: I'm gonna fuck with you! I'm gonna throw some shit at you that you really don't want.'[10]

The *Monster* album sleeve looked to the seventies for inspiration with its garish colours. The sleeve design, a blurry shot of a bear's head in black, pictured against a gaudy, dirty orange background, had an intriguing origin, as Chris Bilheimer, now artistic director at the Athens office, recalls:

> At that point everything that they were putting out would come from Michael and go through me as far as co-ordinating and building actual designs was concerned. Michael would come to me with the ideas and I would build everything. The idea for the cover actually came from a balloon. He came in one day with the balloon and said that he wanted this to be the album cover, and that I should play around with it. I ended up re-photographing the bear head. The balloon is actually green. When I was photographing it I was running off the end of the roll and I had a few frames left. I clicked a few off without even focusing the camera and we ended up liking those best. Both Michael and I are near-sighted so we're pretty used to seeing things out of focus anyway. If you take the cover and turn it counter-clockwise, it makes a kind of devil face. You can see a nose on the left, a mouth at the bottom, a horn on the left side and a giant eyeball! Someone pointed this out to me about six months after the record came out. It's turned it into a kind of Rorschach test for R.E.M. fans![11]

The back cover originates from a section of a photograph of a house. A lot of Southern Victorian houses have eaves, and one of the houses in Athens had a radiating sun pattern in the wood. The rays were painted alternately black and white. Bilheimer photographed the house, doubled the image so it became a sunburst image, transferred it to a television set, and photographed it off the television. It was then turned orange. 'That was the number one edict on the album from Michael, that he wanted it to be orange. It's his favourite colour.'[12]

For the tour Willy Williams, a veteran of Bowie tours and U2 extravaganzas, was brought in as the set and lighting designer. At certain points in the concert, back-projected films would burst into life, providing visual stimulus. All the films bar one were produced by Athens filmmakers Jim Herbert, Jim Cohen, Lance Bangs and Dominic De Joseph, the other one being made by Gus Van Sant. The images of teacups seemingly caught in earth tremors and huge hula-hooping girls looked homespun in the era of *Zoo TV*, but perhaps that was their intention. Stipe was plastered in panda eye make-up. Buck, at 38, could still produce a Townsendesque leap, and Mike Mills, shining like a Christmas tree bauble, even allowed himself to rev up the audience from time to time, as the excellent footage from the official tour video, *Road Movie*, shows. 'Sure, it's all about enjoying yourself out there,' admits Mills. 'You can lift people with the grand gestures or whatever, but you have to keep your tongue in your cheek when you do that.'

Commercially, the *Monster* tour was a huge success, and the *Monster* album, although not quite matching the previous two records, sold around 10 million copies worldwide, reaching Number 1 in both the US and the UK. On a personal level, the tour was bordering on the insane. Buck decided to forswear alcohol in order to try and keep pace with the crazy events going on in front of and behind the scenes. The latter he refuses to discuss. These events must have been serious, and must have been intensely personal, because Buck is an honest and forthcoming interviewee:

'That was a very intense tour, and a lot of weird shit went on. It was so intensive a year that, a month into it, I said, I've got to stop drinking, I've got to be sober for the whole tour. There was so much shit going on behind the scenes that no one really knows about and I'm not going to talk about. Also, I had my new kids with me, and that was hard, and I thought I'm gonna have to be sober for every second of every day because I've got to know that what I'm doing is completely correct. The last week or two I'll start drinking again because it won't matter. Not that I ever drank that much, but I'd like a drink or two before I went on stage and maybe go to the bar with the guys afterwards. But this time, no, I was totally sober the entire time. Every single person on tour drinks, so not drinking really changed my life, changed it in a good way, because I stopped going to bars and now I don't go to bars anymore. If I have a drink it's either at dinner or at the hotel bar.'

Seattle musician Scott McCaughey, originally from the Bay area of San Francisco, was added to an augmented R.E.M. which also included guitarist Nathan December. McCaughey, a big fan of R.E.M., had befriended Buck in Seattle. For his part, Buck was an admirer of McCaughey's band, the Young Fresh Fellows, and the two would form a close personal and professional bond from the early 1990s onwards, with Buck regularly featuring on McCaughey's multifarious recording projects. 'Peter knew that they needed somebody,' says McCaughey in 2001:

They were going to go out on a yearlong tour, and the most important thing is that you have somebody who you get along with [says McCaughey]. Musicianship comes a close second, but it is nevertheless secondary, because if you're going to be sharing 16 hours a day with somebody for about a year, it better be somebody who you can stomach [laughs]! We found we could stomach each other pretty well. They didn't need a virtuoso soloist, they needed somebody like me who can play different instruments fairly well [laughs], so it was versatility not virtuosity that they wanted. After adding me they still felt as if they needed an additional guitarist on the songs I was playing keyboards on, so that's where Nathan came in. I don't think they couldn't have done it without us, but it made a lot of sense to have us so they could do different types of material.

McCaughey was bowled over by the *Monster* album. 'I loved it. Loved it better than anyone, I think,' he claims. 'Nowadays, the R.E.M. guys shrug it off a bit, which makes me mad [laughs], because I worship that record. I listened to that record fifty times in a row to learn how to play all those songs and to get inside it.'

After rehearsals in Atlanta, the band flew to Perth, Australia, and rehearsed for a further five days before opening the tour on 13

January. The night before the tour started, Buck married his girlfriend Stephanie Dorgan after his divorce from Barrie had come through the previous Christmas. Tour support act Grant Lee Buffalo were the in-house entertainment for the day.

In the end, around 50 songs had been rehearsed, and about an hour before each show was due to start, Peter Buck or Mike Mills would perm any 25 from them to form the setlist. 'Whoever starts it passes it on to the other two guys and they all make suggestions, which I love, as it's so spontaneous,' enthuses McCaughey. 'You figure that most people who are out playing arenas make a set before they go on tour, and then just go out and play it every single night. The tech people who work with R.E.M. have to be really on their toes, as they can't plan on what's going to happen on any given night.'

There's certainly spontaneity to the R.E.M. shows. Songs such as 'Losing My Religion', 'Man On The Moon', 'The One I Love' and the encore, 'It's The End Of The World As We Know It', were ever-presents, as were certain songs from *Monster* such as 'What's The Frequency Kenneth?' and the show's frequent opener, 'I Took Your Name'. The beauty of having such a flexible repertoire was that fans learnt to love the unpredictability. The downside was that the shows were not as tightly controlled in terms of pacing as major stadium gigs tend to be. Traditionally, large rock shows are constructed so that they start on a high, with some well-known, fast-tempoed songs, then calm down with some less well-known songs, or some more 'difficult', reflective or acoustic numbers, before building to a hit-laden finale plus encore. R.E.M.'s gigs, in general, lacked this sort of structure. They were not theatrical events, but mix-and-match musical showpieces.

McCaughey was clearly having the time of his life. He regarded Buck as one of *the* premier rock musicians: 'Peter is an incredible guitar player. He blows my mind when I'm playing with him because he's so precise and so inventive that he doesn't have to resort to playing some crazy lead. He's the most consistent musician that I have ever played with. He doesn't really ever have a bad night. He's so focused, he can play a song perfectly twenty times in a row without a problem, which is something that I can't do.' The show was also opened by some major acts, including Sonic Youth, Luscious Jackson, Belly, Grant Lee Buffalo, Radiohead, the Beautiful

South, the Cranberries, Oasis, Echobelly and Paul Weller. You could hardly complain that you weren't being given a great night out.

V

However, the *Monster* tour will be remembered not for the great shows, the music or the return of R.E.M. to the stage after a six-year gap, but for the near-tragedy that took place in Lausanne, Switzerland on 1 March. A third of the way into the set, Bill Berry collapsed in agony. Scott McCaughey:

> I noticed something funny was going on during 'Tongue', but I was concentrating too hard to notice what it was because I was playing organ and that was something that took all my mental facilities to do correctly!
>
> I went across the stage to play guitar for the little acoustic set we usually did with Bill playing bass. We would play 'Country Feedback' and maybe 'Half A World Away' or one of the others that we were able to rotate within that particular set-up. Bill was walking down from the drums to get the bass and, I remember, right when he got near the bass cabinet he just sort of slumped to the ground and sort of passed out. I thought he'd fainted or hit his head on a cymbal when he stepped down from the drums. But I could see that he was severely incapacitated. He was helped off-stage, and we played three or four songs that we would do semi-acoustically without drums. Then we had to decide what to do. Bill was lying in agony backstage, and apparently managed to moan out that we should get Joey [Peters, the drummer from Grant Lee Buffalo, who were opening for R.E.M. at this time], so we dragged Joey out and we did 'Losing My Religion' and five or six other songs that he could fake his way through. Everybody was completely freaked out, we didn't know what to do.

Berry would later comment that he felt as if a bowling ball had hit him on the head. Although he had a history of migraine, this was surely of an unimaginably different magnitude of pain. Berry, whose first concern was that the show must go on, simply told his friends to muddle through as best they could, and with almost two-thirds of the scheduled show left, they played on in the hope that his condition would improve.

After the show, a doctor saw Berry. 'I have never had any idea of a misdiagnosis,' says Mike Mills. Bertis Downs comments: 'The full extent of Bill's condition was not diagnosed until the next day, and when it was diagnosed it was handled with the highest professional standards. But, at a rock show, it's not like you're going to have the greatest brain surgeon hanging out. I don't want to characterise that as a misdiagnosis.'

'Nobody that night diagnosed what it turned out to be,' says Scott McCaughey. 'We were guessing that it was a severe migraine. Knowing Bill, he probably didn't want to go the hospital either. He was probably going, "Oh, I'll be all right." But it was so obvious he was in agony. He was in so much agony, he couldn't move. He was very concerned about the show and the audience; he wanted us to keep playing. That was one thing that came across through the moaning and the pain, he wanted us to keep playing.'

There was obvious confusion, though, concerning the nature of Berry's illness. 'There was someone there who claimed to be a paramedic, and I don't believe he did quite the right thing,' remembers Scott McCaughey. 'I'm not really even sure if this person really was a paramedic. We were led to believe that he was, but there were language barriers. This person spoke English, but you're never quite certain whether you're getting the full meaning. I'm sure at the venue there were ambulances and why he didn't go to the hospital – I don't know what to say about that. I'm sure everyone was trying to do the right thing, and we're really lucky that it turned out OK.'

Peter Buck is far blunter about what he saw as the reality of the situation.

We had to finish the show, which was shocking and weird. We go over and there's a doctor and she says, he has a migraine, and Bill looks at me and says, my head's killing me. Yeah, he was totally misdiagnosed by a doctor who was sitting in the hall. He went back to his room and his wife said, there's something wrong with the guy. It was like four or five hours between the onset and his wife insisting that he went to hospital, but I only saw him for about a minute because they were taking him back to the hotel. He said, 'I'll be OK.' He was talking. I mean, he wasn't unconscious or paralysed or anything. I don't know how confident this doctor was, but she was kind of rolling her eyes and saying, he's had a couple of drinks and he has a headache, big deal. It was not the most sympathetic thing I'd ever seen. But the person is also a doctor, in Switzerland, where they have good healthcare, and she was saying, 'He'll be better tomorrow,' and Bill said, 'I'll be better tomorrow.' It wasn't until around 4 in the morning that they took him into the hospital and gave him a scan.

Berry was diagnosed on 2 March as having suffered a ruptured aneurysm (subarachnoid haemorrhage) on the right side of his brain, and a further aneurysm was also detected.[13] Berry was prepared for theatre, and operated on the following day. The surgeons performed a craniotomy in which the aneurysm was clipped to reduce the risk of re-bleeding.

Berry was very lucky to have been taken seriously ill in a country with possibly the highest standards of healthcare in Europe, if not the world. 'I think we've said, not too inappropriately, that if you're going to have an aneurysm, Switzerland's the place to have it,' says Bertis Downs. 'Lausanne, Switzerland is where aneurysm clipping was invented,' says Buck. 'And the doctor that performed that operation had probably performed it more times than any other doctor on earth. We had just been in Hong Kong and Singapore. We were in Taipei just a week before. Can you imagine what would have happened if we had been in Taipei when the aneurysm happened? Or on the flight back? He might well have died or been paralysed. It would have been bad. It was bad anyway.'

Had Berry not made it through the operation, or if he had survived with his faculties impaired, then R.E.M. would certainly have split up. Buck told the press that he would have given up his career, everything, just to see his friend pull through. And pull through he did. Within a couple of days he was well enough to see the band members at his hospital bedside. 'We were all completely freaked out because nobody knew if he was going to make it through the operation,' says Scott McCaughey. 'When I saw him after the operation, he was hurting, but he cracked a joke, so that was good. I said, "Hey, Bill, looks like you're doing great," trying to be nice to him, and he's lying there with half his skull shaved and a fifteen-stitch scar cross his head. And he said, "If this is good, man, I don't wanna know what bad is!" He kind of moaned out this joke and I thought, well, he's still got his sense of humour. But he was feeling real bad. Eventually, they sent everyone home, except Michael, Mike, Peter and Bertis, who stayed on for the month or so that he was in hospital, just being there for Bill.'

After this kind of major surgery, the critical period is the first five days after the operation, or around the 12th day, when re-bleeding occurs in around 30 per cent of patients, which can lead to permanent deficits or death. By 12 March, just over a week after surgery, Berry was up on his feet, although he was still experiencing severe headaches.[14] The media was informed that Berry was discharged from hospital on 21 March, although it now seems that, in reality, he had left several days earlier and was resting in a local hotel.[15] On 27 March, Bertis Downs reported that 'three weeks to the day after his surgery, Bill played a vigorous 18 holes of golf, and seemed very much on his game. His spirits are good, especially considering all that he has been through.' By mid-April, Berry was well enough to fit in the odd game of tennis and was back practising in preparation for the resumption of the *Monster* tour on 15 May. It had been a remarkable recovery.

'It was only two-and-a-half months later that we were playing two-hour shows,' affirms McCaughey. 'I don't think he was on medication. He seemed to be feeling very good but he took it pretty easy, not so far as the playing went, but as far as the rest of the time. He pretty much rested and went home immediately after the gigs.' The only negative at this time was a cruel hoax fax, from Warner Brothers and on headed notepaper, to KPNT radio station in St Louis, saying that Berry had died. To this day, R.E.M. newsgroups run threads of a 'Bill Is Dead' nature, mostly with tongues very firmly planted in cheeks.

Although normally healthy, later that year two other members of the band decided to give the health insurers and paramedics something to do. Mike Mills had to be admitted to hospital in July, while on the road in Germany. Conveniently for the rest of the group, he fell ill in Cologne, after the others had already flown down to play a rescheduled gig in Prague, home of the best beer in the world, and one of Europe's most intriguing cities. The reason for his hospitalisation was an adhesion following his abdominal surgery the previous year, which caused severe pain. The venue had already started admitting paying customers when the news came through that Mills had been hospitalised. The main concern, according to Buck, was to keeping the word 'bowel' out of the press release.

Mills was well enough to report back for duty within ten days for gigs in the UK and Ireland. The band subsequently returned to play the twice-rescheduled gig at the Sportovni Hala in Prague in August, only for their lead singer to be stricken with considerable pain. 'Michael was in agony during the sound check,' remembers Scott McCaughey. 'He went to the hospital between the sound check and the show and they diagnosed a hernia and they kind of taped him all up. He managed to sing a whole two-hour show with a tear in his diaphragm. I don't know how he did it because he was in a lot of pain. He flew back to Atlanta the following day, where he was neatly tucked back in. Michael couldn't bear the thought of leaving them hanging for the third time. Plus, we ended up spending a lot of time in Prague because it got cancelled before, and we all really loved the city, beautiful city and great people.'

R.E.M. were at the peak of their commercial acceptance. That year the Boston Globe dubbed them 'The Alternative Beatles',[16] and an R.E.M. gig was an epoch-defining event. Here's writer Danny Morrison's poignant depiction of R.E.M. live in Dublin on 22 July 1995:

I have wangled four VIP tickets for R.E.M. at Slane. At Kennedy Roundabout, Belfast, the driver of our bus falls off his seat and out the door. There is still some blood in his alcohol stream and he is answering to the wrong name but so does everyone in this life. To revive him he is given more drink. He comes around, addresses me and says, 'You better drive.' I drive. 'What if you rocked around the clock/Ticked, tocked.' *Automatic for the People* is blasting out the speakers. I look down the aisle, which is full of Martians singing in strange tongues, and it is great to be alive. They drink Dundalk dry then we speed off to 'The Sidewinder Sleeps Tonite'. Slane village becomes global. It is an asylum but there is no aggression. We find our position on the embankment, part of a natural amphitheatre, and the numbers of people innocently enjoying themselves is breathtaking. Night falls. Michael Stipe is illuminated on stage and enlarged on a video screen. As he begins, thousands in the valley below us light candles and there is one anthem. It is of solidarity with the lost and lonely. I look at my sons and my niece and we smile and all stand and join in, one huge swell of humanity. 'When the day is long, and the night, the night is yours alone / And you're sure you've had enough of this life / Hang on / Don't let yourself go, 'cos everybody cries / Everybody hurts / Sometimes.'

There is only one generation – this one. And the meaning of life is our individual little moving slots of time, often converging in or forged in joint experiences, which we look back upon with a sigh, ten minutes or ten years or ten thousand years later.[17]

Despite all the ill-health, the band were not only playing some fine gigs, but also found time to demo and record a new album. Having always preferred to use soundchecks as opportunities to work on new musical ideas, the original intention on the *Monster* tour was to use this space not only to work up new songs, but to track them, and release an album of live recordings (with necessary overdubs) at the end of the tour. However, by the end of the tour, not enough material had been prepared, so the plan was modified, as Peter Buck explains:

We had a yearlong tour going, and I just thought, God, we're just going to play all the same songs, how boring, let's make a new record on the road. Ideally, what I was hoping was that we'd record the last week of the tour and we'd have 11 new songs that we'd do, and then use them for a live record at the end of the tour but, by the end, we only had six new songs in the set, so that kind of fell by the wayside. One of those was 'Revolution', and that was a leftover from *Monster* in any case, so we decided not to use that. But we'd recorded about twenty songs, so we decided to finish them off. I think it's the kind of thing that bands in our position should do. We're one of the bigger bands on Earth and rather than say, let's take a year off, go to Jamaica and make a reggae record, let's really work really hard. I think it's what bands should do. Rather than go out on the road and play their greatest hits, why not write a whole new album?

So, R.E.M. would take some of the performances from the soundchecks and some from the concerts, work them up and add last-minute studio songs conceived post-tour. Reminiscent of the dozens of Frank Zappa albums made that way, it was not an original idea. The main mistake R.E.M. made was to tell the media that some of the new material was in part recorded on tour, since the album, to be entitled *New Adventures In Hi-Fi*, would wrongly be thought of as a road album, containing live tracks 'fixed up' later in the studio. Such albums tended to sound neither live nor studio-based, with elements of both grating to the ears. *New Adventures* was a poor idea, well executed. It wasn't a road album at all, but its music did capture the spirit of what it's like to be away from home, to be rootless for a long period of time.

Although a goodly portion of this new material comprised more nuanced updates on the *Monster* sound, much more of it took the form of spacey, drifty, beat-poet songs. In both their music and, more importantly, their packaging, R.E.M. would retreat quite quickly from the glamour of the *Monster* era. Ethan Kaplan, R.E.M. fan and now webmaster of the unofficial R.E.M. fan site, *Murmurs*, puts it like this:

They got to the brink of superstardom and then retreated. Frankly I'm glad, because a lot of the stuff going on around the *Monster* tour bugged me. It was too much of a media game, and too much of 'we're superstars and untouchable by the rest of the world'. They did this huge promotional push for it which was out of scale to the band itself. It made R.E.M. into a kind of U2. The band was a lot less accessible to people. The Michael Stipe you see in 2002 is completely different from the one you saw in the media in 1995. There was hero worship of Michael Stipe in 1995. Now he's become less brash, less of a media hound. He's in the media much more because of his movie stuff, but he's a lot more funny and personable. It seems like more of his personality is coming out, instead of him just playing with the media all the time. He's done that sort of stuff before, but it seemed to me that he reached the pinnacle of his excess around 1995. He went for it in 1995 because (a) he was coming to grips with himself as a media figure, and going a bit overboard, (b) out of a sense of competition, and (c) because he wanted to. He's never been one to shy away from fucking with people.

VI

Work on the new record continued during the first few months of 1996. Still exhilarated from the reaction to the *Monster* tour, and driven, one presumes, by workaholic Buck's quest to push the band forward, discussions centred on finishing off the record quickly and playing the summer festivals. The idea was quickly quashed by Berry, as Buck recalls: 'At the end of the tour, Mike, Michael and I said, "Let's play the summer festivals in Europe. We could finish this record in March and have it out." And Bill just said no. We thought we could finish the record within a month, but Bill scotched that pretty early on.'

R.E.M., now one of the two biggest rock groups on the planet, were out of contract. Although Downs now suggests that the option of setting up their own label was considered around this time, it appears that re-signing to Warner Brothers was by far the preferred option. Their first period with Warners, from 1988 to 1995, had been a lucrative one, and included two successful world tours and three global album hits. It was time for the band to make this commercial success count in drawing up a new contract, and the new Warners deal was rumoured to be the most lucrative in popular music history. Bertis Downs will not discuss the deal, claiming to be legally barred from doing so, and it is impossible to ascertain with any certainty what the actual figure was. The colossal sum of $80 million was bandied around, a figure that the band has always said did not originate from the R.E.M. camp itself, but from the media. For Peter Buck in particular, it was important that R.E.M., as a rock act, got locked into a new contract when they did. Buck predicted that the current massive commercial success for his band, and other left-of-centre rock acts such as Smashing Pumpkins and Pearl Jam, was unusual in terms of how the industry operated, and might not endure. So, by re-signing when the market for their music was buoyant, he would secure the band's future at a propitious time. His assessment turned out to be spot on.

One person who would not be part of the new Warners deal was Jefferson Holt. The man who, in the eyes of many who have worked for and with the band over the years, had turned R.E.M. from promising college rock combo into world-renowned rock act, left R.E.M.'s employ in early May 1996. Apparently, he turned up for work one day to find the locks on the office door changed. From that moment on, just before the re-signing to Warner Brothers and the release of the *New Adventures In Hi-Fi* album, Bertis Downs was the *de facto* manager of the band.

According to the terms of severance, neither party is allowed to comment on the circumstances surrounding Holt's departure from the Athens office. Cards were printed up at the time which said that Jefferson Holt had split and that both parties were prohibited from speaking about the situation. For a band that prided itself on integrity and honesty, the circumstances surrounding Holt's departure are shrouded in half-truth, innuendo and hearsay, a most unfitting state of affairs for all concerned, including their friends and fans, who have had to patch together a credible version of events from this tangle of misinformation. What we can say with some certainty is that the circumstances of Holt's departure must have been so shocking, and the dissolution so final, that it is now one of the biggest secrets within rock. To this day, Bertis Downs is uncomfortable even talking about his former partner, despite their 15-year-long business association. He refers to Holt, when he absolutely has to, as 'the former manager'.

For his part, Holt reportedly now refers to R.E.M. as 'the band whose name cannot be mentioned', or words to that effect. In 2000 Holt sold off his R.E.M. memorabilia on e-bay, advertising it as the 'estate of Jefferson Holt' in terms usually reserved for the belongings of a dead man. After the traumatic separation, he reputedly told a friend, 'I got bitten by the monster I helped to create.' Had R.E.M. become a greedy, Frankensteinian experiment, too grasping to allow Holt to benefit from a lucrative new record deal? What is for certain is that the period between 1994 and 1996, with its deaths, its near-deaths, its illnesses and departures, dealt a series of blows to the band. From now on, commercially and critically (if not creatively), R.E.M. would be on the slide.

But the biggest shock was yet to come.

10. 'I'M OUTTA HERE', 1996–98

I

For the first time in R.E.M.'s career, business dealings and interpersonal problems were getting in the way of the music. Years of discretion, of operating with laudable intentions, and without rock-star airs and graces, were rapidly giving way to personality clashes and irresolvable tensions. The 1995 *Monster* tour had been associated in the public mind not so much with great performances as with band misfortune, in particular Bill Berry's near-fatal illness. Likewise, in 1996, attention would not be focused on a fine R.E.M. album, *New Adventures In Hi-Fi*, but on the sacking/departure of their ex-friend and manager Jefferson Holt, who had been associated with the band for 16 years, and their re-signing to Warner Brothers. Media speculation concerning the size of the bounty outweighed appreciation of the new music itself, and resulted in under-appreciation of what was a very strong set of songs. 1996 would also be the year in which producer Scott Litt stopped making R.E.M. records. In his case, too, there have been rumours that he was pushed rather than walked. After years of success and good times, the band was having to endure that which it had always been afraid of and had fought very hard to avoid: traditional media speculation, with all the usual clichés – 'management problems', 'money matters' – that came with the territory.

Six years on from the event, a credible version of what happened to Jefferson Holt is still beyond us. Holt left the band's employ just before the re-signature to Warner Brothers, and with a charge of sexual harassment levelled against him, as printed in the *Los*

Angeles Times. Details are sketchy, although it would appear that a few months before the sacking/resignation a female employee had allegedly complained about Holt's behaviour. According to the *LA Times*, 'the employee did not file a lawsuit or register a claim with the Equal Employment Opportunity Commission, but complained to the band that Holt had verbally harassed her with lewd remarks and demanded sexual favours, sources said. Band members questioned Holt, who denied the allegations, and then spent about three months investigating the complaints, sources said. In May, the band called a meeting and asked Holt to leave the organisation, sources said.'[1]

If the allegations are true, then R.E.M. would have been left with no option but to sack him. Sexual harassment in an office which prided itself on its progressive politics, sexual or otherwise, would be totally beyond the pale.

Holt left with a pay-off, and a legal muzzle banning him from further comment. He did, however, say the following to the *LA Times*: 'I've agreed to keep the terms of my agreement with R.E.M. confidential. However, 15 years is a long time, and as time passed, our friendships have changed. I think we found as time passed that we have less and less in common. I've been more interested in other things in life and wanted to spend more time pursuing those interests. I'm happier than I have been in a long time.'[2]

R.E.M.'s prompt action won praise from many. For example, one president of a university feminist organisation wrote:

I think this is a beautiful example of how to handle such a situation. I am sure that it was very hard for R.E.M. to part with Jefferson – a decision with very serious consequences professionally as well as personally – but they did what needed to be done, and got rid of him. Many organisations would not have, as proven in case after case. As for the victim, if she wanted so badly to tell her tale, I think she would have filed a lawsuit or spoken to the press. She obviously wants to keep her privacy, and it is her decision and no one has the right to impose their own agenda onto her. As for protecting Jefferson, if that was their intent, they haven't done a very good job, have they? Everybody knows. What need is there to comment when this is the case? Anything they would say would be interpreted as wrong – either defending their old buddy Jefferson in true boy's club fashion, or backstabbing their long-time friend over a single incident.

In sexual harassment, there are no winners, but I think R.E.M. have done a beautiful job of keeping the losses to a minimum, and they should be applauded for their efforts.[3]

Another source 'close to the band' at the time went on record with a rather different version of events:

The 'official' word is that Jefferson got sick of the music business and decided to get out while he could: apparently a press release has been issued, and the *New York Times* supposedly had a blurb on it as well.

However . . . the highly unofficial version I just got tonight from a Very Good Source is that he was fired by the band yesterday, and was locked out of the office to boot, with Bertis Downs taking over for him, and his usual jobs split up between Bertis and the other office staff members. As far as anyone knows, nothing criminal was involved (in other words, he wasn't embezzling or anything like that); rather, after he made a series of bad business decisions (apparently the same bad decisions repeatedly, in some cases), the band finally decided enough was enough and lowered the boom on him.

Needless to say, the band is hoping desperately that Jefferson won't try and file a lawsuit against them . . .[4]

What is certain is that, in the eyes of many, Holt was, and is, a very popular man. In fact, both Holt and Downs were very well liked within the music business and had a reputation for honesty and integrity. This makes understanding what happened even more difficult, because the various scenarios cast one or the other, if not both, in a very bad light. According to one scenario, which may or may not be hearsay, Holt decided to quit the R.E.M. office over a year before his eventual humiliating exit. At the time of his original decision not to renew his contract, Holt was asked to sign a legally-binding document preventing him from discussing R.E.M. or the terms of his departure. As a result, when a charge of sexual harassment was levelled at him, he was unable to respond.

It would appear that, some time in the early 1990s, the working relationship between Downs and Holt changed significantly. Although it is commonplace in interviews and articles sanctioned by the band to find that Jefferson Holt has been almost entirely erased from the band history, in actuality, as we have seen, he played a crucial role. Peter Buck says: 'We had two managers, Bertis and Jefferson. Bertis has always been the person who did the real work. He's the one who got us a publishing deal, and did our contracts. It was a kind of good cop/bad cop scenario. Jefferson would try and schmooze them and charm them, whilst Bertis would take care of the business. That's the way it worked.'

Yet, for those who worked with the band, it seemed that Jefferson Holt was the sole manager, and that Downs played a different, secondary role as attorney. However, as the 1980s turned into the 1990s, it was Downs who was seen far more frequently with the band in high-profile media situations, whether it be award ceremonies, White House receptions, or local initiatives in Athens, Georgia. Holt, for his part, appears to have withdrawn somewhat from the limelight.

Some of the interviewees for this book have hinted at and speculated upon a behind-the-scenes power struggle between the two in the run-up to a lucrative new record deal. 'I've heard three discrete versions of what happened and I'm choosing to believe the one that suits me the most, based on absolutely no evidence at all!', says ex-producer Mitch Easter with refreshing honesty:

I saw Jefferson this past year. He was involved with this Italian band who were recording here, and he came by, because he is from around here [North Carolina], and he came to see his parents. It was absolutely great to see him. He seemed so unchanged from 1981. I just don't know anything about all the smelly parts, so I'm refusing to give them any credence till I know more. Really, nobody knows, so most comments on the subject are really operating only on the fumes of gossip.

I always liked Jefferson, but I would have to say he's hard to read. He's the kind of guy who probably doesn't have the desire to speak about it. He's pretty canny about how to handle himself. His mom was a politician, and I think he's got a bit of that. I think he's got a lot of reserve, knows what's public and what's private. This is why this harassment thing seems really bogus to me. It doesn't fit with anything I ever saw about that guy. Whereas the power struggle seems to be utterly believable, doesn't it? Bertis was also just terrific, and that's what I'm getting at. I prefer to remember them that way.

I'd like to emphasise how pleasant my dealings with Bertis have always been. He really has always expressed true friendliness towards me, and I do appreciate that. For example, Bertis would let me know when the latest audit would be producing more royalties for me – he seemed really happy to find more money for us. Maybe I'm putting too much good vibes on it, but these communications felt good in the context of the smelly record biz.

Another person who knew Jefferson Holt is Ballard Lesemann, senior rock writer on Athens magazine *Flagpole*. Lesemann used to serve Holt when the former waited tables at the Grit vegetarian restaurant. 'He's a hell of a nice guy, a really thin guy with a striking face. He was always very decent when I met him. That whole PC era was such that, if you cracked an off-colour joke, all of a sudden you were a racist or a sexist. Who knows, maybe someone overreacted? Maybe he overstepped the boundaries?'

Downs and Holt appear to have had very different personal styles. Holt was eccentric, jokey, and could turn on the charm, whereas Downs, the intellectual, was more businesslike and totally uninterested in the rock'n'roll good life, conducting himself efficiently and directly, in a pleasant, undemonstrative fashion.

Don Dixon, former R.E.M. producer, has remained friendly with Holt since the departure:

Jefferson is a great guy. Yes, he and Bertis had fallen out, and I have no idea why. Bertis is a good guy too, but I don't know him nearly as well as I knew Jefferson. How much of that legally barred stuff is true or not, or enforceable, I have no idea. We are basically talking about honour. To this day, Jefferson will not say the word 'R.E.M.' That has something to do with his sense of commitment to whatever document he signed and whatever circumstance. He has always referred to them in print and elsewhere as 'the band that shall not be named', or something like that. This was a gigantic deal to him. Obviously fans are interested in this, but there's a prurient element that I'm not interested in.

I think the split was not so much over money as personal style. It was more over credit. It is my gut feeling that it was probably mostly about weight-pulling. By 'weight-pulling', I mean 'earning your keep', who's doing all the work here, why are you getting all this money if you're not doing the work? That's the only level on which it might be to do with money. I do think it had something to do with Jefferson feeling that he didn't want to be part of it any more. Whether he reacted to that badly on a personal level, creating situations that made it intolerable for him to be still around the office, I don't know.

I think it's probably more likely to be related to a lot of personal stuff. Being successful in this incredibly gross business brings with it a tremendous amount of baggage and pressure. I know that it was not something simple, that it was something that had built up over a number of years. They were all extremely close, and it is my considered opinion that there would not have been an R.E.M without Jefferson Holt.

One conclusion is that it seems to have become clear to Downs that Holt was not working as hard for the band as hitherto. What can be stated with reasonable accuracy is that Downs' role became far more important as R.E.M.'s career progressed. Back in the early 1980s, Holt was manager, Downs merely the guy from the local law school who helped out on a part-time and/or voluntary basis. By the end of the 1980s, Downs was playing a pivotal role in the band's legal and business affairs, negotiating record deals and being very much a hands-on operator. Peter Buck put it like this: 'I can't really comment about why he [Holt] left, but over the years he had become less and less interested in even showing up at the office. Well, he didn't have a desk for eight months. He bought a new desk and didn't show up, so he really didn't need to be at the office for those eight months. Working for us isn't a lifetime employment. I'll hire people and give them raises and keep working with them as long as they do their job and they are loyal. But certain things can happen and you decide that you can't work with those people any more. He's rich, he doesn't have to work any more.'

According to ex-girlfriend and band supporter Ann-Louise Lipman, Holt was an eccentric figure, and a flirt in his own way, but she
casts doubt on whether he would go so far as to abuse anyone
sexually:

There were people in the office who had worked there a long
time. These weren't people who came and went. This was very
curious to me. There's parts that could make sense, but in that
environment? I mean, why would he be doing that there? I
thought he'd found himself when he became R.E.M.'s manager.
It was like a family, and Jefferson was part of that family.

What is known is that one of the band's employees at the Athens
office, Brooke Johnson, left in the spring of 1996, the word being
that she was getting married and relocating to Costa Rica.

'The papers that we signed said we can't talk about it,' says Peter
Buck. 'I'd be taken to court. But there are a lot of rumours out there,
that's for sure. Believe me, I'd love to clear it up, but it's not
something I can do. I personally feel great about everything I did
during that time, and everything the rest of the guys in the band did
during that time, and Bertis did during that time.'

A year later, it emerged that six-time R.E.M. producer Scott Litt
was not required for the band's eleventh album, *Up*. The reason
always given by the band is that Litt no longer wanted to be involved
in production. This may very well be the case, as Litt started up his
own label, Outpost Records, shortly afterwards.

'We worked very well together for all those years,' says Peter Buck.
'It came to the end of the road, mostly through his choice. He was
starting his own record label and he had lost interest in producing
records. When we were doing *Hi-Fi*, I remember asking him whether
he was going to produce all the records on his new label. He told me
that, if he were lucky, he wouldn't ever have to produce a record
again. He wanted to be more like a Mo Austin or Ahmet Ertegun – to
sign artists and build up his own empire. These are perfectly laudable
ambitions. Also, we'd probably come to the end of the road of our
work together anyway. But I'm certainly friends with him to this day.'

Was Outpost ever in the running to sign R.E.M. in 1996? 'Kind of.
I think we were pretty sure we were gonna stay with Warner
Brothers, though we did get other offers, but I do like Scott and his

partner, Mark Williams. But at that stage, I think it was pretty much a foregone conclusion. Scott did sign some great stuff such as Ryan Adams, but his record company got lost in a shuffle when it got merged or something.'

Asked if there had been a falling-out, Mills replies, 'No, not really. Let's just say that there is a lot of water under the bridge. We were all very friendly for the bulk of the time, but we just came to a crossroads; people go in different directions. I'm sorry his label didn't do better. I had some good friends working there and I was pulling for him, but it just didn't work out. Running a label is an incredibly tough business, it's nothing that I would ever try and do.'

Again, with so little hard evidence to go on, it's impossible to explain the situation with any certainty. It is known, however, that Litt's new label had been interested in signing R.E.M., and obviously lost out to Warner Brothers. Moreover, it was suggested by Q journalist Danny Eccleston, writing at the time of the release of Up, that Litt's non-involvement with the new album was a result of his backing the wrong side: 'long-time producer Scott Litt (purged as part of the pro-Jefferson Holt factions when the manager and ex-fifth member left in 1996) . . .' However, Peter Buck says that this was not the case: 'There was a lot of stuff going on, and, essentially, before it started happening, Scott told me that he was going to quit producing records to start his own label. It was an uncomfortable time for every one, but there was no purge.'

Scott Litt politely declined to be interviewed for this book.

II

It may well of course, be a totally unrelated phenomenon, but, since Holt's removal, forced or otherwise, R.E.M.'s record sales have tumbled, and their public profile has been lowered. By 1996, R.E.M.'s three previous records had sold in excess of 30 million units. The next three would sell around a third of this figure, and their lack of marketability in the States would be a recurring theme. The quality of music didn't leave when Holt did, but the band certainly switched from being one of the two biggest rock bands in the world to being a large cult band. It's a transition, one suspects, that the band welcomed.

Buck predicted that dance and rap would take over, particularly in the USA, and that his own brand of rock music would become more of a minority taste. In fact, as it turned out, it would be the boy and girl bands who would rule the roost, but the essence of his prediction was correct: alternative rock would become boutique music, liked by a large cult following rather than a mainstream audience. Rock acts in both the USA and the UK increasingly made music that spoke to this cult constituency and not to the pop charts. Take, as an example, the switch of emphasis from melodic pop to more 'difficult' music made by Pulp, Blur and Radiohead.

The news that R.E.M. had re-signed to Warner Brothers was announced on 24 August 1996, just over a month after it had been made known that the band's former label, I.R.S., had folded. An option that was discussed, but not taken any further, was to team up with the new Dreamworks label. Mo Austin and Lenny Waronker, the two individuals who had brokered the original Warners deal in 1988, had left to work for Dreamworks. But R.E.M. stuck with Warner Brothers on the understanding that, once again, they would have total artistic freedom. In R.E.M., Warners were investing in a brand name that equalled prestige and kudos.

'R.E.M. made a lot of money for Warner Bros early on,' reminds rock critic and academic Anthony DeCurtis. 'They played their original contract out at a time when they were having huge hit records, and it was a contract that was favourable to them in 1989 [sic]. They . . . dutifully followed their contract out at a time when Warner Bros was making a great deal of money. A lot of bands would have renegotiated immediately after a success like that. So some of their last deal was payback. The other thing to think about is that there is still a prestige factor to having R.E.M. on your label. They are a band that younger bands look to as a model. Neil Young hasn't sold a lot of records lately, but it's a good thing to have him on your label.'[5]

The first R.E.M. album since *Fables Of The Reconstruction* presented Warner Brothers with no obvious singles or radio hits. *New Adventures* is at times a sombre and muted piece of music, and a retreat from the melodic pop of *Green*, *Out Of Time* and *Automatic*. At just over 65 minutes, it is also R.E.M's longest album.

The title, *New Adventures in Hi-Fi*, poked fun at what we now think of as the kitsch seriousness of the early stereo era, as typified in this editorial, written in 1951: 'There is so much forced uniformity in our prosperous American life that escaping it becomes an exciting *adventure* [my italics] and a feat to be proud of. And the biggest, proudest group of escapees in the nation, without much doubt, are the people for whom this magazine [*High Fidelity*] is published – the music-lovers, hobbyists, craftsmen and engineers who together have built the sizeable industry known (perhaps regrettably but probably incurably) as *hi-fi* [my italics].'[6]

The commercial fate of the album was sealed when one of its more introverted tracks, 'E Bow The Letter', was released, at the band's behest, as the first single. Buck called the song a 'folk rock dirge', and its Dylanesque vocal delivery and funereal pace made it largely inappropriate for hit radio. With a typically wry sense of humour, the Brits made it the band's highest charting single, in August 1996, and the album itself was also a UK Number 1. In America, the single stiffed at Number 49, a major reverse after five years of commercial success. With sales of around 5 million units, *Hi-Fi's* was a comparatively mediocre performance in the light of the early-1990s successes but, with R.E.M. selling around a million copies of back catalogue annually, the band had hardly hit crisis point.

The strange title references the song's origins. When the music was being developed during the 1995 tour, the working title was 'E-Bow'. An e-bow is an electronic device containing a tiny magnet which can be held up to the guitar string which is vibrating to produce long, sustained, unbroken notes. Buck uses this technique quite expertly on this particular song, giving the guitar a resonance almost like a violin or cello. It pushes the song as close as they dared to the art-rock territory of the late 1970s. According to Buck, Stipe wrote the lyric around an unsent letter, hence the second stage of the curiously nonsensical title. 'His postcards are like scripts to some weird movie that you're only getting the middle of,' added Buck.[7]

The song, and the video, which was shot in Prague, featured a rare appearance by Stipe's hero, Patti Smith. When Smith's husband Fred 'Sonic' Smith died, Stipe called out of the blue in early 1995 to offer his support. R.E.M. cherished Patti Smith's work, and included a version of her 1979 single, 'Dancing Barefoot', in some of their 1995 gigs. In 1996, rather than talk to the press about the new R.E.M. record, Stipe elected to join Patti Smith's tour, where he photographed the singer on the road in some affecting black-and-white shots. The result would eventually be turned into an exhibition and a book, *Two Times Intro: On the Road with Patti Smith*.

Hi-Fi is about distance, physical distance. Many of its songs, such as 'Departure', 'Low Desert' and 'Undertow', have rolling, repeating riffs, and, as they move, they take us along on a journey. They are sonic re-creations of long-distance travel, and capture that seemingly unending and undifferentiated quality of traversing a country, even a continent, by road.

Although R.E.M.'s music is rock music, not dance, it reflects back the hypnotic quality of most dance music, music where overall structures change almost imperceptibly, like one of Brian Eno's art installations of the 1980s. The beauty is in slight variation, as bars of music, or visual images, float and remain static. So, almost all the songs on *Hi-Fi* have this quality: the repeating piano refrain of 'How The West Was Won And Where It Got Us', the great riff rock of 'walk-up Bomb' and 'Departure', the jarring, security alarm-siren musical motif that constitutes almost the whole of 'Leave', and the archly doomy 'Low Desert'.

The CD cover, a black-and-white photograph of the scenery of nowhere in particular, taken through the tour bus window by Stipe, is one of the images which has come to define the band. Nowadays, the image might even verge on cliché. However, back in the mid-1990s, its power was undoubted. 'Michael had taken all these photos on the road while they were recording the music,' says art director Chris Bilheimer. 'So, being that the music was a little bit of a travelogue from that tour, it was decided that the artwork should be as well. He had probably fifteen or twenty photos, and when they were in the studio in Seattle finishing the record, they laid them out on the floor. I was leaning toward that one myself, and Peter walked by and said, "Oh, that one should be the cover," and kept going. I don't even know if he stopped. That kind of clinched it. Usually Peter has zero input or interest in the artwork and to actually have him come forward and show interest it was like, OK, there we go!'

Although there is a good case made by vinyl devotees that mean CD-sized artwork can never match the grandness of a 12″ jacket, the compact artwork that most people saw for *Hi-Fi* was intriguing. The band photo was taken by Bilheimer in the back bar area of the Crocodile Café in Seattle. 'That shot was taken running off the roll. The camera went off, and that's the photo it took. Usually in photography the mistakes turn out a lot better than the planned shots.' The other images are all by Stipe. The diamond shape against black is an elevator door, shot in New York. Another image, on the far left of the CD booklet, is of a Marcel Duchamp unfinished 1923 sculpture, *The Bride Stripped Bare By Her Bachelors, Even*, an abstract work, also known as *The Large Glass*, taken by Stipe at the Philadelphia Museum of Art while on tour. 'The sculpture's on glass, and there's sunlight coming through the window on the other side of it,' says Bilheimer. 'The shot taken by Stipe is not representative at all of what the sculpture actually looks like.' It's an unsettling image, framed through the shape of a cross.

III

If *New Adventures*' musical and visual motifs of motion tie the body of work together, then, within this space, it is as eclectic an album as *Green*. 'The Wake Up Bomb' is an exhilarating reconstruction of the glam era. 'For me, it was a continuation from *Monster*,' remembers McCaughey. 'It was this super, glammy, rock thing, something that Peter, Mike and Bill started playing at sound checks, and another one where Michael came up with lyrics pretty quickly, because we started playing it on tour. We played it live at the MTV music awards in September 1995. We thought it was really cool to go out there and do a brand new song.'

The instrumental track 'Zither' was actually recorded backstage in the men's toilets. Following a beautiful introduction brought in by Berry, 'Leave' explodes into a noisefest. 'The intro is just me and Bill backstage,' says McCaughey. 'Nobody else was around and Bill said, "I've got an idea for a song, play these chords." I got this weird sound from the little practice keyboard we had in the dressing room, then he played the melody on acoustic guitar, and that's exactly what's on the record. We recorded it on a portable DAT backstage. It didn't make it on to the set lists, but it was pretty much finished by the end of the tour. That siren-like noise is an old ARP ODYSSEY synthesiser. I'm holding the octave switch and ramming it back and forth for the entire seven minutes. That's one where everybody asks how my wrist is feeling at the end of the song! It was a mindless task but it did take some perseverance.[8] That's a great song – it seems to be a dark horse favourite of a lot of people.'

'Departure' has the talking jive of Dylan married to a great Buck riff which seems to drift in and out of sync with the rhythm section. 'That was the first new song that we started playing on that tour,' recalls McCaughey. 'It was done in San Sebastian. We flew from Singapore to San Sebastian, a nice little 26-hour trip, and I think Michael wrote the lyrics on that flight. Peter started that riff with Mike and Bill when we were rehearsing in San Sebastian, and Michael came out and started shouting and there it was! And it was immediately put in the show.'

'With *Hi-Fi*, we were trying to do something that no one else had ever done,' adds Buck. 'Which is to go on the road with no songs, and then in the space of a year write a whole collection of songs about being on the road, without spelling out, hey, we're a rock band on the road. Essentially we were trying to capture what modern life is like to us, and to a lot of people – namely that one day you're in one place, the next day you're some place else. In "Departure" Michael sings, "Just arrived Singapore, San Sebastian, Spain, 26-hour trip." I mean, we did that flight. Twenty-six hours with two screaming twin girls in the air and believe me, everyone remembers that flight, then there was a two-and-a-half-hour bus ride. And that record captures it. To be honest, we had the music to "E-Bow" and "Low Desert" written, but no words, before the tour started, but we wrote everything and recorded almost everything on the road.'

Out on a limb, and the standout track on the album, is 'New Test Leper'. The lyric concerns the travails of a chat-show guest, whose self-doubt concerning his faith in Christ is ridiculed by a studio audience, and ends in censorship: 'When I tried to tell my story / They cut me off to take a break.'

I can't say that I love Jesus
That would be a hollow claim
He did make some observations
And I'm quoting them today
'Judge not lest ye be judged'
What a beautiful refrain
The studio audience disagrees
Have his lambs all gone astray?

'It's probably my favourite song on the album,' enthuses Mike Mills. 'It's just a beautiful song, the lyrics are amazing, and, on a purely personal level, it's a really fun song to play on. The guitar is played through a Leslie – a spinning speaker that organs are played through. It's a speaker that spins within the cabinet. They're primarily used for organs, but you can sing through them.'

'I think "New Test Leper" was called "The Sea Chanty" or something like that the two or three times we played it at sound check during the tour,' says Scott McCaughey.

I had forgotten about it until they brought it back at the end of the tour in Seattle. They tracked it there and recorded overdubs. I came in and heard it, and I thought, 'Oh my God, this is amazing.' I happened to be in the studio one night when Michael was re-singing the vocal. I always feel kind of bad about this. He was in the control room with a hand-held microphone with his head right between the speakers. This was a very different way of recording a vocal, not pristine at all, and he was basically doing it by himself. Mike and Scott Litt and I went into the live room, the tracking room, and we were basically jamming, playing 'Wild Thing', and 'Louie Louie', screwing around, and Michael's in there trying to sing this beautiful song. I remember afterwards him playing these three vocals that he had done. They were all incredible, and I said, 'Boy, we were really helping you in there, weren't we Michael!? We were really helping you capture the mood of the song! He could probably hear us slightly because we were banging on the drums and stuff. He must have managed to tune it out, because what he sang was beautiful, and one of those takes was used on the record. Sometimes when he sings, it seems like he likes to be in the room pretty much on his own, so maybe us being out, fooling around, not paying attention, was actually OK.

The title of the album's opener, 'How The West Was Won And Where It Got Us', was another deliberately clichéd formulation, which set the scene for a big story, Western-style. It was another song in that long tradition of classic last-minute additions, recorded in the final sessions in Seattle. 'Bill and I were sitting there, and Bill started playing that drum beat and I instantly started playing those notes on the piano. It's one of those songs that gets written in the time it takes to play it. We wrote it and recorded it that day, and I think Michael wrote most of the lyrics that day too. It really fell together very nicely.'

Buck's plaintive guitar line, actually a bouzouki doubled with guitars, added to the Spaghetti Western/Ennio Morricone trajectory of the song, while the mid-song piece of piano whimsy, despite being thought by many to be a copy of Mike Garson's more manic piano fill on Bowie's 1973 song 'Aladdin Sane', was in fact a nod to Thelonious Monk.

'I love Mike Garson's stuff, and there are similarities between the two,' admits Buck. 'But I said to Mike Mills, "Do Thelonious Monk." Mike started laughing and said, "No way!" So, I said, "No, just do Thelonious Monk as if you were someone for the first time and couldn't play piano. Just thump it!" It was a one-taker. He figured out a couple of notes that worked melodically, but the rest he just hit.'

'I can't play anything like Thelonious Monk,' adds Mills. 'But Monk said once, there are no wrong notes. So, I just tried to apply that philosophy to that solo. I had no idea what I was going to play; I just made it up on the spot.'

The prettiest song on the album, and a minor UK hit single, was the country-tinged 'Electrolite'. 'It was written in Chicago, on a piano in a sublet apartment that my girlfriend at the time was living in,' remembers Mills. 'Most of the piano stuff, although not all, comes from me.'

Prince had his '1999', Blur their 'End Of A Century' and Pulp their 'Disco 2000'; and 'Electrolite' in turn was a typically obtuse musing by Stipe on the millennium, with a star-struck lyric including name checks for 'Martin Sheen', 'Steve McQueen', 'Jimmy Dean' and 'Mulholland Drive', a road which separates Bel Air from the San Fernando Valley,[9] hence the line 'Hollywood is under me'. The ending was seized on by R.E.M. conspiracy theorists as a sign that the band would break up at the end of the decade.[10]

Twentieth century go and sleep
Really deep,
We won't blink

Your eyes are burning holes through me.

I'm not scared
I'm outta here.

The band think it's an underrated piece of work, but there's an overall sense now that the album is flawed. 'Michael still thinks right now that *Hi-Fi* is our best record,' says Peter Buck. 'Looking back on it, I might have cut off a couple of the rock songs, and made it a little more concise.'

For Mills, 'Departure' 'hasn't lasted that well', 'Low Desert' is 'a good song, but a bit grim', 'Be Mine' is 'not as realised as it should have been', and 'Leave' is an 'interesting song, a little bit long maybe'.

'I like the vinyl double album,' says Scott McCaughey. 'It's like a sixties double album. If you have three or four songs on each side and each side is 15 minutes long, it focuses the songs. It kind of makes more sense that way, because CDs, especially when they're over an hour long, it's really difficult to get a handle on them.'

What we now know is that the record was produced, if not by a disintegrating unit, then by one with internal problems. Bill Berry's lack of appetite for the job in hand was being picked up on. 'I think even then, we were all getting inklings about it,' reveals Mike Mills. 'I knew more than the others because I've been so close to Bill. We didn't think he was gonna quit, we didn't think it would get that far, we just thought there were things about it that he was getting tired of.'

IV

Some time in the late summer or early autumn of 1997, Berry told manager Bertis Downs that he wanted to quit. Sessions for the new album were due to start and Berry wanted out. The band had started working on their 11th album at Peter Buck's new home in Hawaii that spring, but Berry's heart wasn't in it. He'd brought in some new ideas, but he found himself pacing up and down the beach, listening to the waves, drifting off, while his band-mates worked on the new songs. Talking to Downs about his personal situation must have been heartbreaking for both of them. Downs and Berry were old buddies even before the emergence of R.E.M. as a force, way back when they were students at the University of Georgia together. Mike Mills, Berry's closest friend, was also told of the decision. Downs asked Berry to reconsider.

These were difficult times for Berry. He had just split from his wife, Mari, and was awaiting the divorce. The album-tour-album circus had finally worn him down. Being in R.E.M. was no longer a pleasure; it was a pain. 'When I had most of my discussions with Bill it was clear that he just didn't want to travel any more,' says Downs.

'He really just lost the desire to be gone a lot. When you're in a band, it's part of the deal, and if you really lose that desire, then what are you doing?'

'He didn't like travelling, eating strange food, meeting new people. You know, all of the things I find so fascinating, he didn't really enjoy,' confirms Mike Mills. 'When he had the aneurysm it made him realise, why should I continue to do something I'm not having fun doing? I think he hated all the other parts so much that it even started to make the music no fun for him, and when the music was no fun, what point was there for him to do this any more?'

At the end of October, the band were due to reconvene in Athens to start work proper on the new record. Buck was excited. Just before travelling to Athens he had demoed a new song, which would eventually become one of R.E.M.'s best songs of the 1990s, 'Lotus'. When he arrived in his hotel, the phone rang. It was Mike Mills warning Buck that some heavy news was planned for the morning. Berry, probably trying to avoid the emotional devastation that he was about to wreak, wanted to break the news of his departure on the phone, but was talked into making a personal appearance.

'I can understand completely why he did it and I think he made the right choice for himself. I think he told Mike beforehand, and was talking to Bertis about it,' says workaholic Peter Buck, a man who, constantly writing and recording with R.E.M. and myriad other musical combos, would probably have found Berry's decision the hardest to accept:

> My understanding is that Bill didn't want to deal with us. He wanted to call us on the phone and say, 'Guys, I don't wanna do this.' I think Mike said, you owe them more. You have to speak to them face to face. I was in my motel room the night before the first day of rehearsals, and Mike called and said, 'Peter, what are you doing?' I said, 'I just got in, I'm a little tired,' and he said, 'Well, we're probably not gonna be doing a lot of rehearsing because Bill has something he wants to talk to you about.' I got the feeling that it was either about leaving the band or that he wasn't ready to make the record. Mike said, 'Well, I just want you to be prepared when you go in there.' I said, 'Well, I appreciate the thought, and I think I know what this is all about.'

Bill just said that he didn't want to do it; it was weighing on his mind and he didn't want to let us down. He actually said that if you guys are going to break up the band because I quit, then I'll do it, but I'll be miserable. At that point we'd already written this whole new record that I felt really strongly about. I said 'Bill, you've gone through a lot of stuff with your aneurysm, and your marriage falling apart. I want you to see a psychiatrist for the month that we're in town and I want you to talk to this guy. If he gives you a clean bill of health that you're not delusional or something, then I'd say it's fine.' I don't know how much he went. He might have gone once or twice, but basically the guy said, he's made a rational choice in his life. You might not agree with it, but he has his reasons, they're good reasons and he doesn't seem to be depressed or having mental problems. He has made a clear decision. That was my only worry – that Bill was depressed about something that wasn't to do with the band. If Bill had called up a year later and said, 'Man, I was totally fucked up back then, I really want to be back in,' then I'd know that we'd done the wrong thing. But every time I see him, or he talks to the guys, he just has no interest in us. So, it was a rational choice. The way he told it to me was that he had been playing professionally for almost 25 years and that he was ready for the gold watch. 'I've been doing it since I was 14 and I'm just tired of it. I don't want to travel, I don't want to play music, I don't want to go to the studios, I don't want to talk to people who don't speak English, I don't want to be famous.'

My feeling is that he was sick of everything to do with the music business, including music. You'd go over to his house, and you'd realise that he hadn't bought a record in ten years. You had to look under chairs to find his old ones. When we had the talk, at the end he said, 'I've been doing this since I was 14 and I'm just sick of it. If I were a policeman they'd retire me now.' He just didn't want to do it. It's not as if he had gone out and done a lot of playing with other people. The whole thing was just too much on his mind. Most people who are in rock bands make that decision when they are about 14 or 15, when music is their whole life, and chasing girls is your whole life too. Get to be 35, and most people don't have a lifetime commitment to making music or even listening to it. It got to the point where

I just dreaded having a meeting where I'd suggest we'd do anything because he just didn't want to do anything. He's one of my best friends, so I'm not denigrating him, but I felt responsible for his unhappiness. It made him unhappy to travel, it made him unhappy to eat foreign food, it made him unhappy to deal with people who didn't speak English, it made him unhappy to be away from home. It made him unhappy to stay up till 11 o'clock playing shows . . . He goes to sleep at 7.30 at night now for Christ sake . . . and wakes up at like 5.30 in the morning! He hates meeting people. I felt really guilty. Anything we'd want to do would make this poor guy miserable.

Mike Mills also describes how the whole situation had become intolerable for all concerned. 'Oh well, yeah, it's frustrating when we're all pulling in one direction and one person is not pulling in that one way. I mean, the thing is, we're all so much in love with being in this band that it was very difficult for us to understand how you could not be. But Bill was, in fact, falling out of love with the band as an entity and as a result he wasn't putting in some of the same effort that we felt he should have been. And you know, it's not because he was lazy, it's because he was miserable. He was writing as much as ever I think but just in general, he was not happy. And, you don't want your friends to be unhappy. It's hard to be around them if they're unhappy, particularly if you feel you're part of the cause.'

For the additional musicians called in for the sessions, the situation had reached almost tragicomedic proportions. Berry had come into the studio at the start of the new sessions and informed them that he was leaving. With Buck, Mills and Stipe now presumably too depressed, or distracted, to work, the augmenters – musicians Scott McCaughey and Barrett Martin, John Keane, and new producer Pat McCarthy – had the task of making a new R.E.M. album without R.E.M. Work went on, half-heartedly, on a song which had been demoed in Hawaii that spring entitled 'Pounce Pony', which was to become the haunting closing song, 'Falls To Climb', before the session was cancelled.

'I think Mike and Peter and Michael were so traumatised with Bill making that decision that they didn't turn up at the studio for a couple of days,' says McCaughey. So basically Pat McCarthy, Barrett,

John Keane and I were kind of sitting there saying "Now what do we do?" It was very odd. We didn't do much. We basically messed around with the song that we had up, "Pounce Pony" and another song which never made it on to the record, called "Drum Sample" which was never quite completed. It was kind of a crazy drum loop with Mellotron and stuff, and that never ended up on anything, which is too bad because it's incredible.'

On his own admission, Michael Stipe, 'fell apart'. If Buck's reaction to Berry's decision was anger, frustration and incredulity that any part of his musical 'family' would want out, and Mills' was one of fatalistic acceptance, then Stipe, as the self-professed 'female heart' of the band, would fall into something of an emotional black hole.

V

Bill Berry's illness, and his jadedness about being in a band, are almost certainly the real reasons behind his decision to quit in October 1997. However, at least two other theories have been put forward. The first is that Berry had simply fallen out of love with the sort of music the band were now making. Responsible for much of the music for songs such as 'Man On The Moon' and 'Everybody Hurts', he saw how the classic R.E.M. blueprint had been changed for Hi-Fi, and, for the new album, risked being destroyed altogether.

'I've heard stories that he was incredibly bored with the music they were doing and he felt left out, but that's just a story,' says Ballard Lesemann. 'It's probably fair to say that his drumming parts weren't as inspired or as elaborate as before – they didn't have the pepper they had in the first three or four records. Even live, he looked like he was going through the motions.'

Another theory is that Bill Berry had become disgusted, not so much with making music, as with the music business. At least one interviewee has suggested that Berry was more likely than the other three to have been upset by the departure of Jefferson Holt, and by the media intrigue that surrounded that departure, which coincided with Scott Litt's leaving too. Was Berry simply wearied by the factional self-interest? We'll probably never know, as Berry, never the most cheerful of interviewees, has largely kept up his anonymity since leaving the band. But it's an intriguing thought, and, until the Athens office reveals exactly what happened in the mid-1990s, it is a theory which will remain only a long-shot bet, at best.

So, R.E.M. were now a trio. It was a blow to band confidence, but the band could survive. Had Stipe left, then R.E.M. could not have survived. However, the loss of one of the three musicians could be overcome. Years earlier they had told the media that, if one of them should leave, then the band would break up. However, they were to carry on, with Berry's blessing. 'In 1997, during the discussion the band had with Bill, he made it really clear that if they were going to split up, then he would continue,' says Downs in 2002. 'They already had quite a batch of songs that they were excited about, and they had a producer in town. They were basically right at the beginning of making a record. Had it happened at any other point, as a result of injury or illness, or in the middle of a tour, or during some down time, then it might have been different. But they were really on the rebound of getting ready to make that record, so they really didn't give it much thought. The three-legged dog has to find out if it can run, and they were ready to try. In Joey Waronker they had a guy who, as a drummer, is a talented and versatile guy who everyone really likes as a person. We had actually known him since he was in high school.'

News of Bill Berry's departure broke on Wednesday, 29 October 1997. 'Physically, I'm in great shape,' said Berry at the time. 'But there was a kind of spiritual ordeal I went through, and I don't know if that's what caused this; it may have. Lying in a hospital bed for three weeks made me look at things a little differently and shift priorities. I used to be so excited about going into the studio I couldn't sleep the night before. But I was getting to the point where I couldn't sleep because I was worried about why I wasn't happy. The idea of doing yet one more tour and spending three months in a studio . . . There's not a window in any studio I've ever been in.'[11]

Michael Stipe told the press: 'It's the end of an era for us, and that's sad. For me, Mike and Peter as R.E.M., are we still R.E.M.? I guess a three-legged dog is still a dog. It just has to learn how to run differently.'[12] Berry and the rest of the band assembled at the Athens office on Friday, 31 October to do a final round of interviews as a foursome. Berry said: 'It first started dawning on me while I was recuperating. I wasn't thinking about quitting the band, but maybe reassessing my priorities and things I wanted to do with the rest of my life. Maybe not so much travel, for one. I had a lot of time to lay around in a hospital bed and think about things. Maybe I started feeling sorry for myself.'[13]

'It's kind of documented that people who have a near-death experience tend to reprioritise,' Stipe told Athens journalist Richard Copley. 'It definitely puts a different angle on your life. I think it's a very courageous move for Bill to make. We're backing him in his decision, as sad as it is. It's a positive, because he'll be a lot happier out of the band, and we'll be able to continue without him with his blessing . . . We've never been about faking it. The reason we're calling everyone together to see the four of us here at this table is that we have nothing to hide. It's a sad strange thing that's happening, but Bill doesn't want to do it any more. There's no hidden agenda, or man behind the curtain.'[14]

With hindsight, the sensible thing would have been for the band to have gone home for a month or two, and re-emerged with some new ideas as to how to move forward as a trio. Instead, desperate to prove to themselves that they were still a band, they rushed headlong into probably the most serious crisis of their career.

At the beginning of 1998, in what was potentially yet another sign that all may have been seriously unwell at the Athens office, it emerged that one of the Athens office staff, the hard-working fan-club director Michelle Rawson, had committed suicide over the Christmas/New Year holiday period. One fan wrote the following account of Michelle Rawson's memorial service on an R.E.M. discussion forum:

'I drove through town to pick up a newspaper and noticed a lot of people walking through the arches wearing all black . . . carrying flowers. They had been at the memorial . . . Now, bear in mind that I've been weepy, depressed . . . for the past couple of days . . . But, as I was waiting at the light, I noticed Bill Berry. Standing by himself. Wearing his dark suit. Waiting to cross the street. It made me cry. I am not sure what part of it made me cry. And Bill wasn't really doing anything other than just standing there, but, for some reason, it was that image of him that sent me over the edge.'[15]

11. 'BE UNAFRAID', 1998–2001

I

A sea of uncomprehending faces. It's June 1998, and R.E.M. are on stage in Washington DC in front of one of the biggest audiences of their lives, 60,000 people gathered together for a good cause – not R.E.M. this time, but Tibetan freedom. It's the band's first public appearance without Bill Berry, and the opening song isn't really a 'song' at all. It's the previously unheard 'Airportman', essentially an instrumental with Stipe's semi-audible hushed tones layered on top.

> He moves efficiently
> Beyond security
> Great opportunity . . . awaits

None of it made any sense, unless you were a devotee of the beautifully mindless repetitions of Krautrock and Eno, that is. Stipe, bare-tummied and swathed in a sarong, looked out at an audience that was being confronted with the stark reality. This wasn't the R.E.M. they had come to know and love. Surely these were imposters?

Scott McCaughey vividly remembers the technically hitched Tibetan Freedom Concert at the RKK Stadium: 'It was not a disaster, but I would say that the audience was probably somewhat mystified! Those 60,000 people weren't expecting us to push a button on a synthesiser and have a little drum machine start up and do a song nobody had ever heard before. That took a lot of balls! With hindsight, it probably wasn't such a great idea, but I've got to hand it to them! R.E.M. are always excited about doing new songs, so we did four songs that nobody had heard before. A lot of the new material then was pretty slow, not real arena rock by any stretch of the imagination. So, it was a little risky. I just remember reading the review in *Rolling Stone*, which said something like, "R.E.M. came out and played not only four slow songs, but four of the slowest songs ever recorded." It was quite funny, actually.'

Although their public didn't know it yet, R.E.M. had just split up and re-formed. Or at the very least had seriously discussed trading in their name as R.E.M. for three solo careers. Band relations had collapsed during the spring of 1998, Berry's departure having had a profound effect both on R.E.M. as people, and on the music they made. As individuals, the three original members descended into glum, warring silence. As musicians, they made music which seemed to belong on someone else's album. Already committed to a process of change, Berry's absence, as Stipe would later comment, appeared to propel the band through two or three albums' worth of development to the point they found themselves in in late 1998, in other words with an album, *Up*, which was a genuine musical departure. Stipe's friend Thom Yorke, himself embarked on a similar quest to redesign the sound associated with his band Radiohead, had encouraged an uncertain Stipe with a friendly phone message.[1] So too did Stipe's hero, Patti Smith. '*Be unafraid*,' she told him.

II

Bill Berry had been the anchor. He was the man most likely to rein in the more extreme tendencies of his fellow musicians. Now the band had to learn how to make a record without him. His absence is all over their eleventh album, *Up*, a dark record, lost in its own world of spiritualism and questioning. With Berry not there, the band pulled in two different directions.

'Bill had a lot of ideas concerning self-editing,' affirms Mills. 'He was very good at keeping us from indulging in too many flights of fancy, and too many self-indulgent things. He had some good musical ideas that often kept us from trying too many different things before we settled on one that we liked. So there were a lot of things that kept us centred and grounded when Bill was in the band. Without him, we all took off on our own little paths, and it turned out that we had to come back together to find a way we could all three could work comfortably together. We lost that when Bill left.'

Buck had always worked rather differently to Mills and Stipe. Like Berry, he was punctual and disciplined. By contrast, Mills and Stipe, with that trait so many rock stars seem to acquire, were habitually never on time, and would start work late and often finish early the next morning. For the new album, it had already been decided that the way forward for the band would be to augment the traditional foursome with outside musicians. Although there was no permanent replacement for Berry, the onus was now more firmly on these musicians to cover the territory he had vacated. Buck soon found himself in the awkward position of being the only member of the original line-up who turned up on time for the sessions. He would begin laying down his musical ideas with Scott McCaughey, Barrett Martin and Joey Waronker while waiting for the appearance of either Mills or Stipe. This was R.E.M. by proxy.

Bizarrely, after he quit, Berry would drop by the studio in Athens, as Peter Buck reveals: 'He'd walk through and go "How ya doin', guys?" He'd hang around a little bit and say "sounds good guys". I think in his own shy way he was trying to get us used to the fact that he wasn't going to be with us, but he'd drop in now and again.'

According to Buck, Mills was going through an uncharacteristically unfocused period in his life, and frustration soon boiled over. For his part, Stipe appeared so traumatised by the recent events that he was unable to write at all.

> That record is an anomaly. Generally Mike's involved at the very beginning. On that record, he just wasn't focused, and Michael was having writer's block. My problem was that we had hired these extra guys to work with us, and we'd get there at one o'clock. Everyone else would wander in at four or five, order lunch and read the newspapers. At that point I would have already cut tracks and overdubbed them. So basically I was making a record without any input from other guys in the band. They resented that, but if I got there at one o'clock, I wasn't going to wait until four o'clock. It got to the point where we were arguing, well, why do this then? It just didn't make any sense really. In addition, people would get focused on little things, and work on, say, one piano riff for three days. It was crazy. 'I'm not going to spend my life like this,' I thought to

myself, 'I'm gonna have a nervous breakdown.' It was frustrating for everyone, though. I think it was frustrating for Mike because, since he wasn't there on time, he wasn't getting to do as much as he normally does. For him it was like, these guys who aren't in the band are getting to play all over the record and I'm not really on it. My feeling was, you know what, you wanna be on the record? Then show up, 'cos that's *all* it takes. People go through a phase where they're not particularly focused on life and that was his. I've had mine too. I was really a kind of workaholic so, no matter what's going on in my life, I'll show up on time and work. I think he was kind of at a loose end, had maybe broken up with his girlfriend. I'm not sure if it was a crisis, but sometimes you're not sure which way you wanna go.

One can imagine the tension: Buck, having finished his initial contribution, hanging around, waiting, thinking he'd much prefer to be back home with Zoë and Zelda than reading the umpteenth book of the week while he did some more waiting. Mills, unfocused, finding himself a bit-part player on his own record. Stipe, nothing to say, no words coming. 'Peter entered the studio with his ideas pretty much ready to go,' is how Mills puts it. 'He knew what he wanted to do; he knew what he wanted it to sound like. I like to listen to things, take my time, and then see what inspires me. All this was downtime for Peter. It was really pointless for him to sit there while Michael and Pat and I tried to listen to things and figure out what to do. He was missing his daughters, and he would rather be with them. We could understand that.'

Of course, the album did get finished, or finished after a fashion. The band now tend to the conclusion that they simply ran out of time on *Up*. The release date had been set for late autumn 1998, and they simply delivered as best as they could when they had to. According to Buck, they could have taken a thousand years and still never have finished it.

When the words and melodies did start coming for Stipe, he wrote in a disturbed and questing, questioning persona. With the aim of writing about how technology and material advancement complemented or contradicted one's spirituality, he produced lyrics that were laden with religiosity and biblical musings. Stipe has claimed that he thought he was working on the band's last will and testament, so bad were the internal politics at the time. The record's emotional closer, 'Falls To Climb' appeared to confirm that the end was in sight:

Who cast the final stone?
Who threw the crushing blow?
Someone has to take the fall
Why not me?

Of course, the band did endure, but not until a crisis meeting had been called by manager Bertis Downs at an Idaho lodge in July 1998. Constantly mindful of what's public and what's private, the band have remained fairly tight-lipped about what went on. Stipe has said in interviews that they 'vomited on each other' for three days, venting their anger and discussing what had gone wrong before finally resolving to continue. It was decided that the band was more important than any individual's hurt feelings. However, it was touch and go. When Mike Mills boarded the flight to take him to the powwow, did he think R.E.M. were splitting up?

Oh yeah. Michael and I were flying out there hoping it wasn't over, but thinking that it probably was. Of course it was difficult. The wisest thing to do would have been to take a little time off and to reassess our situation after Bill decided to quit. But part of going on like that is a reaction against that feeling: no, I'm not going to take time off and take a chance on the band breaking up, I'm going to forge ahead because I want the band to stay together. The reality of it was that forging ahead almost broke the band up. We had no idea how much the working dynamic would change after Bill. We had forgotten how to communicate. What happened was that it brought out the differences concerning the way the three of us work on records. Bill not being there really polarised us and, instead of communicating about it, we dealt with it in bad ways. So basically all that was a chance for us to get together, clear the air, and relearn how to communicate with one another.

III
Up was released in November 1998, to mostly positive notices. They weren't unanimous in their praise, but to say that Up was

poorly received is untrue. Four-star, if not five-star, reviews abounded. This was a crucial period in the development of the band, however, and manager Bertis Downs was more sensitive to it than most, as Ballard Lesemann recalls:

Bertis is fiercely loyal to that band, almost to a fault. He can be so defensive about them that he'll blow up over something really small. In 1998 we wanted to run a big feature on *Up* for *Flagpole* [Athens-based newspaper]. For some reason they weren't going to send out review copies until release date. But we had to have it a week and a half earlier, so we could get it, review it, and run it the week of release, otherwise we'd be a week behind everybody. We finally convinced them to give us a cassette tape copy of the album, so we dubbed off four more cassettes. Four writers ran independent reviews and we made it a cover feature. It's their home-town paper, so this was a major event. Two of the reviews were very mixed, one was fairly negative, one was very positive – you can't get more balanced than that. The reviews were not knocking them personally, but they said things more like 'this record's really drowsy and going in a weird direction', or 'they sure miss Bill Berry', or 'I can tell Mike and Peter sure have been listening to a lot of Beach Boys, but this stuff?', that kind of criticism. Bertis called up and let us have it, and it was like 'calm down, hothead! Hey man, we're all friends here, but we're trying to be legitimate critics.' He talks really fast and he's always got something to do, and I can understand he's got his hands full. But he's a hell of a nice guy – I really admire his assertiveness and his drive, he's totally gung ho and on top of things, but so highly strung some times. On other occasions, he will call up and compliment the editor on an editorial that he agrees with.[2]

By R.E.M.'s standards, *Up* flopped badly in the USA. It sold 117,000 copies on its first week of release there, half that of *New Adventures In Hi-Fi*. By the summer of 1999 US sales figures stood at around 600,000 copies. *Out Of Time* sold 4.2 million in the US alone. Eventually *Up* would sell just over two million copies worldwide. These sales figures were no disaster, but they were well below what was expected of a band of R.E.M.'s stature. It may have concerned

Warner Brothers, but it didn't bother Peter Buck: 'I'm way past the age when selling records means anything to me. In fact, it never really did mean anything.'

This may be so, but the band do appear rather down on *Up*. True, like *Hi-Fi*, it's overlong. Its slumberous pace is oppressive, and in no way can it be said to be an easy listen, that's for sure. However, if you stick with it, it sucks you into its own world. Its melodies are beautiful, Stipe's singing is assured and almost lullaby-like, his voice drifting over the electronica, and the constantly surprising arrangements and weird blasts of sound – guitars camouflaged here, acoustic guitars giving way to trumpets there, the chiming of gamelan bells mixed with the bleats of an obsolete synthesiser to top things off – make this undoubtedly R.E.M.'s most eccentric, yet most personal record to date. Furthermore, 'Lotus', 'Hope', 'Daysleeper', 'At My Most Beautiful', 'Parakeet', 'Diminished' and 'Falls To Climb' must surely be among the band's very best work. 'There's a lot to *Up*,' agrees Mike Mills. 'It takes a lot of work to get inside it. The thing about *Up* is that it requires you to go somewhere, to take a little journey. If you want to understand *Up* you have to go where it is, and that's not a journey a lot of people want to take, it's kind of demanding. But that's OK, because I'd rather make a demanding record than a facile one.'

The album seems now to have something of a cult following, particularly amongst musicians and producers who 'get' the more odd sonic references and can relate to them in terms of the studio craft. Ken Stringfellow, who was brought in to augment the band's live sound for the *Up* tour, is unequivocal in his praise: 'I think it's a total masterpiece. *Monster* is more interested in artifice and exploring the whole issue of personae. It's a little bit cold in a way as these things tend to be. It's a little bit more of an intellectual exercise, whereas *Up* is so human and so emotional.'

According to Stipe, *Up* was a topsy-turvy album, which turned R.E.M.'s musical world upside down: 'The elements in our songs are always the same, going back to *Murmur* – the difference is how it's mixed, how it's arranged,' is how Stipe put it to *Uncut* in 1999. 'Typically, in the past, we'd have 30 tracks of stuff, but the guitar and the drums would take the front seat and everything else would sound interesting but indistinct, occurring somewhere underneath. The difference with *Up* is that the underneath stuff now becomes the stuff on top. And the drum machine takes precedence over the drums.'[3]

On *Up*, Buck traded in his lead guitar not for a mandolin, but for a crappy late-1970s synthesiser. He was fiddling around with synthesisers so old that they had switches labelled 'Rumba' and 'Rock 1', and played dinky little repeating patterns the like of which were last heard a whole musical lifetime ago. *Up* might well be dubbed R.E.M.'s *'New Adventures In Low-Fi'*.

Placing 'Airportman' at the start of the record left nobody in any doubt as to the band's intentions. 'That was probably one of the first ones done,' says Scott McCaughey.

That was recorded in San Francisco at Toast, which is the place where I worked the longest on the record. Peter had gotten this kind of crazy seventies keyboard called the Baldwin Discoverer. You just turn on this little drum machine and there's a tiny speaker in the keyboard. Mike started playing that little keyboard figure, and Peter started doing some feedback. It sort of drifted on, and Michael immediately got some words for it and sang it really quickly maybe even that night or the next day – and there it was! I jazzed through one take of piano going right through that song, and that was pretty much it. I think everyone was kind of feelin' a little Kraftwerk goin' on! It didn't start out that way, but once we got the drum machine and the drifty keyboard figure went down, someone even said that we should put this little low, leapy, farty synth sound on it like Kraftwerk.

On 'Hope' the retro-futurism of the record crackles with invention. Driven on by an unstoppable synth riff it powers to a crunching, awesomely mechanistic finale, exploding into grinding industrial noise at the end. 'That was another song which started life in Peter's attic,' says McCaughey. 'It was originally called "Boomerang", because Peter had this device called a Boomerang where you could record a phrase and the phrase would repeat over and over again, like a primitive sampler. So he recorded this riff on a Farfisa organ, and that's the riff that goes through the whole song. Michael immediately loved it, and came up with a lyric for it. It ended up changing quite a bit, but it is basically just a loop. When Michael got the melody, he asked if it could be in a different key. So we got the Boomerang out again, and the Farfisa. I played the riff in a different key and we reconstructed the whole thing again.'

For his part, Stipe provided one of his most surreal lyrics for the record, sung in a melody reminiscent of an earlier song, 'Suzanne', by Leonard Cohen. R.E.M., always the most upstanding of rock cats, decided that the best policy was to contact Cohen's publishers and give a credit, in much the same way that the publishers of 'Wimoweh' (originally adapted from a Zulu song by Pete Seeger's folk group, the Weavers, and as 'The Lion Sleeps Tonight' a huge for the Tokens and, lest we forget, Tight Fit) were also recompensed.

The only real rock song on the album is 'Lotus'. Its brutal drum sound and great riff have touches of mid-period Bowie, and it is the only song to sound like an actual performance. 'At My Most Beautiful' is a first for R.E.M. on two counts. It's Stipe's first unabashed love song, although once again the addressee is left unspecified. It might actually be a love song to himself, a sort of cool version of 'The Greatest Love Of All'. Secondly, it's the first R.E.M. track that is clearly a tribute, or homage. The song drips *Pet Sounds* and oozes Brian Wilson, and does so gorgeously. What is it about the Beach Boys sound, almost forty years on, that continues to inspire musicians? Scott McCaughey:

> The music from the period is unique, so beyond whatever
> influences initially inspired Brian and the band, that it has
> become almost a genre in itself, one that many, many current
> groups reference and occasionally emulate. The music is
> important to me because it makes me happy. It inspires a sense
> of wonder, and I can listen to it thousands of times and still find
> something new, something miraculous, each time. I think that
> quality, more than anything, is what R.E.M. has been striving
> toward with both *Up* and *Reveal*. Peter and I share a pretty
> fanatical love of the Beach Boys music, and some of Mike's piano
> compositions no doubt display his own love and respect for
> Brian's work (as well as the Beatles, Burt Bacharach, Jimmy
> Webb . . .), and *Pet Sounds* in particular. I think 'At My Most
> Beautiful' was the only truly conscious and obvious nod to the
> Beach Boys – partly because of Mike's heavenly back-up vocals,
> and partly because the band put Charlie Francis (who was
> sought out as recording engineer on *Up* primarily because of his
> brilliant work with the heavily Beach Boys-inspired High
> Llamas) and me to work one evening ladling on *Pet*

Sounds-associated instrumental elements like sleigh bells, banjo and bass harmonica. But everyone felt these were appropriate to the song, it wasn't just an exercise in creating a tribute. And you have to realise, when Michael wrote the wonderful words and melody, I can't imagine he was thinking of the Beach Boys, but was just trying to write the best song he possibly could! When Brian Wilson came to see us at the Greek Theatre in LA in the summer of '99, then yes, of course it was dedicated to him as a loving tribute. Which it surely was.'

'At My Most Beautiful' also made one of R.E.M.'s best videos. The narrative promo is simple and affecting, following the 'bad day', *Out Of Towners*-style, of a young cellist, played by Rain Phoenix, on her way to an audition, with Mills, Buck and Stipe the interview panel.

The overall mood on *Up* is sombre, muted, dark, penitential. 'The Apologist' is creepy, a slow-paced apologia sung over a doomy percussive beat and washes of electronics. Again, Stipe's lyrics, if taken literally, read like a band epitaph:

Thank you for being there for me,
Thank you for listening, goodbye

'There's a lot of crazy sounds going on that,' says McCaughey. 'I love the percussion groove on it. It's got all these, clanky ethnic percussion things going on. Barrett Martin collects percussion instruments from all over the world and we put many of them to good use on that one. I think he was playing something like a bodhran, one of those Irish hand-drum things, although I think it was more of an Egyptian version of it. I know I was playing a bunch of Tibetan bowls that I was clanking together. It's real snaky, that song!'

On the album, 'Walk Unafraid' is a relatively muted piece, yet, when played live, it attains an anthemic, power-pop quality absent from the original. Better is the distinctly odd 'Parakeet' and the haunting 'Diminished', another in the line of last-minute R.E.M. songs à la 'Man On the Moon' and 'Let Me In'. The song also alludes to the modern shamanism of the media and to one of the inspirations behind the group's current musical preoccupations, referencing Brian

Eno's Oblique Strategies cards which, produced in the late 1970s, were a sort of musical I-Ching for the studio:

> I'll consult the I-Ching, I'll consult the TV, ouija, oblique strategies

The album's finale, the stately 'Falls To Climb', sees a confessional Stipe end the album stranded in self-doubt, his words picked out by an ominous military drum beat, the ethereal musical swirling around in curlicues. It's marvellous stuff, but not for the faint-hearted.

'Daysleeper' was rightly insisted upon by Warner Brothers to be the first single, presumably because it was in that classic tradition of R.E.M. songs in 6/8 time, although one of the catchiest songs on the album, the slightly naïve 'Why Not Smile', was surprisingly over-looked at every stage when pondering what on earth might be played on the radio. Shame, since John Michael Stipe was on guitar at the end. 'Daysleeper' nodded off at a peak of Number 57 in the States. In the UK, however, the single surged into the Top 10 on its first week of release, and the band played a number of promotional events at the time of release. The superb video was shot as a photomontage of jerky single-frame images (or stop-motion animation as it's technically called) depicting Stipe, the office worker, leading a life of reversed hours and solitariness.[4]

It was becoming apparent that R.E.M.'s commercial power base was shifting from the United States to Europe, particularly the UK. Ever since *Automatic For The People* failed to reach Number 1 in the USA, the UK market, the fourth-largest in the world, had seen more R.E.M. records sold per capita than any other. The Brits loved R.E.M., the critics showered them with awards, and the fans placed their singles with reasonable regularity into the Top 20. 'There's certainly an intensity of interest in music as culture over there,' says Bertis Downs. 'There aren't a lot of institutes of popular music in America the way there are in England. By far the second-largest section in the fan club is from the UK. From the very early days of playing at Dingwalls and The Marquee in 1983, they've always had an affinity with us. We've been in England on release dates many times doing TV and interviews. There's always been an excitement about R.E.M. in the UK, and we all love being there.'

IV

Ironically, given Berry's increasing discomfort with long tours, the band now decided that the era of the world tour was over. 'It had nothing to do with Bill, we just decided that there would never be a time when we would go out for eleven months at a stretch,' affirms Mike Mills. 'It's just not going to happen. It becomes no fun by the end, and it's just too hard. Peter's got his little girls now, and he doesn't want to leave them for that long.'

The band initially decided to tour *Up*, then changed their minds, worried, in Scott McCaughey's words, that 'it would be too much, it would kill the band'. Instead they committed themselves to a shorter promotional tour, which included some club shows, TV and radio, nothing that would keep them away from Seattle and Athens for any longer than a few weeks. Gigs included Neil Young's Bridge School Benefit Concerts, *The Late Show with David Letterman*, VH1's *Storytellers* and *Later with Jools Holland* in the UK, as well as shows in Germany, Spain, Austria and Sweden. Perhaps mindful of their ageing fan-base, R.E.M. also appeared on an episode of *Sesame Street* singing 'Furry Happy Monsters', with Kate Pierson replaced by a Muppet!

Ken Stringfellow and Joey Waronker (who had played on a few songs from *Up* and at the Tibetan freedom concert from 1998) were now permanent members of the touring group along with Scott McCaughey, a 'veteran' of the *Monster* tour three years earlier. In the spring of 1999, R.E.M. played another dozen or so shows such as the Tibet House Benefit Concert at Carnegie Hall, where they collaborated with Philip Glass and Patti Smith.

The band finally committed to a short tour in the summer of 1999. They weren't doing it to prop up the new album, since *Up* had dropped out of the charts in most countries by this time. They were doing it because they felt like it. 'The tour was long enough to cover a lot of ground, and not long enough to burn everybody out,' points out McCaughey. A short European tour, playing medium to large-sized arenas, many of them open air, was followed by a six-week tour of the States. Fan-club members were given first refusal on two tickets for any venue. 'It's great for the fans and great for us,' said Stipe. 'We're guaranteed people in our eyeline who appreciate the band, and not the promoter's hairdresser's friend.'[5]

Following the long tradition of fantastic support acts, Patti Smith, Suede and Wilco were just some of the big names enrolled to open the evening's fun. The set, as ever, was fast changing from night to night. *Up* staples such as 'Lotus' and 'Walk Unafraid' were set against slam dunks such as 'Man On the Moon' and 'The One I Love', but the hardcore fans marvelled at the occasional reappearance of 'Pilgrimage', 'Cuyahoga' and 'Stand'.

Stipe sang confidently, sashayed playfully and looked far less the media monster of the previous tour. Bathed in the neon glow of the stage design – a back-wall projection of an imaginary advertising hoarding with symbols from across the globe, this was a much less tension-filled show than their previous outing. With the trio augmented to a touring posse of not only excellent musicians but also R.E.M. fans, Stipe, Mills and Buck were pressured into putting some more obscure older songs into the set. They had, in some cases, forgotten how to play them, and needed more than a little prompting by the new musicians, who were more *au fait* with some areas of their catalogue than they were themselves.

Taking a break from rehearsals for the tour, the band and the Athens office were invited over to Berry's house. They found a contented man, happy to ride round on his tractor on his small-holding in Wattkinsville, about half an hour out of Athens, cutting the hay twice a year, sowing, planting, and living a life totally lacking the late hours and manic scheduling of a rock star. 'It was a dinner party, casual style, people from the R.E.M. office and friends and what not,' says Ken Stringfellow. 'There was a buffet and a barbecue, people pairing off in twos and threes, inside and out. He seemed to be familiar with me and the music I played. He seemed very enthusiastic that R.E.M. were doing things even though he, for whatever reasons, couldn't be involved. My impression of him as a person is that he's very shy. To be that kind of personality *and* be on tour *and* doing press – well, my impression is that that would be very difficult for him.'

The tour was fun. Mike Mills was nicknamed 'Trouble' by the tour manager due to his propensity for staying up late. On a visit to Prague, the restaurant menu invited them to partake of a dish called 'Hot Cock'. When a *Q* journalist asked which R.E.M.-er had delighted in this delicacy, 'The singer raised an arch eyebrow and allowed the hint of a grin.'[6] They got to play in an opera house in Vienna, and in front of their home crowd (or as near as dammit) at the Chestian Park Amphitheatre in Atlanta.

For the Atlanta gig, R.E.M. considered asking Bill Berry to play with them, as Peter Buck recalls:

As much as I want to see him, it puts real pressure on him if I ask him to come and do something. We invited him to the show, and considered asking him to play, but Mike said, 'No, he would stress about that for the whole three months beforehand and then he probably wouldn't show up.' So, we invited him to the show, and he stood at the side of the stage. Then people in the audience saw him and shouted, 'Hey Bill,' and Bill waved and after the song was finished he walked out on stage, hugged Mike, Michael and me, then walked over to Joey [Waronker, the tour drummer], and shook his hand . . . and the whole audience was going insane of course . . . then he waved to the crowd and walked off stage. I think he got in his car and drove home, because I didn't see him after the show.

The highlight of the tour was possibly not the occasion when Cerys from Catatonia walked on stage and kissed Mike Mills, though it may have been for Mills of course. It was more likely to have been R.E.M.'s appearance at the Glastonbury Festival. The band had been asked to play the event many times before but, due either to scheduling conflicts or wilful playing-hard-to-get avoidance tactics, they had never appeared there, until 1999, the one year they had not been invited (they simply invited themselves). It's quite common for musicians to describe gigs as 'awesome', 'amazing' or 'the one', but in this case, with thousands of fans singing along to R.E.M. classics, it probably was that bit more special, even for pop stars used to the celebrity junket and the grandiose gesture. 'I was really excited because I got to see Blondie, and the Beautiful South is always fun in England because the crowd are always so into it,' remembers Scott McCaughey. 'By the time we got up there it was dark. We're doing "Everybody Hurts", and there are campfires up there and it's wild. It was pretty moving, and we rose to the occasion.'

The tour finished in Mansfield, Massachusetts. 'This is sort of like the end of summer camp,' Stipe told the 20,000 people there. 'I wish it could go on and on.' Jon Vena of Sonic Net wrote: 'Opening with the *Up* track "Lotus", Stipe took the stage at the Tweeter Center with glitter around his eyes and blue circles painted near his temples.

Stipe was dressed in layers: a long black tuxedo jacket dangled over a white, pinstriped smock, which buttoned over a multicoloured Japanese kimono. Turning to the crowd, he accidentally smacked his head against the microphone.'[7]

V

Work on the next album began in the first few months of 2000. By this point R.E.M. had scored their biggest ever hit in the UK with 'The Great Beyond', a single culled from the soundtrack to the film *Man On The Moon*, which R.E.M. had worked on. Starring Jim Carrey as comedian Andy Kaufman, and Courtney Love as his wife, the film was a critical success. Stipe was executive producer of the film, as he had been for *Being John Malkovich* and *Velvet Goldmine*. 'The Great Beyond' was almost instantly taken to be in the 'classic R.E.M. mode'.

'The lead-in to the chorus is like a chorus, it's that powerful,' says McCaughey who worked on the record. It's like 'Losing My Religion', the whole song is a chorus!' Twenty years on from their first gig, it gave R.E.M. their very first UK Top 3 single.

During 2000 R.E.M. worked in Vancouver, Athens, Dublin and Miami. Michael Stipe, in need of fresh inspiration, jetted off to Israel to soak up the sun and to work on the lyrics for the new album. The mood was optimistic; the pain of making *Up* a memory, and, in interviews, Stipe began to talk more openly and with less apprehension. The band would stay in Dublin for more than two months in a low-pressure atmosphere. U2 were doing some filming at the time for their own record, *All That You Can't Leave Behind*.

'As usual Dublin is a fun, lively place, and there's a lot going on with the Theatre Festival underway,' wrote Bertis Downs. 'Tonight, Radiohead rolls into town for three nights in a circus tent; we are all looking forward to seeing them at the end of their European tour.'[8]

In 2001, some newspapers picked up on the story that Michael Stipe was gay. Not only was this piece of 'news' about as revelatory as discovering that Mother Theresa had been a Catholic, but it was also an old 'new' story. In 1994, Stipe had referred to himself as an 'equal opportunities letch' in an interview for *Details* magazine. In 1999, following the then recent trend of rock stars confessing all in web chats, TV documentaries and video diaries, Stipe, when asked 'Are you now or have you ever been gay?', gave the following unequivocal response: 'Gay? I don't like that term. The very concept of gay puts people in categories. 'Queer' to me is much broader, the idea that something like sexuality is extremely fluid and not capable of being reduced to a category. Am I queer? Absolutely. I have enjoyed sex with men and women throughout my life.'[9]

Stipe's view of sexuality was not unlike that of the outrageously 'out' Boy George, whose homosexuality had been reduced to almost cartoon-like dimensions by his theatrical showboating. The former Mr O'Dowd had said that everyone is homosexual – there are just degrees of homosexuality, and that everyone is heterosexual – there are just degrees of that too. For Stipe, labels were for canned food, not people, and certainly not for himself. He did, however, find the term 'queer' acceptable as a label because of its non-specificity. People could be straight queer, or gay straight.

In her exhaustive study, *Vice Versa: Bisexuality and the Eroticism of Everyday Life*, Marjorie Garber looks at how the use of the term 'queer' had developed in 'metrosexual' circles, 'that is, largely urban and upper middle class. This is perhaps another way of saying that it is a label of some privilege.' She goes on:

Queer chic is now so chic in metrosexual circles that the 'straight queer' is everywhere to be found. *GQ* sketched out a 'Spectrum of Gay Positivity' that ranged from 'Active in Gay Causes' (Barbara Streisand, Elizabeth Taylor) to 'Appropriating Gay Characteristics' (Markie Mark, Prince), 'Professing One's Own Inner Gayness' (Kurt Cobain, Sharon Stone), and 'Pretending to be Gay' (Madonna, certain college students).[10]

This is why some gay men disapprove of the word 'queer', because it is so inclusive, it categorises their experience as being the same as that of lesbians, bisexuals, transvestites and transsexuals.

It's tempting therefore to see Stipe's appropriation of the label simply as the sign of a rich man, with a circle of friends partly drawn from the entertainment industry, picking up on the then voguish word. However, there's no denying that Stipe had become far more open about his own orientation. In 2000, a full year before the media went overboard on it, he said, 'As long as I've been sexually active, I've always been attracted to and slept with men and women. Right now, I've met an incredible man who is an artist, whom I have completely committed myself to.'[11]

Having turned 40, Stipe finally had the self-confidence not to duck the issue in interviews. But his sexuality, if not exactly a non-issue, is nevertheless pretty irrelevant to what we admire him for, which is his music and his art. 'I think he's been pushed into claiming homosexuality or whatever this week's term for it is,' says Stephanie Chernikowski. 'I've heard Michael say, I am gay, I wear dresses, I wear eye make-up. But I don't think he makes that distinction in his own mind. Sexual preference is made to be way too important, especially with artists. He has an incredible hold on the female psyche and I guess he has on the male psyche as well. And I guess that's what's important in art – it's not who he goes home with afterwards.'

VI

A wave of joy. R.E.M. are playing the biggest gig of their lives. It's Rio. It's January. Caipirinhas have been served on stage during the encore. Two-and-a-half years ago at the Tibetan Freedom Concert, the new R.E.M. had foundered, their set marred by technical fuck-ups, and their future uncertain. In Rio, they were self-confident and composed, a functioning unit once again. An estimated 190,000 Brazilians saw R.E.M. that night. It was such a triumph that the corporate nature of the event was almost forgotten. The Festival, staged in partnership with AOL and commencing just 24 hours after the merger between AOL and Time-Warner, surely confirmed that the band were now as much a part of the mainstream Establishment as Bill Gates, MacDonald's and Donald Duck.

Such thoughts were presumably not on the minds of the progressive libertarians in the R.E.M. camp, though the inherent contradiction of the position is problematical. Former Q editor Paul Du Noyer puts forward a powerful argument against the sort of celebrity liberalism he sees R.E.M. as typifying:

I was reading the interview with R.E.M. in the Q May 2001
issue. It prompted me to think about the irritation I was having
with celebrity liberalism, which seems to be a kind of
intellectual laziness with a hint of moral duplicity. The Q
interview took place in the wake of two things: one was the
election of George Bush and the second was the
anti-globalisation protest in Seattle. All the members of R.E.M.

took basically the same line on this, and I thought 'talk about having your cake and eating it'. On the one hand they're content to reap the benefits of belonging to a global American capitalist organisation, i.e. Time Warner-AOL. On the other hand they retain the right to pose as rebels against that system and sneer at the hand that feeds them, which is an especially safe position for them to take, (a) because they live in one of the few nations in the world that affords them the opportunity to become millionaires playing rock music while at the same time posing as rebels against that system, and (b), for rock stars such as R.E.M., all expressions of liberal discontent play extremely well with their audience and through their favourite media channels, such as Q magazine.

It's an entirely pain-free form of rebellion that they're adopting. There's no risk involved in it whatsoever, but quite a bit of shoring up of customer loyalty. And when I read their expressions of how cross they are at the election of George W. Bush, I just hear the sound of Democrat teddy bears being thrown out of cots. It's an expression of petulance on behalf of a liberal elite which includes R.E.M., Julia Roberts and Barbara Streisand, whining because they no longer enjoy the same kind of symbolic hotline to the White House that they enjoyed under Clinton. Clinton was an entirely different character to Bush. I found Clinton to be an obnoxious, posturing hypocrite. He was the kind of politician who fawns upon celebrity and who regards it as key to his appeal that he is down with popular culture. George Bush just couldn't give a fuck about popular culture; the less he seems to be aware of it, the better that plays with his constituency.

It's easy for Buck or Mills to talk glibly of the contradiction of working for AOL/Time Warner and at the same time being on the side of the anti-globalisation protestors, but it's not enough to say it's a contradiction. It's actually so fundamental that you've got to address it or to be accused of hypocrisy forever after. They're quite content to reap the benefits of this economic system, but at the same time reserve the right to posture as enemies of it.

Bono I have more time for, because Bono increasingly shows awareness of the absurdity of what he does and what he is. Bono

I think regards himself as a comical character. Now, I never get any inkling that R.E.M. are aware of their absurdity. R.E.M. strike me as being quite pompous actually. While Bono is committed to his various good causes he also seems to accept the absurdity of a pop star being cited as an authority on these subjects. Bono seems to take his crusading as a duty he has to adopt given his position.

R.E.M. are impeccably liberal. Stipe's sexual identity does them no damage in that respect. They always come across as basically decent, likeable, intelligent people. No journalist that I sent to R.E.M. ever came away saying, 'I hate those bastards,' which could often happen with other artists.[12] I'm sure they are fine people. My cynicism isn't really personal, it's that there is a certain flaw in what I see as celebrity liberalism. You're either for that system or you should abandon it altogether. You confess that you owe your wealth and privilege and celebrity to American capitalism and if you attempt to conceal that by pretending to be down with the anti-global protestors, then there's something flawed in the decision you are taking.

Have R.E.M. become, whether they like it or not, a corporate rock act, and are they aware of the contradictions?

'Certainly,' says Peter Buck, with trademark honesty. 'I shop in little independent stores, buy my records from little independent record shops, shop in the independent bookstore and locally-run groceries. I don't go in big shops, and yet, of course, I'm signed to the biggest label on earth. I can see the contradictions but I don't see why doing business with a big corporation precludes any kind of political activity or anything, in that virtually every person on earth works for a big corporation. A rock journalist who levels criticisms against us probably works for a big company owned by someone who makes cigarettes and napalm. You can think of any major rock magazine and there's basically prostitution ads in the back pages, ads for cigarettes and alcohol. Everyone is touched by that stuff.'

In 2001, Peter Buck had rather more serious matters to deal with than the contradictions of life in a capitalist society. The year would be one of anxiety and depression on a personal level, with the very real prospect of imprisonment at the forefront of his mind. But there would also be a commercial and critical comeback (of sorts) for his band. How ironic, then, that the soundtrack for the year would be provided by the optimistic and humanistic music on the new album, *Reveal*.

12. MUSIC FOR A MARKET THAT DOESN'T EXIST? 2001–02

I

In a sense, we're back where we began, in the record shop that is Peter Buck's mind. For it is Peter Buck, the musical conceptualist in the band, with whom, we suspect, the future course of R.E.M. resides. Buck is now 45 years old. He's been a musician for two-thirds of his life. The music he made in 1982, that vibrant, youthful sound full of possibilities, has long gone. But bloated or uninteresting he is not, and nor is the music he makes. We would not and could not expect it to be the sound of his youth. Too many middle-aged rock stars have fallen into that trap with almost always disastrous results. No, the music R.E.M. now make is becoming to their age and status.

Pop and rock is no longer 'youth' music, and hasn't been for quite a while. Indeed the whole concept of 'youth' detached itself from its biological moorings some time ago. It's not uncommon to find that parents have more left-field minority tastes than their teenage children. A recent ethnographic survey by Christina Williams on young people and popular music came to this gloomy conclusion: 'Popular culture often doesn't have to mean anything but can be handy to pass the time, to fill a silence or to entertain in rather banal ways . . . popular music consumption, like other media consumption . . . is often insignificant and mundane . . . The young people in this study framed the importance of popular music in their lives in terms of routine use rather than emotional investment or identity construction.'[1] 'Banal', 'mundane', 'routine' – it's a depressing litany.

Talking about the R.E.M. single 'The Great Beyond', Michael Stipe told *Dazed And Confused* magazine in 2000 that it was a 'great pop song, but it was made for a radio market that doesn't exist anymore. We are just completely out of step with what's happening.'[2] Their 2001 album *Reveal* proved, at least in the United States, that R.E.M. really were now a genre all to themselves. Their music crossed genres, was above genre, and didn't fit into any of the formats in American radio. 'Nowadays, you've got all these sort of hybrid radio stations and it's all specialised in a way, but it's all monopolistic too because the same companies own all the stations, and it's all garbage,' says journalist Ballard Lesemann. 'If you travel twelve hours across any region of the US and you listen to commercial radio, it's all exactly the same, even down to the announcers, the promos, the "You're tuned into 96 wave FM" or whatever. It's the same voices; it's really ugly, horrible.'

'Clearchanel.com basically own every major market because of Clinton's deregulation of radio,' adds Ethan Kaplan, webmaster of *Murmurs*, the biggest unofficial R.E.M. website in existence. 'And SFX, who are associated with them, own all the venues. So, you have this monopoly on talent and how it's distributed. College radio is basically dead because all the frequencies are saturated.' In a world of dance, rap, boy bands, and the designer angst of metal and hard rock, R.E.M. could not be categorised. Theirs really had become music for a market that doesn't exist.

II

Reveal is a quite different album to *Up*. True, it shares *Up*'s lugubrious pace (and so disappointed some R.E.M. fans who wanted them to speed up and rock out a bit), but its music is more rounded, more confident, and less novel. Cynics might say that a band who had seen its sales figures halve with each successive release over the last decade needed to shore up some consumer loyalty by appealing to their core constituency. But, does that market exist any more? It certainly seems to for their old sparring partners, U2, whose album *All That You Can't Leave Behind*, released in November 2000, had, of course, done exactly that. Three albums of left-of-centre experimental pop had pissed off a large section of their fan base, so, with songsmithery intact and nary a synthesiser, dance groove, or slab of funkoid industrial noise in sight, U2 returned with an album that delighted their old fans. It was, as Bono commented, a big hug, a reassuring arm round the shoulder, a soulful reminder that U2 had returned to their original blueprint. U2 were reapplying for their old job.

The new R.E.M. had a slight whiff of the old. The admittedly terrific 'Imitation of Life' would not have been out of place on *Out Of Time*. A superbly catchy song, with trademark sweet strings, this was R.E.M.'s best single for a decade. 'We even thought about leaving it off the record because it was too R.E.M.,' says Mike Mills. 'We made a conscious decision some years ago to stop writing R.E.M. songs, and we have thrown away many songs because they sound too much like us, whatever the definition of that is! I think you know it when it happens. We felt that "Imitation Of Life" was very much in that vein. But everybody else was saying we were crazy to take it off, so we left it on.'

It may be the most recognisably R.E.M.-sounding track on the album, but it was a beast to get right. Peter Buck had had a version of it, much slower and called 'Fake Trumpet Chorus', as far back as 1999. It seems that Stipe had three goes at coming up with a melody and lyric for the chorus. Version 2 had a mid-sixties pop chorus of 'Baby, oh baby,' which was jettisoned, according to Mills, because 'it wouldn't wear very well', although most of the band thought it was great. The 'fake trumpets' were eventually replaced by the lovely string motif we have now. They tried combination after combination of instruments, at a variety of tempos, but eventually the simplest was the best: they simply handed round the acoustic guitars and everyone in the room played the same line. The result was an aggressive wall of acoustic guitar and a reminder of a bygone age of 'My Sweet Lord' and their own 'Talk About The Passion'.

The lyric Stipe eventually came up with is a trademark piece of writing. On a literal level, it confuses, yet the imagery is so startling, when taken out of context, that it lodges in your head and stays there.

Charades, pop skill
water hyacinth, named by a poet
imitation of life

Later, the allusiveness falls away to reveal a cameo of teenage discomfort, that state of being desperate to impress, yet self-conscious and clumsy, that for some never goes away:

Like a Friday fashion show teenager
Freezing in the corner
Trying to look like you don't try

The single had a distinctive, if not completely successful video, which utilised the techniques of both wide-screen cinematography and pan and zoom. In other words, certain sections of the film were played forward and backwards in a 15-second loop, then zoomed in on, highlighting the narrative. Stipe did a waggle-dance, his arse on swivel mode, Mills entertained in a striped shirt, while Buck sat with a chimp, as you do.

'I can't act and I can't dance, and I don't wanna lip-synch,' says Buck. 'I said, "Why don't you give me a monkey with a ukulele?" It was wearing trousers and was remarkably well behaved. They're actually apes, not monkeys. I call them monkeys too, but I think it would piss them off if they knew what you were saying.'

Reveal is nowhere near as commercial an album as critics made out at the time. 'Imitation Of Life' might have reached Number 6 in the UK, but it was really the only obvious single off the album, with the possible exception, that is, of 'Beat A Drum', which was not regarded as single material by Warner Brothers, despite the most beautiful melody by Mike Mills. 'We did that in Ireland, and it was one of the occasions where a producer can actually come in handy! When I wrote it, what is now the bridge was the chorus. The bridge is the weird key change bit in the middle when the horns play. Pat McCarthy said, we need a bridge, so I went in to write a bridge for it, and Pat said, "Why don't you make the bridge the chorus, and the chorus the bridge," which I did, and it was much better.'

Like much on *Reveal*, the sun comes out, the picnic is going well, but there are storm clouds on the horizon. Images of a tropical idyll are set against images of discomfort and chaos. The lines

Beat a drum for me, like a butterfly wing
Tropical storm across the ocean

are almost certainly a reference to chaos theory. The classic paradigm of chaos theory is the butterfly effect: 'a butterfly fluttering its wings in China triggers a long and complex chain of events that ultimately results in a tornado in Texas.'[3]

This dark side to *Reveal* is nowhere better, although perhaps unwittingly, evidenced than in the artwork. On first inspection, the sunburst motifs, the supersaturated, sunshiny yellow of both front and back, the images of rural contentment, the photograph of a sun-kissed cityscape from the air taken by Stipe himself, are all positive and uplifting. The songs themselves – 'The Lifting', 'I've Been High', 'Summer Turns To High' – talk of uplift, of transformation, of betterment. Yet there's something very wrong. The cover art, for example, is so self-consciously joyous that, like a self-consciously happy song, it is ultimately depressing. Yellow is the colour of the depressed. The unhappy overcompensate by wearing the colour of the daffodil. It's a 'manage-your-depression' front cover, while the blinding white light of the back has echoes of revelation, self-improvement, self-help – in the manner of an advert for the Church of Scientology, or Exegesis.

One song, 'The Lifting', arguably one of the best of their career, actually references such programmes of psychic and spiritual healing:

This conceit, these systems of belief,
Your counsellor agrees,
'You've always marked these boundaries, now you're free . . .'
And with relief

The mantric drum figure reminds us of the Beatles' 'Tomorrow Never Knows', while Stipe's vocal performance is stunning. The moment towards the end of the track when Stipe repeats the word 'never', then, changing the angle of attack, moves the second syllable higher up the scale, is genius.

'I was listening to him work it out in terms of where he went up to that other note, and it was fascinating,' remembers Mike Mills. 'The whole thing was not working until he got to the one where he's doing it now, and it worked! The other cool thing about "The Lifting" is that it was originally done more like "All The Way To Reno", but we decided that it was, in fact, too similar in terms of tempo and rhythm, so we turned it into this funkier thing.'

'In the intro, Scott and I are playing these undersea noises,' adds Ken Stringfellow, 'which surprisingly plays well into the lyrics, where he talks about sunken cities and that kind of thing.'

'I've Been High' is solemn, stately and emotional and, like 'The Lifting', contains some subtle dance textures and beats beneath the vocal. 'In a way, it's the masterwork of the record,' says Stringfellow. 'It's the biggest stretch for them. It's like pushing the boundary of what defines them musically. There's something going on there; it's emotionally compelling and you can interpret it in a variety of different ways. I get a lot of things from *Reveal* that appear to be about personal transformation, and rising, not just from adversity, but from your own boundaries and limitations, the little pitfalls and weak spots that hold you back.'

The album title comes from this song. 'Have I missed the big reveal?' struck Bertis Downs. 'I thought "the big reveal" was just a great phrase from a great song, and then they decided that they just liked the word 'reveal'. Since then, they've made me feel a bit uncomfortable when they say that Bertis named the album. It happens to be their words!'

For 'All The Way To Reno (You're Gonna Be A Star)', Stipe is once again back in character-playing mode, this time as an aspirant female starlet on the road to fame. The music, lush and powerfully realised, has echoes of old-style R.E.M. rootsiness. Another song in the classic R.E.M. tradition, 'She Just Wants To Be', starts organically, with acoustic guitar, and ends synthetically, with computer-driven synth strings melding with traditional orchestration.

'I love that string part,' enthuses Mills. 'We had a great time working with Johnny Tate, the string arranger. The mixture of real strings and synthesised strings works well; removes a little of the saccharine nature of strings.'

The oddest track on the album, and the creepiest R.E.M. track ever cut, is 'Saturn Return'. With his keen interest in astrology, Stipe would obviously have known that, between the ages of 28 and 32, the planet Saturn, disciplinarian of our solar system, 'comes back to check on you', as Kim McCarten puts it. 'It is often a difficult time of soul-searching and self-questioning. For some people, the wake-up call is a short-lived scare, a kick in the ass that motivates them to pursue their chosen path.'[4] He might also have been aware of the 1998 Broadway show, *Saturn Return*.[5] Part of its oddness comes from the fact that it was composed on piano by a non-expert pianist.

'I wrote it on piano,' says Buck. 'It was the end of a demo session actually and I said, "Look everyone, get the weirdest sound on your instrument that you can possibly imagine." Joey and I put this drum loop up, and I just said "Here are the chords." I then said, "We're gonna play it once, and don't worry about playing along with me, just do what you wanna do." We played it one time, and it was a chaotic mess. I was talking to Pat McCarthy about it, and he said, "It's kind of cool. Strip it down to the piano and take whatever you've got and move things around a little." So we took things and ran them backwards and looped things. But it's essentially a total live performance. It sounds on the record like the first day we started working on it.'

'Some of it was pieced together from the demo we recorded in Athens in February, including all that kind of Sonic Youth sounding guitar, which is actually me,' agrees Stringfellow. 'Pat kind of made a collage of stuff I had played on the demo, but the funny thing is that when we were playing the demo I was trying to do my best primitivist Peter Buck kind of thing! It was definitely homaging him to some degree.'

'Chorus And The Ring' was a first take. 'I didn't know the song,' recalls Mike Mills. 'I walked in just as we were about to record it, and so Peter was actually telling me the chords as we were going through it, and I was making up the bass line as we went! I was sitting close to him and he was mouthing the words to me so I would know where to go, and the places I went turned out to be the right ones. It's one of the most exciting moments in music where you don't know what you're going to play but it turns out that wherever your brain goes it's the right thing.'

A slow-paced and rather fine track, 'Fascinating', was removed from the record at the very last moment. 'It's really beautiful,' agrees Mills. 'It has a flute, oboe arrangement but it made the record too long and too slow in the middle, and something had to go.'

'It would fit perfectly on the record,' concurs Buck. 'You do get feedback from fans and friends, and everyone thought our last two records were just too long. I tend to agree with them. When Elvis Costello put out *Brutal Youth*, I loved that record, but I'm not sure I ever heard the last three songs. It was almost 70 minutes long and I don't ever have 70 minutes. When we originally sequenced it, it was another one that was 64 or 65 minutes long, and, we thought, something has to go. There are actual versions of that record floating around on the Internet, as it got to the test-pressing stage. "Fascinating" was Michael's favourite song, I think.'

'Interesting' is just one of dozens of R.E.M. songs that over the years were tracked but never made it on to the end product. Some of the tracks that were weeded out have surfaced on compilations, soundtracks, on reissues of old records, or on the Internet. 'Fascinating', for example, is available for download on the R.E.M. website, *Murmurs*.

In among this treasure-trove of songs which missed the boat first time round are *Out Of Time*-era numbers such as the very fine 'It's A Free World Baby', 'Fretless', the 'It's The End Of The World . . .' style spoken jive of 'Chance'. A whole variety of covers, including Iggy Pop's 'The Passenger', a tremendously hard-hitting version of Leonard Cohen's 'First We Take Manhattan', a poignant live version of 'Wichita Lineman', and a fun-pop version of a song dear to their hearts, 'Wimoweh'. There are some really fine instrumentals too: 'Emphysema', from the *Up* sessions, features an Indian harmonium, 'New Orleans Instrumental 2' is at least as strong as 'New Orleans Instrumental 1', which found its way into 12 million homes on *Automatic For The People*. 'Winged Mammal Theme' swings brilliantly. On 'Mandolin Strum', Buck is like a kid with a new toy, while 'Organ Song', a slowly paced formal piece of church organ music, is unsettling because its romantic sweep could double for music for either a wedding or a funeral.

The Automatic Box, released in late 1993 but now deleted, contained some of these tracks, but what is certain is that, sooner or later, R.E.M. will sit down together and compile an anthology. There are dozens of other songs tracked but never released, while, one suspects, hundreds of other pieces of music never finished off because Stipe wasn't inspired enough to find lyrics and a melody for them.

III

At the time of writing, *Reveal* is regarded by critics and band alike as one of the strongest ever R.E.M. albums. 'I feel good about the fact that when people are going through our pile of stuff whenever our career is over – assuming that people still listen to rock'n'roll when our career is over – *Reveal* will be one of the three or four that they'll pick out of our work and say, oh yeah, that's what the group were about,' says Buck, probably correctly. 'It really caught part of what was going on musically at the time. A whole lot of the dance music that Michael and I were listening to is incorporated into *Reveal*, without it ever being a dance record.'

The punters thought slightly differently. In America, the record sold about the same as *Up*. However, it went Top 3 in Germany, France, the UK and many world territories. With global sales of over four million it re-established R.E.M. as a commercial force. 'The people who bought *Reveal* in America were the ones that needed to hear it,' is how Peter Buck rationalises the poor sales of the record there.

Every day I've signed more copies of *Reveal* than I ever signed for *Automatic*. It's a record that people are fanatical about. The fact that it wasn't a huge hit – well, look what's in the charts. We don't fit in right now. I'm not saying that Warner Brothers did a good job in America because they didn't, but it's kind of hard when no radio station will play your record. The fact is that we're not particularly hip in America, and yet we're up for Grammys, and for every major award around the world, pretty much. And all that means is that the guys who spin the records didn't do it this time, and that's OK. We sold three or four million outside of America. I would put *Reveal* up with *Automatic*. *Automatic* might be slightly ahead in the atmosphere sweepstakes, but then partly that is me, because I know what we were all going through as people. It definitely has a heavier vibe to me than *Reveal*, but *Reveal* was supposed to be a kind of springtime, joyous record which nobody makes anymore. Every other record today is about being pissed off and alienated and about being a teenager. That's great, but, you know, Trent Reznor's just about my age and he's still singing about being in high school, it sounds like. We wanted to go against that.

It was therefore fitting that the highlight of the R.E.M. *Reveal* promotional campaign took place, not in America, but in Germany. On 12 May 2001, R.E.M. played a free concert right in the centre of Cologne. Bertis Downs remembers it as possibly the last R.E.M. concert of its type. 'It was audacious, unbelievable, awesome,' says Downs:

I guess, post September 11, we will never be able to pull anything like that off again. It's just so risky now. I woke up on September 13 or 14, and thought, in today's world, what were we thinking? It was a free show, held in downtown Cologne, right in front of the cathedral. We could see about 20–25,000 people but I'm told that police estimates were 100,000 in the downtown area. You worry about crowd control. You worry about stampedes. You worry about having too many people in one area, those kinds of things. We had professional people there, and the promoter made the thing safe, but it does seem to me that, with all the issues of safety, post September 11, that we're all confronting, we just wouldn't try it again.

The band rose to the occasion that night. They got there at 3 in the afternoon, and basically the whole square was full of fans watching them do their soundcheck. They came back, played for 90 minutes, and it was on MTV live all over Europe. It was one of those transcendent nights. We looked up at one point and there were people 80 feet above the ground in the cathedral, and we wondered how the hell they got up there. We found out later that they snuck in the day before, locked themselves in, crawled out on a little ledge, and watched the band from a bird's-eye view. Fans from all quarters of Europe came to the concert. We met people from Latvia, we met people from Greece . . . It was a special night.

'Find The River' was dedicated to Athens writer and poet John Seawright, who had died of a brain haemorrhage while the band was on tour. Michael Stipe had flown back for the funeral. Jefferson Holt and Bill Berry paid their respects too. Athens was, and is, a close-knit community. 'John was loved by so many people in the community, and died very suddenly this spring,' says Betsy Dorminey. 'He's somebody who was very important to a lot of folk. When John died, Michael made the effort to come back and speak to John's father and mother. He's very unassuming about that. He doesn't come with an entourage or anything or make a fuss. He's willing to grieve with the parents of a friend who died, in a way that's appropriate.'

In 2001 TV and radio show promotion was deemed just as important as committing to a soul-sapping world tour. In August they appeared on *Top Of The Pops* with *Reveal*'s second single, 'All The Way To Reno'.

'There's something sort of deliciously ironic about doing *Top Of The Pops*,' says Mills with a hint of mischief in his voice. 'It's such a historic show, and yet it's usually so full of crap!' The video for the single, directed by Michael Moore, was quite unlike anything else the band had ever done, and was shot during term-time in a secondary school. The stars of the videos, and in some cases the cinematographers, were the pupils themselves. The video split opinion, but to many it was rather touching. It was certainly unique.

The promotional tour had actually started back in a cool, rainy April when the band, numb of finger and screwed of PA, played a set in Trafalgar Square for the South African Freedom Day Concert. The reward for the three members of R.E.M., although not for the auxiliary musicians, was the chance to meet octogenarian Nelson Mandela.

Rehearsals for the concert had been preceded by the arrest of Peter Buck on charges of threatening behaviour, assault, and being drunk on an aircraft.[6] Along with his new guitar tech and assistant, Bob Whittaker, Buck and two other members of the band (presumably Scott McCaughey and Ken Stringfellow) had been on a flight from Seattle to Heathrow. According to the prosecution, Buck consumed an estimated 15 glasses of red wine. Not surprisingly, his behaviour deteriorated somewhat. At one stage he allegedly told the cabin crew 'Another glass, please – I'll collapse after this one.'

During the course of the flight – again according to the prosecution – Buck was politely requested not to drink any more alcohol when it became clear that he was drunk. This request angered Buck, and led to his staggering down the aisle in search of the drinks trolley. However, he was refused any more to drink. He tried a number of ruses to get more alcohol, including offering the cabin crew money. He was by now so incapacitated that he could barely stand. Having staggered to the front of the plane, he then got stuck between two seats and amused himself by playing around with the control panel on the wall which operated the cabin lights and the call bell. Finally he was given a written warning as to his behaviour, which he promptly tore up. Buck still refused to sit down, and tottered around from First Class to Club Class. At one point he tried to put one of his CDs into the service trolley, thinking it was a CD player. He then sat down next to a complete stranger in Club Class, and, on being asked to move, claimed that the passenger was his wife.

If this wasn't embarrassing enough, Buck was then allegedly involved in a scuffle with the cabin crew after aiming a spoonful of yoghurt at them. He allegedly grabbed one of the crew by the neck and yanked his tie, and grabbed a female member of the cabin crew who had tried to intervene, yanking her arm away. During the incident, a pot of yoghurt (rumoured to be lemon flavoured) exploded. Buck then announced his return to the First Class section by overturning a drinks trolley. At this point, he seemed to realise that he had gone too far, and attempted to help clear up the mess. A member of the cabin crew allegedly saw Buck slip a knife up his sleeve, but it was taken off him. Buck ended the fiasco by telling the cabin crew that *he* had been harassed and, declaring that he would be taking British Airways to court, announced 'I am R.E.M. and I can make up a story that I was assaulted.'

According to the prosecution, Buck slept through the final three hours of the flight. On arrival at Heathrow, he was immediately arrested and charged with six offences. On being questioned, Buck remembers having a few glasses of wine and then sleeping all the way from Seattle to London:

'I'm deeply sorry about it, first of all. I got on the plane, having worked 18-hour days, no sleep, didn't see my kids, hadn't eaten that day. I kind of decided that I'm on some sort of vacation for me even though I'm working, and I had three or four glasses of wine very quickly, and fell asleep. And the next thing I know, I was being bundled off the plane, for damage and threats, and I am completely sorry about that. Something woke me up, and I'm covered in cream – yoghurt was involved, and that's all I know, because I've never done anything like this before, and I'm just appalled and shocked at my behaviour and apologetic to the people who had to deal with me.'

Buck was granted bail. The trial began on 13 November 2001, but after a day of opening arguments from the prosecution, Judge John Crocker dismissed the jury.[7] Buck's lawyers argued that there had been an 'abuse of process' during the trial. Buck, deeply depressed by the incident, gave a huge sigh of relief. His defence, although not heard at the time, was that he had taken 35 milligrams of Zolpidem, a powerful sleeping pill, and that the violent reaction of this medication with the initial consumption of alcohol meant that he was not criminally responsible for his actions. The trial was postponed until March 2002.

Many of his friends, colleagues and associates were puzzled. Buck himself had once commented: 'I personally like to drink. I hope to have a glass of wine with dinner and a beer on a hot Sunday afternoon till the day I die – which I hope is about fifty years from now. I think it's stupid, when we've spent so much of our lives gaining control – we don't listen to anyone – to let something that comes out of a bottle ruin your life. And none of us have ever got that far, I think.'[8]

This kind of behaviour by people in the media spotlight is always both simultaneously a surprise (since, by choosing to live a high-profile life, they should know better) and totally expected (since rock stars are egged on to flaunt convention). When 30-something Ian Brown from the Stone Roses was convicted on air-rage charges, the reaction was one of mild surprise. But news that Peter Buck, from a band who had always presented a 'wholesome' and 'law-abiding' image, had been arrested was shocking and, in the end, rather sad.

'We just don't really do illegal things all that much,' Peter Buck had told *Select* in 1995. 'I double-park all the time. But I don't think that helps our cause in being perceived as rock'n'roll animals.'

'It came as a great surprise,' says writer Mat Snow, 'because I never got the impression that he was an angry man – intense, but not angry or abusive. He's always been a guy who likes a beer, but always on a very convivial level.'

'He takes the work really seriously,' says R.E.M. fan and webmaster Ethan Kaplan. 'But everything around it, the press and all that crap, he doesn't take seriously at all. He really respects the fans and stays behind to sign autographs and talk to people. He never puts on airs that he's a multimillionaire rock star. So it's sad that he got all this press about what he may or may not have done. His reputation with the press will always be connected with this yoghurt thing, which nobody knows whether it's true.'

After the incident, Buck simply got back into playing music, and began writing and recording for the next R.E.M. record, now scheduled for 2003. Of course, the terrorist attack on the World Trade Center profoundly affected the band, as it did everyone, and diverted attention away from the promotion of *Reveal* to far more serious matters. In fact, Michael Stipe was in New York with his friend Michael Lachowski during the attack, and was close enough to the disaster to help out: a woman who had fled the building was desperate to contact her parents, and Stipe duly obliged by calling on his cellphone. One of R.E.M.'s songs, 'It's The End Of The World

As We Know It', found its way onto a list of proscribed records circulated to commercial radio after the event. Perhaps surprisingly, 'Anthrax' by the Gang Of Four did not.

IV

Peter Buck had had a personally harrowing 2001. For his fellow band members, however, life as a 40-something rock star was just fine. His friend Mike Mills still has one of his homes in Athens. His son Julian is now 12. Mills plays golf with Bill Berry, and shoots in the high 80s. He professes not to have a tennis game, but every autumn plays a pro-am with his buddy Jim Courier in Austin, Texas to raise money for charity.

'You'll have myself and Jim and we'll play against John McEnroe and Lars Ulrich of Metallica, or something like that. After that Jim will play McEnroe, so you get to see some real tennis as well as us clowning it up out there.' His biggest commitment, outside his immediate loved ones, is still to the band. Funny and self-effacing, he is popular with R.E.M. fans. One fan, Stine Olsen, says, 'Mike is my favourite just because he is such a sweet and nice person. He's always friendly and talkative, and he never says no to writing autographs or joining in for pictures.'

'He's the most personable of the three,' agrees Ballard Lesemann, 'and the biggest partier in the band. He's out there bar-hopping with his pals, having a good time and chatting up the ladies! If you didn't know who they were you could probably mistake them for some mature college drop-outs.'

Bill Berry, once a heavy partygoer himself, with all that entails, is now a gentleman farmer, and happy with his life away from the limelight. That's not to say that he doesn't miss being in the band. 'The way I look at it is that Bill's still a member of this band, he just doesn't do any work or get paid!', laughs Peter Buck.

When I think of us, I think of the four of us. But Bill does not want to do this. A really good friend of mine went up to his house only last week and said to him: 'Bill, do you miss it?' And he said, 'Yeah, I do, but not as much as I'd miss my house if I was out doing it!' In any case, Bill is such a shy person that if he really *wanted* to come back, he'd never tell us. I love Bill; he is definitely a one-off. All the guys in the band and Bertis – if you

asked me what their day was like, I could tell you. And they
could tell you what my day was like too. I have *no* idea what Bill
does with himself. I ask people who have been over to his house
and they say, 'Oh, he's kind of pottering around, fixing things,
and he tinkers with some musical instruments.'

I think part of the reason he left was that his father died
young, and Bill had two separate things in Europe where he just
about died. I think he thought he would die young, and would
have spent his life doing something he didn't want to do. Now
he's in good health, and he's totally relaxed. He's more like he
used to be in the eighties than he was in the early nineties,
where he'd kind of blanked out.

There's no way he could rejoin the band unless we made the
records in his barn, and never toured, and he never did a video or
an interview. When he quit, I kind of offered that as an alternative:
'Hey, well, we'll record with you at your house. If we want to tour,
we'll hire somebody.' He said, 'No, it's too much for me to think
about, I never want to do it.' He's a worrier, and I understand that.
When VH1 did the *Behind the Music* documentary on us, Bill
dithered for a whole month about being involved, and called the
office every single day about it, worried about it, and then came in
and did it, and he was great! Afterwards he said, 'Oh well, that
wasn't so hard.' But it ruined his life for a whole month to think
about doing a twenty-minute interview.

Early in 2002, word was that 'Bill Berry was back in the band'. In
November 2001, an R.E.M. fan had posted a story on rec.music.rem
that Bill had resumed close contact with the band. It read:

I have a relative who lives in Athens and has close ties with the
band. It seems that recently Bill has been jamming occasionally
with the band in Athens and is interested in possibly rejoining.
He was supposed to play a few numbers with the band when
they played in Athens recently, but couldn't because Joey is a
southpaw and Bill is a rightie and they didn't have time to
switch the drums round. But, Bill was at the show and is
currently debating writing/recording with them on the next
album. My source says that if this does happen (and he quotes a
greater than 50% chance), Bill will record the next album with

the band and the announcement that he is back in the band will be made after the recording is finished.[9]

For their part, the band deny this is the case, though given Berry's nervous and vacillating nature, and their own tight-lipped nature, one would hardly expect them to reveal this sort of information even if it were true. 'Well, let me say that Bill and I have always been close,' says Mike Mills. 'The distance between Bill and Peter has always been purely geographical. They never see each other because Peter is in Seattle and Bill never leaves his house, or the area around his house. He's got a bunch of land about a half-hour out of Athens, and has friends and people visit him all the time and he does enjoy riding his tractor and cutting the hay twice a year. I still see Bill, we still play golf together, and we're still just as good friends as ever . . . As far as rejoining, no, I don't think that would happen, because it was too difficult and wrenching for us to come to grips with us being a three-piece, that's what happened with *Up*. As far as coming back into the band, I just don't see it happening because it was just too difficult him leaving.'

The baby of the band, Michael Stipe will forever have to fight against both his own insecurities, and the media's false portrayal of what he is. He is eccentric, and there's no denying this, but so are millions of other people on the planet. Stipe's insecurities stem from the fact that he is largely self-educated. In conversations, he can struggle hard to express himself. In interviews, he constantly refers to his own limited talents. He calls himself a 'college drop-out and magazine reader', and tries to fool us into thinking that he hasn't read a book in years.

For their part, the media tends to portray Stipe as something of a self-righteous and pompous person, as a person who wants the advantages celebrity brings, yet seeks anonymity when it suits him too. While Stipe is as imperfect as the rest of us, most of the interviewees in this book talk of a funny, self-deprecating guy. 'He's very polite, but he has to be familiar with who you are,' says Athens journalist Ballard Lesemann. 'He's a weird fellow too. He looks like a burglar! He dresses weird, and has the total arty towny look.' Stipe is certainly shy, and became 'loud shy' to cover up this basic fact.

Stipe is becoming ever more of a genuine rock hyphenate. He's now a singer-writer-photographer-filmmaker. He has his talents and his admirers. 'I like Michael's photographs,' says Chernikowski. 'Michael can get away with doing things I would love to be able to do but can't because I'm not Michael Stipe: nice shaky camera, soft focus, all the things I love!' Stipe still lives in Athens and is regularly seen out and about. He remains a lyricist with a sense of the enigmatic. Certain phrases, combinations and wordplays work brilliantly well, and he now sings better than he has ever done in his life. Once his songs are in the public domain, he doesn't feel proprietorial about them. They're open to any number of equally valid interpretations. The band members hardly ever question Stipe, or demand to know what certain words mean, perhaps realising that that would be missing the point.

One thing that does seem to have changed is that, after several years of being very much a figurehead and an icon, Stipe is now more than ever concerned with re-establishing contact with old friends. Perhaps it's a sign of getting older, of reaching 40, but he has been keener than hitherto to look back, reflect and reacquaint. Back in Athens he's re-established contact with people like Pylon's Michael Lachowski, now with his own successful design business, and Jim Herbert, still a don at the Art School in Athens. 'I've spent a lot of time with him in the past year and that was after many years of him living his life, and me living mine,' says Lachowski.

About a year ago or so he said that he'd come to the realisation that there were people in town who he needed to make more of an effort to have in his life because he'd screwed up, or neglected them, or whatever. And I was one of them. Another one was Jim Herbert. Really starting from that moment, Michael has made an extraordinary effort to call me, to include me, to invite me. So, I've kind of got to know him again, or, you could almost say, got to know him for the first time. Because, back then, you know, I kind of knew everybody.

I definitely feel that his interests no longer centre exclusively on the band. He's so involved with the film work that he does, and he's been involved in that for so long. He's also involved with other worlds, the sort that are available to him because of his celebrity – being invited to take part in different kinds of events, and charity stuff and film stuff. I think he talks about the film stuff more than anything else. It presents him with an ongoing challenge, whether there are deals to be made, or stuff to be worked out, whereas the music stuff is comparatively more old hat because he's been through the process so many times.

The band continue to play benefit gigs, and the Athens office remains a supporter of proactive, liberal-minded, local initiatives. Although there have inevitably been fallings-out with friends, and bridges burnt, the ties of loyalty that remain are very strong. In the summer of 2001, their former producer, Don Dixon, was taken seriously ill. 'I had a heart attack and I had to have a quadruple bypass,' says Dixon.

I didn't have health insurance, but we figured we would struggle through somehow. I had a conversation with a newspaper writer in North Carolina about my heart attack and the issue of health insurance came up. The Cat's Cradle in Chapel Hill were having this R.E.M. tribute show, and they were intending to give the money to somewhere, but they hadn't figured out who yet. They read this article, called me up and then Bertis got the band involved and they gave me financial support along with the club. Jefferson contacted me as well. Mike Mills and Bertis went to the show there in Chapel Hill and Mitch Easter and his girlfriend Shalini [their band is called Shalini] performed too. I wasn't well enough to go, but I became the focus of it and the guys in the band were incredibly generous and helpful. They put stuff on the website about it, and it really helped a lot to keep me from being in a worse financial position than I am. This sort of selfless, simple help – they weren't doing this to get headlines and to look good, they were helping out because they wanted to – just means that they're good guys.

V
R.E.M. sponsor and publicise charity events like this through their official website, though they were very late to have any sort of web presence. Version 1 of their official website, designed by Michael Lachowski's company Candy in 1999, with some satisfaction announced that: 'R.E.M. are proud to be the last group in the known world to have a webpage. We've worked very hard to achieve this goal.' For many years their web scepticism got in the

way of developing this ambit of their operations, when most global rock acts were heavily involved in various Internet-related projects.

'I think it's symptomatic of the times we live in and the cult of celebrity,' Stipe told *Q* in 1999. 'It's hard enough to separate the work from the person who makes it. I don't want to slam the Internet too much but . . . it can really be a high school chatbook.'[10]

'They certainly had ambigious feelings about the whole enterprise,' reveals Lachowski. 'Part of the feeling that was expressed was that the band felt that it was a band, not an entertainment entity. They don't feel any compulsion to provide a website just because Disney has one. There were already websites out there that covered R.E.M. anyway. The other argument was that it was kind of silly not to have a website in that they had a fan club and ideas and things they cared about.'

The design of the first website was deliberately homespun. 'The concept behind the first site was that it was made to reflect Athens, an Athens sensibility,' records Lachowski. 'They wanted to have some sort of a vibe that it was home-grown, and one of the ways of achieving that was to hire locals to make it. Something that says, this is ours, we made it, it serves the purpose. It's not like we're so stupid that we couldn't work out how it couldn't have been done more slickly. It doesn't necessarily look like something that's coming out of the entertainment capitals, but it's sufficient, it works for us, that kind of "can do" attitude. A lot of the stuff on the site was dumb, and was intentionally dumb.'

In the lead-up to the release of *Reveal*, the original site was dismantled and a slicker site put up in its place. It's still by no means the most sophisticated web presence in rock, as a casual look at the official sites of U2 or David Bowie will instantaneously show, but it's a marker put down by the band in cyberspace.

Luckily for fans, R.E.M. take a pragmatic view of the proliferation of bootleg material on the Net. 'My feeling is that I don't think you can blame it on anybody,' says Peter Buck. 'I once had a conversation with Brian Wilson about *Smile* and putting it out. He said, well, it wasn't the right record to put out, and anyway, anyone who needs to hear it can hear it. It's on bootlegs and if God thinks they need to hear that record then they find a way to hear it.'

The trading network is substantial, and R.E.M. have always had a very large fanatical following. In the 1990s fans such as Paul Holmes in Liverpool with his fanzine *Chronic Town* and Rob Jovanovic in Nottingham with *Rivers of Suggestion*, provided an unofficial information service for the band's admirers. Such initiatives became less and less useful with the rise of the Internet. The band operated a policy of friendly nonco-operation. 'We really didn't get any involvement from R.E.M. themselves,' says Paul Holmes. 'I was told they were reluctant to endorse something that they didn't have any control over. But all the feedback we got from their office was positive.'

R.E.M.'s official website, redesigned and upgraded just before the release of *Reveal*, works in tandem with a larger, unofficial fan site, *Murmurs*, run by a team of R.E.M. fans under the leadership of Ethan Kaplan. 'I started the site when I was 15 in 1995, just to learn html,' says Kaplan. 'Then I started posting news and people started reading it, and I started to update more frequently. In 1998, we added a discussion board and that got the ball rolling very quickly. A lot of the other sites shut down. There has been a lot of bitchiness in the R.E.M. community, but you're going to get that wherever you go. We approach it journalistically. I'd like to think *Murmurs* is alternative independent journalism which is R.E.M.-centred but not R.E.M.-centric.'

Kaplan rightly points out the friendly professionalism of the Athens office, and the exemplary way R.E.M. deal with their fans:

I think a lot of that can be traced back to them hiring David Bell at the fan club office. He's the advocate for fans and a lot of the way the band communicates with the fans is through the fan club. The club now has 10,000 members, and that's why the band is now so much closer to the fans instead of being this monolithic entity on the horizon. It's kind of a personal thing for people.

The office is run like a small business, but it's a multimillion-dollar corporation. Their job is to make sure the guys can do their artwork, their music, with as little fuss as possible. Bertis is like the CEO, the band's like the board of directors, and the office staff keep the wheels rolling. But they don't treat it like that. Everyone feels that they have a part in keeping this thing going and that the fans get what they want and the band can make the music that they want without any of the shit that they don't want to deal with. Every phone call gets returned, no more than two rings per call. I've heard that somebody has called and Mike Mills has answered the phone if no one else does, it's that kind of place. The office looks like an over-zealous fan's apartment. It's not like a corporate decoration thing; it looks like somebody's home and the walls are covered with pictures! You can ascertain how good the band is by the support they have from the people who work with them.

That support team at the office also includes management associate Kevin O'Neil and art director Chris Bilheimer. 'I don't think anyone who's worked here has ever had a background in the music industry,' says O'Neil, accurately reflecting the character of the Athens office which is run by learned enthusiasts rather than industry apparatchiks. Microwave, the long-standing guitar technician, left the band's employ, perhaps after some sort of falling out, in 2000, and his job is now performed by Bob Weber. The former manager of Mudhoney, Bob Whittaker, is Peter Buck's assistant in Seattle, as well as R.E.M.'s tour manager. For his part, Bertis Downs still teaches at the law school in Athens despite his commitments with the band: 'I teach a music law course at law school and I really enjoy it. It's good to be around people who grew up as technology changes. I mark assignments and set exams. I do slant it towards music and the relationships between employers, managers and agents. It's fascinating. It's what I need to do to stay on top of things.' The Athens office is, as one would imagine, a progressive environment in which to work. Not many operations of this sort would, for example, offer male members of the staff paternity leave.

R.E.M. are right to prize the service they give through the fan club. With most fan clubs one gets an impersonal service, a quarterly self-aggrandising glossy magazine, and once-in-a-blue-moon ticket offers in among the constant exhortations to buy, buy, buy the 'exclusive' merchandising. Professionals run them for profit. With R.E.M., you get something different. Having taken the decision to run everything out of their Athens office, R.E.M. put the emphasis on personal connection. Take the Christmas package, for example. Every year since 1988, the band have sent a Christmas present to each member of the fan club, a recording, with maybe a calendar, or some stickers, whatever takes their fancy. 'It's something that the Beatles did, and R.E.M. are continuing the tradition,' says David Bell. 'More than anything else it's an extension of what the band truly feels about their fans. They get this gift every year which quite honestly costs more to mail out than the membership fee does. The fan club in that sense is certainly not about trying to make any money off of anyone. Which, in a sense, is tied up with their community work, their belief in supporting causes. Obviously, R.E.M. have had a very good career in terms of income and all that, but I don't think anyone can accuse them of not giving back, and it starts with the fans.'

The Athens office also actively supports local initiatives, such as Community Connection, which channels resources into a number of social welfare projects. 'They're basically an information and referral centre,' says Kevin O'Neil. 'If you live in Athens or northeast Georgia, you call one central number if you have problems with drug addiction or spousal abuse, or legal or financial problems. They are in touch with non-profit groups all over the state that are able to help you with your problem.'

Very often the Athens office will arrange for a special pre-release party to be held at the time of an album release, with profits going to selected local charities. You'll often find Weaver D's food at such events, automatic for the people, of course. The Wuxtry will be one of the local record stores who will open at midnight and sell the new record. It's this kind of kinship with the band that, in Athens, is unbreakable.

'The listening parties are just for Athens fans – to give the local fan base, the people who have supported R.E.M. from the very beginning, the chance to listen to the record before the rest of the world,' is how O'Neil puts it. 'So we play the album, show videos, documentary footage that hasn't been shown anywhere else yet. We have an auction. In the past we've always had the mayor be the auctioneer.'

Athens remains a friendly town. In an era of standardisation and globalisation it has largely retained its Southern-style bohemian identity. Fans still go on 'R.E.M. pilgrimages', walking the streets in search of Weaver D's. Some fans even end up living in Athens, such as Scouser Paul Holmes:

'Because of the university, there is always a fresh influx of people coming into the town, giving it a good atmosphere, yet it's far enough away from Atlanta to maintain its individuality. Politically, it's still a strange mix. The "townies" are typically liberal-minded Democrat voters, but on the outskirts you've got your typical redneck Republicans who think George Bush Jr is a genius. Then there's the students, driving round in their SUVs that daddy bought them, with the Bush-Cheney bumper sticker. I'll be honest though, I love Athens. Its big strength for me is that it's a town of maybe 50,000 people, with over 30,000 of those people being between 18 and 22. As a result of that, the downtown (and unlike most US towns, it does have a strong downtown) is a good mix of restaurants and bars, small shops and cafés. I think there's just under 100 bars in the downtown alone – and on any night of the week you can find a few that are packed. It really is still a party town.'

VI

Music without compromise!
People look up to them, they think integrity!
You walk in that shadow!
Anti rock stars who mocked their celebrity!
They broke all the rules and were rewarded with the biggest contract in record music history!
They stood united!

This was the litany of sound bites trotted out by VH1 for their *Behind the Music* special a few years ago. It's a profile of the band that *Fiction* has, at times, questioned. R.E.M. haven't always stood united, sometimes they have taken themselves too seriously. Also, being rewarded with the biggest recording contract in history seems to indicate that, rather than breaking the rules, they played the game better than anyone else.

'I can't imagine myself playing to 15-year-old kids when I'm 45.'[11] Forty-five-year-old Peter Buck uttered these 'famous last words' ten years ago, but here he is, still playing to teenagers, particularly if the tens of thousands in the crowd in Cologne are anything to go by. It's one of the inviolable rules of rock – that pop stars simply can't give it up. Playing music, being successful – it's a drug. Although in no danger of becoming a pop tart, Buck now plays with R.E.M. on an increasingly infrequent basis, on one-night stands.

In early 2002, R.E.M. played a successful charity gig to promote gay men's health issues at the Carnegie Hall one week, then played a tribute show to Bono's U2 the next. It's a chance to have some fun and promote good causes, while keeping the band active. 'The premise behind this thing was that all those tribute things are so fucking sanctimonious, so we figured we'd pretend we were so stupid that we think it's a tribute to Sony Bono,' says a mischievous Peter Buck. 'So, Michael, Mike and I wrote this little speech, 30 seconds long, saying all these things that both Bono and [Sony] Bono had done, and then we said, "And this goes out to you, Mr Bono." Bono was sitting in the audience and looked at us, with a "what?" look of incredulity. We played 'I Got You Babe', and everyone looked at us as if we were insane and then Cher came out and everyone started shrieking. They all leaped to their feet and started applauding and she and Michael held hands and sang 'I Got You Babe'. It was really immense!'

Bono himself played an important role as witness in Peter Buck's air-rage retrial, which commenced in March 2002. Many observers had been shocked at the extent and severity of the criminal damage Buck had been accused of, as lurid details of a man so out of control that he attempted to open the plane door at 35,000 feet emerged in the daily reporting of the trial. Bono appeared as the most heavyweight of character witnesses for the beleaguered Buck, and gave testimony to his friend's responsible mien. 'I have never seen him drunk . . . I have absolutely never seen him take drugs,' said Bono. 'I just wanted to stand up and be counted. This is ridiculous. I don't know what must have happened to him. It is certainly a bizarre event and unusual. He is a very quiet man. It is hard to get him to go on tour because he loves his kids so much.'

Stipe too made an appearance telling Isleworth Crown Court, 'He's just not a person who is rude to anyone.' Looking back to his pre-fame teenage years, Stipe told the court that Buck was his 'only friend' – a 'Southern gentleman' who was 'like my big brother'. Mike Mills, Bertis Downs, and Buck's wife Stephanie were also called to the stand to give evidence. Buck was a 'very gentle person', 'straightforward', 'shy . . . very self-effacing'. There was, of course, another side to him – that of the garrulous and sharp-witted man of rock legend – but this side was, for understandable reasons, downplayed. The fact of the matter was that Buck was – and is – a considerate, articulate and witty man. He was certainly no rock hermit, but neither was he a psychotic alcoholic nor a menace to society who should be behind bars. Stipe concluded his evidence with a piece of trademark eccentricity: 'He is a tall man and has got a long nose . . . He can sometimes come across as stand-offish, looking down his nose. But he is the antithesis of that. He is a gentle, kind, incredible person who doesn't look down on anyone.'

In the end, Buck was acquitted. His wife Stephanie and his colleagues Mike Mills, Michael Stipe (looking goofy in a suit and tie) and Bertis Downs smiled to camera, mightily relieved, as the court decided that Buck could not be held responsible for his tranquilliser-induced actions. The jury believed Buck when he said that he had forgotten to mention the sleeping pills on arrest the previous spring, and that his loutish behaviour was the result of a 'drug-induced automatism'. During the trial, Buck had described how he had awoken from his stupor in a police cell, and had been convinced, by the bright lights overhead, that he was recovering from a heart attack in hospital or, as Buck called it, a 'weird Disneyland hotel'. This must indeed have been a nightmare scenario for it to be described in such horrendous terms. For many friends, colleagues and associates who worked with Buck, the whole episode was grotesquely out of character, and it was with some relief that it was consigned to the dustbin of history.[12]

Is the dustbin of history where R.E.M. themselves now reside? They haven't embarked on a world tour since 1995. This is a shame, for R.E.M.'s public needs to see them more frequently and, one suspects, their career needs at least one more big world tour if it is to endure at the level it is now. Oh yes, and there's the little matter of the 'Best Of' compilation that Warner Brothers are so keen to put out. Meanwhile work goes on apace on the next studio album. For Peter Buck, inspiration can strike at any moment, even when it's meal time for Zoë and Zelda.

'Now I have kids, I do a whole lot of writing while they're playing, either in the yard or in the living room. I've just written a song that I'm really proud of and I was trying to get them to eat dinner. All of a sudden I was playing this thing and I thought, "Hey, this is really good," so I said to them, "Now it's time to be quiet, daddy's working." I was in the middle of getting them to eat something they didn't want to eat, like broccoli or something, and I was really excited about it. In the summer I wrote all this super power-pop stuff. Then, after September 11, it's getting a little darker. I'm trying to do something where we extend the songwriting language, where we write songs that don't necessarily go verse, chorus, verse, chorus but go to point A to point B and then end. I'm trying to link things together so that things kind of flow, so there isn't the feeling that there's one song, it ends here, here's another. I played some demos for some friends and they said, this is weirdly, darkly psychedelic.'

The band remain doggedly, determinedly and fiercely loyal to one another. 'They *are* impenetrable,' says Mitch Easter. 'That's something that Don Dixon and I ran up against, but at the same time we had to respect them for it, because it's worked for them. In a way, they're the most "circle the wagons" and clannish bunch of guys you're ever going to meet, which is interesting, because most people aren't like that.'

It's always tempting to detail the peaks and troughs, the rises to fame, the plateaux, declines and comebacks, but, in R.E.M.'s case, this would be a distortion of the reality. Some might argue that *Fables* or *Monster* are slightly weaker than the others, or that *Murmur* or *Document* or *Automatic* somewhat stronger, but the reality is that R.E.M. have never dropped below a certain standard. Why is this?

According to Mike Mills: 'The only reason I could suggest would be that the songs are written by three (or earlier, four) different people in a way at three different times, and then pulled together by a band. In other words, you don't have one guy writing the songs who might go into a slump, who might not be inspired, who might not be creative at one time. Peter and I can certainly pick each other up, and Bill certainly had a lot to do with that as well, providing an odd bit of inspiration with the songs he would write. And then having Michael, who's doing the lyrics and most of the melodies separately. That sort of dynamic helps you avoid having slumps like that.'

Can the band themselves see patterns and progress in their own career? Or have they been so busy doing it, that they have forgotten they have been 'on the job'.

'To me, oddly enough,' says Mike Mills, 'the R.E.M. career almost felt like, in the beginning there were the first two records, which were made with a great deal of innocence and naïvety, in Charlotte with some old friends. I always thought of those two as a piece. And then, after that, in a big way there was everything else until Bill left the band. So, in an odd way, there are two major divisions. The one after *Reckoning* is fairly arbitrary, but it's just in my head. That's where the big adventure really began, everything started to take off a bit more after that.'

Has success changed them as people? It surely must have done. For one, it must have preserved the eccentric Stipe and Buck in their eccentricities. For Peter Buck, success has enabled him to create his own alternative reality. 'I'll be honest with you. I do a lot of things that people who aren't in bands do. I go shopping, pick up the kids from school – I've got to take them to a doctor's appointment this afternoon. On the other hand, I don't think I've been in a bank for ten years. I've never done my taxes, and I don't think I've written a cheque in five years. I've managed to axe myself out of a lot of stuff that I don't think is important in life. I've got two things that are really important to me: my family – both the family related to me by blood and the band family and music. I'm able to concentrate on that all that I want to, and do nothing else. It's not exactly the real world but I don't think it's bad or anything. You do kind of create your own world, and so does everyone.'

However, Buck reckons that success changes those around you more than it does you yourself. 'It doesn't change you, but it changes everything around you. It went from us going into the studio and making records by ourselves, to people assuming their Christmas bonus depends on how well our record does for Warner Brothers, which it does to a certain degree. Success didn't change my tastes, or my ethical system, or the way I looked at the world. It's easier for me to go and buy records if I want to, and I'm relatively sure that I won't have to work again if I don't want to. Of course, I work twice as much as anyone I know. It changes everyone around you, from the record company to people on the street. You kind of forget about it until someone reminds you that you're famous.'

What is it about the music that has so beguiled us over the years? Certainly, it has far less premeditation about it than the music made by a lot of other rock acts. 'My theory is that the records tend to have a life of their own,' is how Mills puts it. 'Once you start making them, they will often dictate to you the direction in which they want to go.'

One factor is certainly the two-stage method of composition. Another reason might be the haunting interplay between voice and lead guitar. 'I think the synthesis which occurs between Peter's guitar and the melody is as important as Michael's voice,' says Stephanie Chernikowski. 'I think that there's an unbelievable rapport between those two. That deep, aching quality is the thing that always captures me. They can do that, and then they can rejoice. They can cover something like Iggy's "Funtime" and it can be funny, earthy, sexy, and wonderfully exhilarating. Then, on an album like *Fables*, they can rip your heart out.'

R.E.M.'s music can indeed gladden the heart, but, more often than not, it takes you into a certain sadness and then releases you, and it's this catharsis that makes it so much a part of the architecture of contemporary pop music. 'R.E.M. project a lot of qualities that not only rock writers but a substantial portion of the rock audience approve of deeply,' is how writer Paul Du Noyer sums it up. 'They do seem to represent this beautiful blend of rootsiness and contemporary awareness. They seem very much of the modern world but rooted in something far deeper, far more ancient.'

The band does have its detractors of course. There are those who think that they are past their sell-by date, and that their lack of commercial success is not an indication of poor promotion, unfriendly radio, or the vicissitudes of fickle public taste, but simply a reflection of the fact that Stipe and co. have outlived their mystique. 'Essentially, R.E.M. have turned into Talking Heads,' is how writer Mat Snow puts it:

Which is to say that, as much as they try to vary their palette of arrangements, their sound palette, their chord palette, they are anchored and utterly restricted by the limitations of Michael Stipe's voice. This is always going to be the case for an act with a lead singer with a rather restricted range. This is why, at his height, David Bowie could do well in so many different sorts of musics because he had a very versatile voice, the voice of a mimic who really could – admittedly in a rather arch way – do rock, do funk, do a number of different things. He was versatile enough to feel comfortable in a number of different chromatic settings or harmonic settings. This is not the case with Stipe, nor with David Byrne, nor, in the end, with the Rolling Stones. The Rolling Stones' signature song is entirely conditioned by the fact that Mick Jagger can only sing in a certain range. That said, within that range R.E.M. got an awful lot out of it for those eight to ten years.

The very least one can say of R.E.M. is that they made great music for a dozen years. This book, however, puts forward the case that they have made almost consistently interesting music for their entire career. Their overall significance is profound. For their generation, those old enough to have rummaged through the record racks in a shop like the Wuxtry (which is still operating under the stewardship of Dan Wall and Mark Methe), old enough to remember punk at first hand, old enough to have lived pop culture (and not just used it as background music at dinner parties, as secondary static to polite conversation), R.E.M. undoubtedly do matter.

As Ballard Lesemann says, 'If you talked to a 20-year-old, with the way MTV has been for the last ten years and the radio and all the Lollapaloozas and Woodstock 99 and all that stuff, they would probably think R.E.M., if they knew them at all, were an old band. But if you asked a music journalist aged 35 and up, they would argue that R.E.M. were probably the biggest US band of the last 40 years.' There's no doubt: Peter Buck, sipping his beer, playing his records and chatting away at the Wuxtry all those years ago, would have settled for that.

NOTES

CHAPTER 1: 'SOMETHING BEYOND THE FLANNEL SHIRT',
1979–80

1. The 'death of rock' debate raged within academia and the print media in the early 1990s. Sociologists began proffering hard empirical evidence of a decreasing investment in pop as lifestyle around this time, and there is no evidence of this trend being reversed as we move from a radio culture to an 'interactive' one. In 1991 Simon Frith wrote: 'A new Gallup survey of Britain's 14–16-year-olds found that the average teenager now listens to pop music for 4 hours a day, 3 times more, it's claimed, than teens spent listening to pop in the mid-1970s. The poll also reveals that pop is now "very low" on a list of "the most important things in life" (after, in order, education, home, friends, money, sex, appearance, work, going out, sport, hobbies and football) . . . This is the post-rock generation gap. The young listen to more and more, and it means less and less. The old listen to less and less but it means more and more. The young are materialist; music is as good as its functions. The old are idealists, in search . . . of epiphany' (Simon Frith, 'He's the one', *Village Voice*, 29 October 1991, p. 88).

2. Jon Savage, *Time Travel: From the Sex Pistols to Nirvana: Pop, Media and Sexuality 1977–96* (Vintage, 1996), p. 5.

3. All quotes in this book are from interviews or email correspondences with the author, unless otherwise indicated.

4. *Rocket Magazine*, October 1986.

5. Alan Reder and John Baxter, *Listen to This! Leading Musicians Recommend Their Favourite Artists and Recordings* (Hyperion, 1999), p. 62.

6. *Amplifier On-line*, issue 10, online edition, 3(4), 1998.
7. Mat Snow, 'Lyrically Dark, Musically Oddball', *Q*, 74, November 1992, p. 58.
8. Anthony DeCurtis, *Rocking My Life Away* (Duke University Press, 1998), p. 44.
9. *Ibid.* p. 45.
10. *Ibid.* p. 45.
11. Julie Phillips Jordan, 'Athens Nightlife Is Alive, Vibrant', *Online Athens*, 28 February 1999.
12. Richard H. King and Helen Taylor (eds), *Dixie Debates Perspectives on Southern Cultures* (Pluto Press, 1996), p. 6.
13. Paul Butchart, the Athens Music Scene, Internet Essay, Love and Squalor R.E.M. http://julie.cloud-8.com/rem/paul 1. html
14. Rosalyn Knight, 'Why is Athens Georgia So Important to Popular Music in America?', undergraduate dissertation (University of Lancaster, 2000), p. 14.
15. Denise Sullivan, 'Eyewitness', *Q*, 96, September 1994, p. 40.
16. 'Stipe on CNN'. http://www.murmurs.com/news/story.php?id=2516, 26 February 2002.
17. Michael Stipe, 'Patti and me', *Mojo*, 33, August 1996, pp. 82–3.
18. Mat Snow, 'Lyrically Dark, Musically Oddball', *Q*, 74, November 1992, p. 61.
19. Adrian Deevoy, 'Saint Michael', *Q*, 104, May 1995.
20. Paul Zollo, *Songwriters On Songwriting* (Da Capo Press, 1997), p. 631.
21. Virginia Pinholster, 26 April 1987, www.onlineathens.com
22. *Rolling Stone*, June 1983.
23. Dave Di Martino, Jim Irwin and Mark Ellen, 'Fables of the Four-Headed Monster', *Mojo*, 12, November 1994.
24. Rob Jovanovic and Miriam Longino, 'Hello/Goodbye', *Vox*, January 1998.

CHAPTER 2: 'WE JUST LIKE THE DOTS', 1980–82

1. Marcus Gray, *It Crawled from the South* (Fourth Estate, 1996), p. 31.
2. I think we can safely say that Buck was joking when he told one journalist in the nineties that R.E.M. stood for 'Rear End Men. We're totally queer', *Details* magazine, February 1995. http://www.geocities.com/SunsetStrip/5582/buckrem.html

3. Paul Butchart, 'A new friend', Love & Squalor R.E.M. http://julie.cloud-8.com/rem/paul3.html

4. Dave Di Martino, Jim Irwin and Mark Ellen, 'Fables of the Four-Headed Monster', *Mojo*, 12, November 1994.

5. According to Rodger Lyle Brown's *Party out of Bounds* (Plume, 1991), pp. 91–4, Kurfurst offered to co-manage with McLaughlin, but the offer was refused, so the B-52's did not replace one manager with another without first seeking a compromise deal.

6. Posting by Paul Butchart on rec.music.rem, 14 February 2001.

7. John Harris, 'Cash For Questions Special', *Q Special - REM Revealed! Artistry! Mystery! REM: the Definitive Appreciation*, 2001.

8. Jim DeRogatis, *Let It Blurt: the Life and Times of Lester Bangs* (Bloomsbury, 2000), pp. 189–90.

9. Andy Gill, 'The home guard', *Q*, 55, 1991.

10. See Rodger Lyle Brown's *Party Out Of Bounds* (Plume, 1991), pp. 171–2 for more details.

11. This was recorded in Seattle at Studio X, the venue for the *New Adventures In Hi-Fi* studio sessions for the Cameron Crowe/Danny Bramson film, *Vanilla Sky*.

12. Mike Mills, reminded of Stipe's appreciation of a certain Belgian novelty punk rock hit: 'Just as a funny aside, I was in a band that covered "ça Plane Pour Moi", with Ingrid Schorr as a matter of fact, and Michael's sister, Lynda. The band was called Mars Needs Women and I think we only played one show, maybe two. This would probably be 1981.'

13. VH1's 1998 *Behind The Music* feature on the band draws attention to the very meagre standard of creature comforts during their first few years.

14. Mike Mills, 'Our town', 1985, reprinted in Clinton Heylin (ed.), *The Penguin Book of Rock & Roll Writing* (Viking, 1993), pp. 402–403.

15. Di Martino *et al*, 'Fables of the Four-Headed Monster', November 1994.

16. Craig Rosen, *R.E.M. Inside Out* (Thunder's Mouth Press, 1997), p. 11.

17. Thanks to John Ellis himself for this information. For the record, this version of 'R.E.M.' was a mixture of hard rock, electronics and dance theatre, with a stage climax involving three dancers in romper suits and masks writhing around on the ground. It

actually sounds far more of the moment than R.E.M.'s 'authentic' pop/rock.

CHAPTER 3: 'UH', 1982–83

1. David Stubbs, 'The right stuff', *Uncut*, August 1999.
2. *Rolling Stone* website.
3. Steve Sutherland, 'When Courtney met Michael', *NME*, 23 January 1999.
4. *Rolling Stone* website.
5. I am indebted to writer and academic Ron Moy for this term.
6. Kipp Teague's The Complete R.E.M. Lyrics Archive, www.retroweb.com/rem/lyrics/song_RadioFreeEurope.html
7. I'm obviously not the first to spot this. See, for example, Deevoy, 'Saint Michael', *Q*, 104, p. 90.
8. R.E.M. Archive: Stipe appears on AOL, August 1994, http://randrews.users.netlink.co.uk/rem/archive/aolstipey.html I have taken the liberty of correcting and editing these quotes, hastily typed as they are, and as emails tend to be.
9. Steve Pond, 'In the real world: rock's most influential college band graduates', *Rolling Stone*, 514, 3 December 1987.
10. 'Stipe On CNN', www.murmurs.com/new/story.php?id=2516, 26 February2002.
11. Can you spot the famous R.E.M. mondegreens such as: 'Chicken fricassee Kenneth', 'A simple bra, found inside my car' and 'I'm not a pot of tea'? Answers to be found at: www.amiright.com/misheard/artist/rem.shtml
12. Don't be afraid. There is actually a very readable book on popular music that makes semiotics almost intelligible. It's Dave Laing, *One Chord Wonders: Power and Meaning in Punk Rock* (Open University Press, 1985). Chapter 3, 'Listening', is the bit you need.
13. See the film *Athens: Inside/Out*, 1986.
14. Theodore Gracyk, *Rhythm and Noise: an Aesthetics of Rock* (Duke University Press, 1996), pp. 104–5.
15. David R. Shumway, 'Rock & roll as cultural practice' in *Present Tense: Rock & Roll and Culture* (Duke University Press, 1992), p. 124.
16. Dave Di Martino, Jim Irwin and Mark Ellen, 'Fables of the Four-Headed Monster', *Mojo*, 12, November 1994.

17. Jon Wilde, 'REM: acts of the year' in *Virgin Rock Yearbook 93–94* (Virgin, 1994), p. 73.
18. *Rolling Stone*, 9 June 1983.

CHAPTER 4: SOPHOMORE, 1983–85
1. No, I didn't know what it meant either. It means 'gain in confidence', so Don tells me.
2. Rodger Lyle Brown, *Party Out Of Bounds* (Plume, 1991), p. 206.
3. For a further discussion of Stipe's photographic imagination, see the section 'Camera' in Marcus Gray, *It Crawled From The South* (Fourth Estate, 1996), pp. 132–40.
4. According to R.E.M. scholar Ron Henry, 'An ancient Chinese folktale about a group of brothers who are tested by an evil emperor has formed the basis of several children's books, entitled either *The Seven Chinese Brothers* or *The Five Chinese Brothers*. In all versions of the story, each brother has an extraordinary ability – such as being able to stretch very tall, to hold his breath a long time, or to swallow an ocean.' Being able to enunciate clearly was obviously not one of the many talents available to these superhuman figures.
5. Mike Mills, 'Our Town', 1985, reprinted in Clinton Heylin (ed.), *The Penguin Book of Rock & Roll Writing* (Viking, 1993), pp. 405–6.
6. Stephanie Chernikowski, 'A Visit to Paradise Garden' (Dilettante Press, 2001), www.dilettantepress.com/articles/finsterwords.html
7. *Rolling Stone* On-line.
8. David Stubbs, 'The right stuff', *Uncut*, August 1999.
9. Adrian Deevoy, 'Saint Michael', *Q*, 104, May 1995, p. 88.
10. The Beach Boys' collaborator Van Dyke Parks was also in the frame at one stage.
11. Jay Boberg of I.R.S. says, however, that he agreed with the band's decision to use Boyd: 'I agreed about the idea of moving on. They had actually introduced the concept of Joe Boyd.'
12. In fact, Boyd originally passed on working with R.E.M. as he was scheduled to work with the Canadian folk artist Mary Margaret O'Hara, but when she cancelled, Boyd fitted R.E.M. into his schedule at very short notice.

CHAPTER 5: GRAVITY, 1985–86

1. Adrian Deevoy, 'Saint Michael', Q, 104, May 1995, p.89.
2. This tradition continues. See, for example, Bill Bryson's admittedly tongue-in-cheek view of the South in *The Lost Continent: Travels in Small Town America* (Abacus, 1989): 'Just south of Grand Junction, Tennessee, I passed over the state line into Mississippi. A sign beside the highway said WELCOME TO MISSISSIPPI. WE SHOOT TO KILL. It didn't really. I just made that up. This was only the second time I had ever been to the Deep South and I entered it with a sense of foreboding. It is surely no coincidence that all those films you have ever seen about the South – *Easy Rider*, *In the Heat of the Night*, *Cool Hand Luke*, *Brubaker*, *Deliverance* – depict Southerners as murderous, incestuous, shitty-shoed rednecks. It really is another country.'
3. R.E.M. Archive: Stipe appears on AOL, August 1994.
4. Rosalyn Knight, 'Why is Athens Georgia So Important to Popular Music in America?', undergraduate dissertation (University of Lancaster, 2000), p. 32.
5. Richard H. King and Helen Taylor (eds), *Dixie Debates Perspectives on Southern Cultures* (Pluto Press, 1996), p. 3.
6. *Ibid.* p. 1.
7. Steve Pond, 'In the real world: rock's most influential college band graduates', *Rolling Stone*, 514, 3 December 1987.
8. *Rolling Stone* On-line.
9. According to R.E.M. expert Marcus Gray in *It Crawled From the South*, pp. 135–6, the origin of the song has more to do with a specific incident and Stipe's interest in minutiae. He quotes Stipe from 1986 as saying that the song 'came from a hand gesture. I just saw it, and then I wrote a song around it. I really focus on detail more than the grand picture, and that detail is what becomes the words of the song. I guess it's left to the listener to spot it, put a frame around it, and see the whole thing.'
10. www.remuk.free-online.co.uk/earlysuccess.htm
11. Steve Pond, 'In the real world: rock's most influential college band graduates', *Rolling Stone*, 514, 3 December 1987.

CHAPTER 6: 'THROWING A BABY INTO ICE-COLD WATER', 1986–88

1. The fifteenth-century heretical religious sect the Lollards were known as the 'Mumblers' on account of their strange talk, while

in the seventeenth century a wing of vocal, political puritans were dubbed the 'Ranters'. The switch for Stipe from quasi-mystical icon to political spokesperson was also commented on waggishly by Q's Andy Gill: 'it's clear he's talking not Complete Bollocks but a more refined, poetic form of Partial Bollocks through which truths hopefully may filter.' 'Positive: Are R.E.M. the best band in the world?', Q, 27, December 1988, p. 135.

2. Craig Rosen, R.E.M. Inside Out (Thunder's Mouth Press, 1997), p. 53.

3. www.oursong.net/about_c_hundred.html

4. David Stubbs, 'The right stuff', Uncut, August 1999, pp. 46–61.

5. Anthony Farrell, Vivienne Guinness and Julian Lloyd (eds), My Generation: Rock'n'Roll Remembered – An Imperfect History (Lilliput Press, 1996), p. 71.

6. Jonathan Buckley and Mark Ellingham (eds), Rock: The Rough Guide (Rough Guides Ltd, 1991), p. 721.

7. Mike Mills, 'Our Town' in The Penguin Book of Rock & Roll Writing (Viking, 1993), p. 404.

8. Jon Savage, Time Travel: From the Sex Pistols to Nirvana: Pop, Media and Sexuality 1977–96 (Vintage, 1996), p. 102.

9. Thaddeus Corneo, 'Guerrilla music: avant-garde voices as oppositional discourse' in Jonathon S. Epstein (ed.) Adolescents and Their Music: If It's Too Loud, You're Too Old (Garland Publishing, 1994), pp. 200–1.

10. Simon Reynolds, Blissed Out: The Raptures of Rock (Serpent's Tail, 1990), p. 98.

11. Michael Azerrad, Our Band Could Be Your Life: Scenes from the American Indie Underground, 1981–1991 (Little Brown, 2001), p. 5.

12. Rolling Stone, 7 November 1985, quoted in www.geocities.com/SunsetStrip/5582/fame.html

13. Robert Draper, The Rolling Stone Story (Mainstream Publishing, 1990).

14. Peter Buck gives some more information here: 'We had an earlier song called "It's Been A Bad Day" that "It's The End Of The World" grew out of. The original had a similar chorus but we couldn't agree on the arrangement. I took the chorus, which we liked, and put it in a different key. I then put a different verse to it so that Michael wouldn't know it was the same song, which it wasn't! And then he rewrote it. But the chords were the same.'

15. Marcus Gray, *It Crawled from the South* (Fourth Estate, 1996), p. 420.
16. The tragic events of 11 September naturally preoccupied all the interviewees for this book. New York-based Stephanie Chernikowski sent the author an email in November 2001 saying: 'For your information: in post 9.11 America, "It's The End Of The World As We Know It (And I Feel Fine)" is becoming the "Amerindie" nation alternative to "God Bless America", having been featured within a week on both *VH1 Presents the 80s* and *The Simpsons* episode last Sunday. They were also the first band I could listen to after 9.11. I had gone to visit friends in Connecticut the first weekend, and when they picked me up, "Lifes Rich Pageant" was on in the car. It was like a warm embrace.'
17. *Q*, 73.
18. *Ibid.*

CHAPTER 7: 'THE MAYOR SAYS HELLO NOW', 1988–91
1. VH1, *Behind the Music*.
2. DeCurtis, *Rocking My Life Away* (Duke University Press, 1998), p. 30.
3. Michael Goldberg, 'The making of *Monster*' (interview with Scott Litt), 1995, www.addict.com/issues/1.02/Cover_Story/Monster.
4. *Rolling Stone*, 514, 3 December 1987.
5. Mat Snow, 'Plink! Plink? Plink!', *Q*, 73, October 1992, p. 74.
6. Stipe told *Uncut*'s David Stubbs in 1999: 'I have a fascination with dreams, obviously, and with Jungian ideas and philosophies – that's part of my vernacular . . . I suspect that our dreams always were like motion pictures and that motion pictures are trying to recreate that world in their clumsy, mechanical way – and that there's a universality to our dreams.'
7. However, as Bertis Downs attests, the inspiration for the song came from a number of other sources, such as *Apocalypse Now*.
8. Andy Gill, 'Positive: are R.E.M. the best band in the world?', *Q*, 27, December 1988, p. 135.
9. Dave Di Martino, Jim Irwin and Mark Ellen, 'Fables of the Four-Headed Monster', *Mojo*, 12, November 1994.
10. Roy Shuker, *Key Concepts in Popular Music* (Routledge, 1998), p. 224.
11. DeCurtis, *Rocking My Life Away*, p. 40.

12. Neil Hannon, '100 years of attitude', *Mojo*, 74, January 2000, p. 75.
13. See Deevoy, 'Saint Michael', for a fascinating profile of Stipe through the ages.
14. DeCurtis, *Rocking My Life Away*, p. 38.
15. Andy Gill, 'The home guard', *Q*, 55, 1991.
16. For more information on her career, see Richard Fausset and Pete McCommons, 'The age of Gwen', *Flagpole* magazine online, 1998, www.flagpole.com/Issues/10.14.98/gwen.html
17. David P. Szatmary, *Rockin' in Time: A Social History of Rock'n'Roll*, 3rd edn (Prentice Hall, 1996).
18. *Rolling Stone*, 15 November 1990.

CHAPTER 8: 'THAT'S ME IN THE CORNER', 1991–94

1. Mat Snow, 'Plink! Plink? Plink!', *Q*, 73, October 1992, p. 71.
2. Adrian Deevoy, 'Saint Michael', *Q*, 104, May 1995, p. 89.
3. Stipe's unwillingness to talk to the press was glossed over at the time by Buck, who argued that the division of labour within the R.E.M. camp simply fell that way. Stipe was in charge of the visual promotion of the band, Mills and Buck the verbal. 'That's his [Stipe's] job. The rest of us, I'm afraid to say, just don't give much of a shit. If it was up to me, the records would come out in white covers and they'd be titled 1, 2 and 3, like Chicago records. Working with Warners on the sleeves is a burden on Michael, but on the other hand Mike and I do the bulk of the interviews. Michael is capable of talking to press and radio for ten hours a day but it makes him unhappy. If Michael said, this year I'll do the interviews and you do the videos, it would be an awful year – shitty videos, monosyllabic interviews.' (Snow, 'Plink! Plink? Plink!').
4. Michael Goldberg, 'The making of *Monster*' (interview with Scott Litt), 1995, www.addict.com/issues/1.02/Cover_Story/Monster.
5. *Ibid.*
6. Paul Zollo, *Songwriters on Songwriting*, expanded edn. (Da Capo, 1997).
7. Goldberg, 'The making of *Monster*'.
8. Gill, 'The home guard'.
9. Adrian Deevoy, 'Saint Michael', *Q*, 104, May 1995, p. 92.
10. Zollo, *Songwriters on Songwriting*, p. 634.

11. Snow, 'Plink! Plink? Plink!'.
12. Zollo. *Songwriters on Songwriting*, p. 635.
13. *Ibid.* p. 634.
14. Apart from 'Fiction', 'Love Songs' and 'Near Wild Heaven', 'Unforgettable' was also considered for a while until it was dropped because of its Nat King Cole association.
15. Peter Buck says: 'When we originally wrote it Michael had the chorus which didn't end up on the record but he couldn't finish it and Michael came up with the lyrics one night and on it went.'
16. Dave Di Martino, Jim Irwin and Mark Ellen, 'Fables of the Four-Headed Monster', *Mojo*, 12, November 1994.
17. 'The thing about *Automatic* . . . and even *Out Of Time*, is we kept trying to make a rock'n'roll record and we kept not making that record,' was how Michael Stipe put it. See Stubbs, 'The right stuff'.
18. Jon Wilde, 'REM: acts of the year' in *Virgin Rock Yearbook 93–94* (Virgin, 1994), p. 73.
19. See Simon Price's excellent *Everything (A Book About Manic Street Preachers)* (Virgin, 1999), pp. 88–9, for a short retelling of the Wire/Stipe incident. Both Wire quotes are sourced from Price's narrative.
20. *NME*, January 1999.
21. Goldberg, 'The making of *Monster*'.
22. The idea of being part of a whole that acts like a single organism, like rats moving as one in a pack, is called in contemporary philosophy the rhizomatic. In a sense rock gigs, in their sense of union, are contemporary articulations of this quality.
23. Snow, 'Plink! Plink? Plink!'.
24. Zollo, *Songwriters on Songwriting*.
25. Snow, 'Plink! Plink? Plink!'.
26. Paul Butchart says: 'The summer of 1980 was one of the hottest summers on recent record, many days of temperatures over 100 F/38C. There were many evenings after the Watt or Tyrones closed when we would hit the local apartment complex swimming pools or head out to the lake named Ball Pump, out in the countryside. Though I should probably admit that I missed some of the more orgiastic swims. We also used to skinny dip at an apartment complex in town called Village Apartments.'
27. Phil Urr, 'Hair loss horror!', *Q*, 27, December 1988.
28. Wilde, 'REM: acts of the year'.

CHAPTER 9: 'LOOK OUT, THERE'S A MONSTER COMING', 1994–96

1. 'Meckel's diverticulum, n, a small pouch-like sac that protrudes from the interior of part of the small intestine (ileum) in about 2% of people. Normally harmless, it sometimes becomes infected and causes a condition indistinguishable from appendicitis. Meckel's diverticulum may also lead to twisting (volvulus) or infolding (intussusception) of the bowel.' (Johan Friedrich Meckel II, German anatomist, 1761–1833). Robert M. Youngson, Collins Dictionary of Medicine (HarperCollins, 1992), p. 383.

2. Charles R. Cross, Heavier than Heaven: the Biography of Kurt Cobain (Hodder & Stoughton, 2001), p. 301.

3. Ibid. p. 331.

4. Ibid. p. 337.

5. Adrian Deevoy, 'Saint Michael', Q, 104, May 1995.

6. The original title, retained right up to the special edition of Monster produced by Chris Bilheimer before the release date, was 'With Love Comes Strange Currencies'.

7. Another song on the album, 'Star 69', although musically pretty generic, continues this theme of surveillance. In certain areas of the USA dialling *69 will call back the most recent caller.

8. In a weird coincidence, R.E.M.'s ex-producer, Mitch Easter, had produced and played on a track, 'Kenneth, What's The Frequency', back in 1987, so R.E.M. cannot really be credited with having originated this bizarre title for a song. The group was Game Theory, led by Scott Miller, and the track can be found on their 1987 double album, Lolita Nation.

9. See www.ratherbiased.com/bizarre.htm for this and an amusing collection of facts and weird statements pertaining to Rather. Try these 'Ratherisms' made on election night, 1996: 'Texas: 32 electoral votes, another of the so-called enchiladas or if not an enchilada at least a huge taco', or 'The re-election of Bill Clinton is as secure as a double-knot tied in wet rawhide.'

10. Steve Sutherland, 'When Courtney met Michael', NME, 23 January 1999.

11. According to the Collins English Dictionary, a Rorschach test is 'a personality test consisting of a number of unstructured ink blots presented for interpretation'.

12. A limited edition version of Monster, in the form of a 52-page hardback book, with artwork by Bilheimer, was nominated for a

packaging Grammy. It didn't win, though Bilheimer points out that this is the organisation that voted Milli Vanilli best new artist of 1991, the year Nirvana broke.

13. It is thought that the propensity to suffer aneurysms at a young age (Berry was just 36 when taken ill) is mainly due to inherited deficiencies. Berry wonders whether a childhood head injury with a baseball may have been to blame. However, one interviewee for the book said, perhaps inaccurately, that Berry's illness was 'his past lifestyle catching up with him'.

14. I am indebted to the coverage given in rec.music.rem Google newsgroup for some of the information about Bill Berry's illness and recovery.

15. See Rob Jovanovic and Tim Abbott, *Adventures In Hi-Fi: the Complete R.E.M.* (Orion, 2001), p. 262.

16. Steven Daly and Nathanial Wice, *alt.culture: an a-z guide to 90s America* (Fourth Estate, 1995).

17. Anthony Farrell, Vivienne Guinness and Julian Lloyd (eds), *My Generation: Rock'n'Roll Remembered – An Imperfect History* (Lilliput Press, 1996), p. 212.

CHAPTER 10: 'I'M OUTTA HERE', 1996–98

1. Chuck Philips, 'R.E.M.'s former manager denies allegations of sex harassment', *LA Times*, 21 June 1996.

2. *Ibid.*

3. Posted by B.J. Richards on the rec.music.rem newsgroup, 12 July 1996.

4. Source quoted on rec.music.rem discussion group: http://orangefox.svs.com/rem/jefferson.txt

5. Miriam Longino, 'R.E.M.: talk about the passion', *The Atlanta Journal/-*Constitution X-site, www.accessatlanta.com/partners/ajc/xsite/rem/index.html, 29 August 1999.

6. Quoted in Keir Keightley, 'Gender, domestic space, and high fidelity, 1948–59', *Popular Music*, 15(2), May 1996, p. 157.

7. Tom Doyle, 'Remember us?', *Q*, 122, November 1996.

8. Most rock acts would simply have sampled this repeating musical motif but, such is the band's commitment to live authenticity, it was obviously not an option seriously considered. It *had* to be played.

9. Craig Rosen, *R.E.M. Inside Out* (Thunder's Mouth Press, 1997), p. 168.

10. A tiresome and pointless debate was initiated by some R.E.M. fans concerning the sequencing of albums. The cover of *Document* has a number 5 on the sleeve. The next album, *Green*, has the number 4 superimposed over the letter 'r'. Stipe says this was a simple typographical error as, on the 'qwerty' keyboard, the letter 'r' is almost directly below the number '4'. According to the fans' 'countdown' theory, the final R.E.M. album would either be number 1, *Monster*, or the 'blast-off' number zero, *Hi-Fi*. Peter Buck had commented to a journalist that the band would break up at the end of the decade and all this, together with the 'Electrolite' lyric which referenced the millennium, was enough to send fans over the edge in their attempts to crack the R.E.M. code. 'Peter Buck says the December 1999 [split up] was a smartass answer to a journalist once, and it's become this big joke,' Stipe said in a rare online appearance, courtesy of AOL, in 1994: 'I reckon we will last longer. The countdown is a silly coincidence. I swear it. Peter Buck says we're going into negative numbers next, so there. I did put the number 7 on each record for a while but started getting strange mail in volumes about it and so we quit. No reason for 7, it was just a cool typo thing (like the typeface on *Fables*).' See http://randrews.users. netlink.co.uk/rem/archive/aolstipey.html
11. Jovanovic and Longino, 'Hello, goodbye'.
12. Tom Doyle, 'A three-legged dog is still a dog', *Q*, 136, January 1998.
13. *Ibid.*
14. See www.athensnewspapers.com/framed.html
15. Extracted from a posting on rec.music.rem

CHAPTER 11: 'BE UNAFRAID', 1998–2001
1. Yorke had sung with R.E.M. at the Tibet Freedom Concert in 1998. Equipment problems marred the actual performance, but Scott McCaughey recalls that the rehearsal was mind-blowing: 'We did "Be Mine", with Thom Yorke singing. Apparently, it was all screwed up at the show. We didn't know this because you don't get a sound check at these festival things, but apparently the guitar that Mike was playing, which was effectively the main instrument of the song, wasn't coming through the PA. We had rehearsed it the day before at DC at some sound station, and

Thom had come and sung it. It was phenomenal. I don't think a recording was made of it, but God, I would love to have a copy. I thought, that could be a hit single. Not that it wasn't great with Michael singing it.'

2. Check out Ballard Lesemann's 'Daysleepy' and 'Automatic . . . for the converted', from *Flagpole*, 21 October 1998, for two reactions to the album. Thanks to Ballard for supplying these.
3. David Stubbs, 'The right stuff', *Uncut*, August 1999.
4. The song's protagonist is, apparently, female. Interestingly, the mid-song piece of whimsy was a field recording by Scott McCaughey: 'We were in San Sebastian for a week on the *Monster* tour, and right by our hotel there was this big sea wall where the waves would come crashing in, and I recorded some of that on my little cassette recorder. There are people walking by talking, and that's part of the sound collage before the last verse.'
5. David Bill, 'R.E.M. having "A Blast", Stipe says', *Online Athens: News*, 27 August 1999.
6. Tom Doyle, 'Out of time?', *Q*, 156, September 1999.
7. John Vena, 'R.E.M. end world tour on "Up" note', *Sonic Net*, 13 September 1999.
8. Bertis Downs, 'Postcard from Dublin', www.remhq.com/new/news.html, 6 October 2000.
9. Andy Pemberton, 'Michael Stipe: cash for questions', *Q*, 152, May 1999.
10. Marjorie Garber, *Vice Versa: Bisexuality and the Eroticism of Everyday Life* (Hamish Hamilton, 1995), p. 63.
11. Rachel Newsome, 'New adventures in hi-fi, pictures and sexuality', an interview with Michael Stipe, extracted from *Dazed and Confused*, *Independent on Sunday*, 16 July 2000, p. 7.
12. Du Noyer, a former editor of *Q*, added: 'I must admit at my time at *Q*, I was deeply grateful to both R.E.M. and U2 for their co-operation with me was of immense benefit to the magazine and probably to them as well. They certainly helped to shore up the magazine during those years. So contrary to whatever cynicism that I have developed I will always be very grateful to them.

CHAPTER 12: MUSIC FOR A MARKET THAT DOESN'T EXIST? 2001–02

1. Christina Williams, 'Does it really matter? young people and popular music', *Popular Music* (2001), vol. 20(2), p. 240.
2. Rachel Newsome, 'New adventures in hi-fi, pictures and sexuality', an interview with Michael Stipe, extracted from *Dazed and Confused*, *Independent on Sunday*, 16 July 2000, p. 7.
3. See http://ask.yahoo.com/ask/20010907.html for a short definition of the theory.
4. See Kim McCarten, 'Saturn Return', www.mergemag.org/1998/saturn.html
5. A musical, according to the *New York Times Review*, of 'lofty aspiration' and an 'upwardly spiralling three-way conversation by Icarus, his father, and the chorus'. Some of these themes appear remarkably close to the lyrical preoccupations of *Reveal*.
6. My account of the alleged incident is based on a transcription of the prosecution's opening speech which was posted on the website, The Smoking Gun at: www.thesmokinggun.com/doc_o_day/peterbuck1.shtml
7. Corey Moss, 'R.E.M.'s Buck to be retried for air rage incident', www.mtv.com/news/article/1451512/20011217/rem.jhtml?headlines=tr, 17 December 2001.
8. *NME*, 24 September 1994.
9. Recmusic.rem, November 2001.
10. Pemberton, 'Michael Stipe'.
11. Snow, 'Plink! Plink? Plink!', *Q*, 73, October 1992.
12. Quotes from the trial have been sourced from NME.com, news.bbc.co.uk, murmurs.com/news and uk.news.yahoo.com

DOCUMENTS

1. PEOPLE

(A) THE INTERVIEWEES
The following either spoke or corresponded with me for the book. A really big thank you to:

Cary Baker	Former National Publicity Director and Vice President at I.R.S. He now runs his own PR company based in LA with Sheryl Northrop, the Baker/Northrop Media Group. http://www.bakernorthrop.com/company
David Bell	R.E.M. fan who put his academic career on hold to run the R.E.M. fan club out of Athens and to build one of the most cordial fan/star relationships in rock history
Chris Bilheimer	R.E.M. art director, he has worked with Michael Stipe on the designs of all R.E.M. album covers since 1994, and is also involved in other aspects of R.E.M. artwork
Jay Boberg	The man who signed R.E.M. for I.R.S. Currently president of MCA records
Joe Boyd	Producer of the band's third album, *Fables Of The Reconstruction/Reconstruction Of The Fables*, and founder of Hannibal records. His production CV includes Pink Floyd and Fairport Convention
Peter Buck	Fast-talking rock journalist manqué and musical conceptualist behind R.E.M. since 1980. Plays

	guitar but refuses to play long solos, thank God. Married to Stephanie; two children, Zoë and Zelda
Paul Butchart	Ex-drummer of the Side Effects, Butchart takes a keen interest in the history of the Athens scene. http://www.athensmusichistory.com
Stephanie Chernikowski	Texan photographer, now resident in NYC, and chronicler of the new wave scene (see her book *Dream Baby Dream: Images from the Blank Generation*, 2:13:61, 1996). She worked with the band in 1986. http://www.stepcherphoto.com
Don Dixon	Co-producer (along with Mitch Easter) of *Murmur* and *Reckoning* and still active as a musician and producer
Betsy Dorminey	Former classmate of Bertis Downs, Athens scenester and R.E.M. supporter. Now works as a lawyer based in Athens
Bertis Downs	R.E.M.'s attorney up until 1996 and then *de facto* manager after the departure of Jefferson Holt. Runs operation R.E.M. out of Athens, Georgia and still teaches at the local law school. He claims to be not in the music business, but the R.E.M. business
George Dubose	Former photo editor at *Spin* and record sleeve designer. Dubose interviewed Stipe in the early 1980s and staged one of the first R.E.M. photo shoots. http://www.hometown.aol.com/dubosephoto/rockphotospg .1.html
Paul Du Noyer	Writer and critic. Founder of *Mojo* magazine and former editor of *Q*. http://www.pauldunoyer.com
Mitch Easter	Producer of *Chronic Town*, and co-producer (with Don Dixon) of *Murmur* and *Reckoning*. Still working as a musician and producer based in North Carolina
Don Gehman	Producer of R.E.M.'s fourth record, *Lifes Rich Pageant*, he made his name as co-producer of several John Cougar Mellencamp records in the 1980s. Still working in record production
Paul Holmes	Ex-R.E.M. fanzine editor. Currently resident in Athens, Georgia

Mark Howard	Engineer on both *Automatic For The People* and *Monster*. Has also worked with Iggy Pop and U2
Ethan Kaplan	R.E.M. ally and webmaster of the excellent unofficial R.E.M. site *Murmurs*. http://www.murmurs.com
John Keane	Musician and producer and provider, on a continued and regular basis, of a home base studio for R.E.M. to demo and record. http://www.johnkeanestudios.com
Rosalyn Knight	Produced a highly readable BA dissertation on the Athens music scene which she made available to the authors for research purposes
Michael Lachowski	Formerly part of the group Pylon, Lachowski's design company, Candy, produced R.E.M.'s first ever website. http://www.candysticker.com
Ballard Lesemann	Rock writer and senior music editor of *Flagpole*, the premier Athens newspaper. http://www.flagpole.com
Ann-Louise Lipman	R.E.M. fan
Scott McCaughey	Seattle-based musician working on a variety of projects (including the Young Fresh Fellows and the Minus Five). Has played with R.E.M. both live and in the studio since 1995. Close friend of Peter Buck's
Mike Mills	Multi-instrumentalist, performer and songwriter with R.E.M. Golfer and occasional celebrity tennis partner too. Unmarried, one son, Julian, born in 1989
Stine Olsen	R.E.M. fan and collector
Kevin O'Neil	Management Associate at the Athens office. Has worked full-time for R.E.M. since 1994
Michael Plen	Currently a top executive at Virgin Records, Plen worked for I.R.S. until 1987 as the label's Promotions supremo
Werner Quadflieg	R.E.M. collector and supporter
Will Rigby	Former drummer with the dB's, who toured with R.E.M. in 1984 and 1987

Ole Skjefte	R.E.M. enthusiast, collector and archivist
Mat Snow	UK rock critic, editor and writer who interviewed the band in 1992 at the time of *Automatic For The People*. Currently editor of *Four Four Two* magazine
Ken Stringfellow	Worked with R.E.M. from the *Up* tour to the present day and recorded with his band, the Posies, as a solo artist and in various side-projects. http://www.kenstringfellow.com
Nikki Sudden	English rock musician who lived with Buck for a short period in Athens and performed live with Buck, Berry and Mills
Hans van der Waal	R.E.M. fan and collector
Dan Wall	Band supporter and owner of Wuxtry Records in Athens where Peter Buck worked for many years
Geoff Ward	Writer, poet, academic, American literature expert and some time R.E.M. fan. His latest book, *The Writing of America: Literature and Cultural Identity from the Puritans to the Present*, was published by Polity in 2002
Weaver D/ Dexter Weaver	Athens-based cook, restaurateur and author who originated the phrase 'Automatic For The People.' http://www.automaticyall.com
Kurt Wood	Local DJ in Athens in the 1980s and champion of new wave music

(B) OTHER CHARACTERS

Next up, those who played a sometimes crucial role in the history of R.E.M. and whose voices have been projected out of various archive sources.

Bill Berry	Drummer and multi-instrumentalist with R.E.M. Left the band in 1997, but rumours abound of a re-formation. Divorced in 1997. Currently to be seen driving a tractor on his smallholding near Athens, Georgia
The B-52's	Athens' first real new wave rock group and sporadic hit-makers to this day

Ian Copeland	Early R.E.M. fan and head of Paragon Booking Agency. Formed a band, the Frustrations, with Mills and Berry in pre-R.E.M. days
Miles Copeland III	Head of I.R.S. Records, the label that had R.E.M. on its roster between 1982 and 1988
Rev. Howard Finster	Self-styled 'Man Of Vision' whose folk art inspired the band. The promo for 'Radio Free Europe' was shot at Paradise Gardens and features Finster himself. Died in October 2001
David Healy	A talented painter, his Dasht Hopes Label funded the recording of the band's EP, *Chronic Town*. Died in a car accident in 1998
James Herbert	Inspirational Athens-based artist who works in the University's Art Department. He produced the art film *Left Of Reckoning* for the band in 1984
Johnny Hibbert	'Radio Free Europe', R.E.M.'s first-ever single, came out on his Hibtone label. Currently works in Atlanta as a lawyer
Peter Holsapple	Singer-songwriter. Opened for R.E.M. in the early 1980s, toured with his band the dB's on the R.E.M. bill in 1984 and 1987, then worked with the band live and in the studio between 1988 and 1991. Rumoured to have split from R.E.M. acrimoniously
Jefferson Holt	R.E.M.'s manager from 1980 to 1996. Possibly the single most important individual in the band's career. A gagging clause signed by all parties at the time of his controversial departure/sacking in 1996 has meant that he has since operated almost reclusively as a record label owner
Scott Litt	The power behind the console. New York-born rock producer who co-produced six R.E.M. albums from *Document* to *New Adventures In Hi-Fi*. Left R.E.M.'s employ to set up his own record label, Outpost (now folded)
Kathleen O'Brien	Girlfriend to both Buck and Berry and early R.E.M. supporter. It was at a birthday party in her honour back in 1980 that the band played their first gig
Gwen O'Looney	Pythonesque of name and liberal by persuasion,

	the R.E.M. camp vigorously supported her candidature for mayor of Athens
Microwave (Mark Mytrowitz)	R.E.M.'s guitar tech for over a dozen years until his departure in the late 1990s. Again, the circumstances of his departure are unknown
Pat McCarthy	R.E.M.'s co-producer on *Up* and *Reveal*
Lynda Stipe	Singer, musician and sister of Michael. Has played with Oh-OK and Flash To Bang Time, and also works as a professional tiler with an interest in mosaic art
Michael Stipe	Visual artist who somehow discovered he had one of the greatest voices in pop. Sings and writes for R.E.M., but increasingly busies himself with photography, art and film production too. He is possibly the single most important male rock icon of the last twenty years (although Bono might have something to say about that)

WORDS

(A) BOOKS ON R.E.M.

For an accessible and well-written account of the band for all newcomers, start with Tony Fletcher's *Remarks* (Omnibus, 1994, currently being revised). If you're already a bit of an R.E.M. nut then Marcus Gray's hugely detailed *It Crawled from the South* is the place for you, and if you've really got the Athens blues, and can't sleep at night without knowing how many times 'Fall On Me' was performed on the *Up* tour, turn first to the fact-fuelled mania of *Adventures in Hi-Fi: The Complete R.E.M.* by Messrs. Rob Jovanovic and Tim Abbott. Denise Sullivan's *Talk about the Passion* is full of insight and oral testimony. Craig Rosen's *R.E.M.: Inside Out* and Peter Hogan's *The Complete Guide to the Music of R.E.M.* offer track-by-track histories of the band. The band's early work is discussed in detail by John A. Platt in *Murmur, Classic Rock Albums*, while the same author's edited anthology, *The R.E.M. Companion: Two Decades of Commentary*, containing over 30 previously printed essays and articles on the band, is an important source. Rodger Lyle Brown's *Party out of Bounds: The B-52's, R.E.M., and the Kids who Rocked Athens, Georgia* is a candid first-hand account of the early eighties Athens scene. After that, the next best place to stop is undoubtedly *Q* magazine. *Q* have offered excellent, if often mildly unquestioning, commentary on the band since the late 1980s, and their 2001 R.E.M. special, 'R.E.M. Revealed!', is a super thing to be sure. Don't forget *Mojo*, *Uncut* and *Record Collector* either. The usual suspects of Cavanagh, Doyle, Deevoy and Gill provide the best coverage in UK journalism (details in the bibliography). In the states, Anthony DeCurtis' work stands out as being the most comprehensive in terms of an analysis of the band's impact and history. The collection of writings, *Rocking My Life Away*, contains two important articles.

(B) GENERAL READING
The following monographs and collections were all consulted during the research and writing of *Fiction*.

Azerrad, Michael (2001) *Our Band Could Be Your Life: Scenes from the American Indie Underground, 1981–1991*, Little Brown.

Beadle, Jeremy J. (1993) *Will Pop Eat Itself? Pop Music and the Soundbite Era*, Faber.

Buckley, Jonathan and Mark Ellingham (eds) (1996) *Rock: The Rough Guide*, Rough Guides Ltd.

Bret, David (1994) *Morrissey: Landscapes of the Mind*, Robson.

Bryson, Bill (1989) *The Lost Continent: Travels in Small Town America*, Abacus.

Carroll, Peter N. and David W. Noble (1977) *The Free and the Unfree: A New History of the United States*, Penguin.

Cross, Charles R. (2001) *Heavier than Heaven: the Biography of Kurt Cobain*, Hodder & Stoughton.

Daly, Steven and Nathanial Wice (1995) *alt.culture: an a-z guide to 90s america*, Fourth Estate.

DeCurtis, Anthony (1992) *Present Tense: Rock & Roll and Culture*, Duke University Press.

DeCurtis, Anthony (1998) *Rocking My Life Away: Writing about Music and Other Matters*, Duke University Press.

DeRogatis, Jim (2000) *Let It Blurt: The Life and Times of Lester Bangs*, Bloomsbury.

Doty, Alexander (1993) *Making Things Perfectly Queer: Interpreting Mass Culture*, University of Minnesota Press.

Draper, Robert (1990) *The Rolling Stone Story*, Mainstream Publishing.

Eddy, Chuck (1997) *The Accidental Evolution of Rock 'n Roll: A Misguided Tour through Popular Music*, Da Capo.

Farrell, Anthony, Vivienne Guinness and Julian Lloyd (1996) *My Generation: Rock'n'Roll Remembered – an Imperfect History*, Lilliput Press.

Flanagan, Bill (1990) *Written In My Soul: Candid Interviews with Rock's Great Songwriters*, Omnibus.

Flanagan, Bill (1995) *U2 At The End Of The World*, Viking.

Garofalo, Reebee (1992) *Rockin' the Boat: Mass Music and Mass Movements*, South End Press.

Gracyk, Theodore (1996) *Rhythm and Noise: an Aesthetics of Rock*, Duke University Press.

Heylin, Clinton (ed.) (1992) *The Penguin Book of Rock 'n' roll Writing*, Viking.

Humphrey, Clark (1995) *Loser: The Real Seattle Story*, Feral House.

King, Richard H. and Helen Taylor (ed.) (1996) *Dixie Debates: Perspectives on Southern Cultures*, Pluto Press.

Lipsitz, George (1990) *Time Passages: Collective Memory and American Popular Culture*, The University of Minnesota Press.

Moore, Allan F. (1993) *Rock: The Primary Text*, Open University Press.

Palmer, Robert (1996) *Dancing in the Street: a Rock and Roll History*, BBC Books.

Potter, John (ed.) (2000) *The Cambridge Companion to Singing*, Cambridge University Press.

Reder, Alan and John Baxter (1999) *Listen To This! Leading Musicians Recommend Their Favourite Artists and Recordings*, Hyperion.

Reynolds, Simon (1990) *Blissed Out: The Raptures of Rock*, Little, Brown.

Reynolds, Simon and Joy Press (1995) *The Sex Revolts: Gender, Rebellion and Rock'n'Roll*, Serpent's Tail.

Rogan, Johnny (1993) *Morrissey and Marr – The Severed Alliance*, Omnibus.

Rogan, Johnny (1997) *The Byrds: Timeless Flight Revisited – The Sequel*, Rogan House.

Savage, Jon (1996) *Time Travel: Pop, Media and Sexuality, 1976–96*, Chatto & Windus.

Sinclair, Dave (1993) *Rock on CD*, Kyle Cathie.

Shuker, Roy (1994) *Understanding Popular Music*, Routledge.

Shuker, Roy (1998) *Key Concepts in Popular Music*, Routledge.

Szatmary, David P. (1996) *Rockin' in Time: a Social History of Rock'n'Roll*, 3rd edn, Prentice Hall.

Zollo, Paul (1997) *Songwriters on Songwriting*, Expanded edn, Da Capo.

(C) ARTICLES ON R.E.M. AND R.E.M.-RELATED TOPICS

Arnold, Gina (2001) 'Ghost tarts and dolphin boys', *Metro Active Music*, 3 January.

Bill, David (1999) 'R.E.M. having "a blast", Stipe says', *Online Athens: News*, 27 August.

Bone, James (2001) 'R.E.M. singer discloses he is gay', *The Times On-line*, 15 May.

Cavanagh, David (1994) 'When R.E.M. are great, they make birdsong sound phony. But . . .' (*Monster* review), *Mojo*, 11 October 1994: 96–8.

Cavanagh, David (1994) 'Tune in, cheer up, rock out', *Q*, 97, October: 92–102.

Cavanagh, David (1996) 'One more time . . .', *Q*, 112, January: 104–11.

Cavanagh, David (1998) 'Come on, he was only the drummer', *Q*, 146, November: 96–104.

Chernikowski, Stephanie (2001) 'A Visit to Paradise Garden', Dilettante Press, http://www.dilettantepress.com/articles/finster-words.html

DeCurtis, Anthony (1992) 'The Eighties'. In *Present Tense: Rock & Roll and Culture*. Duke University Press.

Deevoy, Adrian (1995) 'Saint Michael', *Q*, 104, May: 86–92.

Di Martino, Dave, Jim Irwin and Mark Ellen (1994) 'Fables of the four-headed monster', *Mojo*, 12, November: 70–96.

Downs, Bertis (2000) 'Postcard from Dublin', http://www.remhq.com/new/news.html, 6 October.

Doyle, Tom (1996) 'Remember us?', *Q*, 122, November: 104–17.

Doyle, Tom (1998) 'A three-legged dog is still a dog', *Q*, 136, January: 36–7.

Doyle, Tom (1999) 'Out of time?', *Q*, 156, September: 74–82.

Eccleston, Danny (1999) 'There's life in the old knees yet!', *Q*, 154, July: 46.

Fausset, Richard (1998) 'Automatic . . . for the converted', *Flagpole*, 21 October.

Fausset, Richard and Pete McCommons (1998) 'The age of Gwen', *Flagpole* magazine Online, http://www.flagpole.com/Issues/ 10.14.98/gwen.html, 14 October.

Fresco, Adam (2001) 'Rock star apologises for "air rage" antics', *The Times* On-Line, 24 April.

Gill, Andy (1988) 'Positive: are R.E.M. the best band in the world?', *Q*, 27, December: 135.

Gill, Andy (1991) 'The home guard', *Q*, 55 April: 56–61.

Gill, Andy (1995) 'R.E.M.', in Paul Du Noyer, *The Virgin Story of Rock'n'Roll*. Virgin.

Goldberg, Michael (1995) 'The making of *Monster*' (an interview with Scott Litt), http://www.addict.com/issues/1.02/Cover_Story/Monster

Goldberg, Michael (1995) 'Cyberspace, sex, and the mysterious Stipe-man', *Addicted to Noise*, http://www.addict.com/issues/1.02/ Cover_Story/Q+A/

Gray, Marcus (1994) A remcyclopaedia, *Q*, 98, November: 82–8.

Q Awards (1998) *Q*, 148, January: 44–60.

Hannon, Neil (2000) '100 years of attitude', *Mojo*, 74, January: 75.

Harris, John (2001) 'Cash for questions special'. In *Q, R.E.M. Revealed! Artistry! Mystery! R.E.M.: the Definitive Appreciation*.

Hoskyns, Barney (1996) 'Be seeing you?', *Mojo*, 33 August: 84–7.

Jaymes, Cyd (2001) 'R.E.M. – The R.E.M. DVD Collection', Review, *Dotmusic.com*

Johnson, Steve (2001) 'Time to face facts about celebrity profiles in magazines', 1 June. Chicagotribune.com

Jovanovic, Rob and Miriam Longino (1998) 'Hello, goodbye' [on Bill Berry departure], *Vox*, January.

Junod, Tom (2001) 'Michael Stipe has great hair: based on a true story', *Esquire* Online.

Keightley, Keir (1996) 'Gender, domestic space, and high fidelity, 1948–59', *Popular Music*, 15(2), May: 157.

Kitson, Neville (2001) 'Back on the campaign trail (and they feel fine)', *The Times*, On-Line edn. 27 April.

Longino, Miriam (1999) 'R.E.M.: talk about the passion', *The Atlanta Journal/-Constitution* X-site, 29 August. http://www.accessatlanta. com/partners/ajc/xsite/rem/index.html

Lesemann, Ballard (1998) 'Daysleepy', *Flagpole*, 21 October.

McCarten, Kim (1998) 'Saturn Return', http://www.mergemag.org/ 1998/saturn.html

Moss, Corey (2001) 'R.E.M.'s Buck to be retried for air rage incident', 17 December 2001, http://www.mtv.com/news/article/1451512/20011217/rem.jhtml?headlin es = tr.

Mills, Mike (1985/1992) 'Our town'. In Clinton Heylin (ed.), *The Penguin Book of Rock'n'Roll Writing*. Viking.

Newsome, Rachel (2000) 'New adventures in hi-fi, pictures and sexuality' [interview with Michael Stipe]. Extracted from *Dazed and Confused, Independent on Sunday*, 16 July, p. 7.

Pemberton, Andy (1999) 'Michael Stipe: cash for questions', *Q*, 152, May 1999: 10–14.

Philips, Chuck (1996) 'R.E.M.'s former manager denies allegations of sex harassment', *LA Times*, 21 June.

Rather, Don (2000–2002) Unofficial web site devoted to the US newscaster and journalist, http://www.ratherbiased.com/bizarre.htm

Savage, Jon (1996/1989) 'R.E.M.: post-yuppie pop'. In *Time Travel*, Chatto & Windus, pp. 250–2.

Sheffield, Rob (2001) 'Review of *Reveal*', *Rolling Stone*, 869, 24 May.

Shepherd, David (1999) 'Michael Stipe: international man of mystery', *Q*, 155, August: 64.

Shumway, David R. (1992) 'Rock & roll as cultural practice'. In *Present Tense: Rock & Roll and Culture*. Duke University Press.

Simmons, Sylvie (1998) 'Holy ghost in the machine' [*Up* review]. *Mojo*, 60, November: 92–4.

Sinclair, David (2001) 'Extraordinary things happen when Nelson Mandela puts his name to a concert', *The Times* On-Line edn. 1 May.

Snow, Mat (1992) 'Lyrically dark, musically oddball', *Q*, 74, November: 58–62.

Stipe, Michael (1994) http://randrews.users.netlink.co.uk/rem/archive/aolstipey.html (appearance on AOL).

Stubbs, David (1999) 'The right stuff', *Uncut*, August: 46–61.

Sullivan, Denise (1994) Eyewitness, *Q*, 96, September: 40–3.

Sutherland, Steve (1999) 'When Courtney met Michael', *NME*, 23 January: 16–18.

Urr, Phil (1988) 'Hair loss horror!', *Q*, 27, December: 12.

Wheeler, Gaston (2001) 'Band against band with no loser', *Music Beyond Radio.com*.

Vena, John (1999) 'R.E.M. end world tour on "Up" note', *Sonic Net*, 13 September.

Wilde, Jon (1994) 'REM: acts of the year'. In *Virgin Rock Yearbook 93–94*. Virgin.

Williams, Christina (2001) 'Does it really matter? young people and popular music', *Popular Music*, 20(2): 240–2.

3. SOUNDS

R.E.M. album and single releases (all album releases are italicised):

Title	Label	US release date	Chart position*
'Radio Free Europe'	Hibtone	1981	–
Chronic Town EP	I.R.S.	Aug. 1982	–
Murmur	I.R.S.	Apr. 1983	36 (US) G
'Radio Free Europe'	I.R.S.	May 1983	76 (US)
'Talk About The Passion'	I.R.S.	Nov. 1983	–
Reckoning	I.R.S.	Apr. 1984	27 (US) G; 91 (UK)
'So. Central Rain (I'm Sorry)'	I.R.S.	May 1984	85 (US)
'(Don't Go Back To) Rockville'	I.R.S.	Aug. 1984	–
Fables Of The Reconstruction	I.R.S.	June 1985	28 (US) G; 35 (UK); 30 (Can)
'Can't Get There From Here'	I.R.S.	June 1985	–
'Driver 8'	I.R.S.	Sep. 1985	–
'Wendell Gee'	I.R.S.	Oct. 1985	–
Lifes Rich Pageant	I.R.S.	July 1986	21 (US) G; 43 (UK); 29 (Can); 73 (Aus)
'Fall On Me'	I.R.S.	Aug. 1986	94 (US)
'Superman'	I.R.S.	Nov. 1986	–
Dead Letter Office	I.R.S.	Apr. 1987	52 (US); 60 (UK)
'The One I Love'	I.R.S.	Aug. 1987	9 (US); 51 (UK); 14 (Can); 84 (Aus)
Document	I.R.S.	Sep. 1987	10 (US) P; 28 (UK); 12 (Can); 47 (Aus)
'It's the End Of The World . . .'	I.R.S.	Jan. 1988	69 (US)
'Finest Worksong' (UK only)	I.R.S.	Mar. 1988	50 (UK)
Eponymous	I.R.S.	Oct. 1988	44 (US); 69 (UK); 32 (Aus)
Green	Warners	Nov. 1988	12 (US) 2P; 27(UK) P; 14 (Can); 13 (Aus) P

'Orange Crush'	Warners	Nov. 1988	28 (UK – May 1989), 15 (Aus)
'Stand'	Warners	Jan. 1989	6 (US); 51 (UK); 16 (Can); 72 (Aus)
'Pop Song '89'	Warners	May 1989	86 (US)
'Stand' (re-issue, UK)	Warners	Aug. 1989	48 (UK)
'Get Up'	Warners	Sep. 1989	–
'Losing My Religion'	Warners	Feb. 1991	4 (US); 19 (UK); 16 (Can); 11 (Aus)
Out Of Time	Warners	Mar. 1991	1 (US) 4P; 1 (UK) 5P; 1 (Can); 4 (Aus) 4P
'Shiny Happy People'	Warners	June 1991	10 (US);6 (UK); 17 (Can); 19 (Aus)
'Near Wild Heaven'	Warners	Aug. 1991	27 (UK); 65 (Aus)
'The One I Love' (re-issue)	I.R.S.	Sep. 1991	16 (UK)
The Best Of R.E.M. (UK/Aus)	I.R.S.	Oct. 1991	7 (UK) G; 20 (Aus) G
'Radio Song'	Warners	Nov. 1991	28 (UK)
'It's The End Of The World As We Know It (And I Feel Fine)'	I.R.S.	Dec. 1991	39 (UK)
'Drive'	Warners	Sep. 1992	28 (US); 11 (UK); 10 (Can); 34 (Aus)
Automatic For The People	Warners	Oct. 1992	2 (US) 4P; 1 (UK) 6P; 3 (Can); 2 (Aus) 3P
'Man On The Moon'	Warners	Nov. 1992	30 (US); 18 (UK); 9 (Can); 39 (Aus)
'The Sidewinder Sleeps Tonite'	Warners	Feb. 1993	17 (UK); 99 (Aus)
'Everybody Hurts'	Warners	Apr. 1993	29 (US); 7 (UK); 5 (Can); 6 (Aus)
'Nightswimming'	Warners	July 1993	27 (UK); 71 (Aus)
'Find The River'	Warners	Dec. 1993	54 (UK)
'What's The Frequency Kenneth?'	Warners	Sep. 1994	21 (US); 9 (UK); 10 (Can); 24 (Aus)
Monster	Warners	Sep. 1994	1 (US) 4P; 1 (UK) 3P; 1 (Can); 2 (Aus) P
'Bang And Blame'	Warners	Nov. 1994	19 (US); 15 (UK); 3 (Can); 29 (Aus)
'Crush With Eyeliner'	Warners	Jan. 1995	23 (UK), 55 (Aus)
'Strange Currencies'	Warners	Apr. 1995	47 (US); 9 (UK); 12 (Can); 100 (Aus)

'Tongue'	Warners	Sep. 1995	13 (UK)
'E-Bow The Letter'	Warners	Aug. 1996	49 (US); 4 (UK); 10 (Can); 23 (Aus)
New Adventures In Hi-Fi	Warners	Sep. 1996	2(US) P; 1 (UK) 2P; 1 (Can); 1 (Aus) G
'Bittersweet Me'	Warners	Oct. 1996	46 (US); 19 (UK); 22 (Can); 90 (Aus)
'Electrolite'	Warners	Dec. 1996	29 (UK)
'How The West Was Won . . .'	Warners	Apr. 1997	–
'Daysleeper'	Warners	Oct. 1998	57 (US); 6 (UK); 57 (Aus)
Up	Warners	Oct. 1998	3 (US) G; 2 (UK) P; 2 (Can); 5 (Aus)
'Lotus'	Warners	Dec. 1998	26 (UK)
'At My Most Beautiful'	Warners	Mar. 1999	10 (UK)
'Suspicion'	Warners	July 1999	–
'The Great Beyond'	Warners	Dec. 1999	57 (US); 3 (UK); 25 (Aus)
Man On The Moon . . .	Warners	Jan. 2000	109 (UK)
'Imitation Of Life'	Warners	Apr. 2001	83 (US); 6 (UK); 5 (Can); 32 (Aus)
Reveal	Warners	May 2001	6 (US) G; 1 (UK) P; 4 (Can); 5 (Aus) G
'All The Way To Reno (You're Gonna Be A Star)'	Warners	July 2001	24 (UK)
'I'll Take The Rain'	Warners	Nov. 2001	44 (UK)

†Original soundtrack.
*Sales certifications: S = Silver; G = Gold; P = Platinum; NP = N × Platinum (e.g. 2P).

	Silver	Gold	Platinum	N × Platinum
US	n.a.	500,000	1,000,000	N × 1,000,000
UK singles	200,000	400,000	600,000	N × 600,000
UK albums	60,000	100,000	300,000	N × 300,000
Australia	n.a.	35,000	70,000	N × 70,000

In the US and Australia there is no silver certification, and singles and albums are certified for the same amount. There is no sales information available for Canada. *Source*: Stuart French, with corrections and updates by the author. Thank you Stuart!

A NOTE ON UNOFFICIAL RECORDINGS

By unofficial recordings, I mean bootlegs of course, and, in connection with R.E.M., there's enough to keep you listening 365 days a year until you're an old-age pensioner. Bootlegs are, of course, illegal. However, the band take a rational view on the matter, as indeed they should, given that their guitarist collects them. What I would say, before you venture into laying out serious money, is that very often bootlegs are of substandard performances and of highly dubious sound quality. That said, literally hundreds of shows are in circulation. I think the legendary Tyrone's tape of 4 October 1980 is a pretty essential starting point, given that it provides a snapshot of a band on the verge of something very much better than the tape evidences! A bootleg also exists containing songs from a practice session at the Wuxtry in Atlanta in June 1980. From then on, it's largely take your pick.

Many of the R.E.M. shows which have found their way on to bootleg, via radio broadcast, offer the best sound quality. Apart from that you can trawl through the B-sides of R.E.M. singles for some excellent live performances.

4. VISUALS

There have been six official R.E.M. videos. They are all available on DVD too, except the early compilation, *Succumbs*.

Succumbs (1987) A collection of pop promos from 'Radio Free Europe' to 'Fall On Me'. Includes the James Herbert film, *Left Of Reckoning*.

Pop Screen (1990) Videos from *Document* and *Green*.

Tourfilm (1990) A visual document of the *Green* tour.

This Film Is On (1991) Video accompaniment to their best-selling album ever, *Out Of Time*.

Parallel (1995) Videos culled from *Automatic For The People* and *Monster*.

Roadmovie (1996) 19 live songs from the *Monster* tour.

Tourfilm, *Parallel* and *Roadmovie* are available as a boxed set.

There are two R.E.M.-related films:

Athens Inside-Out (1986) An eccentric look at the Athens scene with interviews with Peter Buck, Michael Lachowski, the B-52's and Jim Herbert amongst others.

A Stirling Performance (2001). This film focuses on the three performances R.E.M. gave at Stirling Castle in 1999 on the *Up* tour, and the impact they had on the local community.

Copies of the band's live TV broadcasts and television appearances and live radio broadcasts are readily available on the fan trading network. The band's concert in April 2001 in Cologne, a portion of which was broadcast by MTV, is essential.

5. VIRTUAL

http://www.remhq.com The band's official site.

http://www.murmurs.com/ The best unofficial site by far.

http://people2.clarityconnect.com/webpages6/ronhenry/remfaq.htm An essential guide is provided at Usenet rec.music.rem by Ron Henry in his Frequently Asked Questions List.

http:///geocities.com/sunsetstrip/5582/index.html A website with content by Lisa Drake *et al.* is devoted to Peter Buck and his fans, Buckheads.

http://www.retroweb.com/rem/lyrcis R.E.M. lyrics managed by Kipp Teague.

http://www.bubblegum.uark.edu The R.E.M. chord archive.

6. TRIVIA

Mike Mills' Top 5 R.E.M. songs of all time (in no particular order):
1. 'It's The End Of The World As We Know It (And I Feel Fine)'
2. 'Losing My Religion'
3. 'Man On the Moon'
4. 'Radio Free Europe'
5. There is no fifth – 'the fifth would rotate,' says Mills.

Peter Buck's Top 5 R.E.M. songs of all time (in no particular order):
1. 'Perfect Circle'
2. 'It's The End Of The World As We Know It (And I Feel Fine)'
3. 'Sweetness Follows'
4. 'All The Way To Reno (You're Gonna Be A Star)'
5. 'New Test Leper'

Says Buck: 'For this day it's a good five, but on another day it'd be a different five.'

INDEX